Hands in Clay

Larry Murphy's hands at the instant he completes a pitcher. At this moment, a clumsy gesture could spoil the perfectly formed pot. He will shape the pouring lip with a quick sweep of a finger.

Hands in Clay

An Introduction to Ceramics

Charlotte F. Speight

Larry Murphy
Technical Advisor

Mayfield Publishing Company

Mayfield Publishing Company
285 Hamilton Avenue
Palo Alto, California 94103

Printing (last digit)
10 9 8 7 6 5 4 3 2 1

Library of Congress Cataloging in Publication Data
Speight, Charlotte F.
Hands in clay.
Includes index.
1. Pottery craft I. Title.
TT920.S685 738 78-22715
ISBN 0-87484-645-5

Editor, Emmett Dingley
Production editor, Janet Greenblatt
Permissions editor, Phyllis Koon
Interior designer, Robert S. Tinnon
Cover designer, Bill Conte
Line drawings by Marisa De Joseph
Production assistant, Chip Geerer

Typography by McAdams Type
Black and white film by Royal Graphics
Color film by Color Tech
Printed by R. R. Donnelley & Sons Company
This book was set in Korinna and Helvetica.

All photos not credited are by the author.

Front Cover

- **A.** Paul Philp
- **B.** Patti Warashina
- **C.** Larry Murphy
- **D.** Miriam Licht
- **E.** Ron Judd
- **F.** Kiln, Thrapsanon, Crete
- **G.** Larry Murphy
- **H.** Larry Murphy
- **I.** Ron Judd
- **J.** Jacqui Poncelet
- **K.** Aldo Rontini

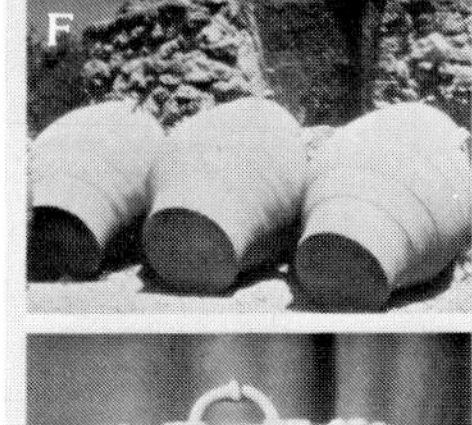

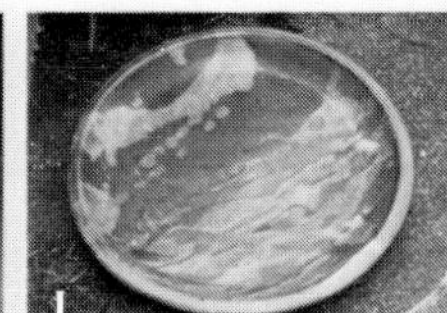

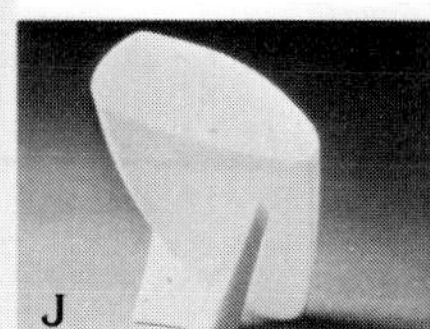

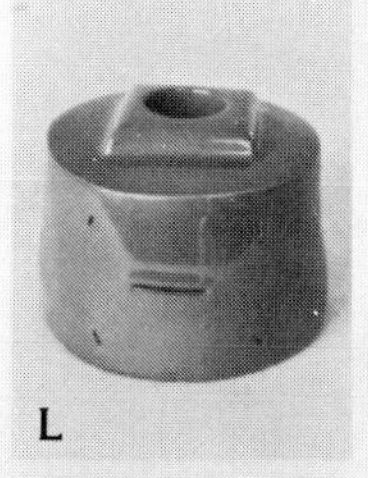

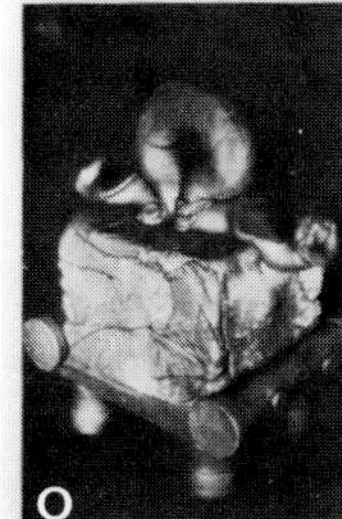

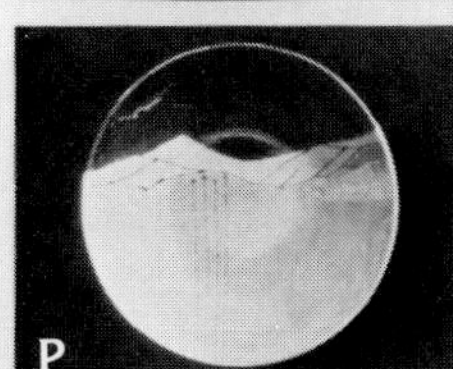

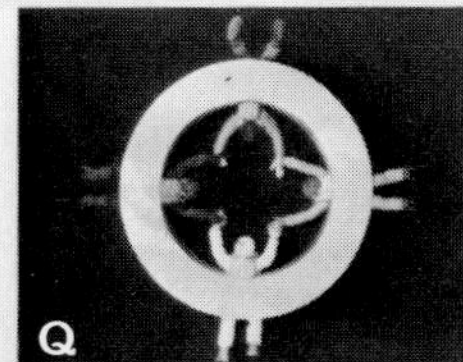

Back Cover

- **L.** Ron Nagle, Quay, Ceramics Gallery
- **M.** Charlotte Speight
- **N.** Michael Cardew, Crafts Advisory Committee, London
- **O.** Ruenell Foy Temps
- **P.** Janet Lowe
- **Q** Ron Cooper
- **R.** Allan Widenhofer
- **S.** Maria Martinez
- **T.** Erik Gronborg

For Martha

Part Two: Your Hands in Clay 155

Preface

HANDS IN CLAY is intended for those studying ceramics for the first time. For some of you this will be in a formal course at a school or college, for others it will be in a less formal craft class or perhaps individually in your home. I have tried to meet the needs of all newcomers to clay by providing the necessary background for a full appreciation of clay as an expressive medium, as well as giving detailed step-by-step explanations of the most common methods and techniques of working in clay.

Organization

The book is divided into a historical background section and a process and methods section, and you may begin with either part or read them concurrently. However, I believe you will develop a keener sense of the inherent possibilities of working in clay if you first study the historical development of ceramics in Part One. I chose the title for this book to emphasize the special relationship that people in all cultures and all eras have developed with this earthy material, believing that you will benefit greatly from seeing how others before you have worked with clay, creating with it useful and beautiful objects.

Scope

Part One describes how clay-crafters around the world have built up a body of ceramics knowledge from experience, and you will learn much that has a bearing on how people still work with clay today. It shows the great variety of uses to which people have put clay—from wine vessels to pipe bowls to decorative tiles—and how ceramics hands down to us a record of history preserved in clay.

Part Two, the process section, starts with the basics of obtaining and preparing the clay and proceeds to the major methods of working with it; from hand building pots to forming sculpture, to working on the wheel and casting. Full chapters are devoted to decorative techniques, glazing, and firing. An additional chapter on glaze calculation is provided in the appendix for those who wish to create their own glazes or to alter available glaze formulas. In it, you will follow a potter through the complete process of analyzing and altering a glaze using chemical calculation. All the necessary charts of chemicals and materials and atomic and molecular weights have been provided in the appendix to assist you in working through your own glaze calculations.

Learning and Teaching Aids

HANDS IN CLAY contains over 500 illustrations, 22 of which are in full color, giving you an opportunity to study the products of centuries of creative interaction between people and clay. Some of these may inspire you, and all of them will inform you. In Part One, the captions accompanying the photographs have been written as short, informative essays, placing the objects illustrated against the background of each culture—the life, the beliefs, the myths of the people who made them. In Part Two, the captions expand on the visual instruction given in the process photographs, explaining in greater detail the technical aspects of each illustration.

I have attempted throughout to explain all new terms and concepts in context; in addition I have keyed these terms (printed in boldface type) into a glossary that has the unique feature of referring you to illustrations that will further clarify the definition. As a further aid, metric and Celsius equivalents are given in parentheses following English measurements and Fahrenheit temperatures. For those of you who want to explore ceramics history or techniques in greater depth, I have also included Suggestions for Further Reading, which can lead you into specialized areas of study.

Objectives and Philosophy

My goal in writing this book was to enable you to discover your own way of working with clay. I believe that to do this you need both the experience of actually working, experimenting, and creating with clay as well as an understanding of what has gone on before. No other book, to my knowledge, brings these two elements together so completely. I hope you find in this book the excitement I feel for clay as a material, and the knowledge and inspiration to create objects with **your** hands in clay.

Acknowledgments

First, I would like to acknowledge the influence of some of my teachers: the kindergarten teacher who first gave me wonderful wet clay to shape; my history teacher, Walter Mohr, who opened the door to the past for me; Maija Grotell, who opened her studio and kiln doors, inspiring me by the example of a sensitive and dedicated potter.

Although I take full responsibility for the book's shortcomings, its strengths reflect the help and energy of many people. I am especially grateful to Larry Murphy, technical advisor, dedicated craftsman, and friend, whose good judgment and advice enriched the book immeasurably; to Jim Stevenson for his many helpful suggestions; to Marisa De Joseph, who put so much time and thought into the line drawings; to Linda Bowen, who cheerfully typed the manuscript and gave me much encouragement; and to my daughter, Martha Wax, for her encouragement and help through many rough spots.

I would also like to thank everyone at Alfred Publishing Company whose enthusiasm and effort carried such a complex project through all phases of publication from initial concept to finished book: my editor, Emmett Dingley, who initiated the idea, who believed I could do it, and who provided aid and encouragement for me to complete it; Morton Manus, president, for his confidence in the project; production manager Bob Tinnon, whose skill and experience were an important part of the process; production editor Janet Greenblatt, whose sharp eye and organizational skills contributed so much; and all the others who helped make the idea become a reality.

There are many other people from whom I received much support and creative energy: potters and sculptors everywhere, who allowed me to photograph them at work and responded so helpfully to my requests for information; museum directors, curators, and staff who gave time and thought to answering my questions, reading the manuscript, taking me through their storerooms, providing me with invaluable material and illustrations. They opened their offices, workshops, and homes to me, welcoming me in and sharing their knowledge. I feel I have many new friends. Thank you all.

Charlotte Speight

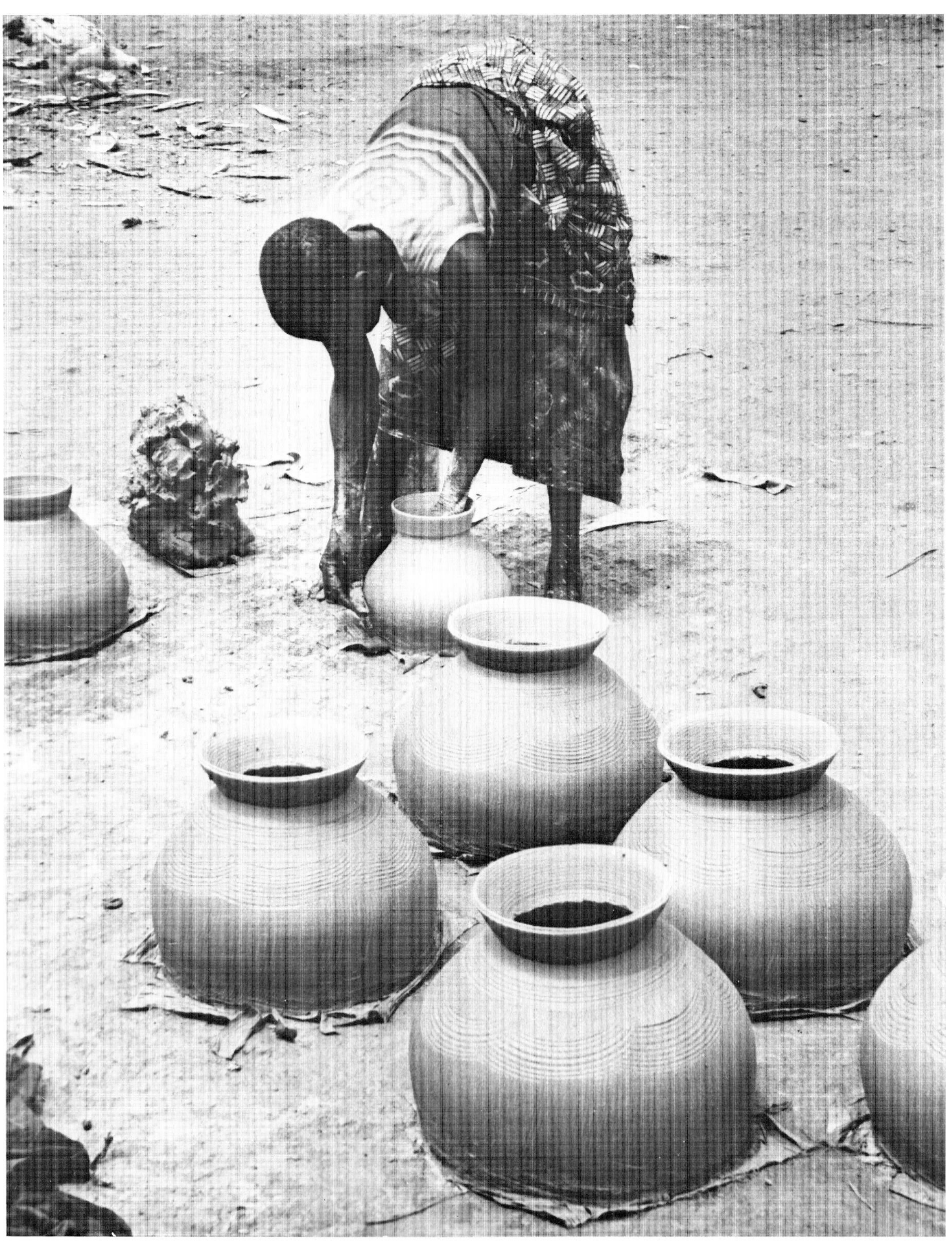

Ashanti potter, Ghana. *Courtesy, Museum of African Art, Washington, D.C., Eliot Elisofon Archives.*

PART ONE

How Clay Was Used in the Past

Chapter One

An Introduction to Clay

Clay feels soft and pliable in your hands. You hold a lump of it, idly pinching and poking it, feeling it take shape almost by itself. It is as if this piece of earth has a life of its own to which you respond with your fingers. Perhaps it begins to look like a human figure; perhaps an animal starts to grow in your hands. You are doing now what people did thousands of years ago. They dug up this sticky earth, shaped it into simple figures, put the figures in the sun to dry, and ascribed religious or magical power to them, worshiping them as symbols of the fruitful mother earth.

Because air-dried clay crumbles when exposed to weather, only fragments of these figures survive, but they represent some of humanity's earliest uses of this basic earth material. They are the beginnings of the craft of **ceramics**, which, as it grew in complexity, grew into an industry that has been essential to the development of civilization. Some early cultures cast metal axes in stone **molds,** but clay was usually used. And modern steel mills still use ceramic materials—fire-resistant bricks line furnaces, and ceramic crucibles hold molten metal.

Figure 1-1 African village women today continue to shape pots using methods that are thousands of years old. *Courtesy, Field Museum of Natural History, Chicago.*

Clay has one intrinsic quality that is all-important to the story of ceramics—its ability to hold the shape into which it is formed. That shape becomes permanent when the clay is heated to a certain temperature, and because of this quality, clay can capture the spontaneous, passing gesture of a human hand, fixing it into an enduring record. A woman in an African village today probably makes her pots with the same gestures used by a Neolithic woman of 5000 B.C. (Figure 1-1).

Push your thumb into a lump of clay, watching how it keeps its mark. When the clay dries, the impression will remain; if the clay were **fired**, this impression could last for thousands of years (Figures 1-2 and 1-3).

A Record of Humanity in Clay

The close relationship between human hands and clay has been invaluable to archaeologists and historians as they try to reconstruct cultures that have disappeared from the earth. Because clay becomes a permanent material when fired, even when it is broken a clay pot or sculpture leaves pieces, or **shards**, that can often be put together again (Figure 1-4). Even if the fragments are too scattered to reassemble, the archaeologist can study the type of clay in the shards, the kinds of decoration used, and the shape of the pottery to learn a great deal about a culture, its degree of technical development, the extent of its trade, and its exposure to migrations, which in turn introduced new techniques. For example, pottery from 6,000 years ago found in Sian, China, reveals techniques and painted designs similar to older pottery found in Russian Turkistan in Western Asia and may have been influenced by migrations from there. Since most archaeological sites are rich in pot shards, the

Figure 1-2 *(Left)* The finger mark of a potter who made a storage jar on the island of Crete around 1400 B.C.still shows in the fired clay. Pushing his thumb into the soft clay, he left a mark similar to the one made in the clay in 1977 by his descendent on Crete (Figure 1-3). Mallia, Crete. *Photo by James McGann.*
Figure 1-3 *(Right)* These thumb prints, linking the centuries, symbolize the long-continuing tradition of human hands working in clay. Thumb print, Thrapsanon, Crete, 1977.

excavator can study a great variety of them, establishing a pottery sequence through the carbon 14 dating of fossils found in these sites. This is a process that dates a once-living organism according to the decrease in radioactive carbon since the organism's death—the less carbon 14, the older the specimen. Once a pottery sequence has been established, it is then possible to date other finds at the site in proper sequence.

Sometimes an archaeologist unearths a clay artifact that suggests a human drama. During the years 1963 to 1965, Dr. Yigael Yadin, professor of archaeology at Hebrew University in Jerusalem, directed the complex excavation of a large fortress and palace built by Herod the Great on top of the Rock of Masada, towering 1,300 feet above the Dead Sea plain. In A.D. 73 this was the site of a heroic last-ditch stand made by 1,000 Jewish rebels against their Roman rulers. These Zealots of Masada withstood three years of siege. Finally, realizing that a Roman break-through was imminent, they decided to die by their own hands rather than surrender. Each man killed his wife and children. Then, according to historian Josephus, they chose ten men by lot "and offered their necks to the stroke of those who by lot executed that melancholy office." The ten men drew lots among themselves to find out who would first kill the other nine and then kill himself.

Figure 1-4 (*Left*) Archaeologists can piece together the fragments of pottery that they find when they excavate ancient sites, reconstructing vessels made thousands of years ago. This buff-colored vessel with brownish black decoration was made about 3500 B.C. in Susa, in what is now Iran. Height 7⅞ in. (20 cm), diameter 7¼ in. (18.5 cm). *Courtesy, The Metropolitan Museum of Art (acquired in exchange with the Teheran Museum in liquidation of the Iranian Expedition, 1948).* **Figure 1-5** (*Right*) A damp clay tablet used as paper by a Sumerian clerk still holds the impression of the marking tool he pressed into it around 2100 B.C. A local doctor, recording some of his favorite medicines, dictated this rather pleasant-sounding prescription to be written in cuneiform characters on clay: "Pulverize the seed of the 'carpenter plant,' the gum-resin of the markasi-plant, and thyme; dissolve it in beer; let the man drink." *Courtesy, The University Museum, University of Pennsylvania.*

Members of the Masada expedition found eleven pottery *ostraca,* or lots, with the names of men written on them. One bore the name of the Zealots' leader, Eleazar ben Ya'ir'. Were these pieces of clay the very lots mentioned by Josephus? We may never know, but we do know that lots like these were used on Masada almost 2,000 years ago for rationing food and assigning duty (Figure 1-8).

Ancient peoples frequently buried clay vessels or figures in graves, where they have been preserved intact. From the abundance of clay objects from different cultures, archaeologists have been able to reconstruct

Figure 1-6 Two girls in Veracruz around A.D.300 pump their swing with looks of absorption. They are also whistles and sound like the toy pottery whistles still made in Mexico today. But they also tell us about the customs of the time; their heads show the wide forehead and pointed chin typical of the people who lived there between A.D. 300 and 700, a characteristic produced by binding their heads in infancy. *Courtesy, Museum of the American Indian, Heye Foundation.*

Figure 1-7 Also from Mexico, the figure of a woman grinding corn on a metate, unaware of her child trying to steal a tortilla from her lap, was made by the skillful sculptors of Colima between A.D.300 and 900. Realistic figures like this reflect the day-to-day events, work, and pleasures of the people of western Mexico so vividly that we can reconstruct almost every aspect of their lives, from their religious rituals to how they waged war or made love. *Courtesy, Museo Nacional de Antropologia, Mexico.*

the history of a period or learn about a society's religion or daily life (Figure 1-10). Scholarly volumes have been written about such clay artifacts, but for us it is enough to experience through them a sense of identification with people who lived in widely separated places and times but whose needs, feelings, and stories were preserved in clay. And so we understand the ancient Sumerian doctor who wanted to keep a record of his remedies. We also enter the world of children at play in ancient Mexico, so much like the world of children today. Homely household chores, temple and house architecture, the war trappings of horses and warriors, tales of heroism—all these as well are recorded in clay (Figures 1-5 to 1-10). It is the talent of the clayworker and the **plastic,** formable quality of the clay itself that make possible such a rich record of human experience.

Figure 1-8 An ostraca, or lot, found by the Masada Expedition headed by Professor Yigael Yadin may be one of the lots used to determine the order of death of the Zealots of Masada, who in A.D. 73 chose to die by their own hands rather than by the hands of their Roman rulers. This action inspired the modern Israeli cry of "Masada shall not fall again." Masada, A.D. 73. *Courtesy, Professor Y. Yadin.*

Figure 1-9 A red and white earthenware house from Peru shows better than any written description how the Moche people built their homes or temples around A.D. 400. They were also skilled at building pottery by hand as well as casting it in two-piece molds, making a variety of spouted jars in animal and human shapes. From the earliest known pottery (around 1220 to 850 B.C.) until the Spanish conquest in 1523, a series of cultures succeeded each other in Peru. Pottery styles and techniques have helped scholars establish the chronology of these cultures. Moche, North Coast, Peru c. A.D. 400. Height 5¾ in. (14.8 cm). *Courtesy, Linden-Museum Stuttgart. Photo by Didoni.*

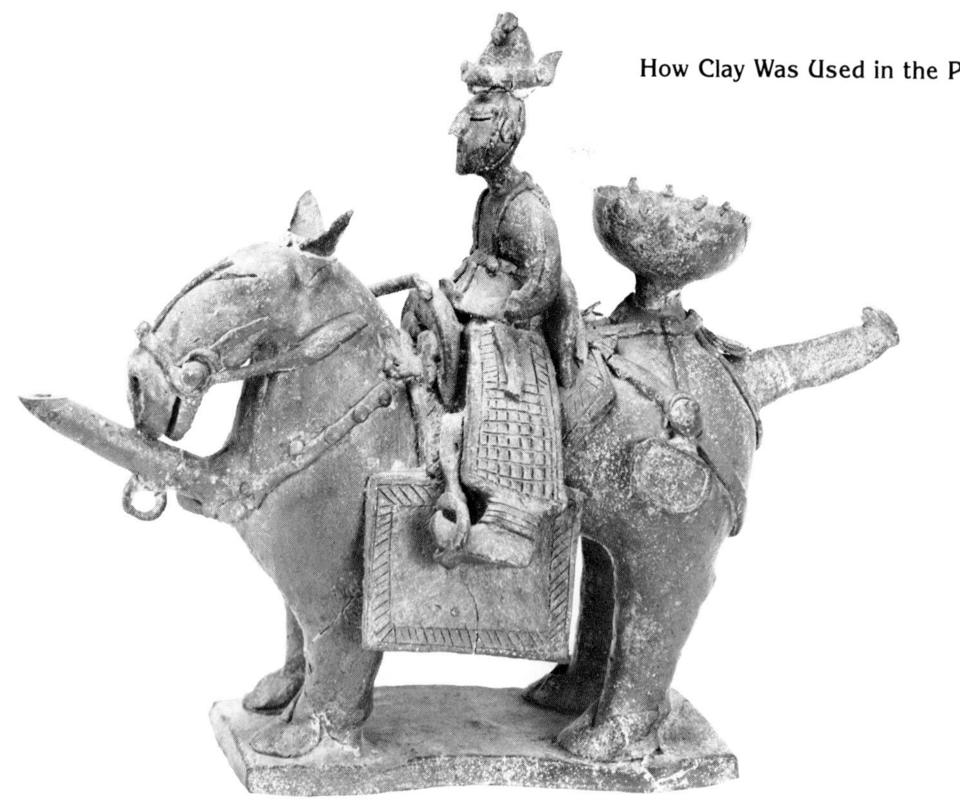

Figure 1-10 Figure of a warrior of the Old Silla dynasty of Korea, found in a tomb. The funnel on the back of his horse and the spout on the horse's chest show that it was a ritual vessel of some sort, probably for pouring libations. The sculptor has also given us a vivid picture of an arrogant fighting man in all the trappings of the period, from his turned-up boots, to what looks like a leather water canteen slung on the horse's rear. Kumryongchong tomb, Korea, 5th–6th century A.D. Height 9¼ in. (23.5 cm), length 11½ in. (29.2 cm). *Courtesy, National Museum of Korea.*

Origins of Clay

Just what is this substance called clay, which tells us so much about the past, and which is still shaped by potters and sculptors into objects that may themselves be puzzled over by future archaeologists? What qualities does it have that makes it adaptable to so many uses? And where does it come from?

From Rock to Crockery

The fertile areas of the earth are covered with topsoil, which is rich in rotted organic matter and makes for good farmland. Under the topsoil, at various levels, sometimes under a layer of rock, there are deposits of clay. Look at cuts where highways have been built to see exposed clay beds; or take a look at a construction site, where pockets of clay may be exposed. Rivers also reveal clay along their banks, and erosion on a hillside may make clay easily accessible (Figure 1-11).

What is clay made of? Our earth's surface is basically rock, and it is this rock that gradually decomposes into clay. Rain, streams, alternating freezing and thawing, roots of trees and plants forcing their way into cracks, earthquakes, volcanic action, and glaciers—all these forces slowly break down the earth's exposed rocky crust into smaller and smaller pieces that eventually become clay.

Rocks are composed of **elements** and compounds of elements. **Feldspar**, which is the most abundant mineral on the earth's surface, is basically made up of the oxides **silica** and **alumina** combined with **alkalies** like potassium and some so-called impurities such as iron. Feldspar is an essential component of granite rocks, and as such it is the basis of clay.

It is this rock origin that makes it possible to fire clay to varying degrees of hardness and to cover it with impermeable coatings of glasslike material called **glaze**. Just as volcanic action, with its intense heat, fuses the elements in certain rocks into a glasslike rock called obsidian, so can we apply heat to earth materials and change them into a hard, dense material. Different clays need different heat levels to fuse, and some, the low-fire clays, never become dense and nonporous (**vitreous**) like highly fired **stoneware**. Each clay can stand just so many degrees of heat without losing its shape through sagging or melting. Variations of clay composition and the temperatures at which they are fired account for the differences in texture and appearance between a **china** tea cup and an **earthenware** flower pot.

Primary and Secondary Clays

Granite, a feldspathic rock covering a large part of the earth's surface, may decompose through weathering without being washed away, forming clay beds on the original sites (Figure 1-12). Known as **primary clay**, these deposits become **china clay**, or **kaolin**, a pure white clay used in **porcelain**, **bone china**, or glazes. "Pure clay" has the following formula,

Figure 1-11 Julian Martinez digging clay from an exposed bed on a mesa in New Mexico in the 1940s. Originally the women of the pueblos dug the clay, but later the men helped, also making or decorating the pottery. Maria and Julian Martinez made pottery together, becoming world famous (see Color Plate 9, p. 146D). Maria, now in her nineties, remembers that in her grandmother's time the potters scattered grain as an offering before digging the clay out with a stick. New Mexico, 1940. *Courtesy, Collections in the Museum of New Mexico. Photo by Wyatt Davis.*

but it is only a theoretical clay, not found in such an unadulterated state in nature:

$$Al_2O_3 \cdot 2SiO_3 \cdot 2H_2O$$

Kaolin is the nearest natural clay to this theoretical clay.

Clay that has been washed away from the original rocks and deposited in beds is known as **secondary clay**. Over millions of years, as the feldspathic rocks of the earth's crust broke down, the particles were weathered down into increasingly smaller sizes, continually being moved down the mountains by rain and streams. As the weathering continued, and still continues, the ever-smaller particles were carried by water, mixed with other minerals and vegetable matter, and finally deposited in river bottoms, plains, or ocean beds. Minerals were added or washed away by the water, altering the composition of the clay. Similar-sized particles were apt to be deposited together to make up a clay bed of a particular mineral and physical composition.

Some clays are made up of rather coarse rock fragments, which, as they decomposed, usually dropped to the bottom of stream beds before the smaller clay particles, forming beds of what are called **fire clays**. These clays are heat resistant and are used pretty much as they come from the ground to make bricks to line furnaces, fireplaces, and **kilns** (Figure 12-7).

Stoneware clay, which is used by potters and sculptors for much of their work (Figures 8-10 and 9-56), is a secondary clay with finer particles than fire clay. As the particles were moved down the rivers, they were mixed with decayed plants, adding potassium, and with small particles of iron oxide. When stoneware clay is fired to a certain temperature, it becomes dense and vitreous.

Common clay is made up of decomposed rocks of all types, along with vegetable material and a considerable amount of iron. This clay varies in color from reddish to yellowish tones, depending on the amount of iron or lime in it. Dug up and used by early potters, it produced the colored earthenware used by Neolithic potters all over the world (Figure 1-32). Clay composition varies from place to place, according to how much of each material was added as the bed was formed, and until people developed transportation that could move the bulky clay easily, potters had to use the type that was nearest to them. Gradually, transportation improved, and as clay-workers accumulated knowledge from experience, they refined and mixed clays to have more control over their color, firing potential, and formability.

Some clays can be dug up and used as

Figure 1-12 Diagram showing how some rocks decompose in place, depositing primary clays, while other decomposed rock particles are moved by the action of water and deposited elsewhere. Usually the heaviest particles are deposited first. Various types of clays (fire clay, stoneware, earthenware, ball clay) are dug from these deposits.

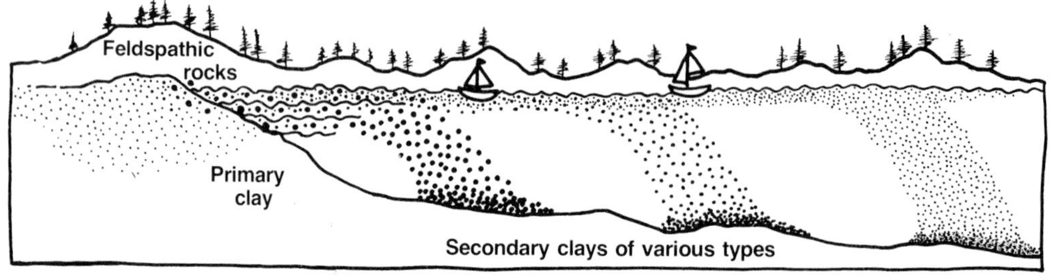

they come from the ground, with very little more preparation than cleaning out large impurities. These are the clays used by our Neolithic ancestors and still used in some traditional villages today (Figure 1-22). However, most clays used by contemporary ceramicists are cleaned, refined, and mixed commercially to produce the best possible **body** for a specific purpose. These are the clays you can buy ready-mixed in dry bulk or plastic bags. When a slight variation in consistency occurs and you curse the manufacturer, remember the problems of the early clay workers who had little choice of available clay and who had to pass on their technical knowledge from generation to generation by word of mouth.

Plasticity of Clay

Stop to think about the difference between fired and unfired clay, and you realize what an amazing material it is. Dampened with water, it is easy to form, holding together as you shape it. Air-dried it is fragile, crumbling easily. Fired, it becomes hard and permanent, keeping its form for thousands of years (Figures 1-14 to 1-18).

What makes clay so easy to shape, or plastic, when it is mixed with the right amount of water? It is partly the fineness of its particles, and partly their flat shape. The film of water between the particles lubricates them so that they can slip against each other, but it also makes them cling together just as smooth pieces of glass will stick together when wet. Water is part of the chemical structure of clay, but it is also part of its physical structure.

Clays differ tremendously in their plasticity; some sticky ones are almost impossible to shape, and others that might work well when used in a semiliquid state for **casting** would never hold together if used less wet for shaping on the potter's wheel. A clay that is a joy to shape on the wheel, however, may not fire easily to the desired density. So the clayworker must take into account many considerations about the qualities of each clay and the desired results. In later chapters we will learn more about what clay can and cannot do, but first let us see how humans first used clay.

Early Uses of Clay

When people found that they could store wild seeds for food and domesticate goats and other animals, they began to leave the nomadic life and turned the campfire into a home-fire. For example, by around 9000 B.C., a transitional village was settled at Jericho near a spring. The simple houses built there contained clay-lined storage pits in which to keep wild grains, although most of the food still came from fishing and hunting. In Jarmo, in northern Mesopotamia, by the seventh millennium B.C., clay-lined pits in the floors were used as hearths, and some excavated pits have been found containing stones, suggesting that these pits may have been used for boiling liquids by putting hot stones in them. Unbaked clay figures found there and in Jericho and the lack of pottery shards indicate that deliberate firing of clay was as yet unknown.

First Uses of Fired Clay

No one knows exactly when or how some long-ago villager figured out that clay would become hard when exposed to fire and could be used to make more convenient receptacles than baskets, skins, or stone bowls. It may have been the result of building fires in the clay pits; or some Neolithic housewife, after smearing a basket with clay to keep out mice, may have set it too near the fire, only to discover that the clay hardened when the basket

Figure 1-13 A Bozo woman from Mali carries her pots on her head, balancing them on a rest made of cloth. Neolithic women probably carried their water or grain in similar fashion. The texture on the lower pot makes it less slippery to lift as well as decorating it. The upper pot shows dark fire smudges from uneven firing. *Courtesy, Museum of African Art, Eliot Elisofon Archives.*

burned. However it happened, the discovery that fire could change clay into a solid substance was responsible for starting potters on the long process of developing techniques of ceramics.

It is likely that women were the first potters, forming the utensils they needed for their own families. Once they could substitute clay pots for nomadic leather or woven containers, housekeeping must have become less of a chore and cooking a good deal easier. Water was probably carried from the spring in pots as village women still carry it today (Figure 1-13).

Agriculture and Fertility

By around 7000 B.C., agriculture and stock breeding were well established in parts of the Middle East. The earth or mother goddess was central to the religion of these early farmers, and some of the earliest examples of baked clay that have been excavated are fertility figures (Figures 1-14 to 1-18). These figurines are characteristic of many agricultural communities around the world, varying in age according to when a particular people settled into villages to farm. For example, by 5000 B.C. in Anatolia, in present-day Iran, Neolithic religious observances aimed toward better crops and herds made use of fertility figures depicting the earth goddess as a young woman, a woman giving birth, and as an old woman.

As time went on and villages in various parts of the world grew larger and life more complex, surpluses of goods were produced and a remarkably wide trade developed. Archaeologists can often trace trade routes by studying fragments of pottery, identifying a style and clay body as coming from a particular locality or culture. It is likely that at that time, when specialization of crafts developed, men became the potters, producing wares for their own village and for trade. As they increased in their proficiency, they formed the clay into a greater variety of shapes, like those shown in Figures 1-19 to 1-21.

Early Methods

It can be said that these early cultures were part of a Clay Age, just as later ages are classified as Iron and Bronze Ages because their main industrial products were made of those metals. Now that we have seen how important clay was in the earliest settled communities, let's take a look at some of the forming and firing methods, following the development of the craft as it progressed in complexity and technique.

Of course no one really knows exactly how the very earliest potters made their pots, and any reconstruction of history involves educated guesses. We can, however, learn something about their methods through microscopic examination of the ceramics found in excavations and by studying preindustrial pottery making in places where potters probably still use techniques similar to those used by early potters. An effort is being made to record these methods before metal and plastic utensils become so universal that pottery for domestic use is no longer made by hand. We can reconstruct from these sources many of the techniques used, as well as the problems encountered, by our earliest potting ancestors. Just how did they set about making a pot?

Clay Sources

The early potter had to find a clay source near enough to be able to carry the clay back to the village—no easy matter at a time when there were no carts or pack animals, only baskets or leather bags carried by hand. Of course, sometimes the clay was brought from quite a distance, as in the Hebrides Islands, off Scotland, in the second millennium B.C., where the clay and the wood for firing were fetched by dugout canoe.

Early farming peoples felt their dependence on the earth, and in many cultures potters would not dig the clay without proper religious observances. In the American Southwest, for example, potters had so much respect for the earth that they actually asked its permission to remove the clay before digging it out with a stick. Mothers taught their daughters the required rituals, calling the earth "Mother Clay" and believing that if they forgot to scatter an offering of meal, the clay might be angry and make them ill. The very early potters probably had similar rituals, for to them the earth was a sacred mother on whom they depended for life and health.

Adding Temper to the Clay

When people first started to make pottery, they probably used the clay just as it came from the river bank or hillside, merely picking out the larger impurities. Later they found they could improve the clay by letting it dry completely, pounding it to a powder, then mixing it with water and spreading it in the sun to dry to a good working consistency (Figure 1-22). At some point they discovered that if they coarsened its texture by adding sand, pounded rock, mica, sea shells, or similar materials, it would be easier to build with and less likely to burst during firing because the air could escape through the pores. The general name for this added material is **temper**.

The kind of temper used varied from place to place, and some clays had natural temper already in them so no other was needed. Around 6000 B.C. in Jarmo, in the Middle East, potters mixed straw in their clay, whereas traditional potters in the American Southwest still use volcanic rock or sand as temper. Experts can often tell the origin of a pottery fragment by examining it to see whether the temper is pounded rock, sand, or some other material. The potter would have found the clay in one place, the temper in another, and pigments for coloring the clay in another, but they all had to be found near enough to the settlement to be carried there.

Figures 1-14 to 1-18 Female figures from many areas of the world and many periods in history. They are usually simple, pinched figures with their features or clothing suggested by lines or dots scratched into the damp clay, or with rolls or dabs of clay pressed onto the figure. Many of them were fertility figures, or figures of goddesses, although we do not know their exact use.

Figure 1-15 Female figure with two faces, Tlatilco, Mexico, 1300–800 B.C. Height 3 in. (7.6 cm). *Courtesy, Museo Nacional de Antropologia, Mexico.*

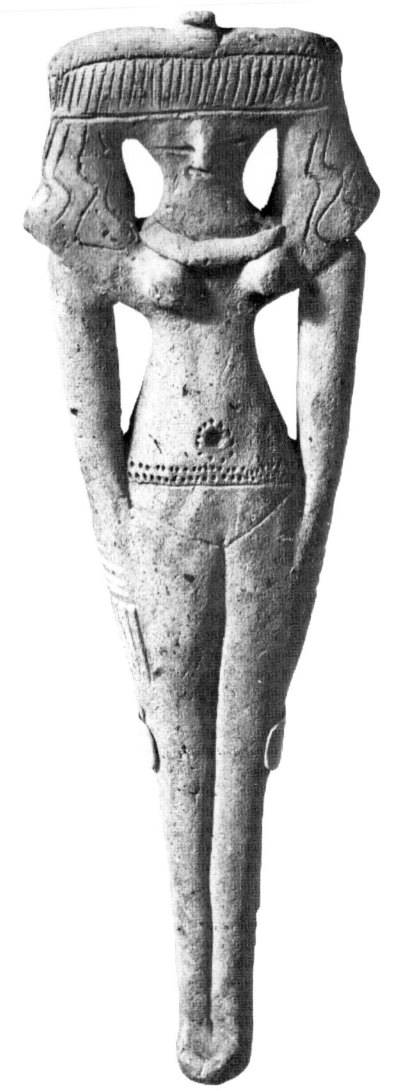

Figure 1-14 Female figure, Middle Kingdom, Egypt, c. 1800 B.C. Height 5⅜ in. (13.5 cm). *Courtesy, The Trustees of The British Museum, London.*

Figure 1-16 Female figure, Tureng Tepe, Persia, 2nd or 3rd millennium B.C. *Courtesy, The University Museum, University of Pennsylvania.*

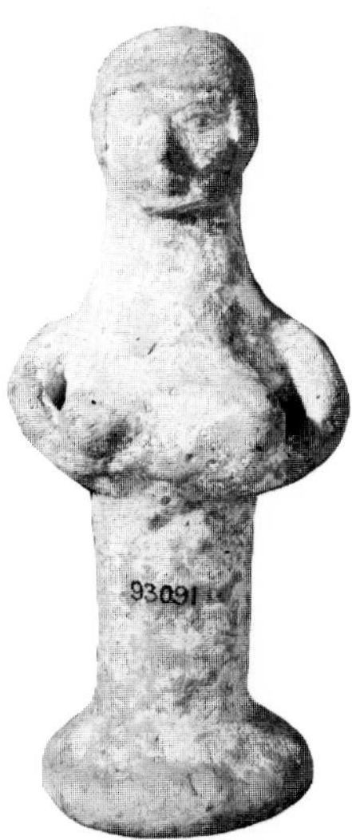

Figure 1-17 Female figure, Bethlehem. 8th–6th century B.C. Height about 7 in. (17.5 cm). *Courtesy, the Trustees of The British Museum, London.*

Figure 1-18 Female figure, bird deity, Egypt, early predynastic, c. 4000 B.C. Height 11½ in. (29.3 cm). *Courtesy, The Brooklyn Museum.*

Figure 1-19 A Bronze Age spouted jar from Yortan, Anatolia, is shaped for safe carrying and easy pouring of liquids. It is decorated with lines that were probably suggested by the leather thongs, or cords, that were used for carrying such vessels. 3rd millennium B.C. Height 9¾ in. (24.8 cm). *Courtesy, the Trustees of The British Museum, London.*

Figure 1-20 Mesopotamian potters made their urns and jars in a great variety of shapes, many of them decorated with paint applied in simple lines and patterns that enhance the form of the vessels and emphasize their curves. Nineveh, Mesopotamia, 3rd millennium B.C. Height 4½in. (11.5 cm) *Courtesy, the Trustees of The British Museum, London.*

Figure 1-21 The humorous shape of this earthenware feeding vessel is emphasized by the painted face. The red and black decoration must have helped a harried mother keep her child amused at mealtime. Cyprus, 10th or 11th century B.C. *Courtesy, Victoria and Albert Museum, Crown Copyright.*

Climate

Climate would have affected the way the potter worked. In the hot climate of Mesopotamia, drying had to be controlled or work done very quickly, but the same problem would not exist for the Bronze Age potter in misty Scotland (Figure 1-23). In the damp climate of humid jungles, the pots might have to be heated to dry them thoroughly before firing, but in other parts of the world pottery would only be made during the warm summer months. Today we can control drying by artificial means, but the early potter was much more influenced by climate. In addition, the type of plants growing in an area affected the eating and therefore the cooking habits of its people, so that their pottery needs were different. Physical factors such as these had an enormous influence on the early potters.

Shaping Methods

After carrying the clay to the village, mixing it with temper, and working it to the right consistency, the potter was ready to start shaping a pot. Probably the very earliest pots were made by women sitting on the ground pinching a lump of clay into a roughly shaped container. When you pick up a lump of clay for the first time, your thumbs seem to sink into it of their own accord, and one hand begins to turn the clay while the other pushes into it, pulling up the sides as you hollow out the interior. Working like this, pinching and compressing the clay, it is easy to shape the clay into simple, thick-walled pots. If the clay is stretched during this process, however, it tends to crack and collapse. It is also difficult when pinching to make a shape that narrows from a swelling body to a tighter neck. Pinching was probably used for generations before someone discovered that it was far easier to build up a pot using some sort of support or mold for the base, adding to it gradually with **coils** of clay.

Figure 1-22 Dry clay piled in the yard of a potter's workshop at Thrapsanon, Crete. This clay will be broken up, soaked, and spread in the sun, allowing the water to evaporate.

Figure 1-23 This Bronze Age earthenware urn from Scotland is decorated with the scratched and punched decoration so often used by early potters. Possibly this type of decoration was a holdover from the patterns formed when clay was pressed into baskets. Along with designs from cords pressed into the clay, this texture appears on early earthenware all over the world. Terradale, Scotland. Height 5¾ in. (14.6 cm) *Courtesy, Victoria and Albert Museum, Crown Copyright.*

Figure 1-24 A Hopi potter in Arizona around the turn of the century shapes a pot with coils, using a basket as base. *Courtesy, Museum of the American Indian, Heye Foundation.*

Figure 1-25 Fiji potters still use a base of grasses and leaves in which to rest slabs of clay as they start to form their pottery. Later, they paddle the pots to force the clay together, using the paddles lying on the mat. *Courtesy, Fiji Museum, Suva.*

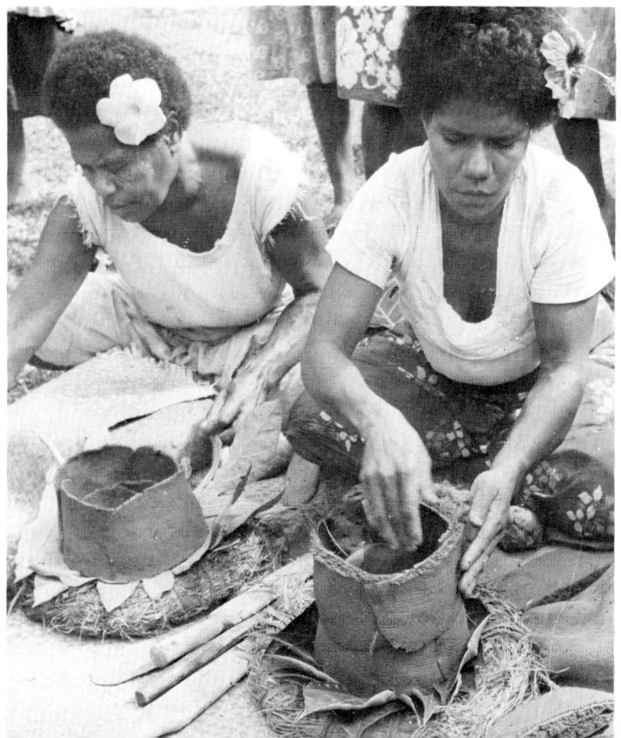

Base Molds

Eventually, potters found that they could shape the base of a pot by patting it out over a rounded rock or in a gourd, or anything hollow, using ashes or leaves under the clay to keep it from sticking to the mold. Early potters used the hollow in a tree stump, the bottom of a broken pot, or a basket as a base mold (Figure 5-16). It seems apparent that people learned to make baskets very early, and many archaeologists believe that this is the reason so much Neolithic pottery was decorated with incised bands of rough texture, suggesting the weave of baskets.

Coils

Rolling the clay between the hands into a "snake" and then building the coils up to a rough shape is the most widely used pottery-building method in traditional cultures today and was undoubtedly the most common method used by Neolithic potters (Figure 1-24). Turning the pot constantly as the coils were added, the potter pushed the coils together to make them stick to each other. Often the coils were beaten with the hand or a wooden paddle, making the walls thinner and forcing the clay particles together (Figures 1-24 to 1-27).

In some country potteries in Japan today, potters shape their pots by holding the clay in the left hand and pounding it with the right elbow. In parts of Southeast Asia, on the other hand, instead of turning the pot itself, a line of people walk around a stand, holding a coil of clay and building it up into a spiral, which is then pounded into shape. In some areas of Africa, a pot is started on a stand or in a hollow tree trunk and the potter walks around it backwards adding the coils. Whatever the method, coiling has had an important role in the history of pot making.

Sometimes, in the process of making a large pot, a potter might find that if too much clay were built up on the base, the walls would collapse from the weight. So the pot was built up only part way, allowing the clay to harden somewhat before adding more damp clay

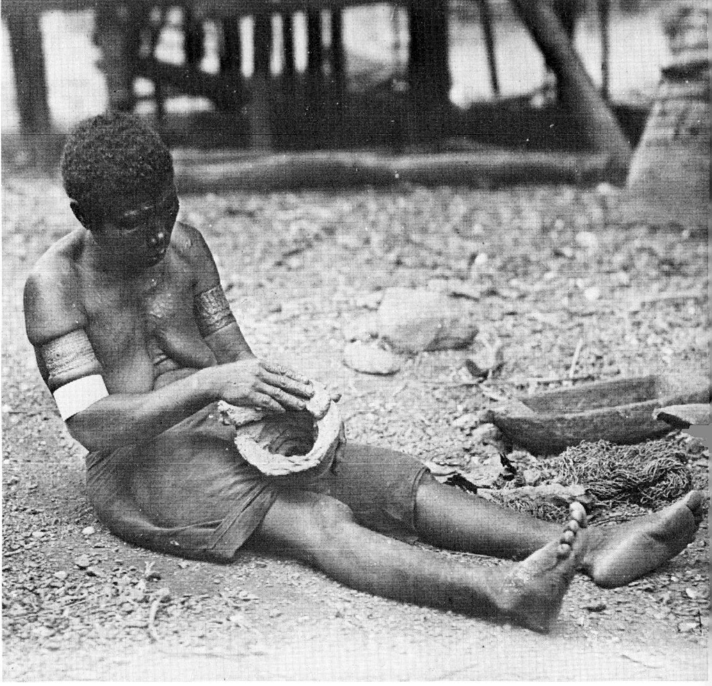

Figure 1-26 A New Guinea woman builds pottery with coils in the simplest way, needing no more equipment for her workshop than her lap and a lump of clay. We can easily imagine that we are looking at one of the world's earliest potters pressing pieces of clay onto the rough pot. Probably she will paddle it later to thin the walls and make the clay particles adhere tightly to each other. Lokanu, New Guinea. *Courtesy, Field Museum of Natural History, Chicago.*

Figure 1-27 In Fiji a potter pounds the formed pot with a wooden paddle while holding a round stone inside it against the walls. In this way she shapes it, pressing outwards where she wants it to bulge, and also makes sure that all the slabs will stick together. In some places the wooden paddles are carved or wrapped with matting or rough cloth to produce a design or texture on the pot. *Courtesy, Fiji Museum, Suva.*

(Figure 1-28). As the coils were added, the potter smoothed them on the inside as well as on the outside, sometimes pressing a rounded stone against the inside of the walls, sometimes smoothing them with the hands (Figure 1-27).

Finishing the Pot

When a pot was completely shaped and paddled, it was ready for finishing. Scrapers made of wood, shell, bone, or a bit of dried gourd were dragged across the pot as it was turned, thinning the walls, smoothing the surface, frequently leaving decorative marks. Sometimes the potter composed these marks into a design or used a smooth stone or piece of leather to polish, or **burnish**, the outside of the pot (Figure 1-29).

None of the earthenware made by early peoples was completely watertight unless it was treated in some way, and potters around the world used various methods to close the pores. **Slip**, a mixture of fine clay and water, was painted on the pot before it was burnished, as is still done in pueblos in New Mexico. But even pushing this fine clay slip into the pores does not make the ware really impervious. Sometimes, in an attempt to solve this problem, the potter treated the fired pot with a mixture made by boiling certain plants, or coated it with pitch from native trees while

Figure 1-28 An Ashanti potter in Ghana starts her pots at the top, then dries them in the sun to let the clay harden enough to support the rest of the coils. She leaves the edges rough so that the added clay will stick. Notice the elegant curving designs and texture, which she forms by sweeping over the damp clay with a toothed tool. *Courtesy, Museum of African Art, Eliot Elisofon Archives.*

Figure 1-29 Polishing stones like the one this potter in Ndola, Zambia, is using were treasured possessions. Often they were handed down from mother to daughter to granddaughter. The burnishing gave the pots a glossy finish, but it also served a functional purpose, pressing the clay particles together and making the pottery less porous. *Courtesy, Zambia Information Services.*

the jar was still hot. This may well be the origin of retsina wine in Greece, where wine may have been stored originally in jars coated with natural resin. Also, cooking in earthenware helps to make it impervious, as does soaking it for a long time in water.

The porosity of earthenware can be an advantage, however. In hot climates, water stored in earthenware jars is cooled by evaporation through the pores, an important consideration in the desert areas of the world, where early cultures were based on irrigation and water was venerated as life-giving. There, cool, refreshing water assumed a religious importance.

Figure 1-30 Much early pottery was decorated with ovals, triangles, circles, and horizontal, vertical, or slanting lines and dots scratched into the clay. Cords were also pressed into the clay to make impressions, and the name of this Jōmon vessel comes from that technique; Jōmon means "cord pattern." Late Jōmon, Japan. Height 3⅞ in. (10 cm), diameter 7 in. (17.7 cm). *Courtesy, the Trustees of The British Museum, London.*

Decorating the Damp Clay

When the pot was finished, the Neolithic potter often took the time to decorate it, especially if it was to be used for ritual or burial. In this period of human development, art was not seen as something separate from daily life. The impulse that led early humans to decorate their tools, clothing, and even their bodies reached into every facet of life, and pottery was no exception. Satisfying shapes might be left plain, but often they were decorated with great inventiveness and imagination. Decoration was frequently applied while the clay was damp, using the most ordinary tools to achieve a great variety of effects. A fingernail pushed into the clay to form a pattern, holes poked into it with a stick, the edge of a shell dragged over it, lumps or coils of clay pressed into it—any of these might decorate a pot (Figures 1-2, 1-30, and 1-31). For example, a pot made in ancient Japan might have indentations poked into the clay to make a textured background for the spirals that were drawn with a sharpened stick or bone, while a Bronze Age potter in Scotland might combine simple cross-hatching and horizontal lines into an effective decoration. Early potters had a keen

Figure 1-31 Water pot from the Fiji Islands shows how raised decoration enhances the appearance of this jar as well as making it easier to lift or carry. *Courtesy, Fiji Museum, Suva.*

Figure 1-32 Pottery vase with tubular handles and purple-painted decoration from Egypt. Late predynastic period. Before 3000 B.C. Height 7½ in. (19 cm). *Courtesy, the Trustees of The British Museum, London.*

sense of form and were skilled at using decoration to accentuate and complement the shape of the pot. The relationship between the form and the decoration of a pot is one of the basic aesthetic problems facing any potter, and it is one that the Neolithic potter solved with sophistication and obvious pleasure.

Decorating With Color

The scratched or applied decoration was enriched by the color of the clay body, which ranged from buff to reddish, light to dark brown, or gray to black, depending on its mineral composition or the firing methods used. Some pots, because of uneven firing, came out of the fire with dark and light, red and black splotches on the outside, a decorative effect still sought after by many potters.

Figure 1-33 Earthenware vessel with spirals painted in red and black, found in a cemetery in Kansu, China. Pan Shan culture, 2500–1500 B.C. Height 13 in. (33 cm). *Courtesy, Collection Haags Gemeentemuseum, The Hague.*

Figure 1-34 Large urn with fish and spiral pattern from the palace at Phaistos, Crete. 2000–1700 B.C. *Courtesy, The Archaeological Museum, Heraclion, Crete.*

The clay-crafter eventually discovered, no doubt by accident, that certain earth pigments could make different colors appear on the fired ware, and as early as the sixth millennium B.C., pottery was washed over with a red color painted with geometric designs.

Various minerals were used in the Neolithic period to paint decorations onto the pottery. These decorations ranged from stylized human figures, fishes, birds, or frogs in the Panpo culture of China to intricate rosettes in Mesopotamia. Many of these painted jars have similar designs, although they were separated by thousands of miles, leading some people to speculate about some yet unknown common decorative ancestry. More likely, the shapes of the pots and the materials themselves suggested the similar motifs. A good example of this similarity is the spiral design that has appeared around the world in pottery widely separated in time as well as place. Scratched into a pot in ancient Japan, it was painted on an Egyptian vessel before 3000 B.C. as well as on early Chinese and Cretan jars (Figures 1-32 to 1-34).

These swirl designs were used on early pottery all over the world, and are still used as decoration today. Perhaps the earliest swirl designs had a religious significance, or perhaps they were used just because their flowing lines expressed nature's own rhythms. The curves of the popular decorative motif fit the shape of the pot, giving pleasure to the artisan and owner, or to the god to whom the vessel was offered.

Figure 1-35 Hollow figure of bull with pouring spout. Amlash, 1st millennium B.C. Height 6⅞ in. (17.4 cm). *Courtesy, The Trustees of The British Museum, London.*

Figure 1-36 Terra cotta horse. Sari Dheri, India, 100 B.C.–A.D. 300. Height 4⅜ in. (11.1 cm), length 4¾ in. (12 cm). *Courtesy, Fogg Art Museum, Harvard University.*

Shape

The ancient and traditional pots shown in this chapter were all shaped to please the hands that would hold them as well as the eyes that would see them. How a piece of pottery feels in the hand is as important as how it looks. The shape, texture, even the weight are all part of

Figure 1-37 Vessels in the shape of birds. Old Silla dynasty, 5th–6th century A.D. *Courtesy, National Museum of Korea, Seoul.*

Figure 1-38 Pottery bird with spout and stopper in the shape of a bird's head. Suto, Losotho. Height 10 in. (25.4 cm). *Courtesy, the Trustees of The British Museum, London.*

the satisfaction we derive from a pot. Our industrialized society may have deadened our tactile sense, but people who still live close to the earth, planting, reaping, sorting, and grinding their food, have responsive fingers, and the pottery reflects this sensitivity.

Acutely aware of the bird and animal life around them, early clay-crafters took a creature's most characteristic aspect, simplified it, and modeled it into clay with vitality and humor. Such clay animals were made throughout history, sometimes as models of possessions to be buried with the dead, sometimes as votive offerings. Others were made as hollow vessels, probably for holding liquid offerings or libations (Figures 1-35 to 1-38).

Early Potter's Wheels

Having seen how early potters built up their pots with coils, shaping them as they turned them in their hands, we can understand how the potter's wheel probably evolved. Picture yourself kneeling or squatting in the sun outside a mud-daubed hut sometime around

Figure 1-39 The sketches show various types of turntables. (1) A potter uses an old broken bowl resting on the ground or a stone to turn the pot while building it. (2) Shaped baked clay base swivels on rounded protrusion. (3) A more evolved turntable with two stones shaped to fit together made it easier for the potter or his assistant to turn it. (4) A turntable revolving in a socket with a wooden or clay wheel pivoting on an axle in a socket. Some village potters still use this type of turntable (Figure 2-4).

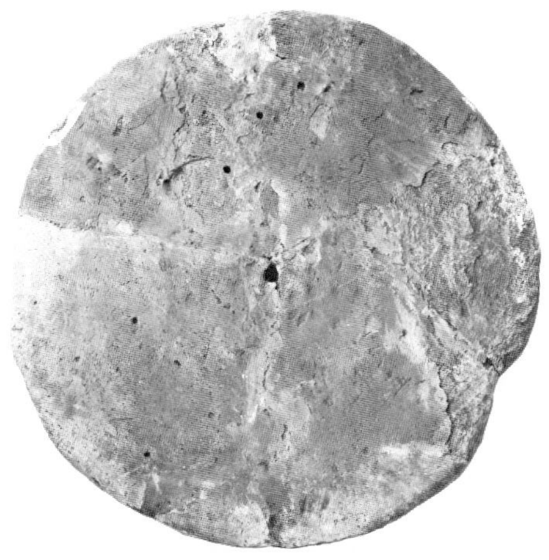

Figure 1-40 One of the earliest pottery-turning devices found. Used by a potter in Ur around 3500 B.C., it may have pivoted on a stone socket set in the ground. Diameter 29½ in. (75 cm). *Courtesy, the Trustees of The British Museum, London.*

7000 B.C., coiling a pot in your lap. Perhaps you have rested the base in an old broken pot, and while you smooth the coils you turn it in your lap. Tiring of this, you might set it down on a stone and realize that it turned more easily there. You have just made a primitive turntable. Eventually someone had the idea of using two stones as a wheel. It may well have taken hundreds of years for this idea to develop into a turntable made from two stones shaped to fit together—the first manufactured potter's wheel. Made from smooth stone like basalt, turntables like these could revolve smoothly as the potter shaped the pot, making it much easier to coil, smooth, and polish it evenly (Figures 1-39 to 1-41).

At some point, the potter put an assistant to work spinning the turntable (Figure 2-20), but we do not know exactly when the turntable evolved into a true potter's wheel. A true potter's wheel must turn fast enough—at least

Figure 1-41 This stone socket and disk made of basalt is of a later date than Figure 1-40, but it shows how a stone bearing would revolve smoothly in a socket. A clay disk on this pivot would turn easily. Similar paired stones, which are probably bearings, have been found in an early potter's shop in Hazor, north of the Sea of Galilee. Stone pottery wheel, Beth-Shan, Israel, c. A.D. 500. *Courtesy, Israel Department of Antiquities and Museums.*

Figure 1-42 Sketch based on an Egyptian carving of the god Khum, showing him using an early kick wheel.

100 revolutions per minute—to give the necessary **centrifugal force** to a lump of clay so that only a light pressure of the hands is needed to make the clay walls rise. In this way, the energy for **throwing** comes from the wheel rather than the potter's hands. Nor can we define exactly what type of wheel it was, or when someone added a lower wheel, which was kicked by the potter's foot to start it whirling (Figure 1-42). Archaeologists have studied the characteristic marks made on pots that are thrown on a true wheel and have set probable dates for its first use—around 3500 B.C. in Mesopotamia, 2300 B.C. in Sumer, after 2750 B.C. in Egypt, and about the same date in China. Potters continued to use the earlier turntables along with kick wheels, however, and they are still used today in various parts of the world (Figure 2-5).

Figure 1-43 Heating pots before firing them in Ogbomosho, Nigeria. Notice the piles of straw in the background, probably gathered as fuel for the firing of the pots. *Courtesy, Field Museum of Natural History, Chicago.*

Firing

Whatever method was used to shape the earthenware pot—pinch, slab, or coil—it eventually had to be fired to harden it. The earthenware clay used in ancient workshops could be fired to a reasonable hardness at a low heat. It matures at low temperatures, never becoming vitrified like stoneware fired at high temperature, and, as we have seen, always remains porous. This low-fire clay was used for making domestic ware throughout the world during all periods of history, and in places where industrial products have not ruined the potter's market, it still supplies the bulk of cooking and storage containers.

Open Firing

Undoubtedly the first earthenware was fired in **open fires** or in pits, much as it is still done in villages in Africa, Fiji, the Middle East, and the American Southwest. First the pots were air-dried. Then, to speed the drying process and to make sure that all the water was driven out of the clay, the potter might have burned dried grass or dung inside the pots (Figure 1-43). Once the pots were thoroughly dry, they were stacked along with the fuel (Figure 1-44). Wood, straw, dung, sugar cane, peat, palm fronds—any combustible material that could be gathered in quantity was used.

Just how to stack, how much wood or straw to use, how long to burn the fire, when to cool the pots, all these problems were worked out slowly with technical knowledge built up over the years and eventually becoming traditions. For instance, the potter may have found that the best time for firing was the evening when the wind had dropped, or that it might work best to fire at a certain time of year. This would become a tradition, unquestioned by potters of later generations who might continue the practice without really knowing why.

Figure 1-44 Firing pots in open fires in Fiji. The pots are simply piled together on the ground, and palm fronds and grasses are piled over them, then lighted. *Courtesy, Fiji Museum, Suva.*

Empirically learned techniques have been the basis of the potter's craft throughout history, passed on in families or through apprentice or slave systems.

Early Kilns

In some places firing was done in pits instead of on top of the ground, giving the potter more control over the heat. By 4000 B.C., in a Neolithic village in Panpo, China, pits with perforated floors separated the pots from the fire (Figure 3-5). Next, potters learned to build clay walls up around the pit, sheltering the pottery from the wind, increasing control over the fire, and cutting down on breakage from sudden temperature changes. By about 2900 B.C. in what is now Israel, potters were building enclosed kilns, and by the same date in China, a more efficient type of kiln was developed with a tunnel that led to a beehive-shaped chamber, creating a forced draft.

The earthenware was fired in these kilns for varying periods of time, depending on the fuel, the kiln, and the number of pieces being fired. Carefully cooled, the pots were taken out of the kiln and possibly coated with natural resin or other material to close the pores before being used.

Figure 1-45 As pottery techniques improved, early potters built kilns to give them more control over the fire and to improve the firing. Vertical kilns with perforated floors above fire pits were used in Mesopotamia as early as 4000 B.C. In these, the heat rose through holes in the floor to bake the pots above. Similar kilns are used in Crete today (see Figure 2-7).

Evolving Techniques

The methods and techniques we have discussed, or ones very much like them, were used by potters all over the world, taking hundreds of years for modifications and refinements to develop. Sometimes migrations would bring new potters to an area and they would teach local potters their techniques. But new ideas are absorbed slowly, and potting in some cultures was so well adapted to the local ecology that methods stayed the same indefinitely. In other places settlements changed from simple agricultural villages to urban centers, causing social and economic changes that affected the production of pottery. In towns, what had once been a home industry became a specialized craft, carried out by men in workshops.

We have compressed thousands of years and many cultures into this discussion of early pottery making and much of it is conjecture based on our study of traditional methods; but there is no question that later ceramics techniques built directly on the discoveries made by early potters. No matter how complex modern ceramics has become, a hand-made pot is still made from decomposed rock, still formed by fingers that respond to the same human desire to make a satisfying shape.

Chapter Two

The Mediterranean World

As early agricultural societies evolved into more complex cultures, new skills and crafts emerged alongside the older crafts of weaving and pottery. In some cultures, metal working and ceramics apparently developed around the same time, each borrowing techniques from the other. Impurities in the clay, fusing when it was fired, or minerals that melted in the heat of a fire, may have suggested to an observant fire-tender the idea of using heat to produce workable metal. Smelting furnaces, at first simple out-door hearths, were later built with much the same construction as early kilns, except that holes were left at the bottom of the furnace walls so that bellows with clay tips could be inserted to pump air into the fire to fan it to the required heat for smelting (Figure 4-2).

Within these new bronze and iron societies, with their improved technology, the craft of pottery making continued to advance, and firing methods and wheels became more efficient. Ceramics had become a true industry, practiced by specialists.

Around the shores of the Mediterranean and on its many islands, in the years from about 3000 B.C. to the early Christian era, kingdoms and empires appeared, flourished, then declined. On the mainland of Asia, in the Fertile Crescent between the Tigris and Euphrates Rivers, a succession of cultures evolved, building elaborate cities based on irrigation of crops and trading of surplus goods. Meanwhile, along the Nile River, the Egyptians built their temples and tombs with the labor of thousands of slaves.

In some of these cultures, clay was used for building with sun-dried bricks, in others for decorating their palaces with ceramic tiles. But in most of them, the potter's energy went into making earthenware vessels for religious rituals and everyday life. Pottery was still fired at low temperatures, and porous earthenware was still the main material used for ordinary domestic utensils.

Egypt

In Egypt, pottery making was carried on in workshops, where specialized master potters would form the ware while their assistants

Figure 2-1 An Egyptian potter's shop, depicted in a mural in a tomb around 1900 B.C., shows the potter and his assistants at work. At the far left, two workers mix the clay with their feet. Next to them are shelves filled with pots and two apprentices loading the kiln. Egyptian kilns were vertical, with an opening at the top. The ware may simply have been piled inside or possibly placed on projecting platforms. In the center of the mural, a helper carries the finished pots in baskets, while at his feet an assistant wedges more clay. The master potter next to him appears to be removing a pot from the wheel, steadying the turntable with his hand. At the far right, two potters form pots, surrounded by finished ware of all shapes and sizes. From a mural in Tomb 2, Beni Hasan, Egypt, c. 1900 B.C. *Courtesy, Egyptian National Museum, Egyptian Service of Antiquities, Cairo.*

mixed the clay, loaded the kiln, and stacked the ware (Figure 2-1). No longer did women make pottery at home to be used by their families. And yet, Egypt's main use of pottery was for everyday ware, because the priesthood and nobility used utensils made of more expensive materials.

Egyptian Glazes

Egypt's most important contribution to ceramics was the discovery of the first glazes, probably by accident. Glazes are compounds of glass-forming minerals that fuse and adhere to the clay body, coating it with what is essentially a thin layer of glass, making it impervious to liquids. Glazes vary in color, hardness, transparency, and fusing temperatures, but, like clay, they are of geological origin. Basically they are silica and alumina, with a **flux** to help the other ingredients fuse. Sand, flint, and quartz are almost pure silica, which at 3270° F (1800° C) would fuse and form glass, but at that temperature the clay underneath would melt. So a flux material is necessary to help the glaze materials fuse at lower temperatures.

The first Egyptian glazed material, known as **Egyptian paste,** was probably discovered by accident when desert sand containing soda ash and potash happened to be mixed with clay. The **soluble** sodium rose to the surface with the water as it evaporated and, when the piece was fired, fused into a glaze. Particles of copper contained in the clay body caused the paste to fire with a shiny blue finish. From this accidental glaze, which was actually part of the clay body itself, the Egyptians went on to make blue and turquoise glazes, which they applied to the surface of the clay. The Egyptians were also expert at glass making and learned to apply their glass techniques to pottery. These early glazes may have been discovered when glass-workers saw how the melted glass coated the pottery crucibles in which it was heated.

The discovery of glazes was an important contribution, which spread to other areas of the Middle East at an early date. These highly **alkaline** glazes of Egypt, however, were apt to crack and peel off. For that reason, they were used mostly on a few ceremonial bowls, on jewelry, and on small sculptures. More successful glazes were developed in Mesopotamia, using lead as a flux, a development we will follow later.

Crete

The island of Crete in the Mediterranean was well situated to dominate trade routes all over the eastern part of that sea. Because of their contact with Egypt, Cretan potters learned the secret of Egyptian paste, and like the Egyptians, they used it mainly for small statuettes or jewelry.

Maintaining a well disciplined navy, Crete was safe from invasion for centuries, and an elaborate and sophisticated culture developed based on commerce with mainland neighbors. Influenced by artistic and religious ideas from Egypt and Mesopotamia, Crete rapidly built up its own lively, colorful culture. Called the Minoan, after King Minos, it lasted from around 2500 to 1100 B.C.

The Cretans worshiped a mother goddess in shrines high up on mountain peaks, where ritual offerings were made to her to ensure the success of the crops. Women, at least those of the upper classes, had more freedom in Crete than in other Eastern cultures, taking part in the ritual sports, dances, and even hunting (Figure 2-2). It is possible that they were also artists, making and decorating religious vessels. They were often portrayed in wall paintings, shown in colorful clothing and participating in sporting and religious events.

The royalty lived in huge palaces whose countless rooms were decorated with brilliantly colored murals; there they enjoyed the comforts of luxurious baths, which were hooked up to terra cotta drainage systems.

Figure 2-2 Priestesses of the mother goddess move in a sacred dance in Minoan Crete, holding one another's shoulders in a gesture still seen in Greek dances today. In the middle stands a musician playing a lyre. The priests and priestesses, usually of noble birth, offered sacrifices, led religious processions to the peak sanctuaries, and arranged ritual dances. Women were active in religious life, participating in the dangerous bull-vaulting, which honored the goddess. Palaikastro, Crete, 1400–1100 B.C. *Courtesy, The Archaeological Museum of Heraclion, Crete.*

Under the palace at Knossos was a maze of storerooms, perhaps the basis of the Greek legend of the labyrinth and the Minotaur. According to the myth, the Minotaur was a half-bull, half-human monster who lived underground at Knossos, demanding a tribute of young men and women from mainland Greece. The Greek hero Theseus escaped from the labyrinth by unwinding a ball of string as he was led through the maze; later he followed the string back out. If you visit these storerooms at Knossos, you will see huge pottery storage jars, or **pithoi,** still in place (Figure 2-3). Made to store grain and oil, they are impressive reminders of the permanence of clay, for they survived the fire that destroyed the palace around 1450 B.C. Around the palace clustered the workshops of the craftsmen, among them the potters who made the pithoi, using methods still followed by potters in Crete today. Watching these potters at work

Figure 2-3 Storage jars, or *pithoi,* underground in the storerooms of the royal palace at Knossos, Crete. The huge jars held grain, oil, and apparently honey, for legend tells us that the young son of King Minos died in Knossos by falling into a huge jar of honey. He was found trapped there with only his legs sticking out. The tall jars were built up of coils in six bands, just as the pithoi are made on Crete today. The rows of raised decoration, in which we can see the potter's thumb prints, marked the joining point of the bands, adding strength. Knossos, Crete, c. 1400 B.C.

Figure 2-4 In Thrapsanon, modern potters still make large storage jars, working outdoors on turntables set in trenches. Like the earlier Minoan jars, they are built up in a series of bands of coils. An assistant potter moves along the row of wheels, adding new coils to each pithos after the earlier band hardens slightly. The master potter follows him, shaping the bands until six bands complete a jar. A helper sits in the trench and turns the wheel. When the jar is finished, the handles are added and designs are drawn. By the next day the thick-walled jars have dried enough to be moved from the turntables, and they then dry in the hot sun until ready for firing in the nearby kiln.

today, we can see how Minoan potters probably made their jars, using turntables and vertical kilns.

Cretan Pottery-Building Techniques

The village of Thrapsanon in the hills of Crete has been a potter's village for generations. One of the older monks at the nearby monastery remembers it fifty years ago when there were over one hundred potters there. Now there are only a handful still using the ancient techniques. They work indoors on smaller pots during the cooler months of the year, but in June they move out to the fields near the kiln, making the thick-walled pithoi similar to those in Knossos (Figures 2-3 and 2-4).

These modern jars are shaped on wheels formed of disks of moisture-resistant plane wood turning on spindles of olive wood (Figure 2-5). In much the same way, a clay potter's wheel dating from around 1700 B.C. probably turned on a wooden axle fitted into a clay socket on its underside (Figure 2-6). The shaft of the Minoan wheel may have revolved in a stone socket in the ground or in a wooden frame like those at Thrapsanon today.

Thrapsanon potters now work in teams, with the master potter shaping the jar on the turntable while an assistant sits in a trench below, turning the wheel.

Figure 2-5 Drawing of a turntable used at Thrapsanon today shows how it revolves in a series of indentations placed along the trench. The tip of the axle pivots in a socket and is also braced by a cross-piece of wood resting on the sides of the pit. The section of the axle that passes through a notch in this plank is wrapped in felt, oiled, and attached to the crossbar with rope. The wheel head is made of plane wood to resist moisture, and the axle is of olive wood, which becomes smooth with friction, thus revolving easily. The handles are grasped by the assistant, who sits at the bottom of the trench and turns the wheel with a movement that is not fast enough to allow the clay to be centered on the wheel and worked through centrifugal force. Instead, the master potter pulls each band up to the needed height, and as the jar grows taller, he sits higher, finally standing to shape the top band. *Drawing based in part on "The Potters of Thrapsano" by Maria Voyatzoglou, in* Ceramic Review, *Nov.–Dec. 1973, no. 24.*

Figure 2-6 A potter's wheel from central Crete between 1700 and 1450 B.C., seen from the underside. A wooden axle was fixed to the center of the wheel and revolved in some type of socket arrangement, perhaps similar to the one used in Thrapsanon today. Vathypetro, Crete. *Courtesy, The Archaeological Museum of Heraclion, Crete.*

Figure 2-7 The front of a kiln at Thrapsanon, Crete, where large jars are fired. Built of stones and covered with clay, it is basically a vertical cylinder built into the ground. Under the floor is the fire pit, and the heat rises through holes in the floor. The doorway will be closed with stones and clay after the jars are loaded, and sheet metal will be placed on top. The length of firing depends on the size and number of jars, but whatever the load, the stoker adds the wood fuel through a hole at the back, building the fire up to the necessary heat.

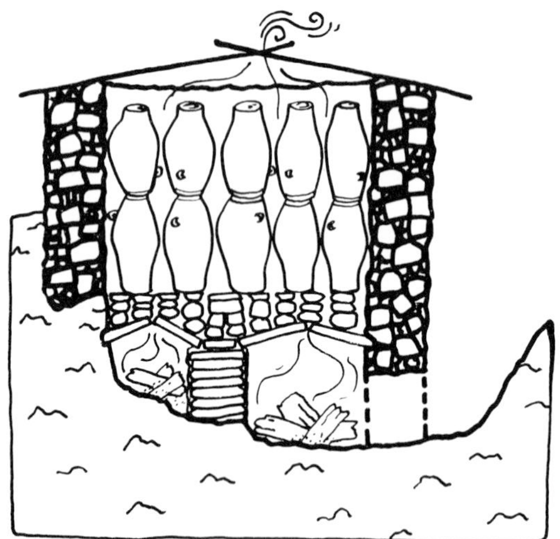

Figure 2-8 Drawing of a Cretan kiln in use today. Its cylindrical form is similar to the kilns of ancient Mesopotamia. Minoan potters probably fired their jars in kilns much like this one, placing pieces of broken pottery over the top instead of sheet metal. The floor of the kiln has holes in it through which the heat will rise from the fire pit below. *Drawing based on observation and on information in the article "The Potters of Thrapsano" by Maria Voyatzoglou, in* Ceramic Review, *Nov.–Dec. 1973 no. 24.*

Cretan Firing Method

The modern-day kiln, made of rocks smeared with fire-resistant clay, is of the vertical type, sunk into the ground with a perforated floor above the fire box. Firing is done with brush wood and is started in the early afternoon and tended carefully until the firing is finished around sunset (Figures 2-7 and 2-8).

This process is the result of empirical knowledge built up over generations, possibly going as far back as 2000 B.C. The young boys helping in the shops today are learning the craft through experience, just as their ancestors did. Hopefully, some of them will stay in Thrapsanon to continue the tradition, leaving their own thumb marks in the clay (Figures 1-2 and 1-3).

Cretan Decoration

Along with the pithoi, a great variety of ceramics was produced on Crete from 2600 to 1100 B.C. Lively dancing figures, cups, offering dishes in many shapes, incense burners, fruit squeezers, tablets covered with incised Minoan script, "teapots" with built-in containers to hold herb leaves, clay seals for bottles of wine marked with personal stamps, caskets for the dead—the list goes on and on (Figure 2-9).

The nature-loving Minoans drew inspiration from living forms of all kinds to decorate these clay products and make them more beautiful. Painted with great freedom, the palm trees, octopuses, flowers, leaves, dolphins, and shells were simplified to follow the curves of the vases and jars (Figures 2-10 and 2-11). Flowing and rhythmic, the painted decorations express the exuberant Cretan civilization with its love of dance, bright colors, and luxury. The potters, by a technique whose secret was lost, extended the usual colors painted on early pottery to a wider range of reds, oranges, and yellows, contrasted with bluish-black. At times the decoration becomes so overwhelming that it distracts our eyes from the shape of the vase, but at its best it is lively, designed to enhance the form of the pot, repeating the curve of a spout or the space between a handle and body (Figures 2-11 and 2-12).

Figure 2-10 Minoan pithos from the palace at Knossos. Made in one of the potter's workshops there between 2000 and 1700 B.C., it is decorated with palm trees, outlined with red against a solid black background. This piece, with its curving palm fronds emphasizing the swell of the body, expresses the love of nature and the vitality so typical of Minoan pottery. *Courtesy, The Archaeological Museum, Heraclion, Crete.*

Figure 2-9 From the Minoan palace at Phaistos comes this vessel with a perforated top and pouring spout, probably used as a "tea pot" for herb leaves like the dittany sold in Cretan markets today as treatment for stomachache. The leaves may have been placed in the strainer, the hot water poured over it to steep the herbs. 2000–1700 B.C. *Courtesy, The Archaeological Museum, Heraclion, Crete.*

Figure 2-11 Dolphin vase, also from Knossos, is an example of how the Cretans adapted marine motifs to pottery decoration. Here, the swirl motif suggests the crest of a breaking wave, while the flowing forms enhance the elegant shape of the jar. It narrows to a graceful base, giving it a lighter quality than the pithos with the earthbound palm trees. 2000–1700 B.C. *Courtesy, The Archaeological Museum of Heraclion, Crete.*

Figure 2-12 Handsomely shaped jar from the Palace at Knossos is almost overwhelmed by its nervously twining decoration of leaves, which distract the eye from its shape. It was made and painted during the later period of Minoan ceramics, just before the disaster that burned down the palace. 1700–1450 B.C. *Courtesy, The Archaeological Museum of Heraclion, Crete.*

Figure 2-13 This jar was found in Mycenae, on the Greek mainland. Perhaps made in Crete and shipped to Mycenae, or made by Mycenaean potters influenced by Crete, it is an example of how ceramics at Mycenae followed Minoan styles. The octopuses twining their tentacles around the jar are stylized and placed on the amphora so that they enhance the vessel's form. 1400–1450 B.C. *Courtesy, the National Archaeological Museum, Athens.*

Mycenae

The Mycenaeans, inhabitants of the Peloponnesus of Greece, were influenced by the art of the Minoans (Figure 2-13), whom they may have conquered; but their military society, which built the huge hill-top citadel of Mycenae, is better expressed by vases like the "Warrior Vase" with its marching soldiers (Figure 2-14). Beginning around 1450 B.C., when Crete either fell to invaders or was destroyed by natural disaster, Mycenae became the dominant power in the Aegean for over 200 years. Mycenaean pottery was found as far away as Egypt, Asia Minor, Cyprus, and Italy, testifying to the commercial power of the Mycenaeans. The king, or overlord, of this aggressive society lived in a fortress palace on the top of a hill in Mycenae, surrounded by an active, commercial town with potters' workshops, goldsmiths, and craftsmen making armor like that shown on the Warrior Vase.

These rich and powerful Mycenaeans held territorial rights on the mainland of Asia Minor, and the Trojan War may very well have been fought for strategic reasons instead of to recover Helen, the beautiful wife of Menalaus. After this war, a long period of disruption followed during which, Homer tells us, Odysseus wandered throughout the Aegean. Actually, a

Figure 2-14 Detail of the painting on the Warrior Vase, a *krater,* or vessel used for mixing wine and water. Mycenaean soldiers in full war-gear, with shields, spears, and plumed helmets, march in formation around its top. The siege of Troy, immortalized by Homer, took place during the period of Mycenaean power, and soldiers who embarked for Troy probably were equipped like these. 1300–1200 B.C. *Courtesy, The National Archaeological Museum, Athens.*

period of migrations and invasions occurred throughout this whole area. From about 1100 to 700 B.C., life was unsettled, and the only record we have of this period is in its pottery (Figures 2-15, 2-16, and 2-17).

Greece

According to a Greek legend, the first pottery wine cup was molded over Helen's breast, which explains the beautiful shapes of Greek pottery. Mythology tells us that Athena, patroness of weaving, was also the inventor of many useful things, including the earthenware pot. For that reason, Prometheus, warring against the Titans, turned to her for help to make extra warriors out of clay. Brought to life by Athena, these soldiers defeated the Titans. In still another myth, a woman was made of clay and given life by the breath of the Four Winds. She was Pandora, whose curiosity got her into trouble when she released the ills of the world from the box. We can see from these stories that clay held an important place in Greek life, and Greek potters produced some of the world's most beautiful pottery.

Geometric Decoration

We do not know when the kick wheel was introduced in Greece, but turntables were efficient enough by 800 B.C. for the potter to build huge vases, severely decorated in a totally new style. They are painted with geometric patterns and simplified human figures, which are totally different from the curving, nature-inspired painting on Minoan pottery (Figure 2-15). The building, decorating, and firing of pots of this size was itself a remarkable achievement. They show a new sense of discipline, a new attention to the relationship between all parts of the vessel, and a desire to fit the decoration to its shape, all features of later Greek art (Figure 2-16). These huge urns, many over four feet high, have a gloomy, ominous quality that suits the seriousness of the times (Figure 2-18). About the only lightness we find in the pottery of this period is in small models, probably toys (Figure 2-17).

Figure 2-15 Enormous urns, like this Attic *amphora,* were placed on graves to hold the ritual libations. Over four feet tall, they are a testament to the shaping and firing skill of Greek potters. No decoration could better complement the shape than these bands of severe, restrained geometric patterns, showing one of the earliest uses of Greek key, or meander, design. 900–800 B.C. *Courtesy, The National Archaeological Museum, Athens.*

Figure 2-16 Detail of a funeral procession on a large krater. The wide band of decoration shows two-horse chariots driven by warriors with helmets and shields. The decorator's brush strokes are clearly seen, filling in the solid black and the cross-hatching on the chariots. Late 8th century B.C. *Courtesy, The National Archaeological Museum, Athens.*

Figure 2-17 Toy horse carrying miniature wine jars shows us that life was not all funerals and war in the Dark Age. The toy could be pushed around on the ground in the way that children today push plastic racing cars on the floor. Chalsis. *Courtesy, The National Archaeological Museum, Athens.*

Figure 2-18 *(Right)* Geometric kraters like this were placed on graves in the Diplyon Cemetery in Athens, serving as memorials as well as ritual vessels. The painting usually included war chariots, soldiers with shields, and rows of figures in the accepted pose of mourning, arms clasped over their heads. In the center is the deceased, lying in state. On this large vase, there is the figure of a woman with a child on her lap seated at the feet of the deceased, a rather homely touch amidst the pomp of the funeral. 8th century B.C. Height 40½ in. (102.9 cm). *Courtesy, The Metropolitan Museum of Art, Rogers Fund, 1914.*

Development of Greek Pottery

It is clear that the potters now had the technical knowledge to produce magnificent shapes, and by the time Greece began to recover from the Dark Age, around 800 B.C., the craftsmen working first in Corinth, later in Athens, were building up a proud tradition. From that time, through the Golden Age of Greece, to the last days of the Roman Empire, the greatest vase makers in the Mediterranean world were to be the Greeks, whose wares would be transported all over the Eastern world and into Europe. Greek wine containers, for example, have been found in sunken ships off the coast of southern France, and the greatest amount of Greek pottery ever unearthed has been found on the mainland of Italy, where some of the most beautiful Athenian vases were sent as export items.

Figure 2-19 Possibly a self-portrait of the potter at work in his shop, painted on the interior of a black-figure cup in the beginning of the fifth century B.C. He sits on a low stool, apparently adding handles to the wine cup on his turntable. *Courtesy, the Trustees of The British Museum, London.*

Athenian Pottery

Athenian craftsmen worked in shops crowded together in the potters' quarter of Athens, called the *Kerameiskos,* which was located near large deposits of red clay, or ***keramos.*** From it comes our word *ceramics.* Most of the potters were foreigners, drawn to Athens from all parts of the Mediterranean because, as the ceramics center of their world, Athens offered them a better opportunity to make a living. There they exchanged techniques, bringing together knowledge from many cultures and enriching the Greek art of pottery. Here, as with other art forms, the Greeks took ideas from many sources, always transforming them into their own forms of expression (Figures 2-19 and 2-20).

Figure 2-20 The drawing shows a Greek potter's wheel from about 600 B.C. with an assistant rotating the turntable. The importance the Greeks gave to ceramics is illustrated by the legend of Talos, nephew and apprentice of the Greek craftsman Daedalus. Talos supposedly invented the potter's wheel, whereupon Daedalus became so jealous that he pushed him off the rock of the Acropolis in Athens.

Important political and sports figures would come to these Athenian shops to order vases commemorating a special event, a victory, the death of an important person, or the winner of one of the Olympic contests. Now, for the first time, pottery was signed by individual artists. The inscription might read "Exekias made this" or "Exekias made and painted this," so we know that some of these accomplished painters were also master potters (Figure 2-21). Some potters became owners of their workshops, painting the vases and cups made by assistants working under their supervision. Although the vases and cups were formed by men, some of the painters were women. Pottery was a commercially important craft, and many potter-painters became famous, showing great pride in the work of their hands in clay.

Figure 2-21 Homeric tales were popular themes for decoration on pottery. A famous black-figure *amphora,* by Exekias, shows Achilles and Ajax playing a game during a lull in the siege of Troy. In this technique of decoration, the black figures were painted on the light clay body, and the lines were scratched through the slip with a sharp instrument, revealing the lighter color underneath. The detail of the flowered cloaks, curls of hair, and decorated armor is drawn with Exekias' masterly touch, always subordinated to the simple, dignified figures of the heroes. All this rich detail, as well as the stylized flowers and hearts on the handles and upper band, is carefully composed on a curving vase, which in itself is a masterpiece of the potter's art. 540–530 B.C. *Courtesy, The Vatican Museums.*

Black-Figure Pottery

The first potters of the new **black-figure** style of pottery worked in Corinth, but soon the Athenians surpassed them in this form of decoration (Figures 2-19, 2-21, and 2-22).

The method used to achieve the contrast between the black figures and the buff or reddish background was a complex one. A special slip—clay containing iron oxides and water, mixed to a creamy consistency—was formulated to paint the figures; the black and red colors were produced through the firing method—a complex alternation of **oxidizing** and **reduction** firings. The reduction atmosphere turned the slip black. Reduction occurs when the flame is smothered and does not get enough oxygen to burn completely. Trying to get more oxygen, the flame will draw it from the metal oxides in the clay slip, releasing the metal in the slip and making the clay change color. After this reduction firing, if the slip were correctly formulated, it would stay black when the kiln was returned to an oxidizing atmosphere. In an oxidizing atmosphere, the fire receives enough oxygen for total combustion, turning the areas not coated with slip back to the usual reddish or buff color. This method requires great care, because the pot can turn all one color if the kiln is not oxidized at the right time (Figure 2-24).

Figure 2-22 Not all black-figure pottery was monumental or solemn. Scenes of the festivals of Dionysos, god of wine, were popular for drinking cups. Originally religious rituals, these festivals later were satyr-plays performed in theaters with actors portraying Dionysos, Silenes, and the satyrs and maenads. *Photo by Hannibal, Athens.*

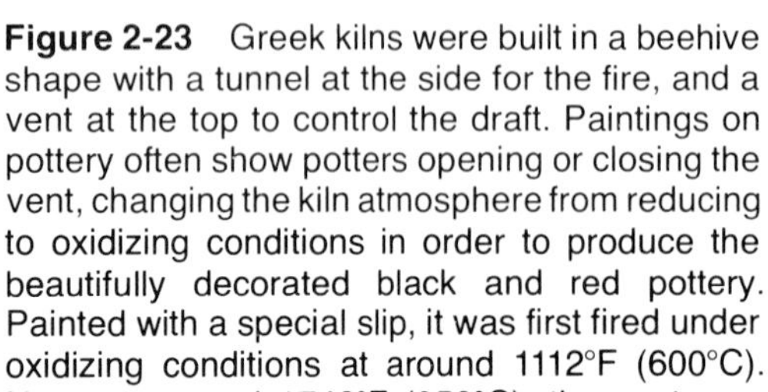

Figure 2-23 Greek kilns were built in a beehive shape with a tunnel at the side for the fire, and a vent at the top to control the draft. Paintings on pottery often show potters opening or closing the vent, changing the kiln atmosphere from reducing to oxidizing conditions in order to produce the beautifully decorated black and red pottery. Painted with a special slip, it was first fired under oxidizing conditions at around 1112°F (600°C). Next, at around 1742°F (950°C), the vent was closed and the fire was smothered. This reduced the ware, turning the whole piece black. When the kiln cooled to a little below 1472°F (800°C), the vent was reopened and oxygen entered, turning the unpainted areas red again.

Greek Pottery Shapes

The master potters of Greece developed highly refined shapes for many purposes, from the large Geometric memorial vase, to the **amphora** (Figure 2-21), which was used to carry liquids and became the accepted shape for commemorative vessels, to the *krater,* in which wine and water were mixed. Other vessels with different shapes held perfume or the oil with which athletes rubbed themselves. These shapes became part of the western

European heritage. Indeed, we can still see a poor reflection of them in the cups and urns presented to winning athletes or carved on gravestones today. They were also traded as far as China, influencing pottery forms there.

Red-Figure Pottery

Around 525 B.C. a new style called **red-figure** pottery appeared in Athens in which red figures were silhouetted against the lustrous background slip (Figure 2-24). This was done by what is called a reserve process, in which the black-firing slip was painted around the figures, reserving the color of the red slip for the figures. The vase itself may have been first coated with a wash of iron or a thin reddish slip. Within the reserved red areas, the details of faces, bodies, clothing, and armor were painted in black lines with a single-haired brush (Figures 2-24 and 2-25).

Figure 2-24 Red-figure painting reversed the earlier technique. Now the potters painted the black around the figures, leaving the figures the red of the clay. Instead of scratched lines, the details were painted in black with a fine brush (Color Plate 2, p. 50A). On this *stamnos,* a vessel originally made to store oil or grain, but here probably used as a presentation piece, Odysseus and his crew resist the beautiful song of the sirens. Odysseus stuffed his oarsmen's ears with wax and had himself tied to the mast so that they would not be lured onto the rocks by the song. The sirens do their best to change their minds, one even flying over the boat, her mouth open in song. Vulci, c. 490–489 B.C. Height 13⅞ in. (35.2 cm). *Courtesy, the Trustees of The British Museum, London.*

Figure 2-25 Tall and cylindrical, the *lekythos* shape was used for funeral vessels, which usually showed the person whose death they commemorated. Now the red-figure drawing became fluid and lyrical. On this urn, a young warrior leads his horse off to the battle from which he never returned. *Courtesy, The National Archaeological Museum, Athens.*

Terra Cotta Figures

The Greek theater, which culminated in the tragedies of Aeschylus, Sophocles, and Euripides, actually grew out of the festivals that were held in honor of Dionysos, god of wine. The bawdy comedies of Aristophanes, performed to enthusiastic audiences in the ancient outdoor theater at Epidauras, remained closer in spirit to the wine festivals. Groups of clay figures depicting actors in the comedies were popular items in potters' show rooms (Figure 2-26), as were small statues of women.

Figure 2-26 Greek actors portray two drunken old men in this terra cotta statuette. Greek comedies were broad and earthy, and the actor's figures were often distorted with padded tights and jerkins. Mid-4th century B.C. *Courtesy, Staatliche Museum, Berlin.*

Figure 2-27 Unlike the women of Minoan Crete, women in classic Greece led a sheltered life within the home. Many small statues of women were made in quantity in Greece or by Greek craftsmen abroad. This one was found in Capua, in southern Italy, and shows two young women playing knuckle bones. Frequently the figure groups were made in molds and covered with slip and painted. Traces of the paint still show on the hair of the figure on the left. Late 4th century B.C. Height 5½ in. (14 cm), length 8½ in. (21.6 cm). *Courtesy, the Trustees of The British Museum, London.*

These **terra cotta** (literally, "cooked earth") statuettes were shipped throughout the Mediterranean from the fourth century B.C. on. Many of them were found in southern Italy, sometimes the product of Greek craftsmen who lived there, and sometimes brought there from Tanagra or other Greek towns where they were made in quantity. Among them, many graceful and elegant figures of women dancing, gossiping, arranging their hair, or caring for children give us a glimpse into the domestic life of Greek women (Figures 2-27 and 2-28). Dancing women were popular subjects, for dance and song were an important part of Greek life. Religious observances frequently included dances; a group of girls might dance at dawn to honor a goddess, or a whole chorus of dancers might sing and dance a hymn of praise. Sometimes a solo lyre player sang to

Figure 2-28 Greek terra cotta dancing figure, found in Italy, shows the freedom of action and motion characteristic of later Greek sculpture. 2nd century B.C. Height 10½ in. (26.7 cm). *Courtesy, the Trustees of The British Museum, London.*

accompany the dancers, and much of Greek lyric poetry was apparently composed for this purpose. Terra cotta reliefs were also mass-produced as offerings at shrines or to be placed in homes for decoration. They, too, show us scenes of home life—a cook in her kitchen, a housewife carefully putting folded garments away in a chest or quieting a child.

Clay in Architecture

Large architectural sculpture in Greece was generally made of readily available marble, although some large terra cotta figures decorated the very early temples. The builders of these early wooden temples also used terra cotta tiles to sheathe the ends of wooden roof beams, protecting them from moisture. Made with vertical grooves to drain off rainwater and protect the wood from rot, these tiles alternated with terra cotta tablets with painted decorations. Later, in the stone temples, these features were copied in marble and became the carved metopes and grooved triglyphs characteristic of the stone friezes running below the roofs of Greek temples.

Greece extended her colonies and trading outposts all over the Mediterranean, using her famous ships to carry conquering soldiers or jars of wine to distant ports. The strange inhabitants the warriors and traders encountered on these voyages fascinated the Greeks, whose intellectual curiosity about the world and desire for new territory and trade led them to be great travelers, and their pottery went with them, influencing potters all over the Mediterranean.

Mesopotamia

While the Greeks were exporting their painted pottery all over the Near East and Europe, on the mainland of Asia Minor clay-craftsmen were experimenting with **lead-tin** glazes.

By the sixth century B.C., tile makers in Babylon and Susa were covering the air-dried brick walls of palaces with brilliant, glazed brick decoration. These blue, brown, and yellow lead-tin-glazed bricks were often made in relief so that the animals or figures would stand out from the background (Figure 3-24). The discovery of lead as a glaze material allowed the potter to make glazes that did not crack like earlier alkaline ones, and the addition of tin made the glazes opaque. This was an important step in decoration, for it meant that the red or buff color of the clay body could be covered, and any colored decoration the potter wanted to apply would show up better. We will see how potters used these glazes later.

The Etruscans

As we have seen, the Greeks were sailors and traders, following the ocean trade routes and roving all over the Mediterranean. Greek contact with Italy had begun quite early—Mycenae traded with southern Italy as early as 1400 B.C. Early Greek traders were attracted to central Italy by the metal ore from its mines, as well as by the forests, a chief source of ship and building timber for the whole Mediterranean. The land was fertile, and Bronze Age farming communities there also developed a metal technology, melting the ore in clay crucibles and using clay molds to produce their tools, agricultural implements, and weapons. This Villanovan culture handed down its pottery-making and metal-working techniques to the Etruscans.

Early Influences on Etruscan Art

The newer Etruscan cities, in what is now central Italy, were settled by people believed to have migrated from Asia Minor. These cities were often built on the sites of earlier Villano-

Figure 2-29 Etruscan pitcher, formed of buccero clay imported from Spain that was said to give a pleasant fragrance to liquids stored in containers made of it. This highly polished, decorated jug, with its animal-head pouring spout, exhibits the typical Etruscan taste for fantasy. 6th–5th centuries B.C. Museo Archeologico, Florence. *Courtesy, Soprintendenza alle Antichita-Firenze.*

van villages, reaching the peak of their civilization between around 700 and 400 B.C. The land around them shaped the people's lives, for its mountains, lakes, deep forests, and fertile reclaimed marshland all provided the Etruscans with the natural resources for a rich culture.

By 750 B.C., a thriving trade with Greece brought quantities of Greek pottery to Etruria, greatly influencing the art that developed there. The Etruscans combined their Eastern love of imaginary animals—sphinxes, winged bulls, and griffons—with the Greek influences, incorporating Villanovan and Greek technology, to produce from this combination of heritages their own energetic art (Figure 2-29). It was an unrestrained expression of the Etruscan love of life and its pleasures along with their preoccupation with death and life after death (Figure 2-31). Even their tombs showed a love of life, for they were painted with brilliant murals of men and women whirling in ritual dances, flute players, and funeral banquets surrounded by trees and flowers, suggesting a celebration of life rather than the solemn mourning seen on the Greek Geometric vases.

Figure 2-30 According to Roman author Pliny, the Greek potter Butades of Corinth was the first to put terra cotta sculpture on temples. When the Greeks brought terra cotta sculpture to central Italy, the Etruscans added their own extravagant vitality, decorating the roofs of their temples with figures of gods and grotesque antefixes. Antefixes were placed along the edge of a roof to mask unsightly ends of tiles. In order to increase the size of the antefixes, the Etruscans surrounded them with brightly painted terra cotta shells. From Temple of Apollo, Veii, 6th and 5th centuries B.C. Museo di Villa Giulia, Rome. *Courtesy, Alinari-Art Reference Bureau.*

Etruscan Sculpture

Clay, which came from the fertile earth, was regarded by the Etruscans as a noble material and was used for the life-sized figures that decorated their temples (Figure 2-33). Originally simple rectangular buildings, Etruscan temples became more elaborate, incorporating Greek features just as the Etruscan religion incorporated Greek gods. Like all Etruscan art, they became an expression of their love of color, of surface decoration, of their intensity of feeling. The Etruscan spirit seemed particularly well suited to the spontaneity of clay, and in addition to making the large temple figures, the sculptors formed decorative tiles and ornaments for their roofs, frequently shaping the clay into grotesque faces or fantastic animals (Figure 2-30). Much of this clay decoration was made in molds, so that the same motifs were repeated frequently. All of it was brightly painted.

Sculptors also made life-sized terra cotta figures of Etruscan nobles to be placed on their coffins. The subjects of these portraits were not shown lying lifeless, but were sculpted in animated poses, capturing a pleasant

Figure 2-31 Etruscan sarcophagus from a tomb at Cerveteri displays reclining figures of husband and wife. Expressive faces and hands were typical of Etruscan tomb portraits, which developed from earlier funerary jars made in the shape of human heads. Found in fragments and reassembled, the sculpture proves how imperishable is fired clay. Photo shows unrestored sculpture. Sarcophagus, Cerveteri, 6th century B.C. Museo Nazionale di Villa Giulia, Rome. *Courtesy, Alinari-Art Reference Bureau.*

moment of their lives, often while they were reclining at a banquet (Figure 2-31).

Later, Etruscan sculptors, influenced by Hellenistic Greek art, became more interested in portraying individuals, and in some of their terra cotta heads we can see the beginnings of Roman portrait sculpture (Figure 2-32). These Etruscan sculptures, dug up during the Renaissance search for antiquities, also influenced later Italian sculptors like Jacopo della Quercia, Niccolò Pisano, and Donatello. Today there are Italian clay sculptors who, although they work in their own contemporary style, continue the vigorous Etruscan earth tradition (Figure 11-29).

Figure 2-32 Etrusco-Roman terra cotta head of a young man marks the change from earlier Etrusco-Greek faces to the more realistic later Roman portrait style. Late 3rd or 2nd century B.C.

Figure 2-33 Free-standing Etruscan sculpture of Apollo once stood on the roof of a temple where brightly painted terra cotta figures and decorative antefixes must have made a lively composition against the blue skies of Etruria. Making such a large figure of clay was a remarkable technical feat, but it was only possible by forming it around the decorated shape between the legs, which provided enough support for the striding figure. Apollo, from Veii, 510 B.C. Height 68⅞ in. (175 cm). Museo Nazionale di Villa Giulia. *Courtesy, Alinari-Art Reference Bureau.*

Rome

The Etruscans, who settled in what is now Rome before the Latins, were the first rulers of that area. Their influence on Roman religion, technology, and art continued long after the Latin Horatio defeated the Etruscan King Tarquin the Proud at the famous bridge over the Tiber.

Nevertheless, a characteristic Roman domestic ware of a type known as *terra sigillata* (literally, "sealed earth") was produced in Roman workshops. It was earthenware, made in what were really pottery factories. (One such factory at Arretium had a mixing vat with a capacity of 10,000 gallons.) This ware was thrown in a mold on a wheel, a technique learned from the Etruscans, and was covered with the same type of slip used on Greek black-figure pottery. However, instead of firing the ware in a reducing atmosphere to turn it black, the Roman potters fired it in an oxidizing atmosphere so that it came out a rich red. It was often decorated with molded figures in relief and was shipped in quantity throughout the Roman Empire. The Emperor Hadrian and Consul Marcus Aurelius were known to have made fortunes out of the pottery factories they owned. These factories also made tiles and other ceramic items for the elaborate public buildings and luxurious private palaces. For example, clay pipes in the walls and floors of the public baths carried hot air from a central wood- or charcoal-burning furnace into the rooms.

Clay was also used in building, particularly in the early days of Rome, when buildings were often made of brick and faced with stone. But by the time of the Roman Empire, terra cotta and brick were no longer in fashion, and marble was preferred for building and sculpture. This attitude was reflected in the boastful words of Augustus: "I found Rome of brick, I leave it of marble."

Chapter Three

The Orient and Western Asia

In the West, we tend to think of history as a direct line, starting with the Neolithic villages in Mesopotamia, moving on to the highly developed cultures of Egypt, Babylon, Crete, Greece, and Rome, and finally arriving at western Europe and America. We are also apt to get the impression that the only place Neolithic people settled into agricultural communities and developed civilizations was in the Middle East and the Mediterranean. It is true that until quite recently we have known much more about early Middle Eastern societies than about those in other parts of the world. This is largely because when archaeology began as a science in the 1800s, it centered on the Middle East; it was familiar ground, made so by the Bible and by Greek and Roman history. In the twentieth century, however, interest in early civilization has extended beyond the Near East and Mediterranean to Africa, the Russian steppes, Eastern Asia, the Americas, and the Orient.

In China, where the early human remains known as Peking man were found, skulls and tools have been discovered near ashes and charred earth, stones and bones, indicating that humans used fire there as early as 400,000 to 600,000 years ago. Excavations in other parts of Asia have also uncovered sites with evidence of the beginnings of agriculture. For example, a cave near the Thai-Burma border was occupied between 5600 and 10,000 B.C. by people who left traces of cucumbers, gourds, peas, water chestnuts, and other plant material. The archaeologists who excavated the caves believe that humans were cultivating plants there at least as early as in the Middle East. In an upper level of this cave, excavators unearthed skillfully made pottery, which the potters had decorated by pressing cords into the clay, combing textures on it, polishing its surface, and possibly even applying a resin finish. Obviously, potters must have been working in that area for a long time to have accumulated so much experience and knowledge about ceramics. These pieces of pottery, along with some very early ones found in Japan, Taiwan, and China, are some of the oldest pottery yet found in the world—between 9,000 and 12,000 years old.

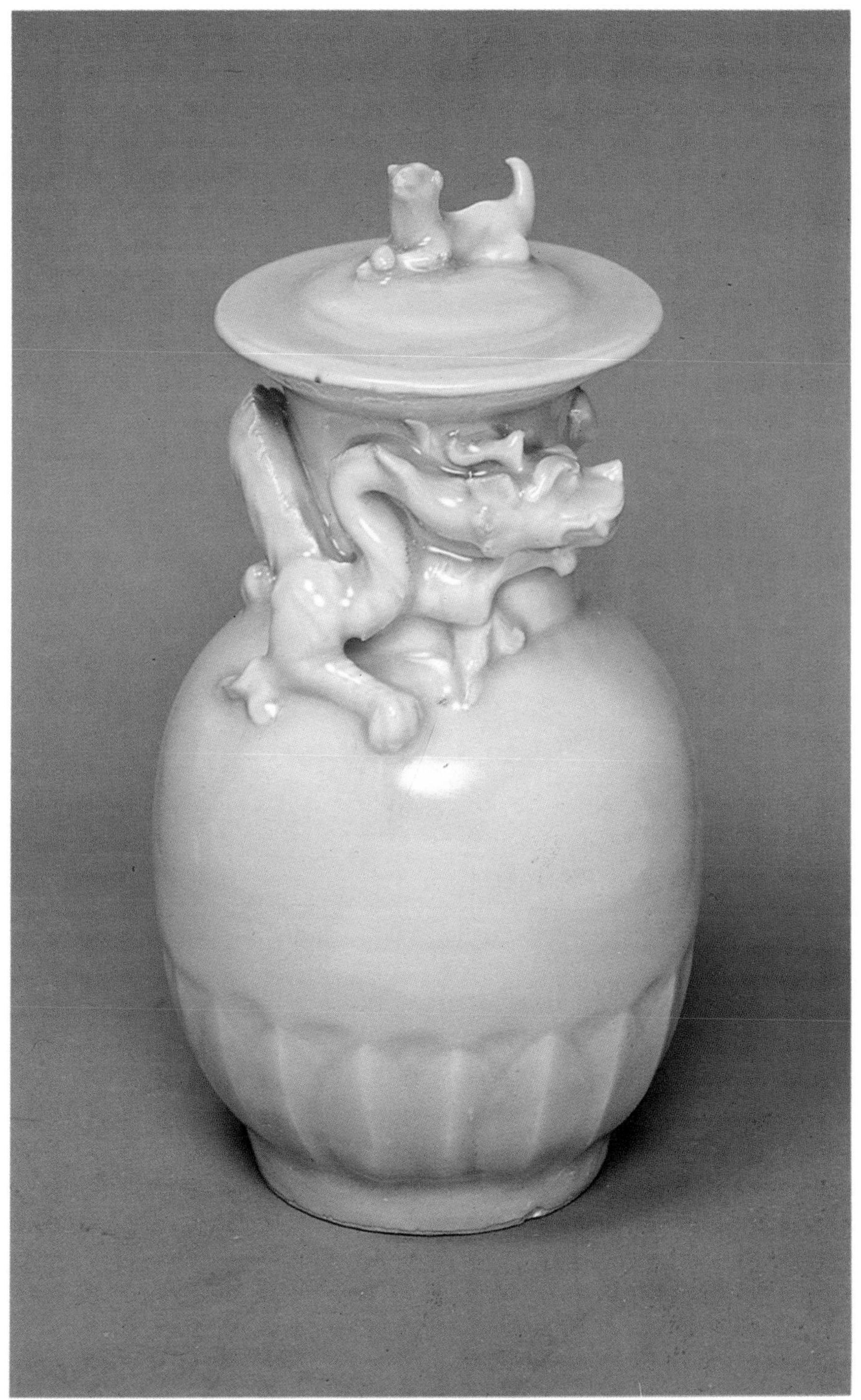

Color Plate 1 Ceremonial jar, China. Porcelaneous stoneware, celadon glaze. Late Northern Sung dynasty, 11th century A.D. Height 9½ in. (24 cm), diameter 5 in. (12.7 cm). *Courtesy, Asian Art Museum of San Francisco, The Avery Brundage Collection.*

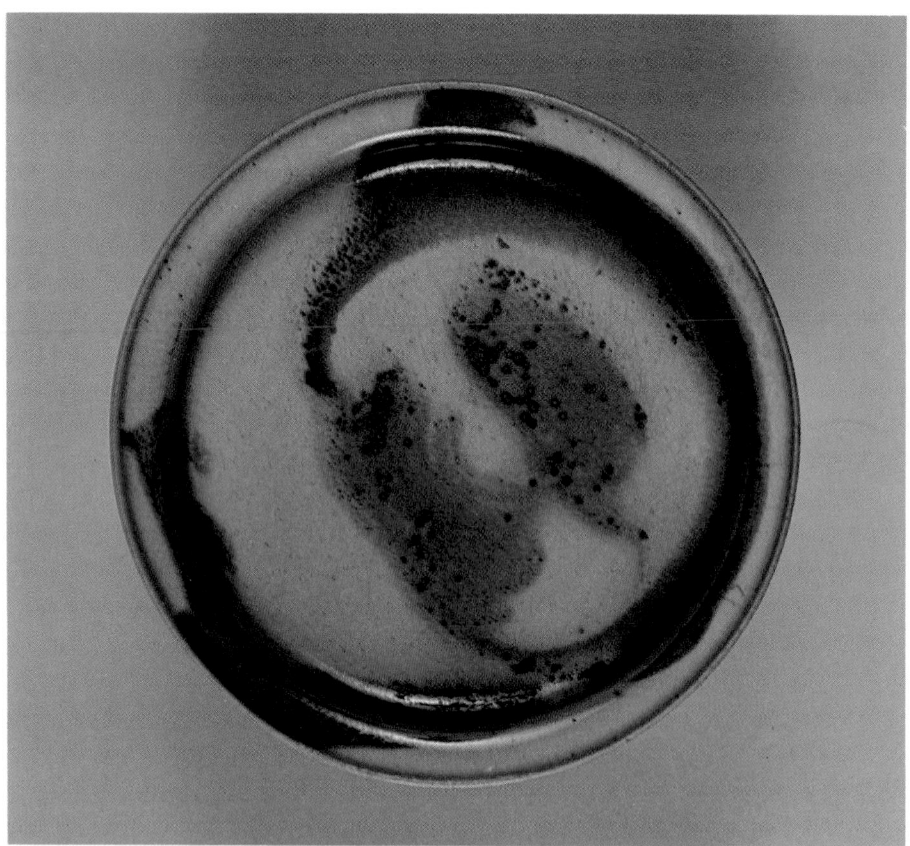

Color Plate 2 Chūn ware bowl, China. Sung dynasty (A.D. 960-1279). Stoneware with lavender glaze splashed with purple. Diameter 7½ in. (19 cm). *Courtesy, Victoria and Albert Museum, Crown Copyright.*

Color Plate 3 Vase with red copper glaze, China. K'ang-hsi period, A.D. 1662-1722. *Courtesy, Victoria and Albert Museum, Crown Copyright.*

Color Plate 4 Alkaline-glazed earthenware bowl, Persia. Black underglaze. 13th century A.D. Diameter 10¼ in. (26 cm). *Courtesy, Victoria and Albert Museum, Crown Copyright.*

Neolithic Culture

As excavations in various parts of the world continue to uncover places where early humans lived, our knowledge of their lives and crafts widens, bringing it into better perspective with the often-excavated Middle Eastern cultures.

China

Between 4,000 and 6,000 years ago, hunters who settled along the Yellow River in central China built up a farming civilization known as the Yangshao. A Neolithic village excavated at Panpo shows us that these people lived in permanent houses, maintained a cemetery, and built pottery kilns.

These farming people were skilled in the crafts, making stone tools and pottery—red earthenware made from *huang tu,* a yellow clay rich in alumina, which they tempered with sand. Their pots were not only decorated with fingernail-impressed designs, but were also painted (Figure 3-1). The painted decorations consisted mostly of geometric shapes and lines, but there were some representations of animals and humans. On the rims of some of

Figure 3-1 Painted pottery urns, low bowls, and jars were made of red clay on a turntable in Neolithic China. The pots were burnished before firing and decorated with mineral oxides in geometric patterns and flowing spiral designs in red, purple, and black. Beautifully shaped and thin-walled, they reflect a highly creative and technically advanced culture. This one was found in a grave in the province of Kansu. Panshan, China, 2500–1500 B.C. Height 13 in. (33 cm), diameter 16½ in. (42 cm). *Courtesy, Collection Haags Gemeentemuseum, The Hague.*

Figure 3-2 Some of the early pots in Neolithic China had three hollow legs, a form that may have developed from three pots joined together. Perhaps the shape of these *li* had a fertility significance, or possibly it was just a sensible way to make liquids boil faster on an open fire. Made from a coarse clay, they were low-fired and porous. The ribbed texture on the legs came from pounding them with rough paddles to thin them. Small clay tools shaped like mushrooms have been found in some places in China; apparently potters held them against the inside of a pot while they paddled the outside. Gray pottery, China, late Neolithic, c. 2000 B.C. Height 6 in. (15.2 cm), width 5¼ in. (13.3 cm). *Courtesy, Asian Art Museum of San Francisco, The Avery Brundage Collection.*

the pots were carefully incised marks, which may have been a method of recording events—possibly the beginning of writing, which was perfected at a very early date in China.

At various places in central and eastern China, potters in the Neolithic period made vessels in a tripod shape with swelling hollow legs, a shape that would influence pottery and later bronze forms for a long time in China (Figure 3-2).

The kilns in which early Chinese potters fired their ware were somewhat different from the early kilns in the Middle East. Many of them were built with a side tunnel in which the fire was lighted; the heat followed the tunnel into a chamber, where the pots were placed. The kilns were not large and could fire only about three or four large pots and about ten smaller ones to around 1470° F (800° C) (Figure 3-3).

By about 2000 B.C., in what is now China, potters of the westerly Kansu Yangshao culture were shaping clay into elegant thin-walled pottery, usually painted with **hematite** powder (red iron oxide) and manganese oxide in a great variety of designs. Many of the designs are geometric, consisting of light and heavy lines in bands, circles, crosses, dots, and triangles (Figure 3-1); others are painted with flowing lines, beautifully emphasizing the shapes of the vessels. Stemmed bowls with lines suggesting the flow of a river, low, wide basins, thin-necked jars, urns decorated with cross-hatched areas alternating with horizontal bands—all of these well-formed pieces were painted in restrained color, mainly black or purple-black with red and brown.

Figure 3-3 Early kilns in China were dug into the earth. Almost horizontal with a side tunnel in which the fire was built, one type of kiln had small heat vents in the floor to distribute the heat around the pots.

Archaeologists debate whether this Yangshao clay culture was influenced by invasions from western Asia, or whether it had moved westward from the central plains of China. When we study Asia and its many cultures, we must keep in mind the tribes that moved constantly through central Asia, passing on new ideas, new artistic forms from one part of the continent to another. Unlike the rich, easy-to-cultivate farming areas along the Nile, the Tigris, the Euphrates, the Indus, and the Yellow River, central Asia was a land of high mountains, wide steppes, and deserts, from which the herd-tending horsemen swept down onto their richer neighbors, sometimes destroying whole civilizations, sometimes becoming assimilated and bringing new ideas to the older communities. Often the reason for these raids was to force the more settled communities to trade the products of their craft, such as pottery, with the nomads, who offered horses in return.

At about the same time, 4,000 years ago, another Neolithic clay culture on the lower Yellow River, called Lungshan, was making black pottery with extremely thin walls. The pottery was made of fine clay, and judging by the thin walls and ridge marks, it was made on a more advanced wheel—apparently a true potter's wheel. Obviously, the potters of that area had made great technical progress. The surface of these vessels is a rich, glossy black, fired in a reduction kiln. The craftsmanship of the cups, stemmed bowls, and *ting* (a type of tripod vessel) is superb. The ting and some of the other shapes of these pots were later to be copied by the bronze-workers of the Shang dynasty.

Japan

At about the time that the potters in Kansu were making their beautiful jars and basins, clay was being used on the isolated island of Japan to make a quite different type of pottery and sculpture, on which the civilization of mainland China apparently had no effect.

Figure 3-4 Bold and strong, this late Jōmon figure is decorated with deeply carved swirls and textured areas alternating with highly polished surfaces. Like so much Japanese ceramic art, it is full of vitality, close to the earth from which it is made. Aomoni Prefecture, Japan, Late Jōmon, 1st millennium B.C. *Courtesy, Seattle Art Museum.*

Called Jōmon, after its "cord pattern" pottery, this period lasted from about 2000 B.C. to A.D. 1000. These Jōmon potters used a coil or slab method, probably without a turntable, to make heavy pottery built of a coarse clay containing a lot of impurities in it (Figure 1-30). It was, as was all early ware, low fired, perhaps in open fires, perhaps in simple pit kilns. Jōmon potters applied the decoration in a characteristic way, reflecting their response to the earthy quality of the material. Heavy and rough, deeply carved or impressed, it contrasts in its vitality and strength with the more refined, smooth-surfaced Chinese vessels (Figure 3-1).

Unlike the early Chinese, who did not make clay figurines, the Jōmon clay-workers made male and female figures, possibly fertility symbols (Figure 3-4). The early Japanese religion was centered on spirits believed to live in trees, rivers, ocean waves—in all of nature—and the people felt they had to keep them happy. These sculptures were probably used for some sort of ritual associated with this religion.

Chinese Technical Advances

In China, many features of the agricultural Neolithic culture were carried over into later periods—among them a preoccupation with ceremony, which developed into rigid rituals governing the rulers and their servants.

Shang Dynasty

The first of the true Chinese dynasties, the Shang, began about 1500 B.C. and placed a central ruler above the local landed lords. The king, supposedly sanctioned by heaven, dominated the nobles, the common people, and the slaves. Cities were built with large religious centers and elaborate palaces where the rulers and nobles lived and held court. The

Shang culture was influenced by the peoples who lived around it in the vast expanses of Asia: tribes from the northwestern deserts, plains, and mountains who worshiped the stars, moon, and sun, sacrificing to them their most prized possession, their horses; northern people who lived in timber houses and had elaborate burial rituals; southern Asians who lived along the banks of the rivers and the ocean, worshiping crocodiles (which may have been the original dragons) and decorating their pottery with stamped designs. All these elements appeared in some form in the culture of the Chinese Shang dynasty.

With the Shang, and later the Chou dynasty, we can see the beginnings of a centralized government alternating with periods of internal war and chaos for many centuries. It was a society in which serfs and slaves farmed the land for the landlords, and artisans produced luxuries for the kings and nobles.

Shang religion was based on the worship of ancestral spirits believed to influence the affairs of humans, and ritual and sacrifice were thought to keep them happy and benevolent. Kings and nobles were buried in elaborate tombs containing ritual bronze urns and pottery, placed there for religious reasons along with the bodies of their sacrificed slaves and horses.

The bronze industry probably took much of its technology from the ceramics industry, and pottery also influenced the shape and decoration of bronzes. Lungshan pottery shapes originally influenced the form of the bronzes, but later, in a reversal of influences, the wine and food vessels cast in bronze for ritual use and for daily use by the aristocracy were copied in pottery.

At Chengchow, a Shang city, the western suburbs must have been the potters' quarter, for fourteen kilns were found there. They were vertical kilns, about four feet in diameter, with a central pillar or wall that supported the perforated clay floor on which the pots were placed.

As kiln technology improved, potters learned to fire at temperatures of up to 2190°F (1200°C), and by around 1400 B.C., the Chinese made the first high-fired pottery, known as **proto-porcelain.** This was a high-fired ware which, although vitreous, did not achieve the translucence of true porcelain. It was made with kaolin, the white primary clay found in large deposits in China, which was later to be so important to the production of Chinese porcelain. This proto-porcelain was covered with a yellowish brown or greenish glaze.

Some Shang pottery was glazed by accident when ashes from the wood fire were carried into the kiln by the heat, falling on the shoulders of the jars; the high temperature caused the minerals in the ash to fuse into a glaze. Learning from these accidents, potters

Figure 3-5 Shang kilns were still dug into the ground, but with a hearth supported on a pillar. By the end of the Shang dynasty, the firing chamber was larger and it was placed above the fire on a permanent grate. Some late Shang kilns may have had domed roofs built up from the permanent low walls each time the kiln was fired.

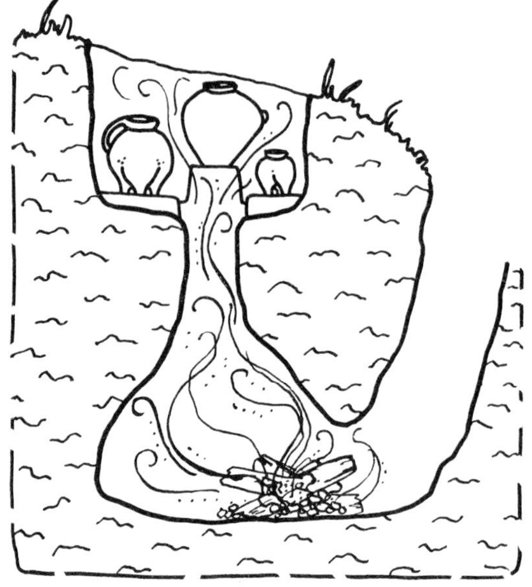

began to experiment with different materials to make glazes. Some of them succeeded in making glazes using feldspar, creating a true high-fire glaze that would fuse with the clay body to make a coating that actually became an integral part of the fired pottery. This was the beginning of the search for refinement in clay bodies and glazes, which occupied Chinese potters for many centuries.

In the later days of the Shang dynasty, when the capital was at Anyang, some very fine white vessels were made of almost pure kaolin in shapes very similar to the bronzes (Figure 3-6). These rare, rather brittle vessels were forerunners of the later clay bodies that would finally lead to the true porcelain of the Sung period.

Figure 3-6 Fine white urns were made of almost pure kaolin during the late Shang dynasty. Fired to around 1832°F (1000°C), they were too fragile for daily use; probably they were ceremonial urns. At Anyang, where they were found, potter's tools were also unearthed, including stamps with dragons and squared spirals. The stamped designs show probable influence from Southeast Asia as well as the influence of animal decorations from cultures in western Asia. On this jar the animal masks are so stylized that it is difficult to make them out on the upper part of the jar. Anyang, Honan, China, late Shang dynasty, 1300–1028 B.C. Height 8 in. (20.3 cm), diameter ⅝ in. (1.6 cm). *Courtesy, Asian Art Museum of San Francisco, The Avery Brundage Collection.*

Chou Dynasty

Following the Shang dynasty, the Chou rulers (eleventh century to 770 B.C.) organized a standing army and a civil service, bringing some stability to the land during their long reign. The ceramics of this period continued along the lines established in the Shang dynasty, and as ancestor worship and court rituals became more elaborate, potters were kept busy filling the demand for ritual vessels. Some of these urns were simple and well formed, but others were copies of metal vessels, decorated with over-elaborate designs.

More important in the story of Chinese ceramics, some workshops were making proto-porcelain into wine vessels, bells, and footed basins, many of them with a greenish glaze. Building on Shang technical knowledge, these potters improved the stoneware body and learned to cover it with a reasonably even, translucent, and resistant glaze—a big step forward. Also, by this time kilns were larger, with quite complex duct systems that distributed the heat around the firing chamber.

During this time, and into the following "Warring States" period, the bronze industry begun in the Shang period continued to flourish, employing large numbers of workers in clay. In Shansi province, excavations of bronze workshops from the fifth century B.C. have revealed pottery crucibles as well as more than 30,000 models and molds used for casting bronze vessels and objects. The models range from small, delicate animals, to large animal-mask reliefs, and the molds were made in several parts. In addition, thousands of terra cotta tiles were produced to roof the Chou cities; they were made in wooden molds lined with cloth to keep the clay from sticking to them, and often they were decorated with stamped or molded designs.

After the Chou, up until 202 B.C., China entered a period of chaos, yet a time of great intellectual ferment. Around 200 B.C., two new philosophies emerged, affecting China's later social, political, and artistic history. Confucius' philosophy, which taught that one could be fulfilled only by following one's appointed role in a rigid social order, was in direct opposition to Lao-tzu's teachings that such discipline and authoritarianism wrongly repressed humanity's natural instincts, which, if followed, would lead to harmony with the universe. The scholarly orderliness of Confucius' teachings and the mysticism of Taoism were both reflected in the art of China.

Chin Dynasty

The Chin, who ruled from 221 B.C. to 207 B.C., conquered all of China, unifying it under a central government. They built the Great Wall of China to keep out marauding northern tribes, using thousands of slaves and war prisoners as laborers to build the Wall and the elaborate roads, canals, and irrigation projects that made possible a unified state. Until very recently, the Chin period was considered unimportant in art, a ruthless tyranny that made little contribution to Chinese culture. But in 1974, Chinese archaeologists excavating the tomb of Emperor Chin Shih Huang Ti made an exciting discovery—a collection of life-sized terra cotta figures of Chin's warriors, buried in battle formation and with full-sized terra cotta horses.

These hundreds of terra cotta soldiers, modeled in their armor, carry real weapons. They are individual portraits, showing the lifelike faces of men long since dead. Originally painted, they are the earliest Chinese realistic ceramics sculpture yet found. Until this treasure was discovered, the change from the formal, ritualistic art of the Shang and Chou was believed to have started with the Han dynasty, which came to power through a rebellion. These newly excavated ceramic figures correct this misconception, showing that the Chin made a real contribution to ceramic art.

Han Dynasty and the Silk Road

Under the Han, beginning in 206 B.C., China entered a period of comparative peace, which lasted until A.D. 220. The Han took from the Chin the concept of a powerful central government, controlling the country with a bureaucracy and a professional army.

We can learn about the lives of ordinary Han people from the grave models claycrafters now made for the landed farmers and warriors—people with rather rural and naive taste (Figure 3-7). From these models of peasants grinding corn or sowing grain, we can reconstruct how they lived and the machines and implements they used.

These Han grave models were lead-glazed, and since lead glazes had been used in Mesopotamia since the sixth century B.C., scholars speculate whether knowledge of them was brought to China over the Silk Road. Established in the second century B.C., this caravan route led from China through Afghanistan to Iran and from there even on to Rome, carrying fine silks and lacquer-ware to the West. Whether some Middle Eastern potters came to China with returning caravans and taught Han potters their techniques, or whether the Han potters traveled to the West and brought back the knowledge, we do not know, but lead glazes appeared in China at this time. It is also true that Chinese bronzes and coins have turned up along with clay tiles and

Figure 3-7 In the Han period, when peasant rebellions were quite frequent, landlords and their families would take refuge in watch towers. This one, guarded by archers and sentries, is a grave model covered with a green lead glaze. Knowledge of lead glazes may have reached Han potters from Mesopotamia via the overland Silk Route which connected China and western Asia at this time. Han dynasty, 2nd century A.D. Height 33¼ in. (84.4 cm). *Courtesy of the Smithsonian Institute, Freer Gallery of Art, Washington, D.C.*

earthenware models of houses in a Chinese-style palace built in southern Siberia. Since these were probably made locally rather than transported such a distance, we can assume that potters did follow the trade routes. At any rate, Chinese pottery was traded across large areas of Asia. Thus the economics of trade are closely related to the Han potter in his shop, who used lead glazes that may well have come from distant Mesopotamia.

Moreover, historical speculations about a society are no longer abstractions when one can look at the actual ridges made by the potter's hands on a piece of clay (Figure 3-9).

Firing and glazing techniques improved during these centuries of experimentation (Figures 3-8 and 3-9). In addition to the lead-glazed grave models, by the end of the Han

Figure 3-8 Kilns were now built with a permanent dome and were designed to direct the heat efficiently over the stacked ware. Instead of letting heat out a chimney directly above the pots, the heat now went over the ware in a down-draft pattern before going up the chimney. This allowed potters to fire at temperatures of 2192°F (1200°C) or more.

dynasty and on into the following centuries, some potters in southern China were making a type of glazed stoneware called Yuëh ware, whose greenish glazes came close to the famous green glaze of the later Sung period. In the ancient kingdom of Yuëh, there were so many potter's kilns firing that a ninth-century poet, Lu Kuimeng, wrote:

> In autumn, in the wind and dew, rises the smoke of the kilns of Yue (Yuëh)
> It robs the thousand peaks of their kingfisher blue.

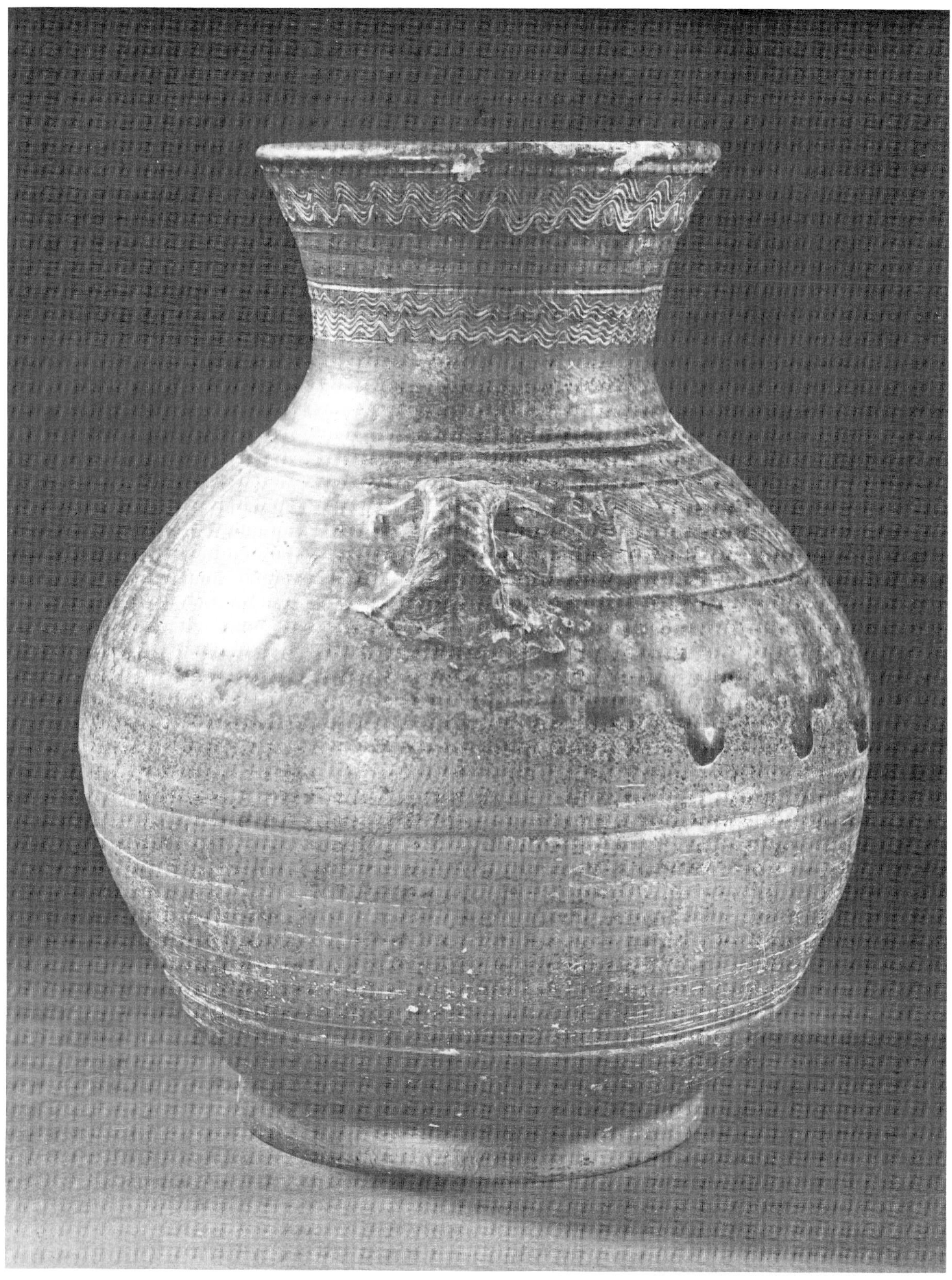

Figure 3-9 (*Left*) By the time of the Han dynasty (206 B.C.–A.D. 220), potters in China were able to fire glazed stoneware. Some glazes, like the one on this jar, were ash glazes, formed accidentally when ashes from the fire fell on the shoulders of the pot. Wood ashes contain alkalies, such as potash and soda, as well as silica and alumina, which fuse with the clay of the pot to form a runny glaze. The mystery of the action of fire on clay and glaze is expressed in a Chinese legend: The god Tung was once a hard-working potter, and while he and his assistants were firing a large and precious bowl, the firing failed. Greatly upset, the potter jumped into the kiln, dying in the flames. After that, the bowls always fired perfectly, so potters worshiped him as Tung the "Genius of Fire and Blast." Stoneware, 200 B.C.– A.D. 221. *Courtesy, Royal Ontario Museum, Toronto.*

After the fall of the Han dynasty, northern China was overrun with waves of nomad horsemen until finally the Toba Wei, a Turkish tribe, brought northern China under its rule in A.D. 439, abandoning their nomadic life and adopting Chinese dress, language, and building styles (Figures 3-10 and 3-11). This Wei dynasty ruled through military officials who became part of the Chinese bureaucracy.

Figure 3-10 Since the Chou dynasty (11th century–770 B.C.), Chinese potteries had been producing quantities of tiles and roof ornaments for buildings. This northern Wei model shows how they were placed on the roofs. The ceramic industry also turned out bricks with designs stamped or molded on them and decorative tiles with scenes of processions, farm life, craft shops, and hunting. These were used to decorate the walls of palaces and temples. *Courtesy, Victoria and Albert Museum, Crown Copyright.*

Figure 3-11 The Toba Wei, a Turkish tribe, conquered northern china in A.D. 439 and ruled it through military officials. These "barbarians," whose western faces were modeled realistically in the Wei sculpture, adopted Chinese customs and clothing. The warrior shown here was painted with red and white pigments over fine-grained, bluish black clay. Wei, 6th century A.D. Height 35 in. (88.9 cm), width 12 in. (30.5 cm). *Courtesy, Asian Art Museum of San Francisco, The Avery Brundage Collection.*

Tang Dynasty

Following the gradual development of clay techniques, we come to the Tang dynasty, which lasted from A.D. 618 to 907. This was a cosmopolitan period in Chinese history, in which outside influences like the Buddhist religion swept over China from India, and the regular communication with central Asia, India, Iran, and the Roman Orient was maintained through trade.

Persian merchants dominated the land trade while Arab and Korean merchants traded by sea, and the ports of Canton and Yanchow had large foreign settlements where people of all races and creeds exchanged ideas and techniques as well as trade goods. Noble Turks came to China, some even marrying into the Chinese royal families. Bringing their retinues of dancers, musicians, and servants, these Turks introduced new faces, new styles of clothing, and new art and music to China. The Chinese were fascinated by the newcomers, and the faces of Persian and wetern Asiatics appear frequently in Tang ceramics. Horses from the steppes of Asia had always been an item of trade, so it is not surprising that horses and the camels of the silk caravans were portrayed in the clay figurines that the Tang potters made in great quantity and glazed with multicolored lead glazes (Figure 3-12).

In addition to the lead-glazed sculpture of camels, horses, and grooms, the Tang potteries produced many small unglazed earthenware sculptures of musicians, dancers, and court ladies (Figure 3-13). Women during the Tang period enjoyed greater freedom than they did in earlier or later dynasties in China. In fact, China was governed for fourteen years by the iron hand of Empress Wu. The upper-class Tang women were well educated, wrote poetry, rode horseback, and even played polo. It was a tolerant society in which Moslem mosques and Zoroastrian temples as well as Nestorian Christian churches and Buddhist temples were built in the capital, Changan.

The potters responded to the demands of their cosmopolitan patrons, working to improve and refine the high-fired wares. In the seventh century, some of the potters working at Hsing-chou managed to make a true porcelain, that is, a ware that is vitrified and translucent, composed of kaolin, feldspar, and silica. The Chinese had large deposits of kaolin and **petunze** or *pai-t'un-tzu,* a white feldspathic rock that was an essential ingredient of their porcelain. During firing at high temperatures, the petunze melts and surrounds the particles of kaolin, which would not otherwise fuse properly. This fine white porcelain was described by a Moslem merchant as thin enough for one to see the sparkle of water through it. It

Figure 3-12 Small ceramic sculptures reflect the cosmopolitan nature of the Tang dynasty. The camels that plodded along the Silk Route to western Asia were cared for by western grooms, who were depicted in realistic detail. Humps and saddle packs were made separately and applied to the camel before it was glazed and fired. Such tomb models were glazed with lead glazes; several colors were applied and allowed to mix freely, so that blue, green, yellow, and brown ran down the sides of the models, creating a mottled effect. Buff earthenware, glazed brown and green, China, Tang dynasty, A.D. 618–907. *Courtesy, Victoria and Albert Museum, Crown Copyright.*

Figure 3-13 (*Left*) Women enjoyed a position of freedom in Tang court life. The slender dancer was modeled in unglazed earthenware. These statuettes were sometimes glazed, or often, like this one, painted. Traces of the pigments can be seen on her clothing. Tang, A.D. 618–907. *Courtesy, Victoria and Albert Museum, Crown Copyright.*

Figure 3-14 Stem cup of white porcelaneous stoneware reflects the refined and elegant taste of the nobles and scholars who collected ceramics. It also shows a Persian origin, probably copied from metal goblets. Chinese metalsmiths had learned from Persia how to make jars, platters, ewers, and goblets out of precious metals, and this stoneware cup was probably made as a cheaper substitute for metal or fine porcelain. Tang, A.D. 618–907. *Courtesy, Victoria and Albert Museum, Crown Copyright.*

was also treasured by Chinese connoisseurs and poets, who called it white as snow or silver and preferred it for drinking tea. At the same time, however, white porcelaneous stoneware was also made as a cheaper imitation of porcelain (Figure 3-14).

Chinese Influence on Korea and Japan

Just as the Tang artisans were influenced by foreign visitors and foreign art, so were Korea and Japan influenced by Tang civilization. Under the Han dynasty, Korea was annexed to China and from then until 1895 was largely a political dependency of China, using the Chinese language until after World War II. The influence of Chinese culture was immense, and all the arts of Korea were originally modeled on the Chinese. While potters in China were experimenting with clay bodies and developing proto-porcelains, large numbers of Chinese immigrants were going to Korea. Among them were undoubtedly some Chinese potters who brought to their new home the forms and traditions of Chinese ceramics and their own experience in clay forming and firing (Figures 3-15 and 3-16). Moreover, ceramic wares from China were exported to Korea, where the Korean potters frequently adopted Chinese bronze-influenced shapes (Figure 3-17).

Beginning in the third century A.D., Japan had contact with both China and Korea. The pottery made in Japan was certainly influenced by Chinese and Korean examples, but the native Japanese tradition was maintained in the *haniwa*—circles of terra cotta figures that were placed around graves (Figure 3-18).

Korean people of Chinese descent moved to Japan, bringing with them knowledge of all the crafts as well as the Buddhist religion, which then became the dominant religion in Japan. Religious and scholarly groups traveled from Japan to China, coming back full of tales of the splendors of the Tang court. From then on, craftsmen, as well as priests, went there to study regularly, sometimes staying as long as twenty or thirty years before bringing their knowledge of China back to Japan. Inspired by the Tang court and by the Buddhist temples in China, the Japanese created a miniature China in the city of Nara, laying it out in the rectangular Chinese manner, building its temples in the Chinese style. Indeed, Nara's collections of Tang art are among the finest in the world, having been preserved there for centuries.

Figure 3-15 Stoneware chariot-shaped vessel from a tomb of the Old Silla dynasty in Korea (5th–6th century A.D.). *Courtesy, National Museum of Korea.*

Figure 3-16 Jar incised with animals from the Old Silla dynasty, Korea, shows the influence of Chinese bronze shapes, but the decoration is free and unrefined. Uljn-gun, Korea, 6th–7th century A.D. Height 16⅛ in. (41 cm), diameter at base 9½ in. (24.2 cm). *Courtesy, National Museum of Korea.*

Figure 3-17 Funeral urns made in Korea show Buddhist influence in the three-tiered knob on the top. First used on the top of the *stupa,* a building that marked a holy spot in India, it was the forerunner of Japanese pagodas. Unified Silla dynasty, 7th–8th century A.D. Height 11¼ in. (28.5 cm), diameter at base 5 in. (12.9 cm). *Courtesy, National Museum of Korea.*

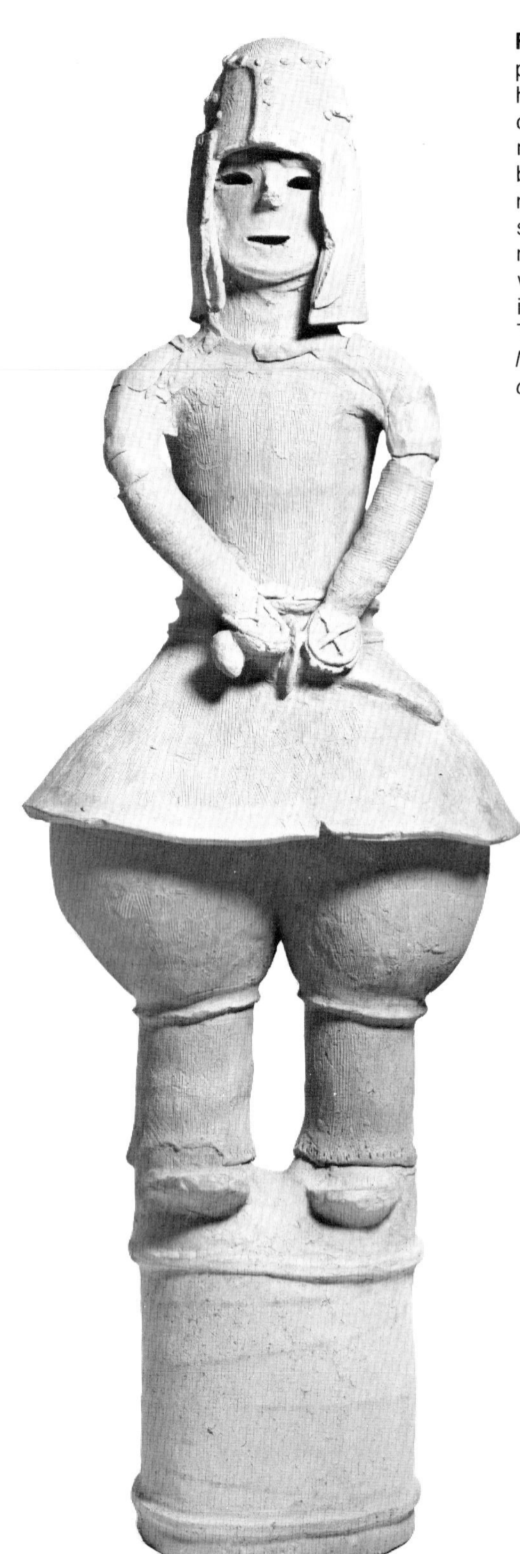

Figure 3-18 Large earthenware figures were placed around the mounded tombs in Japan to hold back the earth. The earliest *haniwa,* or "clay circles," were simple cylinders. Later they were made in the form of horses, warriors, singers, birds, and houses. This warrior wears a helmet, neck protector, and arm protectors, with a Kabutsuchi sword hanging from his belt. His eyes and mouth are holes, giving the face a lively look, as well as helping to keep the clay figure from cracking in the kiln. Earthenware, Fujioka, Japan, late Tumulus, c. 6th century A.D. *Courtesy, Asian Art Museum of San Francisco, The Avery Brundage Collection.*

China: The Sung Dynasty

By A.D. 960, the Sung dynasty had come to power in China, and literature, technology, and science thrived, while the arts became all-important to the courtiers and officials who made up the cultural aristocracy. Painting and calligraphy were studied by every educated person; even the emperors were painters and poets. It was a tolerant society in which the rich were connoisseurs and collectors of the arts, and in this atmosphere of literary and artistic accomplishment, the ceramics reflected the cultivated taste of the upper class. Elegant, formal, and exquisitely crafted white porcelain was produced in several pottery centers—some with as many as 200 kilns. Often it was modeled into ewers, jars, and bowls that expressed the refined tastes of the wealthy patrons.

When Westerners think of Sung porcelain, what usually comes to mind is the green **celadon** glaze, called *ch'ing t'zu* in China (Color Plate 1, p. 50A).* This green Sung glaze was, as we have seen, the result of centuries of experimentation on the part of many potters. The iron oxide in the glaze, when fired in re-

* It is an interesting side note to history that the word *celadon* comes from the name of an eighteenth-century French actor who wore this color green.

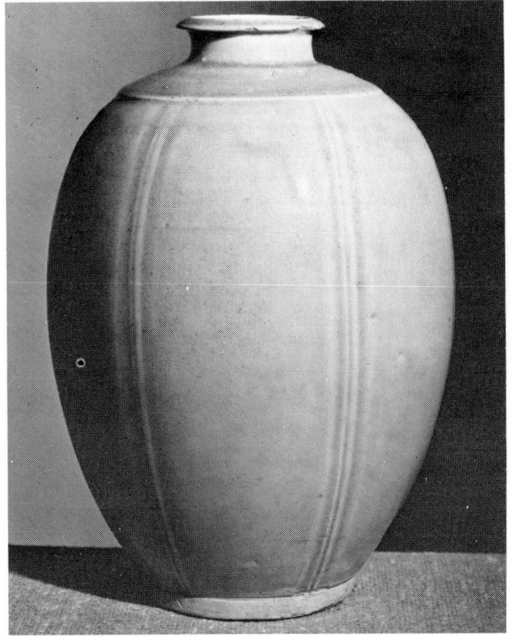

Figure 3-19 Celadon glazes were perfected in the Sung dynasty. When used on elegant shapes like this vase, they were much sought after by collectors. The unglazed base shows that the piece was fired right side up; a good deal of Sung white porcelain was fired upside down so that the bases were glazed but the rim was bare. Often this bare rim was bound with copper or silver, which gave a sharp definition to the edge. Kiangsi Province, China, Sung dynasty, 10th century A.D. Height 9¼ in. (23.5 cm). *Courtesy, Victoria and Albert Museum, Crown Copyright.*

Figure 3-20 Pure white, hard, translucent, and resonant when struck, white Sung porcelain became the standard against which all other porcelain was measured. Because Chinese potters had the technological background of centuries of high firing, as well as the necessary kaolin and petunze, they were able to achieve the purity of clay body and necessary firing conditions to produce porcelain. White porcelain ewer, Sung dynasty, 11th–12th century A.D. Height 7¾ in. (19.7 cm). *Courtesy, Victoria and Albert Museum, Crown Copyright.*

duction, turned anywhere from leafy green to watery bluish green. Celadon was used on both porcelain and stoneware (Figure 3-19).

For centuries, jade had had religious and ritualistic importance in China; the king, officiating at his audiences, held a jade scepter, and lower ranks of nobles held disks of jade. Because the stone was rare and expensive, potters tried for years to find a glaze that would simulate jade, that would duplicate jade's gray-green and green tones. Since celadon-glazed pottery was made in many different workshops, the color of the glaze, the fineness of the clay body, and the elegance of the shapes coated with this glaze vary tremendously. For example, celadon ware from northern China was made of a gray porcelaneous body, fired at a high temperature in a reducing atmosphere, then an oxidizing atmosphere as it cooled, turning the glaze a greenish brown. At the Lungchuan potteries, where the green ware began to appear around 1120, the glaze was used on a grayish white stoneware body fired in a reducing atmosphere. On this ware the glaze was pale olive green.

Figure 3-21 Chambered kilns were now built on sloping ground with several communicating chambers. Each chamber was a separate downdraft kiln, and the heat from one went up into the next higher kiln until it went out the chimney at the end. As a chamber heated to the necessary temperature, fuel was fed through the ventilation holes in the next highest chamber. In this way, each chamber was fired in turn, and its heat was transferred on to the next chamber, preheating it. Thus heat was conserved and large firings could be done with less fuel. The saggars were piled on top of each other, then the kiln was sealed with bricks, with an opening left for feeding the main fire at the bottom.

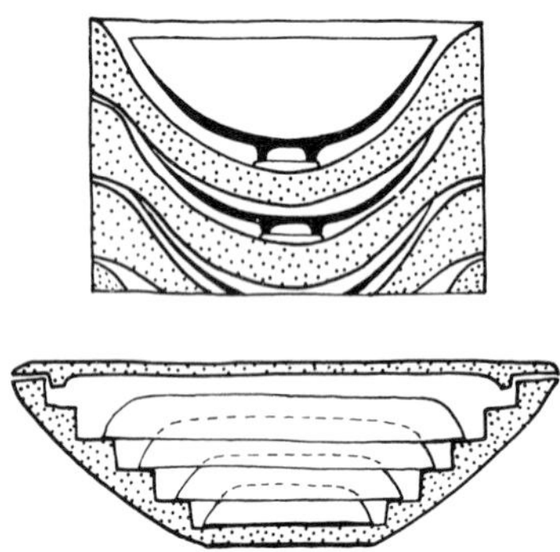

Figure 3-22 Two types of saggars were used to protect the porcelain from dust, ash, and flame.

Now kilns were much more elaborate, often built into a hill in a series of stepped levels, sometimes as long as 165 feet (50 meters) (Figure 3-21). According to contemporary Chinese writers, when the kilns were fired, they looked like giant dragons spitting fire. Most kilns were fired with wood, although some of the smaller ones burned coal. The potters now used **saggars,** fire-resistant containers, to protect the ware from the wood ash, and the Lungchuan kilns could fire as many as 20,000 saggars at one time (Figure 3-22).

By this time, exporting ceramics had become increasingly important to the economy of China, for Chinese porcelain was in great demand all over Asia. That the Arab countries of western Asia bought Chinese ceramics in great quantities we know from the thousands of fragments of earlier green Yuëh ware and white porcelain found in the ruins of the summer residence of the Arab caliphs at Samarra, a palace last occupied in A.D. 883. The uneasy rulers of the Arab world, often afraid of assassination, believed that the celadon ware would crack or change color if exposed to poison. Given the political intrigues of the Arabs, the Chinese porcelain must have been in great demand. Perhaps this idea developed when potters in China discovered that the celadon glaze would crack if not properly formulated to shrink along with the clay body. Ready to learn from accidental effects, they deliberately

Figure 3-23 Sung potters, in addition to perfecting white porcelain and celadon glazes, made black-glazed bowls for the popular Chan tea ceremony. Made of dark stoneware, their brownish black glaze is often mottled or streaked. The spots, known as "oil spots" or "hare's fur," were caused by the crystallization of the ferric oxide in the glaze. Adopted for the tea ceremony in Japan, this glaze became extremely popular there as well; its name became *tenmoku* in Japan. Simple, severe, and heavy, the bowls set off the color of the tea as it was beaten to a foamy green with a bamboo whisk. Bowl, Chien ware, Tenmoku, China, Sung dynasty, 10th–13th century A.D. Height 2¾ in. (7 cm), diameter 7¾ in. (19.7 cm). *Courtesy, Asian Art Museum of San Francisco, The Avery Brundage Collection.*

made glazes that formed a fine decorative **crackle** all over the pieces.

The accomplished Sung potters, in addition to making the classic white-glazed porcelain (Figure 3-20) and soft green celadon ware, perfected other decorative glazes. During this period of intense ceramic production and glaze experimentation, the Chinese exported a great deal of their pottery to Japan.

One type of Sung pottery that had an important effect on Japanese ceramics was a black-glazed ware named after a mountain near Hangchow. Actually *T'ien'mu* in Chinese, the name was changed to the Japanese **tenmoku** (temmoku), the name by which we still call it (Figure 3-23). The thick glaze, which often collects in rolls and drops at the bottom of a piece, frequently has "oil spots," which are caused by the crystallization of **ferric oxide** in the glaze.

During China's Tang dynasty, tea drinking had become very popular, and although many connoisseurs preferred white or celadon teacups, others felt that the black-glazed tea bowls were the most effective background for the foamy green tea. It was during the Sung dynasty that the *Chan* sect of Buddhism emerged, emphasizing, like the earlier Taoists, self-cultivation, quietism, and meditation. This Chan sect, or Zen as it was called in Japan, developed a highly ritualized tea ceremony, the *Cha-no-ya,* in which tea and its attendant rituals became a means of acquiring nobility and purity of thought, a ceremony brought to its highest refinement and popularity in Japan.

Western Asia

Mesopotamia was a center of civilization from very early times, a region where kingdoms and empires succeeded one another in a long, complex political history. Ceramics had an equally long and complex history there with a series of cultures influencing each other's styles of decoration, shapes, and techniques. Aside from painted earthenware (Figure 3-25), already discussed in Chapter 1, a characteristic use for ceramics in that area was in the finish of walls.

As early as 2600 B.C. in Sumeria and Babylonia, tubular pegs of fired clay painted in red, black, and white were pushed into the mud walls in geometric patterns, forming mosaics. In the huge Assyrian, Babylonian, and Persian palaces and temples, brilliantly colored glazed tiles covered the sun-dried bricks, protecting them from weather and adding colorful decoration. On these tiles were figures of humans, lions, bulls, and mythical animals modeled in relief (Figure 3-24). A

Figure 3-24 Tiles coated with tin-lead glaze formed in relief decorated the processional approach to the Ishtar Gateway in the main citadel of Babylon, c. 580 B.C. *Courtesy, Staatliche Museum zu Berlin.*

knowledge of lead and alkaline glazes, as well as the use of tin oxide to make them opaque, had developed early in the Near East. The opaque glaze made it possible to cover up the reddish color of the earthenware, and the white opaque glaze formed an excellent background for painted decoration. The use of these glazes would eventually spread throughout the whole Moslem world and through Spain to Europe (Color Plate 5, p. 146A).

Figure 3-25 Vessel from Nishapur, Persia, was decorated with brown and red on a white engobe covering the red earthenware clay body. 9th century A.D. Height 3 in. (7.5 cm). *Courtesy, Museo Internazionale delle Ceramiche, Faenza, Italy.*

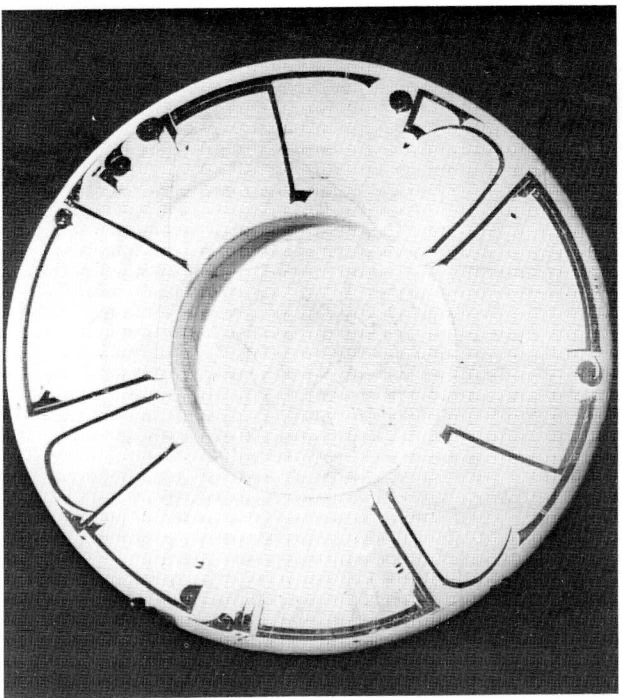

Figure 3-26 Inscription in Kufic script painted in underglaze on slip-covered earthenware makes a handsome abstract design. But it also preaches a lesson: "Deliberation before work protects you from regret." Iran, Samanid period, 10th century A.D. Diameter 14⅝ in. (37.2 cm). *Courtesy, The St. Louis Art Museum.*

Persia

By about 550 B.C., the Persians had conquered large areas in western Asia, extending their empire as far as the Indus River in India and westward to Egypt and Greece. These Sassanid Persians, as they are called, absorbed cultural and artistic influences from the past and from all parts of their empire as well as from faraway China. Combining influences from all these sources with their own taste for the ornate and luxurious, a new Sassanid culture evolved making the cities of Persia the meeting place of two worlds—central Asia, India, and China to the east, and Syria and Rome to the west. Pottery centers established in Samarra, Baghdad, and other cities produced ceramics showing the mixture of all these cultures. After the conquest of Persia and other Eastern territories by the Moslems in the seventh century A.D., the tastes of Sassanid Persia continued to influence Islamic art, and the knowledge of lead-tin glazes was passed on to the Arabs, and through them eventually to Europe.

Islamic Influences

Pottery and tiles were an important part of Moslem art, and through studying them we can learn a good deal about Islamic culture

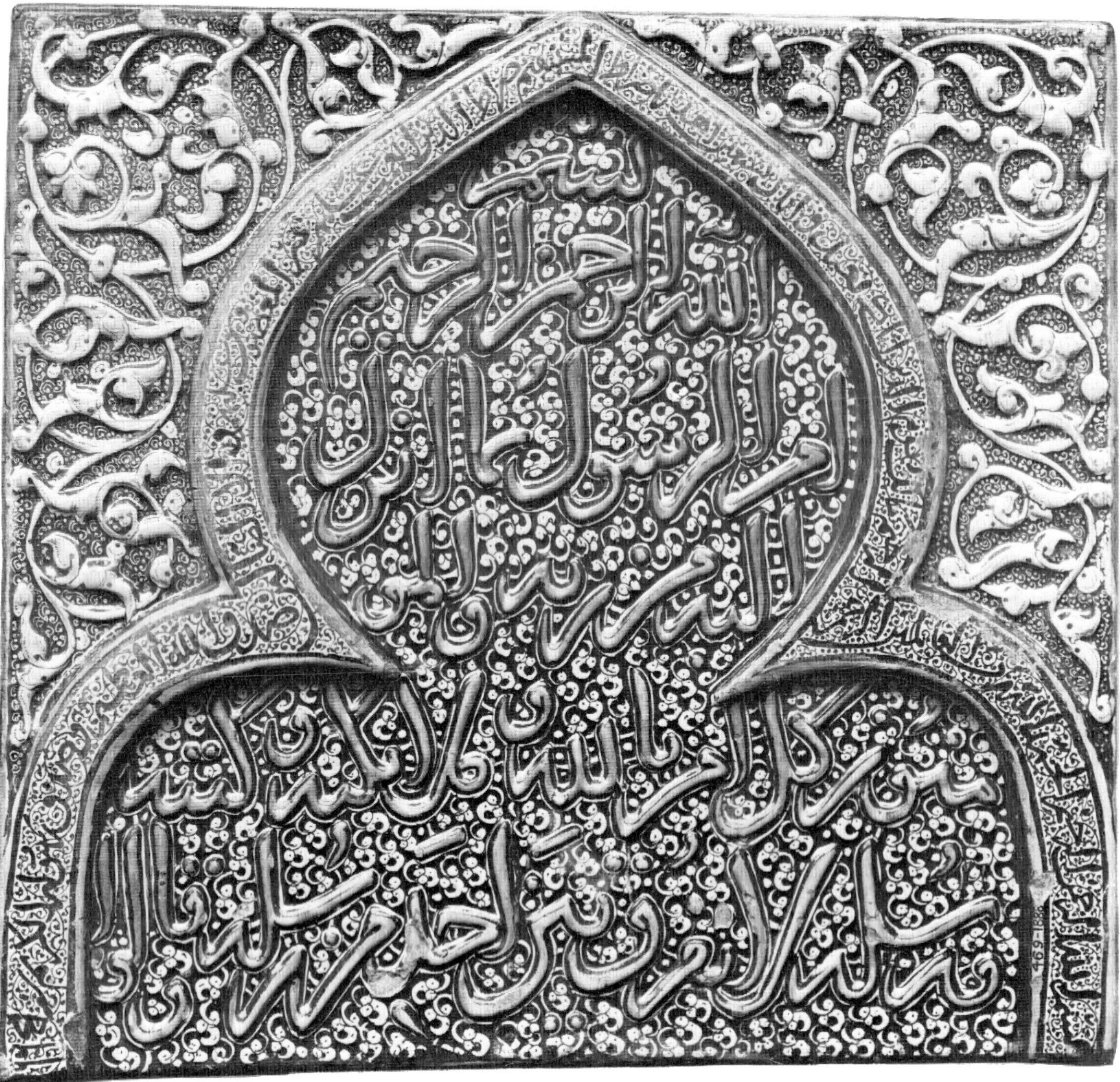

Figure 3-27 Earthenware tiles glazed with brilliant colors decorated mosques, palaces, and tombs in Persia and later throughout the Islamic world. Covered with opaque tin glazes in blues and yellows, tiles were often cut in the shape of stars, leaves, and flowers, then carefully fitted together on the walls. On them twine vines, lotus flowers, and acanthus and palm leaves in twisting, interlaced decorations called *arabesque.* Along with plant decoration, Arabic script was modeled in raised letters or painted in lusters, turning the written word into a work of art. Glazed earthenware tile from a tomb, Persia, 13th century. 21 X 23 in. (53.3 X 58.4 cm). *Courtesy, Victoria and Albert Museum, Crown Copyright.*

and religion (Figures 3-27 and 6-2). In the pottery we can see examples of many of the artistic ideas that later were spread by the Moslems throughout the Mediterranean and on into Europe. The pottery even inspired the famous Islamic poet Omar Khayyám to use a metaphor based on clay to express his attitude toward life. Commenting in the *Rubáiyát* on the brevity of life, he sighs,

> Oh, if the potter makes a jug from my
> dust, let that jug be always full of wine.

The religious text of Islam, the Koran, forbade the portrayal of human figures in mosques, so craftsmen resorted to using leaves, flowers, and quotations from the Koran for decoration, painting them on the colorful tiles used to decorate Islamic architecture. In the Near East, where mosques were built of sun-dried brick, then covered with glazed tiles, the potters of Islam were kept busy making the colorful tiles which sparkled on the domes and minarets, calling the faithful to prayer across the desert. Tiles were also widely used inside the mosques and on the walls of the palaces throughout the Moslem world (Figure 6-2).

It was also against the religious teachings of Islam for metals like silver or gold to be used on earth by orthodox Moslems, because the Koran said that the faithful would be rewarded in Paradise with vessels of gold and silver. So craftsmen looked for a substitute that would give the appearance of metal but still allow its owners to remain good Moslems. Thus they developed a form of **overglaze**—called **luster**—using metallic salts, which, when fired in a reducing atmosphere, become iridescent. The Egyptians had used luster earlier, but it was the Islamic Persian potters who perfected it and used it with such a highly decorative effect (Figure 3-28). As the religious climate of Islam grew less strict, potters began to include the human figure in their decorations, as well as animals and birds, often combining them into fantasy creatures or using animal shapes for ceramic jugs or other objects (Figure 3-31).

Figure 3-28 Opaque white tin glaze made an excellent background for luster decoration. This bowl is painted with yellow luster, which glows with a soft iridescence. Khar, near Teheran. Late 12th to early 13th century A.D. Height 3½ in. (8.9 cm), diameter 7½ in. (19.1 cm). *Courtesy, Victoria and Albert Museum, Crown Copyright.*

Figure 3-29 (*Right*) The black, white, and blue glazes on this Persian bowl were a popular combination with Persian potters. Inscriptions frequently were pious: "Sovereignty is God's," or "Blessings and beneficence." Kashan, Persia, 13th century. *Courtesy, The Metropolitan Museum of Art. Bequest of William Milne Grinnell, 1920.*

Figure 3-30 A water jug in the shape of an animal (or bird?) is covered with white glaze, then painted with luster overglaze. To make this iridescent decoration, metallic salts—copper or silver, for example—were mixed with a paste of gum or clay and painted on top of the glaze. The piece was then given a second firing at about 1112°F (600°C), during which a reducing atmosphere was induced, and the kiln was sealed and allowed to cool. Persia, late 15th or early 16th century. Height 9¾ in. (24.8 cm), length 11¾ in. (29.8 cm). *Courtesy, Victoria and Albert Museum, Crown Copyright.*

Figure 3-31 Foot rasp, apparently used to rub dried skin off feet, made in the shape of a duck. Earthenware, Persia, 16th or 17th century. Length 4¼ in. (10.8 cm). *Courtesy, Victoria and Albert Museum, Crown Copyright.*

Chinese Decorative Methods

As we move across Asia from China to Persia and back, we can see how the developments in art on each side of the continent affected one another. For example, Sassanid Persian designs show up in Chinese silk patterns, and Persian decorative techniques were modified and used by Chinese potters. In turn, Chinese ceramic products were shipped to western Asia, influencing the potters there.

Toward the end of the Sung dynasty, Chinese potters had begun to use many different methods of decoration to add surface interest to their domestic ware. Increasingly interested in this surface decoration, they experimented with colorful high-fire glazes (Color Plate 2, p. 50B), painted floral designs in black under a transparent glaze, and used colored **enamels** over a white glaze. Now Chinese ceramics was entering a new phase of pictorial decoration, one that would have great effect on later European ceramics. As this trend continued, ceramics became more of an industry, with many potteries concentrating on decorated ware for export to the West.

Blue and White Ware

In the fourteenth century, copper oxides were used in China to paint red **underglaze** designs on the domestic ware. But the red was difficult to control, bleeding into the white and often losing its color when fired. So the potters started using a blue pigment derived from cobalt. They painted cobalt on the dried pottery, then covered it all with a semiopaque glaze. When the piece was fired in one firing, the cobalt showed through the white glaze. The native Chinese cobalt had a high proportion of manganese, as well as iron impurities in it, so that it fired to a dark and muddy blue. Persian cobalt, however, contained no manganese, so it was imported from the Middle East and was known in China as "Mohammedan blue." Later, the Chinese were able to refine out the iron from their own cobalt, but since they could not get rid of the manganese, they mixed their cobalt with the imported Persian material (Figure 3-32). Persian cobalt was so rare and expensive that it was used pure only on the finest porcelain, to make blue and white ware of the highest standards for court use.

Chinese blue and white ware became popular all over Asia; shards of it have been found on the shores of the Persian Gulf. As the demand for it grew, much of it was made for export in special shapes copied from Persian metal objects, often decorated with Persian inscriptions.

Figure 3-32 A white porcelain plate made in the reign of Emperor Wan Li is decorated with cobalt underglaze. Mythical beasts in a fanciful landscape were painted on the unglazed body, then the whole piece was covered with glaze. In the firing, the blue color was suspended in the glaze between the outer surface and the clay body, thus acquiring depth and luminosity. Made chiefly in Chingtechen, in official kilns, the best of the blue and white porcelain was reserved for court use and made according to the personal taste of the reigning emperor. Blue and white ware, Wan Li, Ming dynasty, A.D. 1573 –1619. Diameter 12¼ in. (31.1 cm). *Courtesy, Victoria and Albert Museum, Crown Copyright.*

"China" Arrives in Europe

Soon after 1600, a certain type of thin, rather brittle, blue and white export ware reached Amsterdam. This oriental ware caused great excitement, and everyone now wanted "china." Soon the Dutch were importing it by the shipload, and the Chinese now adapted their shapes and decorations to European taste. Europeans became infatuated with **chinoiserie,** with all Chinese crafts, and with Chinese landscape painting in which mountains, swirling clouds, and waterfalls expressed the Chinese appreciation of natural beauty. This type of painting was reflected in the blue and white porcelain, which was now also painted with legendary figures from Chinese literature.

One such legend, much enjoyed by Europeans, tells of an "illustrious lady" trapped on an island by flood waters while waiting for her husband, King of Tsu. The messengers sent by the king to rescue her rushed off without bringing her the king's identifying seal, and without that proof that her husband wished her to leave the island, she refused to go with them, saying, "I see that if I follow you I will save my life, and if I stay here I will perish. But to pass over a matter of such importance in order to escape death would be to fail in courage and fidelity." So the messengers left the loyal lady to die in the rising flood. Popular stories like these were painted on the porcelain, with figures acting out a succession of scenes in a style adapted to ceramics from the continuous scroll paintings of Sung China.

Enamels

By around 1500, enamel painted on top of the glazed surface had become popular in China, making it possible for the decorators to use as many as five colors on one piece. Also called overglaze enamel, or china paint, it is a low-fire glaze colored with metallic oxides. It contains a great deal of lead so that it melts at a low temperature—around 1470°F (800°C). When the enamel is fired, the lead in the body glaze also softens enough so that the enamel melts into it. This form of decoration became so popular that factories were needed to meet the demand for enamel-decorated ware. In these factories the potter no longer decorated his own pieces, and a separation developed between the craftsmen who shaped the pieces and those who decorated them.

In some of the factories where the enameled ware was made, the decorators themselves were so specialized that one man would paint only one part of a design—concentrating on one type of leaf or flower or figure. As many as seventy men might work on one piece of ceramics in a regular assembly line, further separating the potter from the decorator, a separation reflected in the lower aesthetic standards of much of the product. Often now the multicolored decoration totally overshadowed the form of the porcelain in a way that would never have occurred during the Sung period.

Porcelain Glazes

Some potteries in China, however, continued to experiment with glazes, using them on vases and on treasured objects made for the desks of wealthy scholars, such as boxes to hold the red paste with which calligraphers stamped their names on their writings, pots for washing the brushes, and vases for flowers (Color Plate 3, p. 50C). Shaped in simple, classic forms reminiscent of the Sung period, these pieces were the envy of European collectors who spent fortunes to buy them. To compete with Chinese imports, European potters tried for years to copy the thin, translucent porcelain, finally succeeding in the eighteenth century.

Japan

The same type of technical and artistic exchanges that took place between Asia and the Mediterranean world also took place between China, Korea, and Japan. Japan owed much of her early ceramic technique to China, and through Japan we in the West inherited some of these techniques and attitudes. But Japan expressed her own spirit, changing and adapting the techniques brought from China.

Nature and Life

From very early times, the Japanese believed that supernatural beings had been created by the gods at the same time as humanity's creation. In the Shinto belief, these *kami* gave life to everything that existed. Just as the stars, the ocean, the mountains, and the plants all had life breathed into them by the kami, so too, the skill of a swordsman, a fisher, an archer, or a potter came from them. This sense of life, which the hands of the potter passed on to the clay, was an important characteristic of Japanese ceramics, one that was never completely lost, even when foreign influences were at their strongest.

Divided as the country is into islands, mountains, and steep valleys, and isolated from the mainland by the ocean, Japan never developed as strong a centralized government as China, and its political history is one of intense rivalry between clans, of almost continual civil war. Eventually, a centralized government did develop in which an emperor reigned, but the real control was in the hands of the Shogun, whose military power kept the clans somewhat under control.

Through all the upheaval of civil wars, Mongol invasion attempts, and innumerable clan battles, the potters continued to work, absorbing outside influences, slowly transforming them into shapes that expressed the true Japanese spirit. The life of the potter reflected the rural attachment to the land, the family, and the clan. A family of potters would live on the same piece of land for generations, digging their clay from the same bank, firing their kilns at the same place. As a result, the Japanese potter developed an intense personal relationship with the clay, a relationship with the land and all nature. The Japanese saw the clay and the potter as one, both animated by the same life-force. This love of nature was as important in shaping the sensibility of the Japanese artists and craftsmen as were the native Shinto and the imported Buddhist religions.

Figure 3-33 Comparing this early Japanese stoneware jar with the Han jar (Figure 3-9), one can see how much early pottery in Japan owed to Chinese influences. But there is a vitality in the way the narrow neck sits on the swelling body that suggests the characteristic Japanese relationship with the clay. This later led to greater freedom and expressiveness in Japanese ceramics. 9th or 10th century A.D. *Courtesy, Victoria and Albert Museum, Crown Copyright.*

Foreign Influences

Indian Buddhism, which came to Japan from China in the sixth century A.D., was modified there, for the Japanese were too much of the earth to accept totally the Buddhist teachings about the unimportance of material things. For example, the sutras of India were changed in Japan into spells that were recited to ensure good health, bring rain for the crops, or ward off fire and drought. In the same way, the foreign potters who came to Japan bringing new ideas and new techniques influenced the local potters, but within a generation or two the new ideas were absorbed and changed.

As we have seen, after the end of the Jōmon period, Japan's ceramic craft was greatly influenced by Korea, which in turn had learned much of its ceramic technique from China. Indeed, many of the Korean potters who came to Japan were of Chinese ancestry.

With the influx of Korean craftsmen and the true wheel they brought with them, Japanese ceramics changed radically (Figure 3-33). Besides the wheel, the Korean potters brought with them an accumulated knowledge and experience in building kilns and firing. These superior skills of the Korean craftsmen were recognized by the Japanese, who hired them to update the local craft of ceramics, much as a nonindustrial country today will hire foreign experts to teach modern techniques. Japanese scholars and potters also went to China to study. Japanese tradition tells us that the Buddhist priest Tōshirō Kato Shirozaemon went to China to study ceramics, bringing back clay when he returned in about 1227. Later, it is said, he found good clay in Japan and established a pottery in the Seto area, still the largest pottery-producing area in Japan.

Whether or not Tōshirō really was the founder of the Japanese pottery industry, many new workshops were established in Japan that fired stoneware in kilns modeled on the Chinese and Korean sloping kilns (Figure 3-34). The earliest of these were made by roofing over a ditch dug into the hill, allowing the heat to rise through a narrow firing chamber about seven or eight meters long. Sometimes called snake kilns because they were made in one long tunnel with no dividing walls to separate them into compartments, they produced pottery that was meant to imitate the celadon and black and brown of the Sung glazes. But the Japanese potters, lacking the centuries of experience of the Sung potters, made a coarse type of impressed or incised ware with a green and sometimes a yellow glaze. In the 1500s, the Japanese general Hideyoshi brought back potters as prisoners from his Korean campaign who helped to improve the techniques of Japanese ceramics.

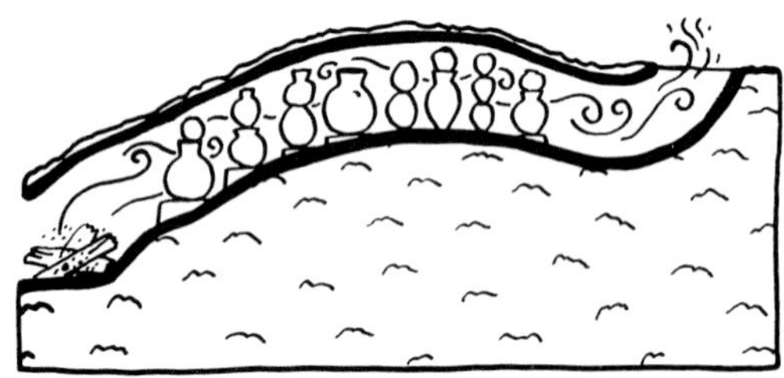

Figure 3-34 Snake kilns were modeled on similar Korean kilns. In them, the pots were packed on top of one another, on circular stands with slanting bases to keep them level on the sloping floor. In some kilns, the ware was placed in saggars. Eventually, the Japanese used chambered kilns and today unchambered kilns are found mainly in Korean villages.

The Zen Tea Ceremony

The Chinese import that exerted the greatest influence on Japanese ceramics was the tea ceremony. The Chan sect of Buddhism, called Zen in Japan, was brought to Japan by returning Buddhist monks around A.D. 1200, becoming an integral part of the Buddhist search for enlightenment in Japan. According to the Japanese tea master, Sen no Rikyu (1521-1591), "Tea in a humble room consists first and foremost in practicing and attaining Buddhist truth according to Zen." The first tea seeds in Japan were planted on a hillside near Kyoto by a Zen monk, the tea bowls were introduced by another monk, and the teahouse where the ceremony was performed was designed by yet another Zen monk. These teahouses, set in a beautiful, stylized garden, were approached by stepping on irregular, moss-covered stones. The guests crouched to enter the low door, leaving the outside world behind, and humbling themselves in preparation for a ceremony that expressed the Zen ideal of simplicity and refined poverty.

By the sixteenth century, Kyoto was the center of the tea culture, making *chato,* or tea ceramics, which included bowls, jars, flower pots, incense containers, and tea caddies, all made in accordance with Zen teachings (Figures 3-35 and 3-36). The tea master Sen no Rikyu preferred the simple rice bowls of Korea, which had been made long before the tea ceremony became popular, choosing them for their roughly formed, simple shape and their practicality. Tea bowls were first made in Japan in the sixteenth century by a Korean potter who had married a Japanese woman and settled in Kyoto. After he died, she continued to make the bowls. Her son Chojiro (1515-1592), following in the tradition of his parents, was honored by Rikyu as a master potter. His son Jokei was given the right to mark the character **raku** (pleasure) on the bottom of his bowls, and from then on succeeding generations of the family made the bowls, using the treasured mark into the twentieth century.

The brown and black glazes, which originally came from Sung China (Figure 3-23), were adapted to tea ceramics, taking the Japanese name *tenmoku.* Instead of copying the formal shapes of the Sung ware, however, the Japanese potters formed theirs into deliberately irregular pottery, hand built rather than wheel thrown. Tea enthusiasts also delighted in the accidental effects that occurred during firing in the small, square kilns, admiring the cracks, pits, and variations in the glaze. A studiedly simple effect was sought by the potter, and each bowl expressed the character of

Figure 3-35 Bizen ware was made of coarse, low-fired clay, fired gently over a long period of time because of its low heat resistance. Its surface varies from rough and unglazed to bright and glossy—rather like polished wood. In one piece, colors may range from greenish to matt, unglazed black, with red patches caused by the fire. The pots were packed in straw, or bags of straw were placed in the kiln, to achieve these fire patterns. This seventeenth-century Bizen jar has the typical uneven shape, pitted glaze, and dark fire splashes admired by the Zen tea masters. Earthenware, Japan, 17th century A.D. Height 8 in. (20.3 cm). *Courtesy, Victoria and Albert Museum, Crown Copyright.*

Figure 3-36 (*Right*) Classic Japanese raku tea bowls were carved, not thrown or coiled. A thick shape was pinched out, dried somewhat, then sculpted to the final shape, producing a bowl with no joints—a practical consideration because raku was subjected to great temperature changes when it was placed in and taken out of a red-hot kiln. Each *chawan* (tea bowl) was an individual piece, but all followed strict rules about the shaping of the lip, the "tea pool" in the base, and the interior spiral that leads the tea to the drinker's mouth. The coarse clay body did not conduct heat quickly, and the gentle, slow warming of the hands by the hot tea was part of the enjoyment of the ceremony. Guests examined the shape of a bowl, for its feel in the hands was as important as its looks. Raku, earthenware with black-brown glaze, Japan, 17th century. *Courtesy, Victoria and Albert Museum, Crown Copyright.*

its maker. The names of the potters were known, and famous bowls were also given names; some of them are now classified as National Treasures of Japan.

Among the treasured tea ceramics are the tea caddies in which the finely powdered tea was kept. Freshly ground for each party, it was dipped from an earthenware jar called the *cha-ire.* Kyoto was not the only area that produced tea wares, and some of the most famous tea caddies came from the Bizen kilns, which fired a rustic type of pottery greatly valued by tea masters (Figure 3-35).

Both the raku tea bowls and the **Bizen** tea ware have had a strong influence on our contemporary Western pottery, especially since the resurgence of Zen Buddhism. Potters all over the world now use tenmoku glazes and fire Bizen-style pottery, looking for accidental effects in their work, while raku-type firing has become so popular that special equipment is now manufactured for it (Figure 12-18).

Porcelain Industry in Japan

The Japanese did not limit themselves to the Bizen and raku wares. At the beginning of the sixteenth century, a Japanese potter, Gorodayu Shonaui, visited China to study the porcelain industry there, hoping when he came home to find the necessary ingredients for porcelain in Japan. The imported technique of porcelain-making remained mysterious and exotic, inspiring the story that Shonaui's pots contained the bones of his assistants as one of his necessary ingredients!

Around 1605, an immigrant Korean potter, Ri Sampei, found kaolin in the Arita district of Japan, and the district suddenly became the center of a porcelain industry that by 1664 shipped 45,000 pieces of porcelain a year to Holland from its port at Imari. Now the Japanese used the chambered sloping kiln similar to the Chinese kilns (Figure 3-21). So many trees were cut down to supply the kilns with fuel that the government finally restricted the building of new kilns. At Arita, the techniques of underglaze with Mohammedan blue and the use of brilliant overglaze enamels were copied from the Chinese. Working with a natural sense of design and skilled brush work, potters there made enameled ware of great beauty. But, as in China, the need to cater to Western taste and to produce in quantity to fill the demand led to a factory situation. Large-scale production lowered the standards. Western taste demanded garishness rather than subtlety, so that much of the eighteenth-century and nineteenth-century export porcelain was decorated to appeal to this taste.

Figure 3-37 One type of later Chinese kick wheel was rotated by an assistant who provided the power in an ingenious manner with his feet while hanging on to a rope dangling from the roof of the workshop.

Figure 3-38 Kenzan, the potter, signed the low, square tray on the base, while Kōrin, his brother, signed it on the upper left, above his freely painted scene of iris near an "eight-part bridge." Nature was the main inspiration for the decorations that Kenzan or Kōrin painted on bowls, trays, and boxes. Often the painting was kept to one side, leaving a large area undecorated for contrast and balance. Stoneware tray by Ogata Kenzan, decorated by Ogata Kōrin, Kyoto ware, Edo period. Height 1⅛ in. (2.8 cm), 8⅝ in. (21.7 cm) square. *Courtesy, Smithsonian Institution, Freer Gallery of Art, Washington, D.C.*

Ogata Kōrin and Kenzan

Despite the over-decoration, there were some potters in Japan who continued to work with a close personal involvement with the clay, forming their pottery with restraint, decorating it with graceful brush painting, using underglaze and overglaze techniques in a simplified, truly Japanese manner. Kyoto was no longer the center of court life, for the capital was now at Edo (later Tokyo), and the local lords had to attend court there or send hostages. Many noble families in Kyoto became impoverished, and some of them had to earn their living by teaching painting, poetry, or music. But the aesthetic traditions of Kyoto continued, and two potters and painters of wealthy background, Ogata Kenzan (1663-1743) and his brother Kōrin (1658-1716), applied their highly developed taste and sensitive visual awareness to ceramics (Figure 3-38). These two brothers often worked together, both of them signing a piece. Sometimes working under the patronage of nobles, sometimes alone in great poverty, the potter Ogata Kenzan used a white clay body, or a colored clay covered with a white slip, as a soft background for the brown or black oxide designs that he or his brother would paint. These were painted freely with masterly brush strokes, simplified to the fewest possible lines.

Later (1615-1868), Edo period potters who worked in this tradition were greatly influenced by Kenzan (Figure 3-39). The Kenzan name was handed down to potters considered worthy of it, and in the twentieth century, an Englishman, Bernard Leach, was named Kenzan VII (Figure 6-30 and Color Plate 12, p. 210B).

Many of the potteries in the nineteenth century became factories, trying to turn out cheap "china" to satisfy the demands of the growing middle class in Europe and America. As methods were devised to speed production (Figure 3-37), as specialization within the process developed, the finished piece became the product of many people, and the personal relationship of potter and clay was lost.

In Chapter 6 we will see how the same separation developed in the Western world. However, in Japan, as in the West, there were potters working in small studio-workshops with a few assistants, who continued to limit their production to what they could directly control, keeping the personal tradition alive. These small workshops produced ceramics that were appreciated by knowledgeable collectors and critics, and in 1927, in Japan, the artist-potters were recognized in the 8th Imperial Exhibition of the Arts. Their work was shown in a separate category, placed on a

Figure 3-39 A late Edo plate from Shigaraki shows the nature motifs widely used in that period to decorate everything from pottery to sword guards. Waving bamboo, painted in free, sparing brush strokes, was a popular motif. Shigaraki, Japan, Edo period. *Courtesy, The Fogg Art Museum, Harvard University.*

Figure 3-40 Chambered kiln in Mashiko, Japan, shows the newly glazed ware. *Photo by James Aliferis.*

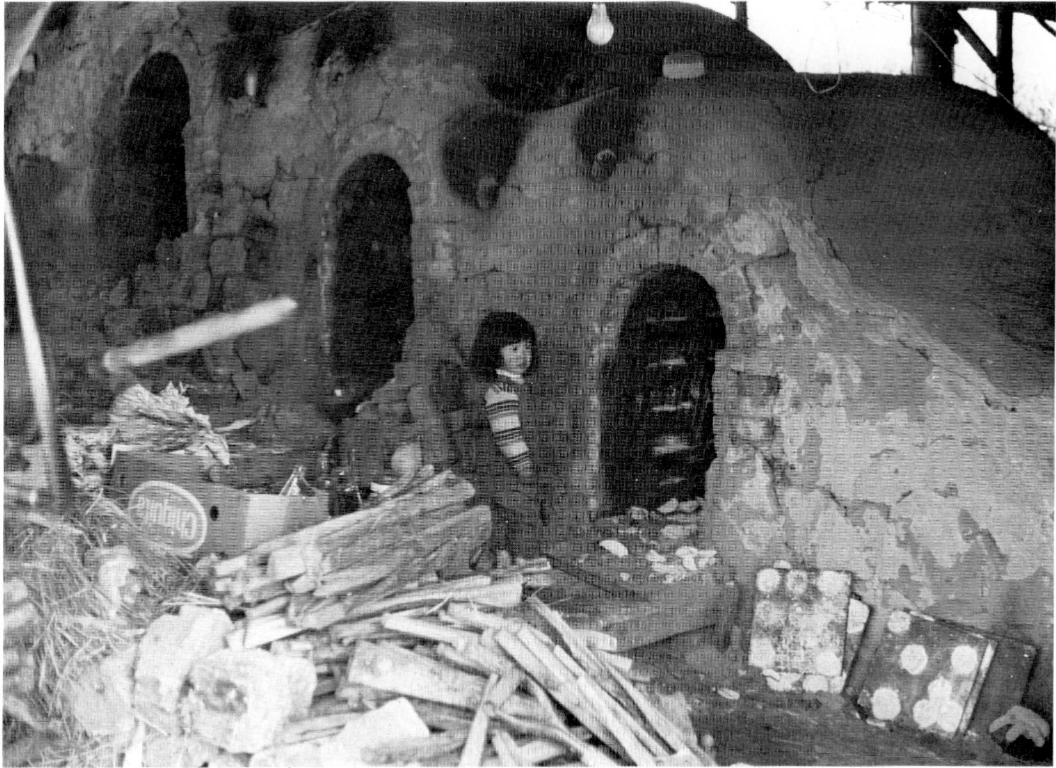

Figure 3-41 Climbing chamber kiln in Mashiko, Japan, 1977. *Photo by James Aliferis.*

level with sculpture and painting. It is this tradition of Japanese pottery that has influenced so many Western potters in the twentieth century. It is perhaps best known to Westerners through the craft of Shoji Hamada, who worked in the early 1920s in England with Bernard Leach, returning to Japan in 1924. There, in Mashiko, he worked alongside the local potters (Figures 3-40, 3-41, and 6-31). A master potter, whose pieces are in museums all over the world, he kept close to the inherited traditions of folk art in Japan. He also traveled and taught throughout the world, as well as teaching in Mashiko. His ideas of simple, honest beauty have influenced potters everywhere.

Chapter Four
Africa

Africa, like all the major continents, has seen a procession of peoples moving across its land for thousands of years, hunting its wild animals, driving herds to new grazing lands, moving on in search of a better place to live. In the process, newcomers have pushed the original inhabitants or earlier immigrants ahead of them, resulting in a complex intermingling of peoples and racial strains.

The African continent is vast, encompassing many types of natural environments. Wide, open grasslands, hot, dry deserts, deep rain forests, and cool mountain woodlands—all are part of Africa's rich natural heritage. Just as the land is infinitely varied, so are the people who have lived on it. Their life styles, their beliefs, their ceremonies, their legends, and their arts also vary from place to place, from people to people. In this limited space we can only suggest the rich variety of life on this continent, and we must recognize that we cannot speak of African art and African ceramics as if they were the products of a single culture.

Clay and Metalcraft

Since archaeological excavations and studies in Africa are comparatively recent and few, there are undoubtedly many fragments of pottery and sculpture still under its soil waiting to be found. Until then, our knowledge of the history of clay working in Africa will be far from complete.

Figure 4-1 (*Right*) Ancient Nok sculptors shaped clay into faces that speak to us with a sense of urgent life. The images look carved out of the clay, suggesting that the Nok artists may have based their forms on earlier wood carvings. Almost life sized, these figures are a remarkable technical achievement; the sculptors obviously had a long tradition of firing behind them, for it is difficult to fire such large sculptures without cracks. The clay was heavily tempered—you can see the particles in the clay body—to keep the figure from bursting in the fire. Nok culture, 2nd–1st century B.C. *Courtesy, Jos Museum, Nigeria.*

At one time the Sahara Desert was grassland, supporting herds of animals, and it was the home of semisettled pastoral peoples who covered the walls of caves with paintings and carvings of elephants, rhinoceros, buffalo, horses, and camels, as well as domestic cattle. They also made pottery, which has been found along with the cattle paintings, dating from between 4000 and 1200 B.C. As the desert grew drier, both cattle and people moved on, leaving behind them only the bones of animals and their lively representations on the walls, reminding us that this was once a rich grazing area.

Eventually, groups of people on different parts of the continent settled into a way of life based on the domestication of animals and agriculture, allowing them to develop metal and clay crafts. As in several other early cultures, in parts of Africa the clay crafts and metal working seem to have developed side by side. That the techniques of firing clay and metalworking were developed concurrently is not surprising, since both crafts are fire related (Figure 4-2). In Upper Nigeria today, for example, the wives of the iron-workers are the potters of the society.

Figure 4-2 African metal workers used clay for crucibles, molds, and bellows tips. This rough clay tip would have fitted over the end of a wooden bellows pipe to protect it from the heat as it was pushed into the fire. Some tips were formed and decorated with great care, while others, like this one, were merely utilitarian, made of coarse clay that could stand the temperature changes. Height 3 in. (7.6 cm), width 2¾ in. (7 cm). *Courtesy, the Trustees of The British Museum, London.*

Nok Sculpture

In northern Nigeria, near the village of Nok, and at Taruga, furnaces and iron tools dating from around the fourth or fifth century B.C. have been found along with fragments of almost life-sized terra cotta sculptures of humans and animals (Figure 4-1). The technical knowledge required to build such large pieces and fire them safely indicates that people must have been working with clay there for a long time. Whether the sculptures represent important persons or ancestor figures, we do not know. The bodies of these human figures are simplified, decorated with strings of beads, and the faces are stylized but extremely expressive.

The Nok was one of many cultures in Africa to develop a royal court art, centering around the king or chief. Sculptor-potters in these societies were retained by the court to produce a variety of ceremonial and status objects in addition to ancestor figures. It was believed that if the traditions represented by the ancestors were not adhered to, misfortune would result. The traditional patterns of respect for ancestors were changed in these royal cultures so that the forebears of the king, rather than a family's own ancestors, were revered.

The women in some of the small groups that live in this area today make pottery similar in shape to ancient Nok pottery and also make sculpture for grave memorials and ritual purposes. Thus it is possible that they are the inheritors of the Nok culture; but, as yet, that is only conjecture, like so much else in the story of African ceramics.

Ile Ife Sculpture

One of the courts had its center in the city of Ile Ife in southwestern Nigeria, where the Yoruba peoples produced a rich and lively royal art from around A.D. 800 to 1400. There have been no archaeological finds as yet that can fill the gaps in our knowledge about the years between the end of the Nok culture and the flowering of the Ile Ife culture, and possibly there is no connection between the two. But there are some similarities between them that suggest that the Nok terra cotta figures may have influenced Ife sculptors. For example, the two cultures were the only ones so far discovered in Africa to make large-scale terra cotta sculpture, and both of them simplified the bodies of their figures, using similar designs in the beaded decorations on the bodies (Figure 4-3). However, it is quite possible that there is still-undiscovered early sculpture elsewhere on the continent which, if found, would change any existing theories of interchange between cultures.

Figure 4-3 Ife sculptors worked in a more realistic style than the Nok. Ife and Nok were the only African areas where large human-figure sculptures have been found. The dates of the Ife sculptures are uncertain—probably some time between A.D. 600 and 1200. Ife. Nigerian Museums. *Courtesy, the Trustees of The British Museum, London.*

Benin Sculpture

By the eleventh century A.D., the sculptors of Ile Ife were skilled in bronze casting, which relied on ceramics for molds and crucibles. As in China, skill in clay sculpture and bronze casting were closely related, although the methods were different. According to local tradition, Iqu-igha, a talented Ife sculptor, introduced the casting process to the nearby city-state of Benin at the request of its king. There, too, sculpture became a court art focused on the king, preserving the memory of historic happenings and images of the royalty and their ancestors. Benin sculptors also made portrait heads of terra cotta, perhaps as clay models for the bronzes.

In Africa, as in so many other societies throughout history, what we call "art" frequently served ceremonial and ritualistic functions (Figure 4-4). Humans often express through ritual objects their feelings about the supernatural or about natural forces they cannot control. Such ritual objects are often believed to have the power to protect, control, or intercede with supernatural spirits.

Figure 4-4 A *mogyemogye,* or "jawbone" pot, made as a container to hold the wine that was poured over the Golden Stool of Ashanti. According to legend, the stool fell from the heavens, bringing good fortune to the Ashanti. Gold was important to the Ashanti. Gold dust was used as money, and gold objects were symbols of royalty and divinity. The decorations on this handsome pot are similar to those used on Ashanti gold work. Abuakwa, Ghana. Height 18 in. (46 cm). *Courtesy, the Trustees of The British Museum, London.*

Figure 4-5 The Ibo, who live on the west bank of the Niger River, placed sculptures and sculpted pots like this on altars dedicated to Ifijiok, the Yam spirit. The figures show the chiefs, their wives, their children, and attendant musicians. Ibo, Osisa, Nigeria. Height 13¾ in. (35 cm). *Courtesy, the Trustees of The British Museum, London.*

Figure 4-6 (*Right*) The Ashanti also made terra cotta sculptures that were placed in graveyards—they were apparently used in funeral ceremonies or as memorials to the dead. This one was sculpted over 150 years ago by a clay-craftsman of the Kwahu, an Ashanti group. Kajebi, Ghana. Height 15 in. (38 cm). *Courtesy, the Trustees of The British Museum, London.*

Ritual Ceramics

In Africa, ritual objects were often associated with the passage from one period of life to another—from childhood to adulthood, from life to the world of the dead. Many of the ceremonial objects were used by the male secret societies governing the initiation into manhood, while others were related to the puberty rites of the women. Still others were used in ceremonies, festivals, and rituals dedicated to the spirits of crops and fertility. For example, in the Ibo village of Osisa, on the west bank of the Niger River, ceremonial terra cottas were placed on the outdoor village shrines dedicated to Ifijiok, the Yam spirit (Figure 4-5).

Other ceremonies also required sculpture or pottery, such as the initiation of the leather artisans of the Korhogu region. There, unbaked clay figures were realistically modeled in order to teach the initiates the necessary lessons. And in Ghana, among the Ashanti, potters made several types of ornamented pots to be used in burial or other rituals. One type, the *abusua kuruwa,* was placed along with a cooking pot, utensils, and hearthstones near the grave. In it was placed hair that all the blood relatives of the deceased had shaved off their heads. The Ashanti also put clay sculptures of heads in their graveyards, probably as memorials (Figure 4-6).

One unusual terra cotta head, the only one of its kind found in Africa so far, was discovered in the Luzira Hills near Lake Victoria in Uganda (Figure 4-7). This head was found near iron artifacts, but it is believed to be only a few hundred years old. Its purpose is unknown, reminding us that our knowledge of sequences, dates, origins, and meaning of so much of African ceramics is incomplete and that much more information is needed before we will have a clear picture of its consecutive development.

The Crafts in Everyday Life

In Africa, as in many other preindustrial cultures, art was not separated from everyday life and the crafts were not isolated. Rather they were a harmonious part of people's lives. The domestic implements of ordinary people, as well as those of chiefs and kings, were shaped with care and embellished with decoration. A Yoruba poem that celebrates equally the beauty of fast-running deer, children, a rainbow, and a well-swept veranda, says, "Anybody who meets beauty and does not look at it will soon be poor." It is taken for granted that just because an object is useful it need not be ugly. The artist is not divorced from the people who use the product, and although some may be more skilled than others at weaving, pottery making, singing, or dancing, what would be considered a special talent elsewhere is thought to be a normal human ability in Africa.

Figure 4-7 An unusual clay head from Uganda, unlike any others yet found in Africa. Probably it is a few hundred years old, although as yet nothing is known about the culture from which it came. Luzira Hill, Uganda. Height 7⅛ in. (18 cm.) *Courtesy, the Trustees of The British Museum, London.*

Figure 4-8 (*Above*) Tobacco pipe bowls were made of clay in animal shapes throughout a wide area in Africa. Attached to long hollow stems, like this Shilluk pipe, they were modeled as birds, leopards, and other animals. The incised cross-hatching typical of their decoration was often emphasized with white chalk or ash. Sudan. Length of bowl 3⅛ in. (8 cm). *Courtesy, the Trustees of The British Museum, London.* **Figure 4-9** (*Left*) Another pipe bowl, fashioned as an elephant, is made of highly burnished black pottery with the usual cross-hatching in contrast. Usually, pipes or ceremonial objects were made by the men. Batotela, Zambia. Height 1¼ in. (3 cm). *Courtesy, the Trustees of The British Museum, London.*

Figure 4-10 Drums of all types have been important in most African cultures. An example from Lybia consists of a simple clay pot with a skin stretched tightly over it. Lybia. Height 6 in. (15 cm). *Courtesy, the Trustees of The British Museum, London.*

Figure 4-11 These clay cattle are representations of the *bos indicus,* an animal that no longer exists in the area. Sometimes the figures were fired, sometimes the children played with them unfired, waging mock battles with them. Rhodesia. Height 2¾ in. (7 cm). *Courtesy, the Trustees of The British Museum, London.*

Figure 4-12 Tiny, burnished, black pottery figures from Ethiopia depict the daily life of a Hebrew tribe, as well as Old Testament stories. (*Left*) A woman grinds grain while a child peeps over her shoulders. Compare this with a similar scene sculptured in western Mexico. (Figure 1-7). (*Center*) A woman carries water from the spring or river in a clay pot. (*Right*) A bed with the Star of David, and two figures said by the sculptor to be Solomon and the Queen of Sheba. Ethiopia. *Photo by Mogens S. Koch, Horsholm, Denmark.*

Traditional Pottery Techniques

Our knowledge of early pottery techniques in Africa is scant, but we are able to study the traditional methods still followed in villages today, and we can assume that they are based on centuries of accumulated tradition and experience (Figures 1-1 and 4-1). Although it is unwise to generalize, there are some factors that make for similarities in the techniques used throughout the continent. Within these similarities there are of course great variations.

Pottery in Africa is, and always has been, hand built. Neither the true potter's wheel nor the sophisticated type of turntable on an axle developed in the Middle East or China was ever used there, except in ancient Egypt. The kick wheel has only been introduced very recently in a few workshops (Figure 4-15). So, too, the kiln as it existed in China and the Middle East was never used in Africa. With a few exceptions, pots have always been fired on the open ground (Figure 4-14).

Figure 4-13 Demonstrating traditional methods at the Field Museum of Natural History, in Chicago, Ladi Kwali of Nigeria builds and decorates a water pot. (*Top Left*) She narrows the neck after building the body, adding coils that she presses tightly against the walls. (*Top Right*) She has shaped the neck and the rim is almost complete. (*Left*) She adds decoration around the neck by pressing into the damp clay with textured tool. *Courtesy, Field Museum of Natural History, Chicago.*

Probably the first pots were made by women who needed them for cooking, storing food, and carrying water (Figure 1-13). But, unlike some other parts of the world where villages became towns, then industrialized cities with a complex technology, African society until recently stayed largely rural, in touch with the earth. Life there did not call for a sophisticated technology. For example, the domestic earthenware pots made by village potters were better adapted to cooking over an open hearth, for porous and coarse clay bodies allow the ware to expand and contract, reducing the likelihood of cracking. In earthenware jars, some holding up to sixty quarts, drinking water was kept cool by evaporation. Because no need existed for a higher-fired ceramics, it was not developed. Today, however, where African nations have developed an urban middle class, a few workshops cater to their needs and to the needs of the tourists, making glazed stoneware (Figure 4-15).

In Africa, clay was shaped for many purposes: pots to hold honey beer, palm oil lamps for cult shrines, pots to dye fibers in, pots for babies' baths, and terra cotta pipe bowls, as well as human figures (Figures 4-7, 4-8, and 4-9). And musicians in many parts of Africa still use drums whose ceramic sound chambers mark the rhythm for dance or ritual (Figure 4-10). Small toys for children were made of clay, while often the children themselves dug clay and shaped it into animals as they played by the river (Figure 4-11).

Just as other cultures in southern countries have for centuries used mud or clay in building, in Africa it has been used for mosques and storage buildings as well as houses, which are often decorated with elaborate sculptured clay reliefs on the outside. In agricultural societies, where it is important to protect the grain from weather and rats, clay has been used since early times to line grain pits or to make large storage jars. In the same way, Africans make rodent-proof granaries that are raised from the ground on stones and have clay floors.

Outside Influences

The interior of Africa remained largely isolated from European influences until the nineteenth century. There were, of course, earlier invasions, migrations, and trade with other peoples whose art styles either changed or were absorbed into indigenous styles.

The Cretans, Greeks, and Romans all came to northern Africa, and the Kabyle pottery of Algeria is decorated with white, brown, and black designs that are remarkably similar to ancient ware made in Bronze Age Cyprus, suggesting that there may have been a lingering influence from there. The Coptic Church in Egypt and Ethiopia, whose Christianity dated from the earliest days of the religion, had an effect on local ceramic styles, reflecting also Byzantine and Roman influences. In addition, the Moslems brought with them to Africa their religious rules against representation of human forms, changing the styles of ornament in the areas that were converted to Islam. From the time the Portuguese came to Africa in the 1600s, local Christianized communities quite often reflected the new teachings in their arts, while in Ethiopia a tribe of Jews depict Old Testament characters in their sculptures (Figure 4-12). But just as China and Japan absorbed and modified the Buddhist art that came there from India, so has Africa absorbed and modified the artistic ideas that have come to the continent throughout history.

Clay Techniques Today

In Africa, men and women usually have distinct roles and rarely do the same work. For example, pottery making is generally reserved for women, and where men are involved in it they frequently make only a special type of pottery or use a different technique. As in the American Southwest, the women generally taught the girls, handing down the empirical knowledge of generations. The hands of African women traditionally dug the clay, prepared it for use, and shaped it, often according to rules or taboo. In Ghana, among the Shai people, every house has a potter, all of them

Figure 4-14 Firing in Africa has traditionally been done on the open ground. Here, Ashanti women of Ghana arrange pots for firing, building up several layers with fuel between them. Sometimes as many as 300 pots are fired at one time, using wood, grass, millet, or straw, as fuel, while at other times one large pot is fired alone. Potters in some villages dig channels to improve combustion, but in only a few places in western Africa is a low wall built around the pots as a rudimentary kiln. Ghana. *Courtesy, Museum of African Art, Eliot Elisofon Archives.*

women. There, the men used to make the ritual clay pipes, but certain taboos forbade them to make the domestic ware. In earlier centuries the pits where the Shai dug their clay were under the control of priestesses who presided over the rituals governing its removal. For instance, clay could only be dug by women who had passed puberty. On the other hand, there are peoples among whom the men make pottery and the women are forbidden to come near them during certain parts of the process. Another rule forbids Ashanti women from making any pots with human decoration. The reason given is that a woman who did this once became sterile because she had made an image of a human instead of bearing a child. And in Kenya, no one can take photographs of pots going to market for fear they will crack.

Hand Building

Almost every type of hand-building technique is used in Africa. Sometimes the base of a pot is started by molding the clay in some sort of base mold, leaving it to stiffen somewhat, then turning it upright so that the rest of the pot can be built on it with coils. Conversely, pots are sometimes made by forming the upper section first, turning it over to stiffen, and when it is ready, building coils onto it upside down (Figure 1-28). The Ashanti women, however, use no coils at all, making the whole pot by pulling up the sides from a lump of clay, walking around it backwards as they build it. In other areas, the potter forms the base by hollowing out a lump of clay with her fingers, then building the walls. Others start the base by pressing clay into a mold on which ashes or leaves keep it from sticking, pounding the clay with a stone, a wooden beater, or sometimes a specially formed clay pestle. Or the base may be formed in a gourd or in the bottom of an old pot and turned with the hands or feet as the pot is built. In several areas the hollowed-out stump of a tree or an already-fired pot makes a base mold at a convenient working height (Figures 1-1 and 4-13). But in other areas, the potter works on the ground, bending over the pot.

As the coils are added, the clay is pressed or beaten together, the pot is smoothed on the inside, and the outside is either decorated or smoothed with the fingers, a metal scraper, a shell, a bit of dried gourd, or a piece of leather. There are some potters who finish their pots by burnishing them with stones or seed pods, rubbing until the surface is polished. Sometimes the clay body has been tempered with mica or covered with a slip containing mica before it is burnished, and as a result the finished pot sparkles when the bits of glistening mica catch the light.

Among the African ceramic treasures in the storerooms of the British Museum is a modest box labeled "African female potter's tools," collected in the 1880s. The box contains only a piece of metal for scraping, a wooden tool for making designs, smooth stones for polishing, a pointed shell for punching holes, and a corn cob and seed pods for impressing designs. Similar to tools used in the American Southwest, they are mute reminders that potters all over the world have shaped and smoothed clay pots in the same fashion for thousands of years (Figures 1-29 and 5-19).

Depending on local tradition, potters use a variety of decorative techniques and styles (Figure 4-13). They may scratch their designs into the damp clay with a knife or stick, press them into it with twisted or plaited straw, or roll repeat designs on the clay with a carved wooden wheel or even a corn cob.

Finishing

In many villages the potters coat fired pots with resin, palm oil, or mixtures made from boiling leaves, reducing the porosity of the pots and often changing the color of the red clay body to a dark brown. This vegetable material, originally applied all over a pot to seal it, is now sometimes used for decoration only, applied in patterns of bands, lines, or triangles. For example, the unusual marbled effect on the pots made by the Bakongo tribes are made by splashing vegetable matter onto the sides of the pots while they are hot, after firing. Obviously this was done for decoration, since it does not cover the whole pot.

Similarly, a great variety of decorative steps and techniques have evolved, some of which had their origin in function. Thus the impressed, carved, or raised designs on a water pot make it easier to lift a wet, slippery pot full of water. In Uganda, the shape of calabashes, which were originally used as containers or ladles, are now copied almost exactly in clay, while other tribes carve lines on their pots, copying the laced pattern originally made by the fiber or leather thongs with which water gourds were carried. Water or milk pots from Botswana are decorated with patterns that contrast dark-toned graphite-burnished triangular designs with areas of the untreated red clay body. The Ibo of Nigeria, on the other hand, color only the raised bands undulating around their large-bellied vases. Whatever method is used, each region or group of peoples stays within its decorative tradition, repeating the same types of designs.

Figure 4-15 A contemporary potter in a workshop in Zambia uses the local stoneware clay on a kick wheel. Several workshops of this type have been started in African countries to meet the local demand for more durable pottery. In addition to producing contemporary domestic stoneware, the potters build pots in older shapes, decorating them with traditional designs. In Nigeria and Ghana, workshops started by British potter Michael Cardew brought European techniques to Africa. *Courtesy, Zambia Information Services.*

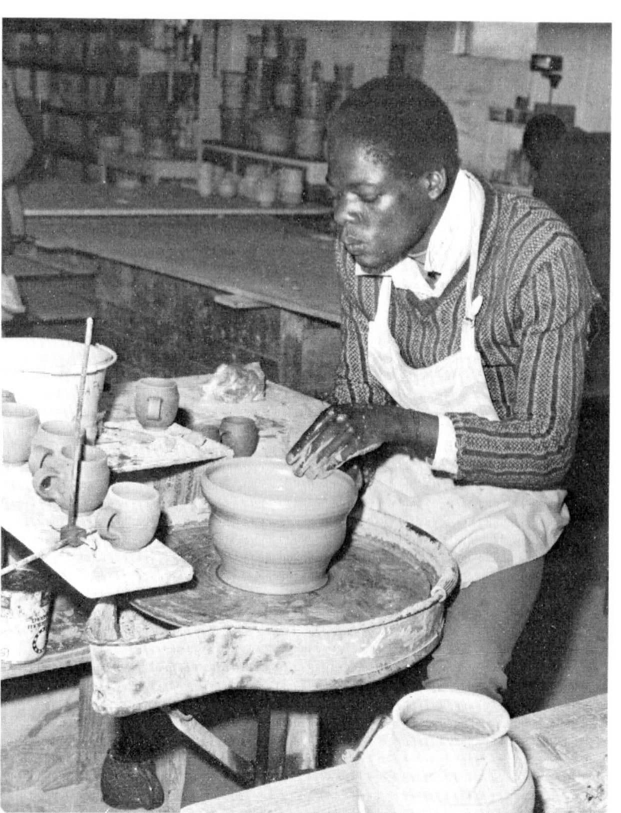

Firing

After the pots are dried in the sun, or in some cases in a cooler spot with other pots placed over them, they may be heated by burning grass inside them before firing (Figure 1-43). Almost all pottery firing in Africa is done in an open fire (Figure 4-14). The length of time of a firing varies from place to place, according to the size, number, and thickness of the pots, and may last for several hours or only a few minutes. Indeed, there are some potters who fire their pots very lightly, and the housewife who buys one fires it a second time when she gets home.

Changing Crafts in Changing Times

Hundreds of thousands of pots are produced by these traditional methods in Africa—the Shai potters in Ghana make over one-half million a year, selling them to neighboring villages. Women potters frequently carry their fired pots on their heads for ten or fifteen miles to market them.

All over the world, traditional crafts have been changed or lost as societies have changed. What will happen to the craft of pottery in Africa as the continent becomes more industrialized and urban is uncertain. Recently, several workshops have been set up to adapt the shapes and decorations of older African pottery to wheel techniques, producing glazed stoneware (Figure 4-15). Many African potters, like Ladi Kwali (Figures 4-13 and 10-5) and Abasiya Ahuwan of Nigeria, are deeply committed to their traditional heritage but are also using new techniques. From potters like these, new styles of ceramics are emerging, combining old and new techniques and forms into an art that is expressive of present-day Africa.

Chapter Five
The Americas

Thousands of years ago, hunters from Asia tracking mammoth, bison, and other large animals crossed over a land bridge to the American continent. When the glaciers of the Ice Age melted, about 8,000 years ago, the water they released flooded this land bridge, creating in its place the Bering Strait; thus we know that these hunters must have come before that date.

They brought with them stone tools, arrows tipped with chipped stones, and a type of spear thrower that appears again much later as a ritual object in the stone and clay sculpture of several native American cultures. The remains of a primitive hunting-gathering people have been found in central Mexico dating from around 10,000 to 7000 B.C. This indicates that the migrations of people from the Asian continent must have started considerably earlier to reach as far as Mexico by this date. In waves of migration, they spread out into the North American Great Lakes area, the Plains, the Mississippi Valley, and the East Coast.

But other bands of migrants roamed further south, some of them eventually reaching the tip of South America. In their wanderings, they encountered high plateaus, snow-capped mountains, and dense, humid jungles. Small groups stopped along the way, adapting their lives to the different environments. The settled descendants of these early hunters became the artisans, potters, and sculptors who contributed their skills to the advanced and sophisticated cultures that later flourished in Mesoamerica and the Andes region of South America. (Mesoamerica is a name coined by archaeologists to include central and southern Mexico, Guatemala, El Salvador, and parts of Honduras.)

As time went on, the groups of people scattered throughout the Americas developed such varying racial characteristics, languages, religions, and art styles that it is sometimes hard to remember that they originally came from the same stock. There are, however, some features common to all the civilizations that flourished in Mesoamerica. Most of them cultivated maize, used hieroglyphics, built large stone monuments, created calendars, and understood and used some form of mathematics. In their attempt to control the environment, improve their crops, or ensure the continuation of the race, they developed religions oriented toward fertility, centering on gods that were the personifications of animals or humans. A priestly class became powerful, dominating the society and imposing the organization necessary to build large stone ceremonial centers, including impressive pyramids, temples, tombs, and sometimes palaces and ritual ball courts.

Mesoamerica

The high plateau of central Mexico, dotted with lakes and covered with grasslands, at one time attracted large numbers of grazing animals. On these pastures, with snowcapped mountains towering above them, groups of hunters moved from place to place, following their main source of food. But about 8,000 years ago the climate began to change and the large animals disappeared, so that the hunters were forced to gather seeds and grasses to supplement their food. This led to the cultivation of crops, and by around 5000 B.C., these people had domesticated squash and chili and learned to grow maize, which became the staple food of that region.

Throughout the ancient civilizations of North and South America, the cultivation of maize preceded the growth of urban civilizations. Plenty of corn stored away meant that people had the leisure and security to engage in crafts or organize the communal effort required to build large religious buildings, irrigation projects, or cities. As the young maize plants pushed through the earth each year, were watered by rain, and the ears ripened in the sun, the promise of food and life was renewed. This yearly event led the farming villages to express their hopes for good crops, their fears of drought, and their gratitude for sunny skies and rain in ceremonies and offerings to their fertility gods. Out of these ritual needs grew their architecture, their carvings, their ceremonial vessels, and their music and dance.

The vast groups of buildings used for ritual and government purposes required large numbers of artisans to paint and carve the walls, and these societies also used the skill of ceramic artisans to shape the often elaborate burial and offering urns. Most of the ceramics that have survived came from tombs, where they were protected from breakage, so we get the impression that all ceramic production was devoted to religious objects. But we know from wall paintings, sculpture, and a few *codices,* or illustrated historical books, that simpler vessels for storage, cooking, drinking, and other household uses were also made. All early potters of the Americas worked with hand-building techniques, using simple turntables, for the potter's wheel did not appear on the continent until it was brought by later European settlers. The potters shaped their vessels with coils and modeled the figurines by hand, or pressed clay into molds to speed up production.

The Olmecs

Many of the common features of the various Mesoamerican cultures are believed to have come originally from the Olmecs, whose civilization was centered in the eastern coastal regions of Mexico between 1300 B.C. and A.D. 300. From their urban centers there, the Olmecs traded with other cultures in jade, kaolin, turquoise, and shells, bringing along with their trade goods new concepts of religion, including the cult of a jaguar god believed to control rain and fertility.

They improved existing technology in both agriculture and the crafts, made accurate astronomical observations, and irrigated or drained their coastal land with large engineering projects. Their ceremonial centers included courts for a ritual ball game, and at one of them, the Island of La Venta, they erected enormous stone heads, which they brought on rafts across sixty miles of water. These huge heads have the characteristic petulant Olmec faces, which look at us with such a sour expression. The Olmec mouth, with its downturned lips, also appears on the plump seated figures modeled realistically in clay (Figure 5-1). This characteristic mouth appears in a lot of sculpture, both stone and clay, throughout the whole of Mesoamerica, testifying to the widespread influence exerted on the technology, art, and religion of other peoples by this vigorous early civilization.

Figure 5-1 Usually coated with white or cream slip, many of the Olmec terra cotta figures appear to be infants, or baby-faced adults, often with a cleft in the top of the head. One Olmec stone carving shows a woman mating with the jaguar god, and since the Olmecs believed that the jaguar was the source of all life, it is believed by some authorities that these clay figures represent were-jaguars, offspring of that union. Olmec, Las Bocas, State of Puebla, Mexico. Height 3 in. (7.6 cm). *Courtesy, Museum of the American Indian, Heye Foundation.*

Tlatilco

Around 1300 to 900 B.C., on the Central Plateau, near present-day Mexico City, a village named Tlatilco was the center of a culture that borrowed some of its technology and artistic ideas from the Olmecs but produced its own

Figure 5-2 Two-headed or double-faced women, whose significance we can only guess at, were quite common among the figurines found at Tlatilco. This figure, with its carefully arranged bangs, headband, and lock of hair falling on the shoulders, shows traces of the color that usually decorated these clay images. They probably had some fertility meaning. Tlatilco, Mexico, 1300–800 B.C. *Courtesy, Museo Nacional de Antropologia, Mexico.*

Figure 5-3 Maya athletes wore protective belts, helmets, gauntlets and knee pads when they played the ritual ball game. Players were usually forbidden to use their hands or feet, so the ball was kept in motion with their bodies. In the great Maya ball court at Chitchen Itza, there is a stone ring on each side, and the team who got the ball through it won immediately. Jaina, Campeche, Mexico, A.D. 700–800. Height 6 in. (15.2 cm). *Courtesy, Museo Nacional de Antropologia, Mexico.*

style of ceramics. Because of the large amount of clay sculpture and pottery found there, it has been suggested that Tlatilco was a rich village surrounded by less affluent villages. Its tombs yielded handsome, polished black pots, decorated jars, and quantities of female figurines (Figure 5-2).

The potters scraped, polished, and stamped their pots, or decorated them with textures made with the edges of shells traded from the Olmecs. They separated these decorated areas with incised lines, sometimes rubbing red hematite powder into them after the jar was fired. They also painted the pottery with red, yellow, and white geometric designs or with stylized snakes or jaguar claws—another Olmec influence. One interesting type of jar from Tlatilco had a double-necked pouring spout formed like a stirrup, a shape that appeared again later in Peru as well as in the North American Southwest. The unusual shape was probably carried to those areas through trade or migration (Figure 5-13).

The sculptors who worked with the region's abundant clay modeled it into human figures, which were buried in large quantities in the tombs. The bulk of the figures portray large-hipped women, most of them naked, some wearing short skirts, some painted with lines suggesting tattoos, clothing, or body paint. The Tlatilco sculptors showed a great interest in female hair styles, and the hair of all of these figures is elaborately dressed (Figure 5-2). Many of the figures show women dancing or carrying children on their backs or in their arms or playing with a dog. The most unusual figures are the ones with two heads or two faces that share a third eye; we do not know the reason for these dual faces.

Male figures of musicians, acrobats, and dwarfs, and masked figures, probably representing priests or shamans, have also been found in the tombs. Among them is the very earliest clay sculpture of a ball player wearing the padding that was characteristic of their costumes. This same ritual game is also represented in paintings and sculpture of other Mesoamerican cultures right up to the time of the Spanish Conquest in 1520 (Figure 5-3).

Maya

The Mayan civilization, which lasted over 2,700 years from its beginnings in the tenth or eleventh century B.C., produced some of the most remarkable ceramic art of Mesoamerica. Indeed, according to the *Popul Vuh,* the sacred book of the Quiche Indians in Guatemala, who still speak Mayan, the very first manlike creatures were modeled out of clay by the gods. The gods destroyed these clay people, however, since they could not think, and finally, "only maize was used for the flesh of our first fathers." Maize-centered, like other Mesoamerican cultures, the Maya also worshiped the Chacs, the rain gods, along with the gods of wind and sun. Earth and sun, clay and water, and maize—all important elements in any agricultural society. Even when the Mayan society became extremely complex, it recognized that without the rain and sun, famine resulted, and the old gods were still worshiped along with the new.

An advanced civilization, capable of charting the movements of the planet Venus with only one day's error in 6,000 years, the Maya recorded past history on stone monuments using hieroglyphics and an accurate calendar predating our modern calendar by over a thousand years. Well-preserved stone pyramids and temples, as well as many gold, jade, and clay artifacts, have been unearthed in the jungle area of Mexico and Guatemala where the Maya lived.

The ceremonial pottery of the Maya was quite simple in shape, but was elaborately decorated with paintings in black, red, and white on an orange background. These paintings show the priests, warriors, and nobles in ornate headdresses, engaged in rituals, raids on other tribes for prisoners, and the sacrifices which followed, sacrifices probably also linked to fertility.

A few surviving codices and observations by priests who came with the conquering Spaniards have told us a great deal about the Mayan society. But one of the best sources of information about Mayan life is the large number of terra cotta figurines buried with the dead on the Island of Jaina, opposite Yucatan. Expressive, lively, and beautifully crafted, these clay sculptures show us notables in their huge headdresses, which force them to sit or stand in dignified poses, and elderly statuesque ladies wearing heavy jewelry looking as if they are dressed for a festival. But they also show us the everyday life of ordinary people. Women cooking, weaving, caring for children, the old, and the ill—all come alive in clay.

Perhaps most lifelike of all are the ball players (Figure 5-3). Only a few inches tall, these figures capture all the excitement and action of the game, which was eagerly watched and bet on by the spectators. Common to almost all Mesoamerican cultures, ball courts were always placed near the temples; apparently the game often ended in the sacrifice of one of the players, so it is believed to have had a religious significance. The rules varied from culture to culture, but throughout Mesoamerica, the ball, perhaps symbolizing the sun, was passed from player to player from one end of the court to the other.

The Mayan civilization eventually lost its vitality; its cities declined, were deserted, and were finally overgrown with jungle. But the influence of the Mayan culture, like that of the Olmecs, was felt in other parts of Mesoamerica.

Veracruz

On the Gulf Coast, in central Veracruz, a culture developed from about 500 B.C. to A.D. 900 that centered in Remojadas and later in El Tajin. The Remojadas culture produced a large number of clay figures, many of which were joyful and smiling. Such a cheerful frame of mind is rare in Mesoamerican art, and thousands of figures, seemingly stopped in the middle of a belly laugh, have been found in Remojadas.

Some of the figures have the emblems of life and movement on their headdresses, so they may have had some connection with life-giving rituals. The earliest ones were solid, modeled by hand, but later ones were made in molds or built up hollow by hand into almost life-sized figures. Many of the smaller figures were made as whistles, others as toys or rattles (Figure 1-6). Although the wheel was never developed for transportation in Mesoamerica, some of the clay toys were made with wheels so that they could be pulled along. Looking at the figurines buried in the graves in this region, one gets the impression of a fun-loving people who faced life and death with a smile.

Teotihuacan

On the Central Plateau, north of Mexico City, loom the impressive ruins of the sacred city of Teotihuacan. Rising steeply from the flat plain, the pyramids stand as mute reminders of the bustling city that flourished there from 100 B.C. to A.D. 850. There, the priests, who also controlled the government, served the deities associated with water, fertility, and agriculture. Tlaloc, the rain god, was called upon to water the crops tended in the great Valley of Mexico by peasants who lived in scattered huts around the city.

The city itself, unlike many other Mesoamerican religious centers, was a residential center, as well as the focus of religion. The potters and sculptors lived in a special area given over to the crafts, while the priests and nobles lived in palaces. The pottery of Teotihuacan that has survived is simple, often shaped like cylinders with three feet, decorated with sculptured jaguars or human heads. The vessels are formal and ritualistic in feeling, and their shape and decoration have led some scholars to suggest a link with Chinese Shang dynasty bronze urns. Some of these clay vessels were coated with plaster and painted with images of the gods in brilliant color, in the same way that the stucco walls of the temples were painted.

Small clay figures and masks were made to be placed in the graves, and hundreds of these have been found at Teotihuacan. At first they were modeled by hand, but the demand apparently became so great that they were later made in molds.

Figure 5-4 Grayware Zapotec funerary urn. The earliest of these urns were hand modeled, but later they were mass produced in molds. State of Oaxaca, Mexico. Height 13½ in. (34.3 cm). *Courtesy, Museum of the American Indian, Heye Foundation. Photo by Carmelo Guadagno.*

Zapotec

From around A.D. 300 to 900, near present-day Oaxaca, the Zapotecs built a great ceremonial center at Monte Alban. There is some dispute about the earlier settlements there—either they were strongly influenced by the Olmecs, or possibly the Olmec civilization actually began in the valley there and radiated outward. In any case, the Zapotecs, themselves greatly influenced by the culture at Teotihuacan, built a great religious center high on a hilltop.

Ceramics played a large part in the religion of the Zapotecs, even in as lowly a form as the pots needed to carry water to the thousands of laborers struggling to build the pyramids, temples, and ball court 1,200 feet up the mountain; there was no water on top of Monte Alban. A variety of pottery has been found there, some linked in style to Teotihuacan, others to the Maya.

But most characteristic of the Zapotec style are the elaborate sculptured urns made to accompany the dead who were buried in cave tombs at Monte Alban (Figure 5-4). These ritual urns held fire, incense, food, or water offerings for the gods who were represented on them. Jaguar figures were also modeled into large, imposing offering urns, some as tall as 33 inches. Their snarling faces, with menacing fangs, testify to the mixed fear and worship with which the jaguar god was regarded by the pre-Columbian peoples of Mesoamerica. Figures of women also appear on the urns, possibly representing goddesses. They are dressed in a style of clothing still worn by the Zapotec women in Oaxaca, including a *quechquemitl* over the shoulders, necklaces and ear ornaments, and colored cords braided into the hair. Toward the end of the Zapotec period, many of the urns were formed in molds and the standard of craftsmanship declined.

The Zapotec culture itself declined between A.D. 800 and 1200, and Monte Alban was eventually taken over by the Mixtecs, who were more noted for their gold work than for their ceramics.

Aztec

The most recent, and shortest lived, of the cultures in central Mexico was the Aztec, who came from the north and founded a modest village in the Valley of Mexico in A.D. 1325. It grew rapidly into the great city of Tenochtitlan, whose wide avenues, network of canals, aqueducts, and drainage systems astounded the Spaniards when they arrived in 1520. On the center of an island, now Mexico City, stood a great ceremonial center surrounded by a wall, a ball court, shrines, and sacrificial altars.

Aztec trade was extensive, and food stuffs and raw materials, as well as pottery, hides, herbs, and jewels from the surrounding conquered towns, poured into their busy markets. The Aztecs dominated their neighbors, demanding tribute from them and raiding them to procure the constant stream of sacrificial victims needed for their religious rites. They believed that the sun god needed human blood to gain strength for his battle with his jealous brothers and sisters, the gods of the stars and the moon. So daily sacrifice was essential to sustain him.

Aztec art owed much to the surrounding cultures, especially the Mixtec of Oaxaca and Puebla, from whom they took the craft of painted pottery—a delicate orange ware decorated with gray, yellow, or white. Much of their pottery probably came from other places as tribute; in the surviving Aztec codices, colored drawings show the tributes of feathers, skins, fabrics, food, and plants, often carried to the city in pottery vessels. Other paintings on agave paper depict babies being baptized in simple pottery tubs, tripod urns with food in them, and elderly people drinking their daily allotted ration of the Aztec liquor, pulque, out of wide, shallow pottery cups. All the usual domestic pots appear in these paintings, giving us a clear idea of how important clay was in the daily life of early Mesoamerica (Figure 5-5).

Figure 5-5 Aztec women used household pottery in their daily lives in much the same way as Mexican village women today. Here, a housewife grinds corn on a metate, while a few tortillas cook on the earthenware platter on the hearth while others await their turn. An olla cools her water by evaporation through porous earthenware. Aztec pottery was hand built, for it was not until the arrival of the Europeans that the potter's wheel came to Mesoamerica. *Redrawn from a Spanish codice.*

Western Mexico

In the area now covered by the states of Michoacan, Guanajuato, Jalisco, Colima, and Nayarit, the villages were isolated from the other Mesoamerican cultures and show only a few traces of Olmec and Teotihuacan influence in their sculpture. Also, they were not as deeply involved with religious ritual, nor did they develop as powerful or wealthy a priesthood as other societies. No monumental religious centers were built here, and few stone carvings remain.

What has remained is a wealth of clay figurines that were buried in tombs throughout the vast area. From around A.D. 300 to 900, sculptors made clay figures ranging from solid miniature animals to hollow human figures 30 inches (75 cm) high. These clay people are modeled in all the varied activities of their everyday lives (Figures 5-6 and 5-7). Clay models of rabbits, armadillos, mice, and parrots, along with houses, temples, and ball courts round out our picture of their culture. Although these figures were buried in the underground shaft tombs, it was not primarily a ritual art. To see how these western artists were more concerned with portraying life on earth than with pleasing the gods, compare one of the figures with the stylized Zapotec funerary urn (Figure 5-4).

Although there is great similarity between the sculptures from the western areas, there are regional differences of custom or style. For instance, we learn that the women of Nayarit usually went naked or sometimes wore a short skirt, but always dressed their hair carefully and wore large ear plugs and usually a necklace. The men, on the other hand, were often shown wearing light armor woven from fibers, carrying clubs and spear throwers. Frequently the people of Nayarit are shown in what are almost caricatures, and the ill and deformed among them are sculpted in an exaggerated manner.

In Jalisco, on the other hand, where the sculptors worked with less exaggeration, people are shown more realistically; a woman nursing her child, a young man looking into a mirror, an old man carried in a litter, and singers and dancers all bring us closer to life in this beautiful part of Mexico (Figure 5-7).

In Colima, highly skilled sculptors also modeled a happy people, seemingly at peace with their environment, apparently not feeling the need for god figures to lead them into the afterlife.

With the arrival of the Spaniards, amid their horses and guns, the old cultures of Mexico were destroyed; since then, the

Figure 5-6 The flat heads modeled on figurines were not a distortion, but the result of binding the infant's head almost at birth. This nursing child, however, has such a thin head that it is hard to believe it could survive such an exaggerated distortion. Magdalena, Jalisco, Mexico, A.D. 300–900. Height 17½ in. (44.5 cm). *Courtesy, Museum of the American Indian, Heye Foundation.*

Figure 5-7 Clay figures, none more than 7 inches (17.8 cm) tall, were made to be placed in graves in western Mexico between A.D. 300 and 900. One man, wearing a snake and feather headdress, may be a priest or shaman; he beats paddles together to accompany the dance of the man to his left. Although we sense the reality of life in the figures, the grouping may suggest relationships that never existed. Jalisco, Mexico. *Courtesy, Museum of the American Indian, Heye Foundation.*

ceramic arts of Mexico have been greatly influenced by the Hispano-Moresque styles brought there by the new cultures. Tiles, wheel-thrown pots, and bowls are all colorfully decorated with motifs very similar to those brought to Spain by the Arabs (Figure 6-1). Earthenware ollas still cool water in Mexico, and vestiges of the ancient Mesoamerican cultures remain in the pottery toys and whistles that are still made in some areas. As recently as twenty-five years ago, these were the only toys the village children owned, but now they are primarily made for the tourist trade.

Figure 5-8 (*Left*) This woman, who wears bracelets, head band, and ear plugs, apparently has painted or tattooed her body and face. The hollow clay figure, just over 6 inches tall, still retains some of its original red, black, and white color. Jalisco, Mexico.

The Isthmus Area

In the narrow neck of land between the two Americas, in what is now Panama, Costa Rica, and parts of Colombia, the rich gold mines yielded quantities of the shining metal. Although simple pottery found in Panama has been dated as early as 2000 B.C., during the time when Mesoamerican and Peruvian cultures were building complex stone cities, gold was the important art medium for the people of this area. Sometimes hammered, but also cast, the gold was formed into the fantastic supernatural creatures of their religion. Here clay had a functional purpose; the early goldsmiths used two-part ceramic molds to cast their beautiful solid-gold ornaments.

Later the pottery made in the province of Veraguas in Panama was outstanding for the refinement of its shape and decoration (Figures 5-9 and 5-10). These potters, working in the centuries just before the arrival of the Europeans, hand shaped bowls, jars, and pedestaled urns on which they painted stylized animals and gods. Their forceful decorations complement the elegant forms and are set off by horizontal bands and scrolls. Birds, turtles, serpents, and crocodiles were painted on the buff ware in red, black, and purple in a rhythmic style unlike Mesoamerican or Peruvian pottery.

This sophisticated ceramic craft was lost when the Europeans arrived, in the same way gold-working methods were lost. Today, in the villages of Panama, women still hand build their domestic pots as their ancestors probably did, but make them in only a few simple shapes. Digging the dry clay from nearby deposits, pounding it, sieving it, and kneading it with a small amount of sand, they use it to build up a pot with coils, then pound it with the flat of the hand. Some of these traditional potters still make pots with three legs, an echo of earlier days when clay was formed into a great variety of shapes for religious or funerary purposes.

Figure 5-9 Polychrome bowl with painted decoration representing the crocodile god. Veraguas, Panama, A.D. 1000–1500. Height 9¾ in. (24.8 cm). *Courtesy, Museum of the American Indian, Heye Foundation.*

Figure 5-10 Pedestal vessel, painted with seven animal heads. Veraguas, Panama, A.D. 1000–1500. Height 10 in. (25.4 cm). *Courtesy, Museum of the American Indian, Heye Foundation.*

South America

Toward the end of the glacial period, bands of hunters made their way along the western coast of the southern continent. Some of them found hospitable land in the low fertile valleys of the rivers that break up the long coastline, while others wandered into the high mountain plains and valleys; still others had made their way into the humid dense jungles on the eastern side of the towering Andes mountains.

In the two main western areas of coast and plateau, the descendants of these hunters settled into farming and fishing villages, cultivating maize. These early peoples did not have pottery, but they formed fertility figures and figures of birds and animals out of clay, leaving them unbaked.

Just where in South America fired pottery was first made is uncertain; perhaps to the north in Ecuador, or Colombia, perhaps in the eastern jungles. Recent finds in Ecuador suggest that farming cultures producing pottery developed there at least as early as in Mesopotamia. The story of the many ceramic cultures that succeeded one another from prehistoric times to the Spanish Conquest of Peru in 1533 is a confusing one. There are still areas in this vast continent where there has been little excavation, while other parts of it have been studied more thoroughly; thus the picture that emerges is apt to be uneven. The coastal areas are best known, the highlands next, and the eastern jungles just barely.

Nevertheless, between around 1800 and 900 B.C., people on the north and south coastal areas of western South America had settled into the large villages that provided the basis for the later urban societies. Technical improvements were made in agriculture, weaving, pottery, and stone architecture. The pottery of this period was well made but usually simple, with only a little decoration, generally geometric.

Figure 5-11 A Paracas potter in Peru, some time between 900 B.C. and A.D. 200, cleverly combined relief sculpture and incised lines on this stirrup-spouted vessel, whose shape may have originally come through trade from Tlatilco in central Mexico. The bird and human face motifs with which it is decorated were often used in pottery of the Andes region. Paracas, South coast, Peru, 900 B.C.–A.D. 200. Height 7½ in. (19.1 cm). *Courtesy, Fine Arts Museums of San Francisco, M.H. De Young Memorial Museum.*

By around 900 to 600 B.C., the pottery was more elaborately decorated, and at that time, in the southern Paracas area, potters formed the clay into stirrup-spouted vessels, bridged bottles, and whistling jars, shapes that would be used for centuries by the potters of the Andes region (Figure 5-11).

Chavin

During these centuries, the Chavin empire was established, dominating a large area. It was inspired by a new religious cult that possibly spread from the eastern rain forests. The Chavin rulers built a huge stone religious center at Chavin de Huantar, in a high valley. Here sculptors carved a monumental image of a human with a smiling, fanged mouth as well as other god images. This stone sculpture influenced the art of surrounding and later peoples, and a great deal of the pottery of the central Andes would later be made in the shape of humans and animals, much of it clearly influenced by Chavin stone carvings.

Moche

As the Chavin empire declined, local artistic styles flourished, varying from valley to valley, and the ceramic artisans experimented with a variety of methods and materials. Among these, the Moche potters of the northern coast were most productive around A.D. 400, although their style was developed as early as 200 B.C. and lasted until around A.D. 600. The liveliness, inventiveness, and skill with which they modeled their sculptured vessels was outstanding (Figure 5-12). Stirrup-spouted drinking vessels or water jars were their most typical shape, and they made them in a wide range of images—realistic portrait heads, fanged god faces, animals, fish, crayfish, humans in crouched poses, and houses and temples (Figure 1-9). These Moche sculptor-potters were technically adept, and they hand modeled or used molds with equal skill. Whichever method they used, Moche ceramics rarely became standardized. Earlier Andean pottery had often been painted with resin after the clay was fired, but now the Moche used slips of red and black clay to decorate their pots before firing, usually burnishing them.

Figure 5-12 Sculptured head is actually a stirrup-spouted jar whose face is a portrait, possibly of the person with whom it was buried. The turbaned noble has a tattooed face and neck band. Moche potters formed their pottery in molds after first making a model in solid clay. They pressed two slabs of damp clay onto the front and back of the model, allowed them to harden slightly, removed them, then fired them. This formed a two-part mold into which they pressed damp clay to form two sections of the jar. Next, these were joined to make the hollow jar, and handles and spout were attached. Details of face or body were added by carving into the clay while it was damp, or by adding clay, individualizing each jar. Before firing, the potters burnished and painted them with slip. Mochica culture, Trujillo, Peru, A.D. 200–600. Height 12 in. (30.5 cm), width 6 in. (15.2 cm). *Courtesy, Museum of the American Indian, Heye Foundation. Photo by Carmelo Guadagno.*

Nasca

Another local culture to appear after the decline of the Chavin empire was that of the Nasca on the southern coast, whose people built shrines, adobe pyramids, plazas, and cemeteries, wove and embroidered intricate textiles, and painted their pottery with brightly colored symbolic decoration (Color Plate 8, p. 146C). Theirs was a highly creative and religious culture, in which the cult of the dead assumed importance. Their bodies were buried with rich metal ornaments, wrapped in embroidered cotton, and accompanied by painted pottery, which often had the same type of stylized patterns as the weaving. The realistic type of modeling done by the Moche was not popular with potters here, who concentrated instead on painted decoration. The thin Nasca ware was made into bridged spout bottles, small bowls, and simple cylindrical jars resembling modern flower vases (Figure 5-13).

Figure 5-13 Nasca potters often shaped their water jugs into bridged shapes like this. The flat, stylized painting of a mythical bird is set off by black lines around each area of colored slip. Nasca, south coast, Peru, 200 B.C.–A.D. 600. 8½ X 6½ in. (21.6 X 16.5 cm). *Courtesy, Fine Arts Museums of San Francisco, M.H. De Young Memorial Museum.*

The story now becomes even more confusing, with competing religious and political movements and shifting centers of power between A.D. 600 and 1000. Finally, two cities, Huari and Tiahuanaco on Lake Titicaca, became the dominant powers. Tiahuanaco was the center of yet another new religion, with immense stone pyramids, temples, and underground rooms with carved pillars. Although many artisans were gathered there to make feathered objects, metalware, fine weaving, and ceramics, their designs were rather limited and the art as a whole had none of the variety or imagination of the Nasca or Moche work. For some reason, around A.D. 800, the highland cities were abandoned, and as the population of the coastal regions declined, new regional art styles abounded.

Chancay

One of the new cultures (around A.D. 1000), that of the Chancay Valley on the central coast, produced pottery with highly decorative, geometric designs in black and white. Sometimes these designs combine three-dimensional modeling with painted animals reduced to squares, rectangles, and triangles (Figure 5-14).

Figure 5-14 Monkeys, cats, and other animals were painted on pottery in the Chancay Valley in a style that reduced them to geometric patterns. These animals, which also form the eyes of the modeled head, were probably cats, and may have had religious significance. Chancay Valley, Central coast, Peru, A.D. 600–900. 5 X 5 in. (12.7 X 12.7 cm), *Courtesy, Fine Arts Museums of San Francisco, M.H. De Young Memorial Museum.*

Chimu

Bringing the story closer to historical times, in the mid-fourteenth century, the Chimu rulers on the northern coast extended their power far beyond the boundaries of what had been the Moche sphere of influence. The ruins of Chan Chan, the Chimu capital, cover more than eight square miles, with streets, squares, pyramids, and palaces divided into ten districts surrounded by enormous walls made of sun-dried brick. This brick was covered with clay plaster and carved in designs of geometric shapes and stylized animals. In this luxurious city, hundreds of artisans made gold mummy masks and other objects set with semiprecious stones, as well as producing intricate jewelry by casting it in one- or two-part ceramic molds.

Although the Chimu were fine metalworkers, they were not quite as gifted in ceramics, and their attempts to rival the old Moche pottery were not very successful. They used molds to create their stirrup jars, producing them in large numbers and in the process losing vitality. Most of the Chimu ware was a highly polished black, occasionally red, without any applied painted decoration (Figure 5-15). The themes of their pottery decoration were mostly secular, depicting the daily life of humans and the animals that lived around them.

Figure 5-15 Whistling jars were popular with Chimu-Inca potters. The water made a whistling sound when the jug was tilted. This one is made in highly polished black ware. Attempting to re-create the Moche style, the potters were not as gifted as those earlier artisans, and the modeling is not as sophisticated. Chancay Valley, Central coast, Peru. *Courtesy, Fine Arts Museums of San Francisco, M.H. De Young Memorial Museum.*

Inca

The Inca empire rose in one century from a small, unimportant group of people fighting with their neighbors to an awesome power that maintained military and administrative control over a huge area from Chile to Ecuador. Their engineering genius provided them with an elaborate communication system of roads and fortresses, as well as government centers, and palaces and temples of massive stone blocks that were cut so carefully no mortar was needed.

Their incredible gold treasures were their downfall, for the Spaniard Pizzaro, seeing them, looted the palaces and temples. Inca pottery, on the other hand, was functional, painted in simple, geometric designs. This was probably because the nobility used silver and bronze dishes and goblets, while only the poorer people and the large army that policed them used pottery. Since much of the pottery that survives was apparently government issue to military posts, it is rather standardized.

The Inca rule and the complex urban cultures of South America came to an abrupt end in 1533 when the Spanish entered Cuzco. Since that time, as in Mesoamerica, the local populations of South American villages have made domestic pottery in simple shapes for their own use.

Folk Traditions

When the Spanish arrived in what is now Latin America, bringing with them new culture and new pottery technology, the impact on native clay cultures was as abrupt as the arrival of Korean and Chinese potters in Japan. New techniques modified the native clay traditions, and changes in religion, life style, and eating and cooking habits brought new shapes to the pottery. In some isolated areas, pottery reminiscent of the utilitarian ware of earlier cultures persisted, but the high level of artistic activity that produced the ritual vessels associated with earlier cultures was interrupted.

Today, new changes in living have again brought new technology to this region. As in other areas of the world, traditional potters can now compete with metal and plastic only when they can make their pots more cheaply than merchants can sell the new, lightweight, unbreakable pots and containers. However, in isolated valleys high in the Andes, transportation is still so difficult that families still make pottery for their own use.

Elsewhere, large cooking vessels, water storage jars, and vessels for making certain traditional foods and beverages are still made of earthenware.

The traditional potter's techniques in present-day South American villages are variations of the methods we have seen elsewhere in the world. Most of the ware is hand formed, although some potters use homemade wheels similar to those used in Crete today, or occasionally they use modern kick wheels. Bases are formed in old bowls, which are revolved on a flat stone or the ground, sometimes pushed with the hand, sometimes with the toe, like the earliest turntables. In one area, pots are made on a clay turntable that revolves on a protruding base (Figure 1-39). In another, slabs of clay are draped over the bottom of an old pot covered with burlap, where they stiffen into shape. Elsewhere, slabs are pressed into flat molds to make large platters. In still another area, pots are paddled on the outside much as women in Fiji paddle theirs (Figure 1-25).

Firing methods vary from open firing with straw, grass, wood, or dung to simple updraft kilns similar in construction to the Mediterranean kiln whose design was brought by the Spaniards (Figures 1-45 and 2-7).

The cultural disruption that occurred with the arrival of the Spaniards broke the tradition of decorative and ritual clay vessels in which the Moche, Chimu, and Nasca cultures excelled (Figures 5-12 and 5-13). Recently, in parts of Peru, a new interest in native cultures has led some potters to make imitations of Nasca or Inca decorative pieces. Elsewhere, in Chile and Colombia, for example, some potters are using molds to make sculptural groups of human figures, birds, and animals for the tourist or export trade. Some family workshops where mother, father, and children do all the forming, firing, and finishing have developed their own recognizable decorative styles. Whether these family workshops will continue as the children are tempted into other jobs is a question faced by traditional potters in villages all over the world.

North America

The earliest inhabitants in the southwestern area of North America, known to us as the Basketmakers, probably received their stimulus for pottery making from Mexico, for the pottery decoration on certain early pottery from Arizona shows many motifs similar to those in Mexico.

Apparently, groups of people pushed up from Mexico into the Rio Grande Valley of the American Southwest, meeting and mingling with the earlier settlers there. In any case, there was a close enough contact with Mexico's more northerly cultures for their influences to be felt. For example, the adobe houses built under overhanging cliffs in New Mexico and Colorado have their exact counterparts in northern Mexico, built at about the same time.

Pueblo Legend

A Pueblo legend gives us a more colorful story of the beginnings of pottery in that area. According to Cochita tradition, pottery making was learned from a mythical Clay Old Woman who was sent to the village from Shipap, the underworld, the place from which all people originally came. Clay Old Woman mixed the clay with sand, softened it with water, and then began to coil a pot while her husband, Clay Old Man, danced and sang. The village people watched her carefully as she built the pot, but when it was about a foot and a half high, Clay Old Man broke it with his foot. She chased him around the village, retrieved the pot, made it

into a ball of clay again, and built another pot. From this one, each person of the pueblo took a piece of clay and started to make pottery, following the steps Clay Old Woman taught them. Now, they say, if the people of Cochita forget to make pottery, two masked dancers come to remind them about the day they gave clay to the pueblo. Whether you prefer the archaeological or the mythical version, there is no doubt that the craft of pottery making has played a large part in both the sacred and the domestic life of the Pueblo peoples.

Early Pueblo Clay Craft

In the region where present-day New Mexico, Colorado, Utah, and Arizona meet, the descendants of the Basketmakers merged with new peoples from the south, and between A.D. 700 and 1100, began to build permanent clusters of homes, some of whose ruins still stand. These were the first *pueblos,* the Spanish name for these villages. The same name, capitalized, has also been used by outsiders as a name for the inhabitants.

There the potters made pottery that was thin, beautifully shaped, and decorated with painted designs. From A.D. 1100 to 1300, a complex urban culture developed in which architecture, weaving, and pottery were refined. It was a time of technical and artistic achievement.

Figure 5-16 (*Left*) Seated outside her house at the turn of the century, a Hopi woman made her pottery with simple tools, like those still in use today. A basket for support, a board, a lump of clay, a tin of water, and a half circle of dried gourd are all she needed to form pots. Living in remote western villages, for 600 years the Hopi have made pottery with yellow-orange decoration painted directly on the polished clay body rather than on slip. Hopi woman, Arizona. *Courtesy, Field Museum of Natural History, Chicago.*

It would be impossible here to describe all the varying decorative styles of Pueblo pottery, for although there are certain traditional techniques that have continued throughout the history of ceramics in this area, the artist-potters of different villages devised different designs to enhance their pottery. The crafts of the Pueblos were living arts, developed to meet the needs of their daily or ceremonial life (Figure 5-20). At various times in their history, their pottery has reached a peak of creativity, declined, and then been renewed, often more vigorously than ever. New ideas, new influences, new needs have sparked changes in the decoration or shape of the pots. Whether the influences came from Mesoamerica, from the Spaniards, from contact with other tribes, or from the arrival of tourists when the railroad came in 1880, the Pueblos have usually taken these new ideas and changed them to fit their way of life.

The cultural flowering from around A.D. 1100 to 1300 was ended by a twenty-two-year drought, and the population shifted to other less arid locations near the present pueblos. Despite the disruptions, the potters continued to work, shaping their ware by hand and using a glaze to decorate it. This was a glossy coating, a true vitreous glaze. It was only used for decoration, never for waterproofing the whole pot. The secret of this method was lost around A.D. 1700.

From around A.D. 1600, when the Spaniards first settled in this area, until the present, so many new ways of life, new power structures, and new religious influences came to the area that the Pueblos had to struggle to maintain their traditions. Despite the chaos, the craft of pottery has been continued, maintaining a characteristic Pueblo attitude. Modern Pueblo potters, like their forebears, see themselves as united with the land and the environment, drawing their creative values from them.

Clay Digging

Although, for purposes of space, we must speak of the Pueblos as having one culture, there were differences between the villages in the way that they dug, prepared, and finally shaped the clay. Generally, however, the women, who were the potters, dug the clay out with sticks, speaking to the earth, asking its permission, for the Pueblo people felt that the clay had life and feelings. Sometimes they had to travel quite a distance. In Santa Clara, for example, the clay, *Na p,* was gathered at a place called *NA Pi i we,* about a mile west of the pueblo, while the tempering material, *Shunya,* was found about seven miles away. Once dug, they had to be carried in a basket or hide container back to the pueblo, where a great deal of work went into the preparation of the clay. The dry lumps had to be pounded and the stones and other impurities removed, and often the clay was ground on a stone until it was fine, just as the maize was ground.

Tempering Materials

Next the gritty material, the temper, was mixed in (Figures 7-8 and 7-9). It was measured by experience—so many handfuls to so much clay. The temper coarsened the texture of the clay, allowing the air to escape so that the pot would not burst in firing.

Each pueblo or area had its own kind of temper. The Zuni, for example, have always added ground-up broken pottery to the clay, each generation thereby incorporating a bit of its own history into its pots. On the other hand, the potters of Taos and Picuris needed no temper, for there were abundant bits of mica already in the local clay. Other pueblos have used volcanic sand or have laboriously ground lava rock into a powder to add it to the clay. Mixing was done with the hands, and sometimes the feet (Figure 7-8).

Pueblo potters did not age their clay as the Chinese did. Once mixed, it was wrapped in a damp cloth or sometimes buried in the ground to keep it out of the sun until the potter was ready to use it.

Coiling

Coiling was the traditional method of pot building, and the base of a pot was molded in a basket or a *puki,* a shallow, fired bowl (Figure 5-16). The sides were built up straight, then pushed outward into shape (Figures 5-17 and

Figure 5-17 Maria Martinez of San Ildefonso, in a photo taken around 1940, shapes and thins the walls of a pot with a bit of dried gourd shell. She carefully presses outward from the inside with her left hand, forcing the clay into the beautiful curve characteristic of her pottery. She uses a pottery bowl as a base under the pot: potters kept a set of base molds for different types of pots. Water jars were started in molds with a convex area so that the bottom of the jar would be concave, fitting the head for carrying. (See also Figure 7-26.) San Ildefonso, New Mexico, c. 1940. *Courtesy, Collections in the Museum of New Mexico. Photo by Wyatt Davis.*

7-27). The potters made large, wide- or narrow-necked storage jars to hold maize, occasionally with clay lids, dough bowls that would hold a week's supply of bread dough, narrow-necked water jars, shallow, flat bowls, canteens, and many types of swelling, globe-shaped vessels, as well as some special shapes. For example, Santa Clara pueblo potters make a special double-spouted wedding vessel with a bridged handle reminiscent of South American spouted jars (Figures 5-15 and 5-21). According to tradition, drinking jars like these were used at weddings as recently as forty years ago, but it is not known if it was devised then or if it was a traditional shape. At a secular celebration, after the bride and groom had each drunk from one side of the jar, it was handed around for all the men to drink from the groom's side, all the women from the bride's.

Ceremonial vessels, sometimes made, or at least decorated, by the men, were often made in particular forms, according to their use in the sacred rituals. Many of these ceremonies have remained secret, so we do not know the use of certain types of vessels or the meaning of their symbolic decoration. Pitchers, rectangular bowls, footed bowls (some with handles), low bowls (some with sculptured figures of frogs), and small thin-necked jars believed to hold the sacred corn pollen—all these were used in the sacred ceremonies.

Clay sculpture was not common, although a few pots were made in the shape of birds or had animals sculptured on them. But as the tourists came to buy curios, by 1890 some potters began to make human figurines, and today this sculptural tradition continues in Cochita pueblo (Figure 5-18).

Figure 5-18 Helen Cordero, of the Cochita pueblo, continues a tradition of sculpted figures started there in the 1880s. Her brightly painted storyteller sits with eyes closed, chanting with open mouth while delighted children climb over him. *Courtesy, U.S. Department of Interior, Indian Arts and Crafts Board, Washington, D.C.*

Finishing

After the pot was shaped, it was dried away from the sun, and the potter watched for cracks, mending the little ones with damp clay but discarding the pot if large ones appeared. Finally, it was smoothed again with a piece of broken pottery, or later, metal. Then it was coated with slip to cover the rough, coarse texture of the clay body and to provide a smoother base for painted decorations.

Figure 5-19 Maria Martinez polishing a pot using a smooth stone. She rubs the slipped surface with even strokes, painstakingly developing a rich, glossy polish. There is no glaze on her pots, and the remaining slight marks of the stone add vitality and depth to the finish. Collections of rubbing stones in various shapes and sizes were handed down through generations of potters; it was bad luck to lose one. (See also Color Plate 9, p. 146D). San Ildefonso, New Mexico, c. 1940. *Courtesy, Collections in the Museum of New Mexico. Photo by Wyatt Davis.*

The slip was usually red, white, or off-white, made of fine clay that could only be found in certain places. The white slip was basically kaolin, while the cream slip was bentonite. Those pueblos without adequate slip clay near them traded with others for it. After the slip was applied, the pot was burnished with smooth, curved stones of various sizes and shapes or sometimes pieces of leather or rags (Figure 5-19). Less often, the damp, uncoated clay body was puddled, a method of stroking it with a stone to float the finer clay particles to the surface, giving it a smoother finish.

Decoration

After the slip was burnished, the design was painted, using various types of pigment. Fine mineral-colored slip, and vegetable paint have all been used. The mineral-colored slip usually fired to shades of dark brown, black, or sometimes red, and the vegetable pigment burned black during firing. Called *guaco,* it was made by boiling new shoots and leaves of the Rocky Mountain bee plant into a syrup. Hardened and formed into a block, it could be kept for years and mixed with water when needed. Traditionally, the paint was applied with a brush made from chewing bits of yucca leaf to the desired consistency; nowadays, commercial brushes are sometimes used. The dull black decoration, which contrasts so handsomely with the glossy finish of contemporary Santa Clara and San Ildefonso pots, is produced by painting designs with fine slip on top of the polished surface, then firing it in a reducing atmosphere, which turns the whole pot black. The slip paint comes out **matt** while the burnished surface of the pot stays shiny (Color Plate 9, p. 146D).

Decorative motifs have varied throughout the years from geometric and symbolic designs painted in black on white, to flowing polychrome (many-colored) decorations (Figure 5-20). Stylized bird, animal, and plant forms, the sacred twin clowns, symbols of clouds, rain, and lightning, plumed serpents, and feathers are some of the images displayed (Color Plate 9, p. 146D). The meanings of many of the symbols remain a secret, or the original meanings have been lost. For example, most Pueblo pottery has bands of color or

Figure 5-20 McCartys water jar, named for the Acoma village in which it was made. This nineteenth-century pot is decorated with several colors—the flowing bands that swing around its swelling shape are painted in two shades of orange. Informally decorated, the walls of these jars were thin, so that they would not be too heavy to carry when filled with water. McCartys, New Mexico, c. 1890. Height 9¾ in. (25 cm). *Courtesy, Museum of New Mexico, School of American Research. Photo by Arthur Taylor.*

black lines around it, and these encircling lines, sometimes called the "spirit path," almost always have a break in them somewhere. Although some say the break was put there to keep the soul of the pot from being imprisoned, other scholars say that the true meaning is lost.

Firing

After the pot was decorated, it was ready for firing. The traditional methods of firing have remained very much the same, except now that most of the pottery is produced for decorative purposes and not intended for domestic use, it is fired at a cooler temperature than in earlier times. Like the potters of Africa, Fiji, or other traditional cultures, the Pueblo potters fire in the open, using available local fuels—cow or sheep dung, wood, or even some soft coal in the Hopi area (Figure 5-21). Nowadays the pottery is placed on sheet metal, and sheet metal covers it, but basically it is the same open firing method used by potters all over the world. Usually it is done in the evening or

Figure 5-21 Julian Martinez pulls a double-spouted wedding jar from the coals. Around 1918 Julian and Maria Martinez began to fire burnished red-slipped pots in a rather cool reducing atmosphere. The pots, which had been painted with slip, emerged from the coals shiny black with dull black decoration. Maria shaped the pots into forms that became famous, and Julian decorated them. Later, their son, Popovi Da, did the decorating. San Ildefonso, New Mexico, c. 1940. *Courtesy, Collections in the Museum of New Mexico. Photo by Wyatt Davis.*

Figure 5-22 (*Left*) Dark, burnished pottery, usually with incised decoration, was typical of the Mississippi Valley culture called the Mound Builders. Compare the pattern of swirling lines with the spiral patterns on pottery from other cultures as widely separated as Crete and China. Found near Natchez, Mississippi. Height 6¼ in. (15.9 cm). *Courtesy, Museum of The American Indian, Heye Foundation.* **Figure 5-23** (*Below*) Pottery pipe bowls from various tribes. (*Top Left in Photo*) Pipe bowl representing a frog, from Illinois. (*Top Right*) Pipe from Cayuga County, New York. (*Bottom*) Pipes with flaring bowls from the Nacoochee Mound. White County, Georgia. *Courtesy, Museum of the American Indian, Heye Foundation.*

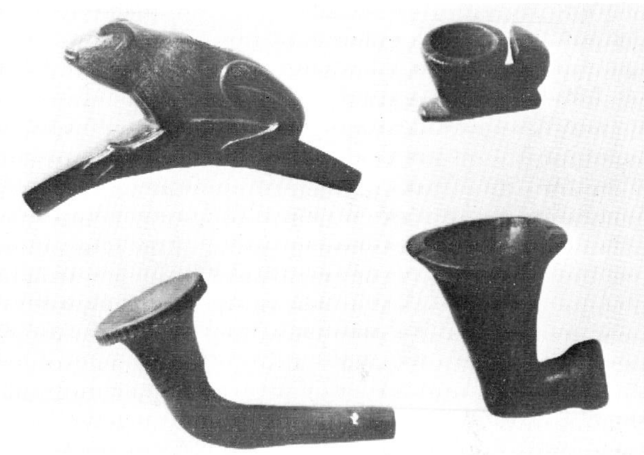

morning to avoid a wind that could cause the fire to burn unevenly, possibly causing breakage. The firing generally takes from around thirty minutes to an hour and a half, after which some potters leave the pots to cool in the fire, while others rake away the coals and remove the pots with long sticks.

Today, Pueblo men and women continue to make pottery, handing down the tradition to younger members of their families. The potters change their decorative styles, adapting to new needs or to new markets. But their innate respect for the earth, for the life-force in what others consider inanimate objects, still permeates their work.

Clay Craft in Northern Tribes

The other groups of native North Americans that spread out over the Great Plains, Southeast, Mississippi Valley, and East never developed as complex a pottery craft. Their life styles were different; they did not cultivate maize, and after the arrival of the horse with the Spaniards, many tribes went back to a semi-nomadic hunting life.

In the Mississippi Valley, one group, possibly influenced by weak echoes of Mesoamerican pyramids, built large earth mounds. Called the Mound Builders, these people also made the most skilled pottery of the more northern regions of North America (Figure 5-22). Some of the northern tribes used simple pottery vessels for cooking and made bowls for the pipes so often used in their ceremonies (Figure 5-23).

Chapter Six

Traditions in the West

We have seen how the art of ancient Greece and the advanced techniques of her artisans exerted a strong influence on Roman ceramic art. Then, as the Roman Empire declined, new ideas and new influences appeared. The Christian religion, brought to Rome by early missionaries from Judea, incorporated into its early art classic influences from both Greece and Rome. Byzantium (Istanbul), from its position on the shores of the Bosporus, between eastern Europe and Asia, passed on to the West artistic concepts and styles that had come to it from India, from Egypt, from Persia, and from the ancient cultures of Mesopotamia. And while these two cultural streams—the classical and the oriental—merged in the art of medieval Europe, Islamic art was also spreading westward.

Hispano-Moresque

The art of Islam reached Europe when the Moors crossed over from North Africa around A.D. 700, occupying a large part of Spain for nearly 800 years. The art style that resulted from the combination of native and imposed styles is known as Hispano-Moresque. The potters who came with the invaders brought with them their knowledge of glazes and lusters as well as Islamic decoration (Figure 6-1). Potters have always been among the first settlers to follow invading military forces, for new communities of immigrants soon had to replace their fragile cooking pots.

In Spain, the Islamic potters found the tin they needed to mix with their lead glaze to make it opaque. The Assyrians had known of this **opacifier** as early as 1000 B.C., and this knowledge had been revived in Persia in the eighth century A.D. and passed on to the Arab world (Figures 3-26 and 3-27). The Moors brought this knowledge with them to Spain, where the artisans used it to make brilliant-colored glazes to coat both pottery and tiles (Figure 6-2). Although the spread of Islam in northern Europe was halted by the French in A.D. 732, the Moors remained in Spain until 1609. There they built luxurious palaces and richly decorated mosques, continuing the architectural traditions they had brought with them from the East. In the courtyards of palaces like the Alhambra, brilliantly glazed tiles made a colorful background for the play of water in the many fountains that cooled the hot summer air (Figure 6-2). The decoration of these tiles was based on plant forms and on the decorative script of the Koran (Figure 3-26). This type of decoration became the predominant style in Islamic art because the representation of human figures was forbidden in the mosques, and when tiles and pottery were made for secular rulers and their palaces, the tradition was usually continued.

The Hispano-Moresque potters continued to use plant motifs in decoration (Figure 6-1). The opaque lead-tin glazes with which they painted the tiles and pottery were colored with oxides. Between the ninth and sixteenth centuries, throughout the Islamic world, potters evolved a variety of colors from whatever oxides were available; blue from cobalt, green from copper, purple and brown from manganese, and yellow and brown from iron were all used successfully. If red was desired, it was usually added as an enamel overglaze. These oxides were either added to the basic lead-tin glaze to make a colored, opaque glaze or painted onto the raw white background glaze and fired with it in one firing. The resulting opaque glazes covered the pinkish buff of the earthenware clay body, adding brilliant color and an impermeable coating to the surface of the tiles, bowls, and jars. In addition, the Islamic potters who came to Spain brought with them from the East the techniques of metallic luster overglaze, using it on tiles as well as on the large and impressive bowls and vases they made for their wealthy customers (Figure 3-28).

Figure 6-1 Dark green, yellow, and gray-blue on a white, opaque, tin-glazed background decorate this Hispano-Moresque plate. The Moslem edict against portraying any living creature applied only to mosques, so that on pottery the decorators were able to portray animals and even humans, as well as floral designs. Tin-enameled earthenware, Spain, 15th century. Diameter about 9 in. (22.9 cm). *Courtesy, The Metropolitan Museum of Art, Rogers Fund, 1930.*

Figure 6-2 The Alhambra, or "Red Castle," was built in the thirteenth and fourteenth centuries as a palace for the Moorish rulers in Granada, Spain. There, the *azulejos*—colorful, patterned tiles—covered the lower parts of the walls, adding geometric and calligraphic ornament to the fanciful architecture. The Court of the Lions, Alhambra, Spain. *Courtesy, Spanish National Tourist Office.*

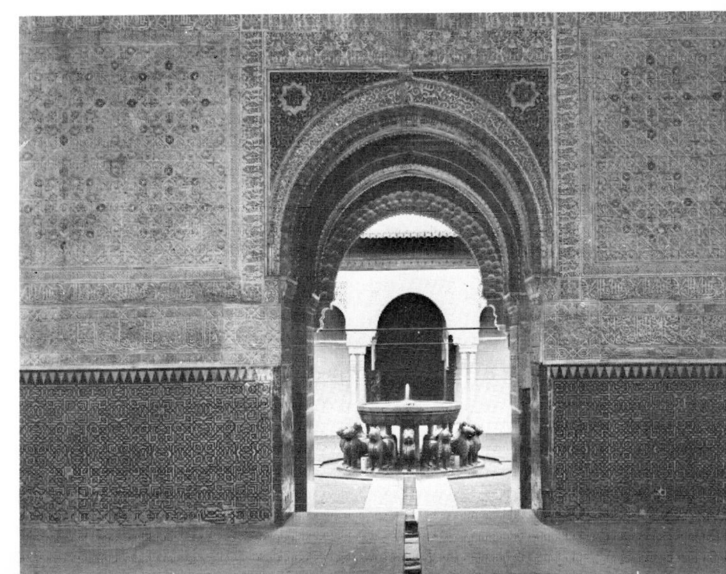

Italian Maiolica

In Spain, the region of Valencia became one of the most important pottery centers, and even after the expulsion of the Moors in 1609, potters there continued to use Islamic techniques and decorative styles. Much of their best decorated, tin-glazed earthenware was shipped to the Balearic Islands, then shipped elsewhere from the port of Majorca. That is why the Italians called all white-glazed earthenware **maiolica** (or **majolica**). It was shipped to many parts of Europe, but especially to Genoa and Pisa in Italy. There, the numerous princes, cardinals, and popes bought the beautifully colored bowls and plates from Valencia to display on their tables, walls, and shelves.

Figure 6-3 Deruta was one of the centers of ceramics in Italy where techniques learned from the Moorish potters in Spain were used to create pottery known as maiolica (or majolica) (Color Plate 5, p. 146A). Cesare Borgia, ruler of Umbria, was also Archbishop of Valencia, the leading pottery center in Spain. Through contact with Spain, the Deruta potters learned to make their glazes opaque with tin and to use lusters that gave the ware a metallic appearance. This dish is decorated with mother-of-pearl luster outlined in blue. Earthenware, Deruta, Italy, 1530. Diameter about 10 in. (25.4 cm). *Courtesy, Metropolitan Museum of Art, Gift of Henry Marquand, 1894.*

Soon, Italian potters were trying to copy the maiolica. Good clay had always been available in Italy, and records dating back to as early as 1330 mention tin as a main ingredient in potter's glazes there. Slowly, their knowledge of glazing techniques was perfected, and by the turn of the fifteenth century, the production of white and colored maiolica had spread through a large part of Italy (Figure 6-3). The bisqued earthenware was dipped in a glaze containing lead and tin oxides and silicate of potash that was often obtained by mixing the sediment collected from wine-making vats with sand. After this white base glaze dried, the colors were painted on and the piece was fired. If lusters were desired, the metallic oxides were painted on after the piece was glaze fired and then fired again in a reducing atmosphere. The cities of Faenza, Deruta, Vicenza, Siena, and Perugia all had active pottery workshops, and by the time the new ideas of the Renaissance had become established in Italy, potters in those places had learned to make glazed pottery that was impermeable, colorful, and practical (Figure 6-3).

Because the new glazed ware could be easily washed, it was at first especially popular in pharmacies for jars containing herbs, medicines, oils, and ointments. But soon it was used for more elegant purposes. Now the wealthy merchant-princes and banking families could afford luxury, and they liked to display their wealth and buy the latest novelty. As a result, the new products of the potters' workshops were in great demand and were even considered elegant enough to be given as gifts to the Medici: Lorenzo the Magnificent, writing to Robert Malatesta in 1490, thanked him for a gift of the new Italian maiolica, saying, "They please me by their perfection and rarity, being quite novelties in these parts, and are valued more than if of silver, the donor's arms serving daily to recall their origin."

The earliest maiolica was at first decorated with simple geometric designs—

cross-hatchings, circles, and dots—but soon other types of ornament were used. Oriental motifs, traceable back to Persia, and northern medieval decoration appeared along with classical and Renaissance decorative motifs (Color Plate 5, p. 146A). In the pottery region of Bologna, where the presence of the University of Bologna made for a tradition of manuscript decoration, many of the designs on the earthenware were twining flowers, curling tendrils, and leaves, which show the influence of Gothic illuminated manuscripts from the monasteries of northern Europe (Figure 6-4).

Figure 6-4 In the sixteenth century, Faenza became the leading maiolica center of Italy. There, Gothic and Renaissance influences merged to create a characteristic Italian style. Decorative pottery objects were painted with rich colors; dolphins entwined in the tendrils of vines were an especially popular motif. Pilgrim bottles like this were tied to the harness of a traveler's horse with a cord passed through the handles. Faenza, c. 1540. Height 13⅝ in. (34.6 cm). *Courtesy, Cleveland Museum of Art. Gift of J.H. Wade.*

Changing Pottery Techniques

During the medieval period, pottery techniques remained basically the same as they had been in the classic world of Greece and Rome. The kick wheel had spread through the Mediterranean world and was used along with the turntable (Figure 6-5). Apprentices learned their skill in workshops, and traditions were handed down by master potters to their apprentices. One of these masters, a sixteenth-century Italian potter named Cipriano Piccolpasso, wrote *The Three Books of the Potter's Art,* describing his own methods and those of other potters (Figures 6-6 through 6-9). He tells how to form pots on the wheel, how to finish them properly, how to build a kiln, and how to fire it, giving the reader the benefit of his years of experience. We learn, for example, that now the pivot of the wheel axle

Figure 6-5 Medieval potter, redrawn from a fifteenth-century playing card, uses a notched tool to make a decorative texture on the outside of the jug. Note the pile of clay at her feet and the way the wheel head is supported.

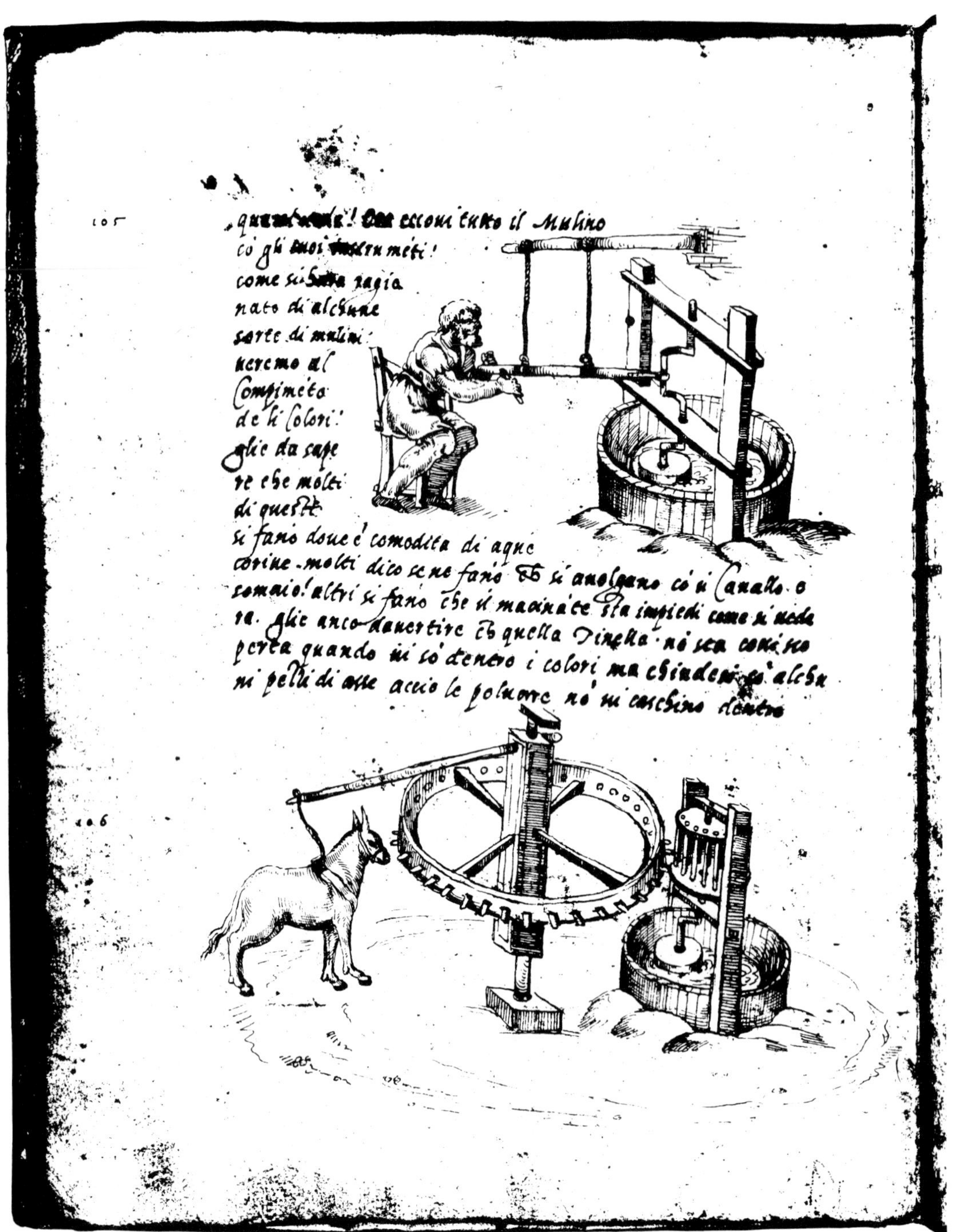

Figure 6-6 *The Three Books of the Potter's Art,* by Cipriano Piccolpasso, is a storehouse of information about sixteenth-century Italian pottery techniques. Here he illustrates mechanical devices used to speed up the mixing of clay and glaze materials. Italy, c. 1556. *Courtesy, Victoria and Albert Museum, Crown Copyright.*

Figure 6-7 An Italian potter's shop of the sixteenth century shows the kick wheels rotated with the foot. Piccolpasso tells the reader that the diligent artisan works as carefully on the outside surface as on the inside, smoothing the ridges of clay that are apt to appear as the vase rises. Cipriano Piccolpasso, *The Three Books of the Potter's Art,* c. 1556. *Courtesy, Victoria and Albert Museum, Crown Copyright.*

was tipped with steel and revolved on a flint socket or on a plate of strong steel. In addition, the bearing near the top of the axle was wrapped with oiled leather, making it turn more easily and making it possible for the potter to produce the earthenware in greater quantity.

Since it is difficult to narrow the neck of a vase or jug from a swelling body, potters often make them in two pieces, joining the two parts with slip while they are still damp. According to Piccolpasso, these sections were also sometimes joined after the first bisque firing, with a coating of glaze to stick them together. To speed the production even more, bowls were sometimes shaped upside down on a convex mold on the wheel, and their walls were scraped and thinned by holding a template against the side of the piece while it was revolved on the wheel. The wheel was also used for decorating pots with incised designs, which were formed in the damp clay as the potter held a notched tool against the pot.

Just as wheel techniques were improved, kilns were now larger, more complex, and built in a horizontal design (Figure 6-8). They were wood fired, requiring the help of several assistants to keep the fire going for the long hours needed to fire the ware (Figure 6-9).

In the early days of maiolica production, many of the paintings on the plates and bowls were done in the "austere style," simple, flat paintings of people with facial details and clothing outlined with dark brush lines. In these representations, there was no attempt to show perspective, and as a result, the figures

Figure 6-8 Now kilns were built of brick, with an arched opening to the fire chamber. Holes in the floor allowed the heat to rise through the stacked pottery. Cipriano Piccolpasso, *The Three Books of the Potter's Art,* c. 1556. *Courtesy, Victoria and Albert Museum, Crown Copyright.*

Figure 6-9 (*Right*) The ware has been stacked in the upper chamber and the door has been bricked up. The master potter directs his assistants to pile in more wood, while he times the firing with an hourglass. Cipriano Piccolpasso, *The Three Books of the Potter's Art,* c. 1556. *Courtesy, Victoria and Albert Museum, Crown Copyright.*

on the early maiolica remain on the flat plane of the plate. Toward the end of the fifteenth century, however, when potters were striving for elegance and were anxious to use the latest styles, the earthenware changed. Fewer utilitarian pieces like the drug jars were made, and presentation pieces meant to be displayed rather than used became one of the most important products of the workshops. These *piatti di pompi*—display plates—were placed on furniture and shelves, and some can even be seen in some of the Italian paintings of the period. Souvenirs and gifts of all types were made in the potter's shops—two-handled vases, wedding bowls with portraits of the betrothed on them, dishes with paintings of women and children, to be filled with appetizing food and given to women who had just given birth—every occasion was an opportunity for display.

As time went on, the white-glazed surface was seen as a mere background on which the painter could apply the new methods of painting illusionary space. Perspective and shading made the mythological figures, the cupids, the dolphins, and the Renaissance architectural backgrounds all stand out in three-dimensional relief. Pottery decorators now signed their work and modeled it on the paintings of their more famous Renaissance colleagues, such as the painter Rafael. These scenes from history and from Roman and Greek mythology were no longer colored drawings, but became elaborate paintings that overwhelmed the ceramic background with little regard for its shape.

Sculpture

While Renaissance painters were concerned with producing the illusion of space on the walls and ceilings of palaces, religious buildings, and chapels like the Sistine Chapel, sculptors were also modeling the freestanding human figure. In the medieval period, the human figure had been painted or carved only as part of church architecture to tell religious stories to the illiterate congregation. Now, classical influences and the new humanism led artists to paint and carve images of humans with more concern for their individual beauty or personality. Clay, as we have seen, had been used by the ancient Etruscans to model life-sized figures for their temples and tombs, and the Romans had also

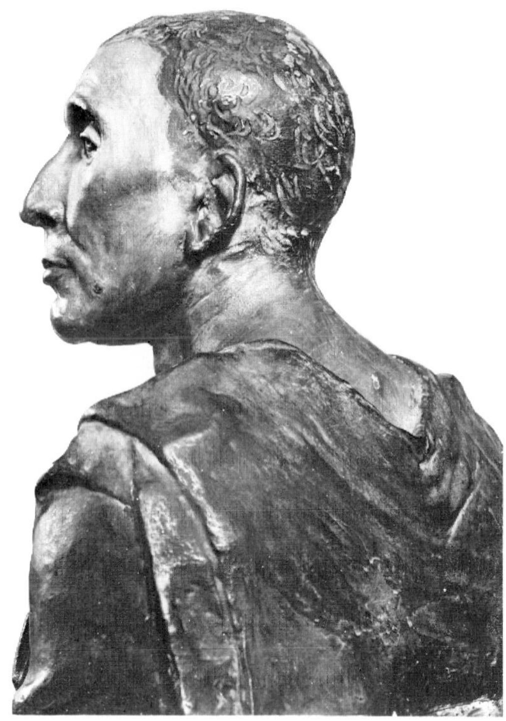

Figure 6-10 This terra cotta bust attributed to Renaissance sculptor Donatello probably represents Niccolo da Uzzano, leader of a group of merchants who tried to resist the rising power of the Medici in Florence. Portraits like this continued the ancient terra cotta tradition of the Etruscans and represented a break with medieval religious sculpture. *Courtesy, Alinari-Art Reference Bureau.*

used it occasionally for their portraits. The sculptors of the Renaissance period generally used clay for the models from which bronze statues were to be cast; but also, although less frequently, they used terra cotta for pieces of sculpture that could be fired as works of art by themselves (Figure 6-10).

In Florence, in the mid-fifteenth century, the sculptor Luca della Robbia was impressed with the colors that could be obtained with opaque glazes. He saw the possibility of using them to make his sculpture more lifelike and experimented with colored glazes on terra cotta reliefs. As the first person to try the new colored glazes on large pieces, he used them primarily on his colorful medallions of the Madonna and Child surrounded by wreaths of flowers and fruit, still seen on buildings in Florence today (Figure 6-11).

Figure 6-11 Luca della Robbia (1399–1482) applied brightly colored opaque tin glazes to large terra cotta reliefs of Madonnas, prophets, and saints, which were used to decorate buildings in Florence, and his family carried on the tradition into the sixteenth century. Andrea della Robbia (1455–1525) made the frame for this medallion, decorating it with fruit and flowers in a style that was typical of the family's work. "The Virgin Worshiping the Child," wall plaque, 15th century. *Courtesy, The Philadelphia Museum of Art. Purchased by the W.P. Wilstach Collection.*

For centuries, the artisans of Islam had been especially skilled tilemakers, and architects had made use of their products as a versatile material with which to surface and decorate buildings. In Italy, too, glazed tiles were popular. Used in churches and palaces, they covered floors with colorful decorations in blue, orange, green, and purple, with medieval floral motifs and Persian and classical motifs; all these appeared together with coats of arms, animals, snails, symbolic references to well-known figures of the day, and tools of trade; anything, it seemed, might be painted on the tiles, making them into a colorful record of Italian Renaissance life.

Northern Europe

Northern Europe and the cities of Italy engaged in trade with one another, as well as periodically waging war with one another. Travelers moved between the two areas with remarkable ease, whether on military campaigns or as visitors. Northern artists came to Italy to study the classic remains being dug up, and Italian artisans went north to work. For example, potters from Faenza went to France, and it was from the name of their town that France later applied the word **faience** to its own tin-glazed earthenware. Gradually, the Italian style of maiolica spread throughout Europe.

The history of pottery in northern Europe is in some ways similar to the story elsewhere, but in other ways it is different. Neolithic and Bronze Age potters there had made urns and vessels by hand, decorating them with the usual Neolithic patterns of incised lines and textures. Hand-built black vessels with incised lines often emphasized by white chalk, funerary urns painted with swirls, rough pots with overall fingernail textures—all these had appeared in northern Europe, from Scotland to Denmark to Hungary (Figure 1-23). Many of them were shaped with a fine sense of form and were decorated with sensitivity to the relationship between that form and the applied decoration. But a continuing tradition of fine pottery making had not followed the Neolithic period in northern Europe. Ancient urban centers like those in the Mediterranean had not developed there, and the pottery that was produced locally never compared technically or artistically with that of the classic world of Greece.

When the Roman legions conquered large areas of "barbarian" northern Europe, they brought with them their own ceramic techniques. Local potters probably worked with the Romans, and most of the pottery produced in the Roman-occupied territory consisted of rather rough copies of that made in Rome. The wheel was introduced, and some of the techniques of the Mediterranean were adapted to the local clays. For example, clay had been deposited in large beds in southern England by a vast river that had washed down decomposed granite from the hills. Neolithic potters had used it, and later the Phoenicians had dug it up and exported it. The Romans also found it and used it in small kilns in the area, producing a slate-colored ware.

After the Romans left, most of northern Europe forgot the wheel for several centuries during the Dark Ages. However, by the mid-seventh century, potters were again using the wheel in England, and all through the medieval period, the potter's wheel was used there to make jugs (Figure 6-12). These jugs formed a large part of the medieval potter's output, for at this time ordinary people ate off wooden plates and drank out of horn or wooden cups, while the nobility used metal plates, goblets, and bowls. The jugs were rough and crude in technique, but strong and bold in shape, and their incised decoration was fresh and varied. Some of this local utilitarian ware was glazed and some of it was decorated with designs in slip. The only glaze known in Britain at this time was a lead powder

Figure 6-12 The jugs made in medieval England (c. 1300) were sometimes decorated with incised lines made with a notched tool (Figure 6-5), a roulette, or a carved wooden stamp. Lead was applied in the form of a powder—galena—which combined with silica in the clay during firing, forming a glaze. It usually fired yellowish, but other colors were also produced with the addition of copper, manganese, or iron. Height 14⅝ in. (37.2 cm). *Courtesy, Fitzwilliam Museum, Cambridge.*

called **galena,** which was dusted on before firing. This produced a transparent glaze, often colored with oxides, which did not hide the clay body color, but which adhered to the surface, making the earthenware watertight.

The Romans had brought with them the firing techniques of the Mediterranean, and most medieval kilns remained very much like them—vertical kilns with some sort of perforated floor resting on a central pillar, a fire underneath and a vent at the top. However, horizontal kilns were also developed in several European countries. In the horizontal kilns, pots were stacked on the floor of the firing chamber and a temporary vault of turf, or clay smeared on a wicker support, was built over them. Later, horizontal kilns were built of brick (Figures 6-8 and 6-9).

Roof tiles and bricks had been made by the artisans in Roman settlements in Europe, and during the Middle Ages, brick became an important building material in areas where there was little native stone. In addition to roof tiles, medieval craftsmen also made painted tiles which told stories from the Bible, or showed portraits of the saints, bishops or nobles associated with the church. Some of these were made with an inlay technique in which white clay was inlaid into red clay, producing white line drawings of figures in elaborate Gothic architectural settings.

Rhenish Stoneware

During these years, when local potteries in Britain and France were making simple, rough, lead-glazed earthenware jugs, potters working along the Rhine Valley developed the first stoneware in Europe. This Rhenish stoneware, made possible by the discovery and utilization of available stoneware clay, was fired in horizontal kilns—some of them merely the simple turf-covered kilns.

The abundant wood in northern forests helped potters there attain and hold the high temperature in the kiln needed to fire stoneware, and the potters gave the vitrified stoneware an additional surface by glazing it with salt. To do this, they threw salt in the kiln when it had reached a high heat, whereupon the intense heat immediately vaporized the salt. The sodium in the vapor settled on the surface of the stoneware, where it combined with the silica in the clay, forming a glassy substance, sodium silicate.

Since the Rhine was navigable, the potteries could export their ware easily, and many of these **salt-glazed** stoneware jugs reached England. Rhenish potters guarded the secrets of their methods jealously, but eventually the potters in England learned how to make it.

Faience

Meanwhile, however, the white-glazed ware from Italy became popular in northern Europe, and potters from Faenza went to France to work. From the Italian potters the craftsmen of France and the Low Countries learned Italian glazing methods and used glazes in the multicolored Italian style. There was a big market in Europe for glazed and painted white earthenware in the Italian style, and French potters called it faience, after the town of Faenza. There was one individualistic artist in France, Bernard Palissy, who experimented with glazes and developed his own unusual techniques and style to make elaborate display plates that influenced later European artists (Figure 6-13).

In northern Europe, glazed maiolica tiles became popular and were adapted to new uses. Instead of providing cool floors as they did in Italy, here they were often used to cover the stoves that heated the chilly rooms during the northern winters of Germany and the Low Countries (Figure 6-14).

Figure 6-13 Bernard Palissy (1510–1590), a French glass painter who became interested in pottery, was so determined to develop new glazes that at one time he sat up for six days and six nights tending his kiln. When he ran out of wood, he fed the garden fence and tables and chairs to the fire. He said of his years of glaze experimentation, "At the end of ten years time I became so thin that my legs had no roundness of shape left about them. . . . as soon as I began to walk, the garters with which I fastened my stockings used to slip down. . . ." Bernard Palissy, or in his style, France, 16th century. *Courtesy, The Metropolitan Museum of Art. Gift of J. Pierpont Morgan, 1917.*

Figure 6-14 In the late fifteenth and sixteenth centuries, northern European potters made tiles for the large stoves used to heat the drafty houses. Frequently the tiles were molded in relief, like the ones on this stove. The repeat pattern tiles are glazed in green, while around the middle of the stove runs a border of figures on multicolored tiles. Austria, 1589. *Courtesy, Philadelphia Museum of Art. Gift of Henry Dolfinger.*

European Blue and White Ware

Around 1600, the first shipments of blue and white Chinese porcelain began to arrive in the West, and the potteries in Italy and elsewhere, especially in the Low Countries, began to make cheap imitations of it in earthenware. Since European potters had not yet discovered the secret of porcelain, and the imported Chinese ware was expensive, there was a ready market for cheaper imitations. Potters all over Europe began to decorate their tin-glazed ware with cobalt to produce blue and white imitations of Chinese porcelain (Figure 3-32). Although this style was used in many places, it became especially associated with the town of Delft in Holland, and this type of pottery was called *delft ware* whether it was produced in Delft or elsewhere.

As usual, political events were responsible

for the spread of ceramic styles. For example, William of Orange became king of England as well as king of the Low Countries in 1689, and potters from Delft went to England at that time, taking their methods with them. Other influences, like that of Bernard Palissy (Figure 6-13) and French faience, also spread throughout Europe. This maiolica, faience, and delft earthenware was thick, and not transparent like the porcelain from China, but the white opaque glaze was a good background for cobalt blue decoration, and the fired glazed covering produced a relatively inexpensive ceramic that had the appearance of the white oriental ware.

A great variety of objects were made from the tin-glazed earthenware; drug jars, tiles, mugs, barber's dishes, bowls for the bleedings so popular in medical practice, and wig stands all reflected the new rage for Chinese-inspired decoration (Figure 6-15).

Figure 6-15 After the blue and white Chinese porcelain came to Europe, the town of Delft became the pottery center of the Low Countries. The breweries of Delft were in economic difficulties so it was decided to turn them into potteries and teach the unemployed brewers to become potters. From this grew the industry of delft ware. This wig stand, made of white glazed earthenware painted with cobalt, shows the influence of the Chinese style of decoration. Netherlands, 17th century. *Courtesy, Victoria and Albert Museum, Crown Copyright.*

English Traditions

Tea was another Chinese import, and like the Japanese potters who adapted their products to the tea ceremony, the new social habit affected the work of English potters. New shapes were developed to pour the novel tea, and coffee from Arabia, which became the fashionable beverages in English drawing rooms and coffee houses.

While the popularity of tin-glazed ware continued, the increasing demand for all types of ceramics both for display and for use led local potters in England to make quantities of lead-glazed earthenware decorated with slip—a technique that remained popular well into the eighteenth century and is still used today by studio potters on stoneware. Less sophisticated than the Italian- and Chinese-influenced decorations, the designs on these jugs, presentation dishes, birth souvenir cradles, and mugs were either **trailed, feathered,** or incised in **sgraffito** technique, all methods that continue to be used (Figures 10-15 to 10-20).

The secrets of stoneware bodies and salt glazing eventually reached England from Germany, so potters there now had the technology to make high-fired, nonporous, acid-resisting ceramics—a big improvement over the easily chipped earthenware. They experimented with different types of stoneware

Figure 6-16 In the early eighteenth century, the potteries in Staffordshire, England, adapted the German technique of salt glazing to small sculptured figures. Stiff and self-conscious, often seated on benches or church pews, the figures pose for portraits in their best clothing. Made of a dense, white stoneware body, the details of their faces and clothing are accentuated with dark brown clay slip. Salt was thrown into the hot kiln, where the heat of the fire vaporized the salt, which combined with the silica in the clay body to form a glaze. Pew group, Staffordshire, c. 1730. Height 6 in. (15.2 cm). *Courtesy, Fitzwilliam Museum, Cambridge, England.*

bodies, using them for teapots, coffeepots, and jugs of dark red and dark brown stoneware, but they also developed a fine, white stoneware body that was well adapted to pressing or casting in molds. In the early eighteenth century, this technique was used to form small sculptures decorated with slip, as well as useful ware (Figure 6-16). This English tradition of salt glazing stoneware was brought to the American colonies by settlers, where it was used widely until advancing factory technology pushed it into the background. Recently it has been revived by studio potters (Figures 11-21 and 11-22).

Porcelain in Northern Europe

In the meantime, the secret of porcelain had been discovered in Germany around 1710 by Johann Fridrich Böttger, who was originally a chemist and alchemist. The king of Saxony and Poland had ordered him to try to make gold to fill the depleted royal treasuries, and during his unsuccessful search for materials from which to make the precious metal, he became interested in clays. His experiments eventually led to the first European ceramics factory, in Meissen, Germany, where he made stoneware teapots, cups, and bowls that were so hard they could be decorated by cutting on a lathe. Finally, he discovered kaolin in Saxony, and after much trial and error, succeeded in making porcelain.

Two quite different factors gave an impetus to the ceramics industry in France. In 1709, Louis XIV was in need of money, so he had all the royal gold and silver ware melted down, leaving himself with no appropriately elegant tableware. He then commissioned the potters of Limoges to make faience of the Italian type to replace it. Also, in the mustard-manufacturing town of Dijon, potters were kept busy making the faience jars in which the mustard was shipped. Thus, royal pride and French taste in food contributed their part to the growth of the potter's market. In France, too, the race was on to find the secret of porcelain so that local producers could compete with the flood of Chinese imports. Finally, the French and the English also found kaolin, enabling them to make their own porcelain and compete with the Chinese imports.

Although England was behind other European countries in developing porcelain, the potters there experimented with clay bodies, producing a variation of the classic porcelain formula. In addition to making a true translucent porcelain called **hard paste,** which was fired at a very high temperature, they made another type called **soft paste.** This fused at a lower temperature because it contained bone ash, which acted as a flux to promote fusion. Still in use in England today for bone china tableware, it has recently been explored as a material for studio pottery and sculpture (Figures 8-36, 8-37, and 10-12).

These developments in German, French, and English ceramics influenced other countries in Europe. In Denmark, for example, in the eighteenth century, the ceramics industry at first was almost completely supervised by French and German technicians who had brought their own styles and techniques with them. Since Danish clays did not fire well, raw materials were also imported for use in the Danish faience factory. By the middle of the eighteenth century, porcelain was manufactured at a factory in Denmark, using techniques brought there by a French potter who had come in 1759 to work for the king. The king had ordered him to let two of the local technicians learn the secrets of porcelain before he returned to France, and in 1779, the factory became the Royal Copenhagen Porcelain Factory, as it is still called today. What happened in Denmark is just one example of the competition and secretiveness that were typical of the ceramics industry after the arrival of Chinese porcelain, an intensity that makes one think of the space-age rivalry between Russia and the United States after Sputnik.

The Pottery Industry

An English potter, Josiah Wedgwood (1730–95), has probably had a more profound effect on the world's dinnerware than any other single person, for he transformed the English potteries from craft workshops to a mass-production industry that used steam power and large-scale distribution methods, making it possible for ordinary people to af-

Figure 6-17 Influenced by classic art rather than porcelain from China, this black basalt vase from the Wedgwood pottery was made of stoneware colored with manganese and was so hard that it could be cut or polished on a lapidary wheel. Josiah Wedgwood said of this blackware, "The black is sterling, and will last forever." Basalt ware, c. 1775. *Courtesy, Trustees of the Wedgwood Museum, Barlaston.*

ford attractive, easily washed tableware. In addition, he experimented with a variety of clay bodies, developing black **basalt ware,** which was created in classically inspired vase shapes (Figure 6-17).

The detailed story of the china factories is beyond the scope of this book, but a few comments provide interesting side lights on the social changes occurring in England in the eighteenth and nineteenth centuries. For example, the development of transportation played an important part in the pottery industry: by 1777, a canal brought cheap transport to the door of Wedgwood's new factory branch; and Wedgwood urged other pottery owners to join him in building a good road to join the main London road so that wagons could carry their ware easily. In the process of manufacturing large amounts of tableware, the pottery-producing areas of England became polluted with the fumes and smoke that poured from the kilns, for one pottery might have two dozen kilns in operation at a time. The bottle kiln (Figure 6-18) was the preferred shape at this time, and ways of speeding production were developed as Europe moved into the Industrial Revolution. Molds, potter's wheels sped by mechanical inventions, steam power harnessed to turn mixing machinery, and rows of workers in an assembly line attaching handles to finished pieces or painting designs on the ware were characteristic sights in the factories.

In the nineteenth century, the Industrial Revolution absorbed expert potters into the factory system, and "progress," which became the goal, consisted of being able to make more and sell it cheaper. Only in the small, local potteries were the traditions of individual craftsmanship kept alive. In some isolated areas of northern Denmark, for example, the women had always made domestic pots by hand, forming them on boards on their laps and firing them in open peat fires in much the same way the Neolithic potters of Denmark had made and fired black burnished pottery.

In other countries, throughout history and up to the present day, local potters in isolated, nonindustrialized areas have continued to make a great variety of country objects, from milking pans to bean pots to cricket cages, using the traditional earthenware techniques (Figure 6-19).

Figure 6-18 (*Above*) Bottle kilns were the most widely used kilns in the British pottery towns in the eighteenth and nineteenth centuries, until they were replaced by tunnel kilns in the twentieth century. They were basically a simple up-draft design, but with modifications that increased their efficiency, making higher temperatures possible. The bottle-shaped outer structure increased the draft to the inner kiln and gave protection from the weather to the men placing the saggars. Some regulation of the heat was made possible by a system of metal doors on the fire mouths and dampers. In this model of an eighteenth-century kiln (made in 1950, by C. Shufflebotham), workers can be seen carrying ware to the kiln and stacking the saggars into piles that sometimes rose to 30 feet. *Courtesy, City Museum and Art Gallery, Stoke-on-Trent.*

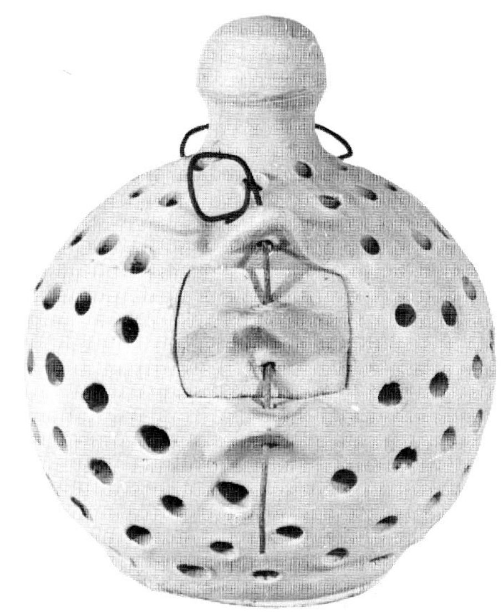

Figure 6-19 (*Right*) Crickets were kept in this cage, providing a "music box" for children. Other earthenware objects included pottery cages to hold snails being prepared for human consumption and shelters for rabbits while giving birth. *Courtesy, Museo del Pueblo Español, Madrid.*

Figure 6-20 German settlers in Pennsylvania made plates of earthenware covered with slip or glaze. Lines were either drawn into the slip in a technique called sgraffito, or slip or glaze was painted on the ware. Dates, names, and inscriptions usually ran around the edges of the plates, which were frequently decorated with birds. George Hubener, Pennsylvania, 1786. *Courtesy, Philadelphia Museum of Art. Gift of John T. Morris.*

America

When potters came to America as colonists in the seventeenth century, they brought their expertise with them and soon established kilns in New England, Pennsylvania, and Virginia. In New England they used the local glacial clay to make coarse earthenware, which they glazed with lead. Very little of this has survived, but enough kiln sites have been excavated to show us that every town had a potter who made earthenware for the nearby housewives.

Usually, the potter was a farmer or fisher who dug his clay in the fall, dried it in the winter, and made pottery whenever he could spare the time. The master potter would do the throwing while a couple of assistants, often his sons, would do the rest of the work. The earthenware was thrown on a kick wheel, then glazed with red lead, which was ground with sand in water in a glaze mill consisting of two granite millstones. The potter added cobalt, manganese, or iron to the transparent glaze to give color to the pieces, applying the glaze in spots, streaks, or splatters. Slip decoration was also popular, and jars, jugs, washbasins, pie plates, crocks, and porringers were all trailed or painted with simple designs made up of freely painted lines. None of the decoration was elaborate, probably because of the Puritan attitude toward the frivolous; but it is clear that in addition to making necessary, useful objects, the New England potter wanted to make them as attractive as the material and the social mores allowed.

Although pottery making was generally a male occupation in the colonies, a good deal of the decorating and glazing was done by women, and apparently some women were potters as well. In 1716, for example, an advertisement spoke of women potters who had arrived as indentured servants and were available for hire, and there are records of a Grace Parker who ran a pottery after her husband's death, trying unsuccessfully to bring stoneware to New England. Other colonies had other traditions, and the type of decoration on their ceramics was influenced by the areas in Europe from which the settlers came (Figure 6-20).

Stoneware

Stoneware clay existed in some parts of America, but not in New England. The potters in New York, Pennsylvania, and Virginia who found local stoneware clay guarded well the secret of its manufacture into pottery. New England and upper New York imported finished stoneware from these other colonies, but as settlements spread, stoneware clay from New Jersey could be shipped to potteries that were near navigable water—such as those in upper New York near the Hudson River and Bennington, Vermont. After 1820, the Erie Canal and a network of waterways made these potteries even more accessible, and a ceramics industry developed there.

The English produced more refined china, which was shipped across the Atlantic to fill the American need for tableware, so American potteries concentrated primarily on utilitarian pieces based on a simple cylinder shape (Figure 6-21). In the days before home canning, these crocks were needed to store the pickled and salted food on which a household depended in the winter months. Since this stoneware was now salt glazed and the resulting ware inert, with no lead in the glaze, it was impervious not only to liquids but to acids as well. Every good housewife had a storeroom full of pickled vegetables, salted butter, and pork, as well as stoneware jugs and bottles full of vinegar, beer, and whiskey.

As workshops expanded, labor-saving devices were brought in and the work became more specialized. The master potter would throw the basic shape, then the finisher would take over, carefully smoothing the inside and outside, possibly using a carved wheel or **roulette** to make impressed decorations in the damp clay. The handles would be put on by a third person, and yet another would apply painted decoration using a slip cup or a brush. The slip cup was a small pottery flask with a thin neck in which a quill was inserted (Figure 10-15). Used for oxides or slip, these cups made it possible for the person decorating the ware to trail the slip quickly onto the raw clay, making designs that often reflected the interests of the people for whom they were intended. Patriotic designs, flowers, birds, American eagles, full-rigged ships, chickens scratching in the barnyard, grazing deer were all drawn with various degrees of skill.

This ware was then placed in a kiln for a single firing, which ended with salt being thrown in the kiln to glaze the ware. When salt vaporizes, it gives off an irritant gas, and there are records of complaints from citizens living near the salt kilns where the ware was fired. Fired in a brick-lined kiln, with wood as the fuel, the stoneware was slowly brought to white heat in one firing without a preliminary **bisque** firing to drive out the water. The kiln operator had to regulate the wood fire carefully so that the pots would not burst at this point, bringing the kiln to the necessary temperature to volatize the salt. When the ware was ready to take the glaze, the salt was thrown

Figure 6-21 Potters in upper New York State and Vermont specialized in stoneware crocks decorated with chickens, eagles, and shore birds as well as patriotic symbols. Stacked sometimes six high in the kilns, the cylindrical crocks underneath were thick walled enough to support the weight. The whole operation of firing and salt glazing these crocks took from six to eight days. Height 11½ in. (29.2 cm), diameter 11½ in. (29.2 cm). *Courtesy, New York State Historical Association, Cooperstown.*

in, and in the words of one local potter's instruction manual, "When fit to glaze, have your salt dry. Scatter it well in every part of your kiln, during this act you must keep a full and clear blaze so as to accelerate the glazing and give the ware a bright gloss. Stop it perfectly tight and in six days you may draw a good kiln of ware." The fire would be kept burning, with the kiln kept at high heat, until finally, after six or eight days for the whole operation, the kiln was opened—hopefully to reveal a kiln full of perfect ware.

As in England, after the Industrial Revolution the potteries in the United States became factories too, and the small workshop could not compete with the low prices of the factory-produced goods. The artisan now performed just one function in an assembly line, losing any sense of personal identification with the final product.

Figure 6-22 An early nineteenth-century ink stand from the Royal Copenhagen Porcelain Factory in Denmark was simple and functional. *Courtesy, Museum of Decorative Art, Copenhagen. Photo by Ole Woldbye.*

Arts and Crafts Movement

In the 1800s, however, a number of artists and art critics, rebelling against the machine and the pompous ugliness of Victorian taste, preached a return to the handmade ware. Led in England by William Morris and John Ruskin, they urged craftspeople to return to preindustrial crafts, to respect the material in which they worked, and to join in an arts and crafts revival that would beautify their surroundings. A reformer as well as a designer, Morris felt that the human spirit could not survive in such a materialistic world, and his solution was handicraft.

The influence of the Romantic movement led many of these artists to return to the past, to the Middle Ages, to Persia, and to the early Italian Renaissance for inspiration for the designs on their painted wall tiles, decorated plates, maiolica fireplace tiles, and fountains. These were all an attempt to re-create the world as it was before the arrival of the machine. Escapist as they were, these artists did draw attention to the decline of the arts and crafts and to the plight of the artist and artisan.

Before mass production and specialization had separated the maker from the product, the artisan potter had been a part of the mainstream of life. The men and women who worked with clay had automatically filled the basic needs of the everyday community, whether for vessels to place on the altar of a god or for a simple pot for cooking over a wood fire. The potters had dug the clay, handling it with care and respect, forming it into traditional or functional shapes. They were not concerned with the place of the artisan in society, for their place in it was secure and important. Now, however, artist-potters had to find a place in a world that was rapidly becoming machine oriented.

Influenced by the crafts movement, some of the large ceramics companies hired artists

Figure 6-23 An earthenware plate with a realistic seascape painted with a thick glaze is an example of how late-nineteenth century artists turned to decorating ready-made pottery. Using ceramics as a background for painting, they began to bring artists into the craft of pottery making. Niels Skovgard, Denmark, 1888. *Courtesy, Museum of Decorative Art, Copenhagen.*

to design for them, making what was called art pottery. Like the presentation plates of the Spanish and Italian maiolica, much of this was heavily ornamented, made to be looked at rather than used.

Other artist-potters, turning away from the ornamented tradition that had dominated European ceramics ever since Italian maiolica and Chinese blue and white ware had become so popular, turned to simpler shapes influenced by Sung Chinese porcelain. They experimented with the brilliant glazes of the Orient, often developing their own special glaze effects (Figure 6-25). In Denmark, where even in the early nineteenth century the Royal Copenhagen Porcelain Factory produced some simple, functional objects (Figure 6-22), some artists, on the other hand, were attracted to pottery as a surface on which to paint (Figure 6-23). They took the vigorous useful earthenware of the country potters and painted it in styles that represented a sharp break with current ceramics decoration (Figure 6-24).

Elsewhere, artists who started as china painters became dissatisfied with the shapes available to them and designed pots for the professionals to throw. Still others, drawn through their interest in decoration to realize the importance of the form of a piece, decided to become potters themselves (Figures 6-26, 6-27, and 6-28).

Figure 6-24 Thorvald Bindesböll decorated this large vase at the Copenhagen Earthenware Factory at Valby in 1893. It was painted in black and white and incised with a sharp instrument using the sgraffito technique. The black is rich and dark, while the white is so thin that in many places the yellowish clay body shows through. Bindesböll painted on professionally thrown earthenware with simple and abstract designs that anticipated later European ceramics. Denmark, 1893. Height 22¾ in. (58 cm). *Courtesy, The Museum of Decorative Art, Copenhagen. Photo by Ole Woldbye.*

Figure 6-25 Some European potters in the 1890s began to create simple shapes and to experiment with glazes. This vase by J.F. Willumsen of Denmark is an example of this return to overall glaze and form. Stoneware, 1897. *Courtesy, Museum of Decorative Art, Copenhagen.*

Figure 6-26 English-born A.W. Finch had studied in Belgium with Henry van de Velde, a leader in the arts and crafts reform movement at the turn of the twentieth century. Finch later went to Finland, where he designed for the Iris factory at Porvoo. Around the same time other Scandinavian factories, like the Arabia Factory in Helsinki and the Gustavberg in Sweden, began to hire artists to design for them. Ahead of their time in design, Finch's bowls, vases, and dishes influenced later pottery in Scandinavia. A.W. Finch, c. 1900. In The National Museum, Finland. *Courtesy, Arabia, Finland.*

Figure 6-27 Adelaide Alsop Robineau came to pottery through china painting. Bored and frustrated with decorating other people's work, she first cast her pieces, and then began to work on the wheel, encouraged by her potter husband. She worked for hundreds of hours carving her vases, and sometimes fired one piece as many as seven times to get the glaze effect she wanted. As a result, her output of art pottery was small. (*Above Left*) Indian vase. Height 14½ in. (36.8 cm). (*Above Right*) Cloudland vase, U.S.A., c. 1900. Height 12 in. (30.5 cm). *Courtesy, The Detroit Institute of Arts. Gift of George G. Booth.*

Figure 6-28 Some potters at the turn of the century returned to the Orient for inspiration, but rather than copy highly decorated later Chinese ware, many of them worked at developing glazes and forming shapes reminiscent of Sung porcelain. Ernest Chaplet, France, 1906. *Courtesy, The Museum of Decorative Art, Copenhagen.*

Sculpture

From the Renaissance on, most of the important sculpture in the Western world was generally carved in stone or cast in bronze. Although some Renaissance artists in Italy created life-sized terra cotta religious sculpture, most employed it for small busts or portraits (Figure 6-10).

Working in clay, however, was an important part of the sculptor's craft, for many of the original sketches, as well as the final models from which bronzes were made, were formed of clay over an **armature.** This is a framework of wood, metal, or other rigid material, which supports the damp clay and keeps it from collapsing under its own weight as the artist builds it up. Pressing the moist clay onto the armature, the sculptor can make pieces that would be impossible without a support. For example, a rearing horse supported on only two thin rear legs could not be built up unless it were done over some sort of framework. Clay with a heavy wooden armature inside can rarely be fired successfully, so this method of construction was used only for the original model. A mold was then made from the model so that the final piece could be cast in bronze. (A few small fired terra cotta figures from Tang China were x-rayed and found to have the remains of wood or even metal armatures inside them, but this is an exception.) This method of working is still used by sculptors today, and if you will look at the surface of a bronze sculpture closely, you may see the mark of the artist's fingers in the clay.

Terra cotta and porcelain were used widely from the seventeenth to nineteenth centuries to make small press-molded or **slip-cast** sculptures, which were often colorfully decorated and glazed (Color Plate 7, p. 146B). These were extremely popular as ornaments in palaces, mansions, and cottages throughout Europe and the United States. In wealthier homes that could afford porcelain, glazed figures of shepherdesses and shepherds, Psyche and Cupid, and fruits and vegetables graced the elegantly carved tables in the parlor; while the kitchen dresser of a cottage might be brightened with a salt-glazed stoneware group (Figure 6-16), a Toby jug, a figure of some current military hero, or a representation of events nearer to home. These small sculptures were either made by pressing clay into a mold or slip casting it. Slip casting was done by thinning the clay body with water until it could be poured into a porous mold. Potters and sculptors still use some of these methods today to cast sculpture or pots, frequently painting them with underglaze or overglaze colors (Figures 8-36 to 8-39, 10-26, and 11-26).

The Turn of the Century

In the late nineteenth century, some art school graduates began to turn to ceramics, setting up small workshops where they could form, glaze, and decorate their pieces themselves, or at least supervise all stages. Now the story had come full circle, and the artist-potter was back in the small workshop situation of preindustrial days. But although romantics might yearn for lost traditions and attempt to restore the past by returning to preindustrial styles of art, it was clearly impossible for the new artist-potter to become again an unsophisticated village potter working in response to a neighbor's needs. Too much had happened in the world, and the potter was part of it. Now, any craft worker had to face the conflict between the machine and human hands, between the need to form clay with honesty and integrity and the economic problems of competing with cheap, machine-produced goods.

How this conflict has been faced, resolved, or avoided is part of the story of clay in the days following the arrival of machine technology in the nineteenth century. At this

Color Plate 5 Lead-tin-glazed plate from Deruta, Italy, c. A.D. 1530. Diameter 8 in. (20.6 cm). *Courtesy, Indiana University Art Museum.*

Color Plate 6 Brush-decorated bowl, Japan. 18th century A.D. Height 4½ in. (11.4 cm). *Courtesy, Victoria and Albert Museum, Crown Copyright.*

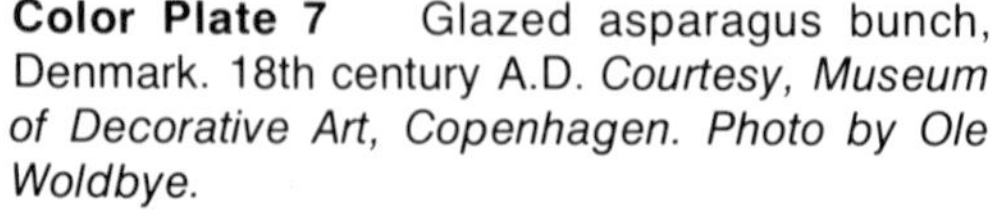

Color Plate 7 Glazed asparagus bunch, Denmark. 18th century A.D. *Courtesy, Museum of Decorative Art, Copenhagen. Photo by Ole Woldbye.*

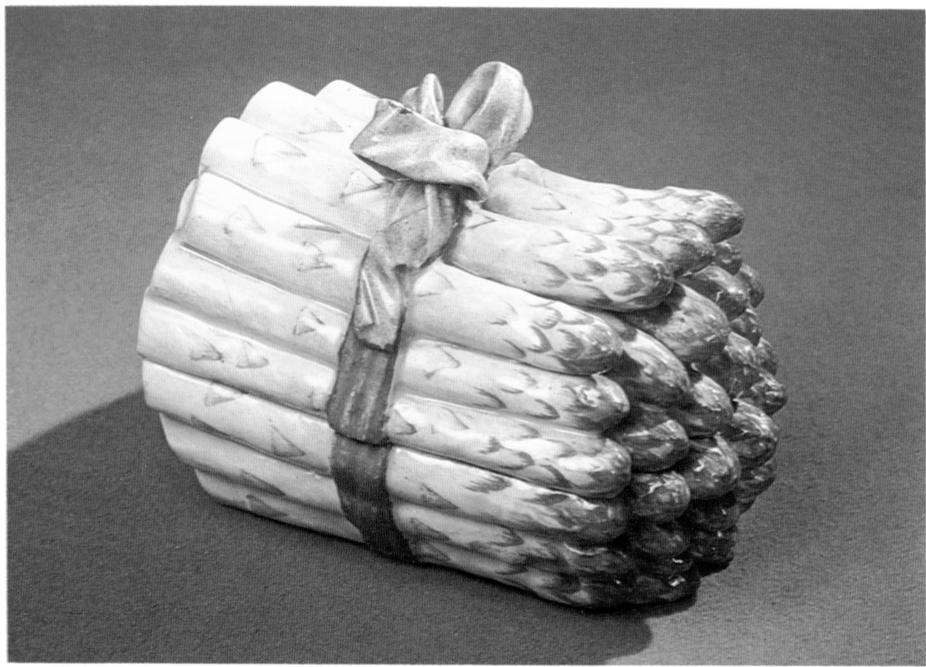

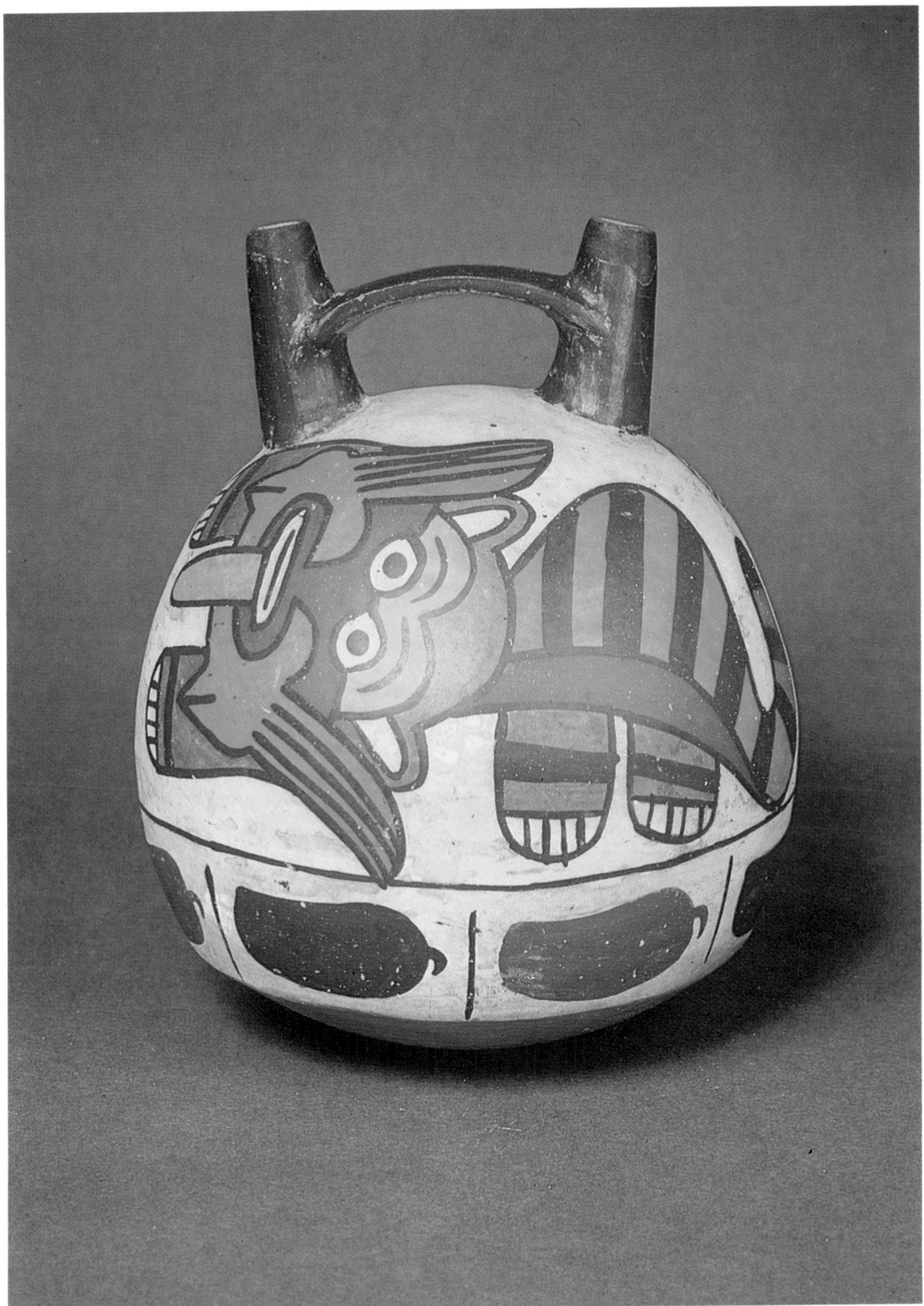

Color Plate 8 Spouted jar from the Nasca Valley, Peru. Decorated with wild cats and fruit. Height 8 in. (20.3 cm), diameter 6¾ in. (17 cm). *Courtesy, Museum of the American Indian, Heye Foundation.*

Color Plate 9 **Maria Martinez,** U.S.A. Coiled bowl. Slip decorated by her son, Popovi Da, 1957. Open-fire, reduction. Height 3½ in. (8.9 cm), diameter 5 in. (12.7 cm).

Color Plate 10 **Michael Cardew,** England. Slip-glazed earthenware with trailed decoration. 1938. Collection of Katherine Pleydell-Bouverie. *Courtesy, Crafts Advisory Committee, London. Photo by David Cripps.*

time, anyone drawn to clay crafting as a lifework was faced with questions that would never have occurred to the Minoan, Islamic, or Japanese village potter. Is the clay-crafter an artist who should be less concerned with the useful, who should be considered equal to a painter or sculptor? Or is clay primarily a functional material that should be used to make useful pots? Where does the line between art and craft lie? What life decision does a clay-crafter make—to create one-of-a-kind pieces to be displayed in urban galleries, or to produce repeat utilitarian ware in quantity?

Figure 6-29 Art school trained, English potter W. Staite Murray taught himself to make pottery in the early 1900s and in the 1920s and 1930s, he taught ceramics at the Royal College of Art, where he influenced many younger potters. Not interested in making useful ware, he insisted on the importance of ceramics as an art medium. W. Staite Murray, "Wheel of Life" vase, c. 1939. *Courtesy, Victoria and Albert Museum, Crown Copyright.*

The 1920s

These questions were faced by several young potters in England in the 1920s, and they came to different decisions. For example, W. Staite Murray, trained in an art school, exhibited his pieces in galleries along with painters and sculptors, having no interest in making useful pots (Figure 6-29). Art school graduate Bernard Leach, on the other hand, was greatly influenced by the folk pottery of Japan, where he studied with the sixth Kenzan (Figure 6-30). Seeing the potter's craft as part of that tradition, he came back to England in 1920 to found a pottery in Cornwall. With the help of a fine young Japanese artist-potter, Shoji Hamada (Figure 6-31), he set up a pottery workshop, and with members of his family, he settled down to make pots for use. Greatly influenced by the artistic philosophy of the Orient as well as by Korean, Chinese, and Japanese pottery, Leach was also drawn to the simple slip-decorated earthenware made by English country potters (Figure 6-30).

Although Leach is best known for his stoneware made in muted earth tones, he has explored a great variety of decorative effects throughout his long life. His influence, through his work, his pupils, and the wide popularity of his book, *A Potter's Book*, has been immense.

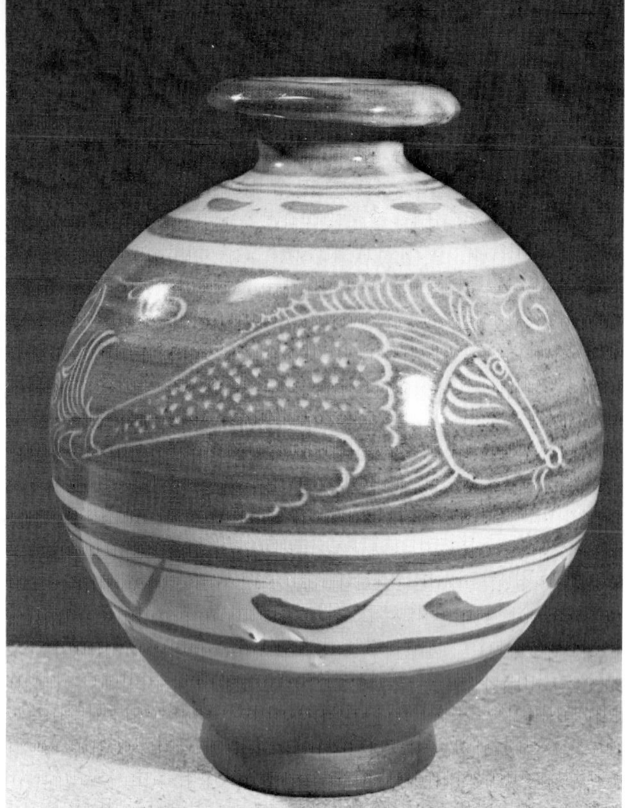

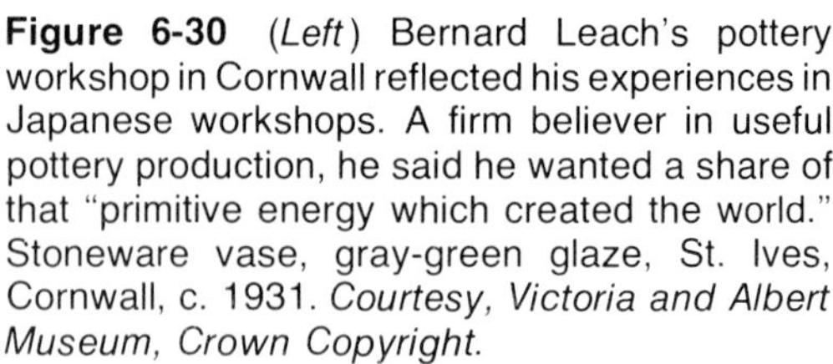
Figure 6-30 (*Left*) Bernard Leach's pottery workshop in Cornwall reflected his experiences in Japanese workshops. A firm believer in useful pottery production, he said he wanted a share of that "primitive energy which created the world." Stoneware vase, gray-green glaze, St. Ives, Cornwall, c. 1931. *Courtesy, Victoria and Albert Museum, Crown Copyright.*

Figure 6-31 Shoji Hamada went to England to help Bernard Leach set up his kiin. Both men were dedicated to the production of useful, folk-inspired pottery, and their lifelong association created a bridge between Eastern and Western ceramics. (*Below*) Hamada decorating a vase. *Courtesy, Foreign Ministry of Japan and Consulate General of Japan, Los Angeles.* (*Right*) Piece by Hamada made in 1931. *Courtesy, Victoria and Albert Museum, Crown Copyright.*

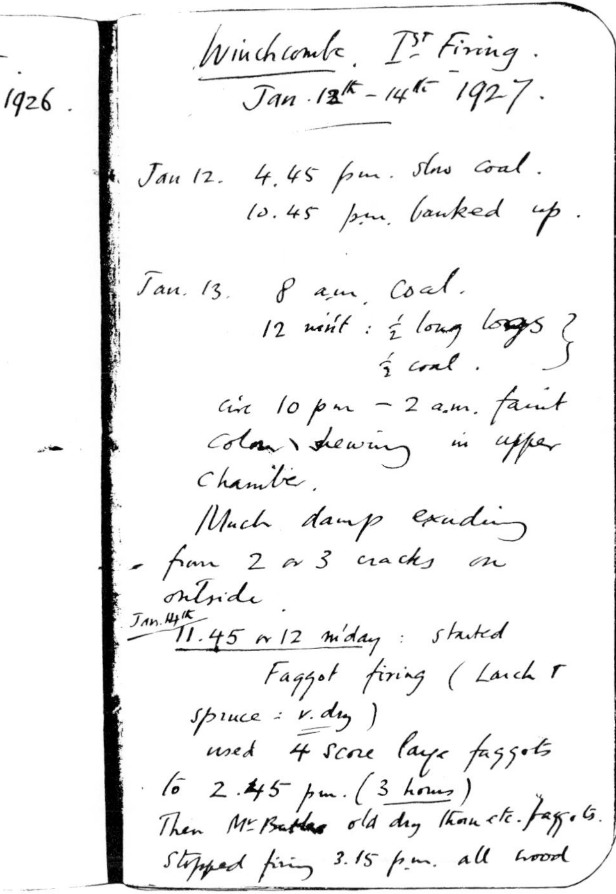

1926.

Winchcombe. 1st Firing.
Jan. 12th – 14th 1927.

Jan 12. 4.45 pm. slow coal.
10.45 pm. banked up.

Jan. 13. 8 a.m. Coal.
12 mid't: ½ long logs ?
½ coal.
c. 10 pm – 2 a.m. faint colour showing in upper chamber.
Much damp exuding from 2 or 3 cracks on outside.

Jan. 14th 11.45 or 12 m'day: started Faggot firing (Larch & spruce: v. dry)
used 4 score large faggots to 2.45 pm. (3 hours)
Then Mr [illegible] old dry thorn etc. faggots.
Stopped firing 3.15 pm. all wood

Figure 6-32 Michael Cardew, a former assistant of Leach's, makes domestic ware, often slip decorated. His attitude toward pottery is that instead of self-expression, the potter should strive to "express the universe." Gray-green glazed stoneware, c. 1949. *Courtesy, Crafts Advisory Committee, London.* **Figure 6-33** In 1927, Michael Cardew fired his first kiln at his new pottery. This page from his kiln book records in detail the steps in that firing, giving us a glimpse of the long, hard hours of work in a potter's day. *Courtesy, Crafts Advisory Committee, London.*

Over the years, at the Leach workshop, hundreds of assistants and pupils, under the careful supervision of Leach and later his wife, Janet, have been trained in production pottery. There they learned to make each piece, no matter how tiny, express the Leach philosophy of "the straightforward, the natural, the innocent, the humble, the modest" (Color Plate 12, p. 210B).

One of Leach's assistants for three years was Michael Cardew, who then went on to set up his own kiln in Gloucestershire (Figure 6-32), where he worked in stoneware, making slip-decorated tableware (Figure 6-33 and Color Plate 10, p. 146D). Cardew considers himself a country potter—one of the "earthenware people" as opposed to the "porcelain people." He is also a highly articulate man, whose belief that pots can proclaim that life is good has inspired young potters from Nigeria, to aborigines in Australia, to American college students. He is well known for starting workshops in Ghana and Nigeria, where potters like Ladi Kwali (Figure 10-5) learned to make stoneware from a local clay in addition to the traditional earthenware shapes in which they were already skilled.

These two British potters, Leach and Cardew, represent one current in the stream of influences that converged in the twentieth century. On the other hand, city potters, as Cardew calls them, represent another current. More urbane, influenced by contemporary art movements, these potters and sculptors had less interest in making domestic ware (Figures 6-30 and 6-31).

Figure 6-34 Patrick Nordström was designing for Danish ceramics factories by 1914. His shapes were simple and his glazes rough textured, a combination that would become very popular in Scandinavia and later in the United States. Stoneware pot with wooden lid, c. 1929. *Courtesy, The Museum of Decorative Art, Copenhagen. Photo by Ole Woldbye.*

The 1930s and 1940s

With the disruption of life in Europe in the 1930s, fine potters like Hans Coper (Figure 9-66), Lucie Rie (Figure 11-3), and Marguerite Wildenhain emigrated to England and the United States, enriching the craft in both countries with their artistry and technical knowledge. When we look around at the available ceramics education in the United States today, it is hard to believe that in 1938, when California potter Laura Andreson wanted to widen her knowledge to include the wheel, she had to wait for the arrival of Gertrud and Otto Natzler from Vienna a year later to learn the skill. The University of California at Los Angeles, where Andreson taught coil building and slip casting, had such a wheel, but no one knew how to use it!

In the eastern United States, enough interest in ceramics had lingered from the days of the early crafts revival movement so that when Maija Grotell arrived from Finland in 1927, she was able to get a job teaching ceramics at the Henry Street Settlement House. She was eager to become an artist-potter herself, and as a teacher she wanted to bring ceramics to the level of an art. It took years of dedication on the part of many artists like Maija Grotell before ceramics was seriously accepted as an art form, no longer relegated to hobby status. Later she taught at Cranbrook Academy of Art, a school that was ahead of the times in teaching the crafts on an equal footing with painting, sculpture, and architecture. There, her disciplined craft and her years of innovative research into glazes inspired several generations of ceramics students (Figure 6-35 and Color Plate 11, p. 210A).

Figure 6-35 (*Left*) Maija Grotell holding a roughly textured, gray-green stoneware pot. Its swelling form is emphasized by splashes of blue glaze contrasting with a glossy black interior. *Courtesy, Maija Grotell Research Fund. Photo by Charles Eames.*

Art Styles Influence Ceramics

While these potters were making their influence felt on new generations of students, the contemporary movements in painting, sculpture, and architecture were influencing ceramics as well as other crafts (Figures 6-36 through 6-39). When artists like Henri Matisse, Pablo Picasso, Marc Chagall, and Fernand Leger turned to designing or decorating one-of-a-kind ceramics, clay moved into the art gallery, becoming an acceptable medium of self-expression. This trend was resisted, and still is, by some people who felt it perverted the true use of clay, but as the freedom to use any and all materials accelerated in the arts, clay was no exception.

On the other hand, the Bauhaus School, founded in Germany in 1919 and influential there until it closed during the Hitler regime, taught a doctrine of "form follows function." Believing that applied decoration had no place on any contemporary product, whether it was a building, a chair, or a coffeepot, the Bauhaus artists influenced the design of factory-produced goods in the late 1920s and 1930s, as well as the work of many individual potters. Reflecting the changing attitudes, Scandinavian factories like Arabia and British factories like Wedgwood began to introduce lines of simple, functional tableware, while the Museum of Modern Art in New York gave Good Design awards to the best-designed industrial products every year. Also, in an interesting

Figure 6-36 Not all Scandinavian potters in the 1930s were devotees of Bauhaus functionalism. Axel Salto, who in 1924 was designing highly decorated vases for Bing and Grøndahl Porcellaensfabrik, continued for many years to make one-of-a-kind pots covered with rich glazes over sculptural, organic forms. In the 1950s, he also designed a simple, elegant white dinner service for Den Kongelige Porcellaensfabrik, on which the restrained decoration was highly stylized. Modeled and carved vase, warm brown glaze, c. 1931. *Courtesy, The Museum of Decorative Art, Copenhagen. Photo by Ole Woldbye.*

Figure 6-37 Cubist art of the 1920s, along with other contemporary art movements, made its influence felt on ceramics as well as on industrial design. Danish potter Christine Swane decorated this plate with a line design inspired by paintings of Picasso and Braque. Plate, c. 1931. *Courtesy, The Museum of Decorative Art, Copenhagen.*

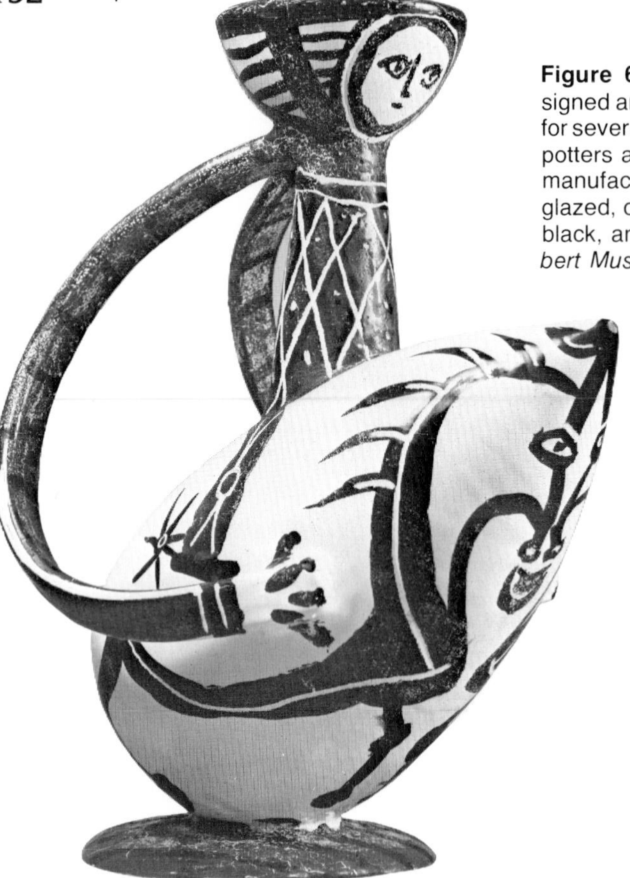

Figure 6-38 "Cavalier," a composite pot designed and painted by Pablo Picasso. He worked for several years with Susan and Georges Ramié, potters at Vallauris, painting on pieces that they manufactured to his designs. Some were brightly glazed, others, like this, painted with red, brown, black, and white slip. *Courtesy, Victoria and Albert Museum, Crown Copyright.*

development, several ceramics factories, like De Porcelyne Fles in Delft, Bing and Grøndahl in Copenhagen, and Arabia in Helsinki, instituted experimental studios. The artists who worked in these programs were given freedom to create their own one-of-a-kind pottery or sculpture (Figures 7-61, 7-62, and 8-25), while at the same time maintaining a relationship with the factory. In some cases they designed for the factory, in other cases they used the factory facilities for their own work—the amount of give and take between craft and industry varied from company to company.

Where in all this ferment of new methods and new artistic concepts could the individual who worked with clay find a path? Artists and craftworkers throughout history have been influenced by new artistic ideas and techniques from other cultures. From the "Mohammedan blue" underglaze used by the Chinese in their own characteristic way, to the tin glazes of Spain and Italy that were transformed by Dutch potters into a local style, to the German salt-glazed stoneware that became a crock for Vermont pickles—all these methods from

Figure 6-39 Portrait plate painted by Henri Matisse, made at the Susan and Georges Ramié pottery in Vallauris, France. The drawing is in black with some sgraffito, and the face is left in the reserved clay body color against blue. 1948. Diameter 16⅞ in. (43 cm). *Courtesy, Museo Internazionale delle Ceramiche, Faenza, Italy.*

other lands were incorporated and slowly transformed by local artisans into new styles that filled the needs and expressed the outlooks of their own cultures. So, too, the artists of the early twentieth century gradually absorbed and integrated new ideas from so many sources, keeping their own integrity as well as their own individual sense of form, color, and decoration.

Today's Freedom of Expression

Now, in the second half of the twentieth century, as the interest in clay as a material for production pottery and for self-expression has grown, the craft has come to reflect the general freedom of the whole contemporary art scene. As more and more artists worked in clay as potters or sculptors, they explored or developed new techniques as well as reviving old techniques and using them in new ways. Today's clay worker has a bewildering choice of techniques and artistic philosophies from which to choose. From coiled African water pots (Figure 4-13) to fiberglas-reinforced sculpture (Figure 8-26), from raku (Figure 12-20) to sand and clay sculpture (Figure 8-48), the past and present offer an almost unlimited freedom.

As you learn the fundamentals of clay working, you will face this choice; so as you learn how to throw a pot, how to glaze, and how to fire, think about your place in the long procession of human beings who have worked in clay. In Part Two, you will see examples of how others have used this new freedom of the last few decades.

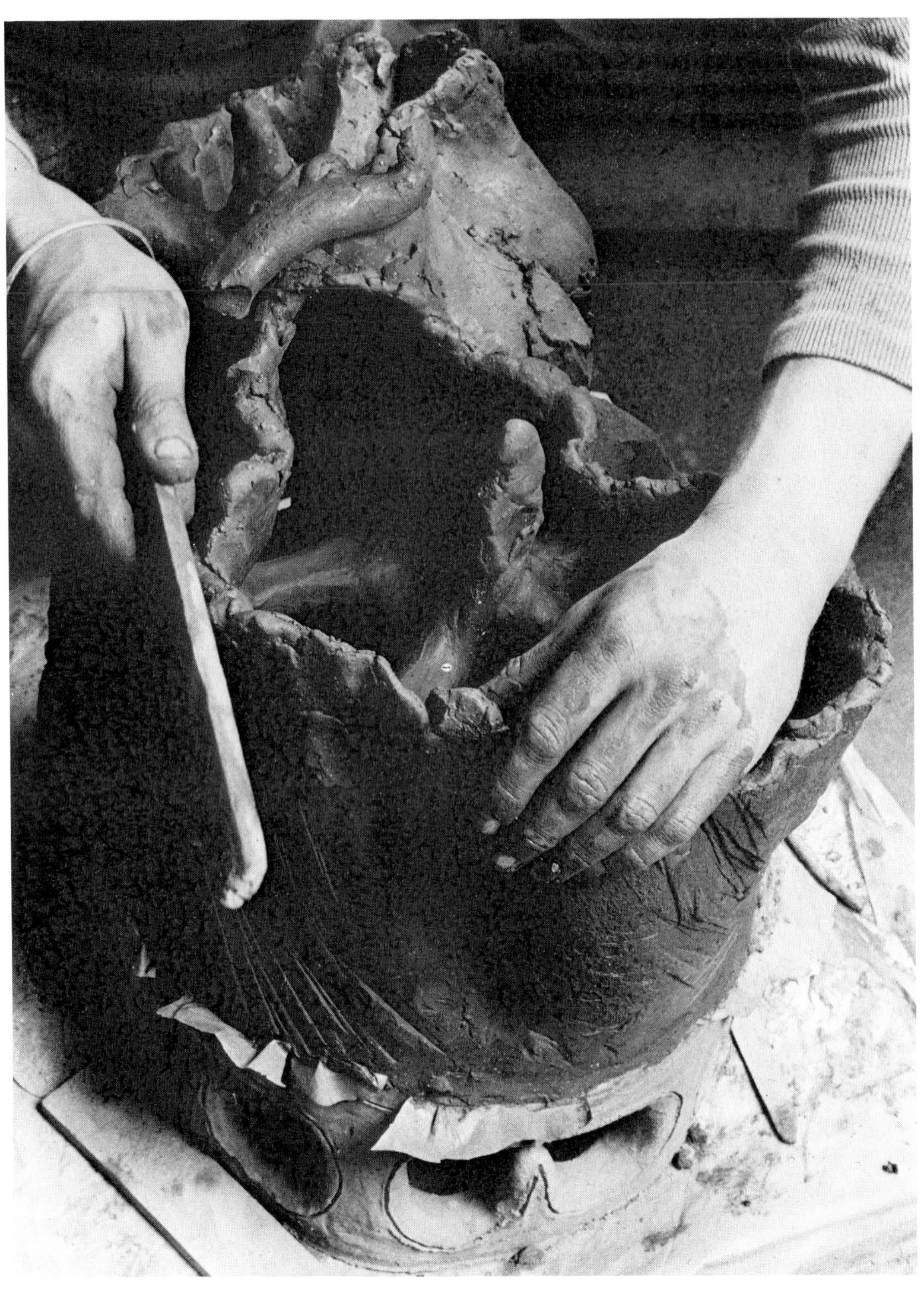

Hands working in moist clay have shaped it into sculpture or pottery for thousands of years. Nicholas van Os, Netherlands, 1978. *Photo by Frits van Os.*

PART TWO

Your Hands in Clay

Chapter Seven

Preparing Clay and Hand Building

Hands—patting, pinching, pulling, and poking clay—have formed useful, beautiful objects for thousands of years and are still leaving their imprint on clay today (Figure 7-1). Now that you are joining this long line of clay crafters, which stretches back to Neolithic times (Figure 7-2), you are faced with the question of how you will discover your own way of working with clay. Potter, poet, and dancer Paulus Berensohn* says:

> It's the person working with clay that matters to me; the connection each of us makes to it. It's awesome, this clay; as if it were the "stuff" of imagination.

As a person living in the twentieth century, you are exposed to an incredible amount of stimulus from the past, from other cultures, from other craftspeople. Museums, galleries, and books show you techniques from the past, and every month when the ceramics magazines come out, you can see work by contemporary potters and sculptors almost as

Figure 7-1 Lawrence Jordan, of the United States, uses a variety of hand-building techniques as he builds up his pots. *Photo by Louie La Fonde. Courtesy of the artist.*

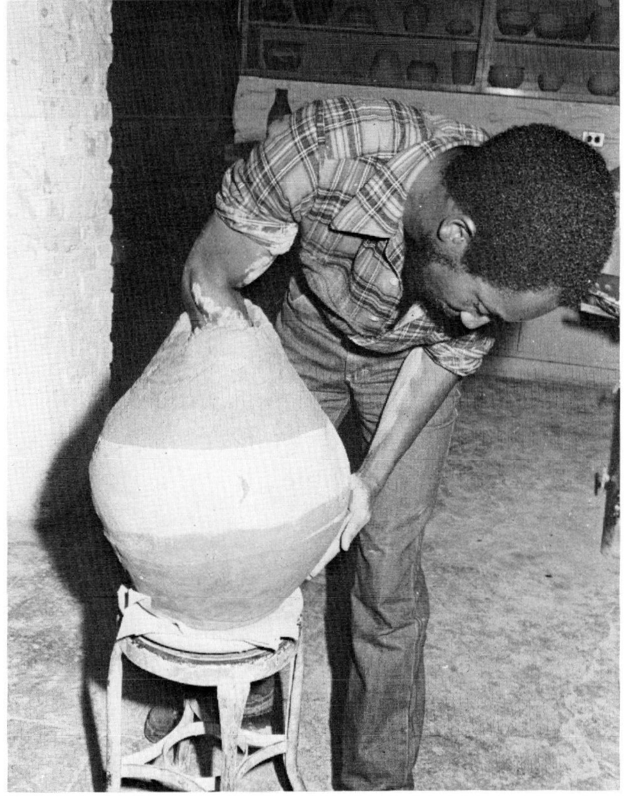

* Paulus Berensohn is author of the book *Finding One's Way With Clay* (New York: Simon and Schuster, 1972).

Figure 7-2 Around 4700 B.C., along the River Yarmuk, in what is now Israel, a Neolithic clay crafter pinched clay into a fertility figure. *Courtesy, Israel Department of Antiquities and Museums.*

Figure 7-3 Bricks of silica will protect NASA's space shuttle from intense heat during re-entry into the earth's atmosphere. *Courtesy, NASA.*

soon as they open their kilns. You can even read technical journals and learn about the ceramics materials used in industry and space technology (Figure 7-3).

Exploring Clay

Controversy, strong feelings, and a good deal of scorn often divide clay-crafters of varying beliefs. One has only to read the letters in crafts magazines to see how strongly some individuals feel about their own ways of working. It can be confusing to the beginner. But where you find yourself in the midst of today's strongly held beliefs and conflicting viewpoints depends on your discovery of what feels right for you. In the words of poet, potter, and teacher Mary Caroline Richards,

> Our pots do bear our spirits into the world. Clay is basically the same material that it was in 6000 B.C., and you can use your hands in the same way as the first person who shaped it. But you are unique, and how your hands reflect that special quality will indeed bear your spirit into the world.*

As you read through Part Two of this book, looking at the pictures of people working in clay, studying their methods, remember that other people can do only just so much to help you find yourself in relation to clay. The rest is up to you.

Explore the clay, see what it says to you. Listen to it, find out what it can do, and what you can do with it. There are many ways to experience clay. Swiss potter-sculptor Ernst Häusermann, for example, takes his students camping for a week near a clay pit (Figure 7-4). There they live with clay, working to-

* Mary Caroline Richards, *Centering in Pottery, Poetry, and the Person* (Middletown, Conn.: Wesleyan University Press, 1964).

Figure 7-4 Ernst Häusermann, of Switzerland, takes his students camping near a clay deposit to learn about clay by living with it. *Courtesy of the artist.*

Figure 7-5 Dancer Jere Graham slides and slithers in creamy, colored slips, becoming a piece of moving sculpture. Crossweaves Dance Company, U.S.A. *Photo by ISHA.*

gether to build caves, houses, and slides. In another clay experiment, a group of California dancers see how the wet clay feels on their bodies, pouring it, sliding in it, dancing a celebration of wet earth (Figure 7-5). You may not explore clay in just these ways, but you can take lumps of it and squeeze it in your hands to see how it responds, what it does when it gets wet, how far you can push it before it collapses, or what you can do with collapsed clay; how thin you can pinch it, or what happens when you work it until the warmth of your hands and the air rob it of moisture.

Only you and the clay can really tell each other how you are going to work together. Thus the information offered in the remainder of this book is intended to help you discover your own way of working, not to dictate absolute rules. "For an artist," says U.S. sculptor Stephen De Staebler, "the most valuable motto would be 'No rules'."

Clay Bodies

You will probably want to start off using premixed commercial clay bodies, each of which has been carefully formulated for a particular use and labeled with its firing range. Digging out your own clay or mixing your own clay body from dry ingredients is probably best left until you have had some experience with ready-mixed clays. However, a little knowledge of the way clay bodies are developed and how they behave will take away some of the mystery surrounding clay.

As we saw in Chapter 1, clay is made up of particles of decomposed rocks, often mixed with materials such as iron or organic matter. It may vary from coarse to fine, from white to red or brown, responding in various ways to your hands, to drying, and to the fire of the kiln. Some clays can be used pretty much as they are dug out, cleaned of large particles of impurities, while other clays need a good deal of preparation. Mixing up a batch of clay is very much like mixing dough for bread. In fact, the experienced potter in a workshop operates much of the time like an experienced cook who has learned the culinary basics and now mixes ingredients in a try-it-and-see spirit.

A clay body, then, is a mixture of clay and other materials, either worked as it comes from the earth or prepared by the user. You will probably not try to mix clay bodies until you have had more experience with clay, but some understanding of how they are developed will help you understand whatever clay you use. Obviously, what you are going to do with the clay makes a difference in the body you will use. For example, if you are planning to make coiled pots and fire them at a low temperature, you will not use a high-fire porcelain clay, but rather a somewhat porous earthenware; whereas if you plan to throw on the wheel, you will need more-plastic clay.

Shrinkage and Warping

Very fine clays shrink more when they dry than those with larger particles, so you would not use a fine body like porcelain to build large, thick sculptural forms. On the other hand, if you were building a large piece of sculpture to be fired at a high temperature, you would use a stoneware body with a lot of temper or grog in it so that it would be less likely to crack in drying or firing.

Plasticity

Shrinkage rates of clays vary, and in mixing a clay body this is an important consideration. **Ball clays,** for example, shrink a great deal and cannot be used alone, but they are important additives to less-plastic clays like kaolin. The amount to be added must be carefully worked out to give the necessary plasticity without adding so much that it causes too much shrinkage. Clays to be thrown on the wheel must be more plastic than sculpture clays, so they are made with as little nonplastic material like flint or feldspar as possible and with additional plastic material such as ball clay or bentonite.

The firing temperature also affects the plasticity of clay, for necessary flux materials like feldspar or talc, which help the clay body to fuse in firing, make it less plastic and therefore harder to throw. If you want to throw porcelain on the wheel, you may want to increase the amount of ball clay to make it workable. But since ball clay fires to gray tones, in so doing you may sacrifice some of the whiteness of the porcelain.

Aging Clay

Clay, like bread, is improved by the action of bacteria. It needs to be left alone for a period of aging after it has been mixed, allowing the water to permeate the particles completely. If the clay is aged for more than a few days, bacteria start to form. These bacteria develop acids and gels and secrete enzymes that help break the clay into smaller particles, increasing its plasticity. Two weeks will probably ripen the clay, although most potters say the longer the better. Legends tell us that ancient Chinese potters prepared clay to be put aside for use by their sons and grandsons. And Michael Cardew tells of some clay that did not throw well. Leaving it behind when he went off on his travels, he came across it years later and found that it had become plastic, a joy to form on the wheel.

Color

Color is also a consideration in choosing one's clay. Since iron acts as a flux, earthenware containing a lot of iron can be fired at low temperatures, but it fires to buff, brown, or red. We saw how potters, first in the Middle East, then in Spain and Italy, used opaque white tin glazes to cover the reddish colors of earthenware clay (Figure 6-1). Until porcelain making was finally mastered in Europe in 1710, the Chinese were the only ones to develop a white clay body. The kaolin in China happens to be very plastic, so Chinese potters did not have to add much ball clay, which meant they could make very pure white porcelain.

You will want to consider the clay body color in relation to what you are going to make. If you are using stoneware for sculpture, or if you want to leave parts of a piece unglazed, the color that iron gives to the clay may be desirable. Also, the amount of iron in the body will make a difference in the way a glaze looks after firing. For example, the same glaze may appear very bland on one stoneware body and rich on another that has a larger amount of iron in it. In other cases, iron may darken or dull the color in a transparent glaze.

Maturing Temperatures of Clay

The **maturing** temperature of clay bodies varies tremendously from low-fire earthenware to high-fire porcelains. Because stoneware and porcelain bodies are fired at high temperatures, they require less flux material to fuse. But if, for example, the local stoneware you buy or find requires a somewhat higher temperature than you wish to use, you can add some flux to help it fuse at a slightly lower temperature.

Feldspar, which has a higher maturing range than iron, is used as a flux material in stoneware and porcelain. Of course, if you wanted to lower the maturing temperature a great deal, you would not use stoneware, but a low-fire body. Earthenware, the common red clay used throughout the world, does not require high temperatures, since the iron in it acts as a flux at lower heat.

Formulating Clay Bodies

You can see that many considerations enter into the mixing of clay bodies. Special needs, like making slip for casting or mixing a clay body that can stand up to the temperature changes and stresses of cooking, present other problems.

How does the experienced potter formulate a clay body? Largely by changing ingredients in small batches of clay and testing them. In order to make records simpler and tests more accurate, it makes sense to change one ingredient at a time, testing its effect on wheel throwing, casting, sculpture, or whatever you wish. Then comes the firing. Since most people who make their own recipes for clay already know a good deal about what the ingredients do, the tests will probably be within the range of possibility; but until the clay goes through the fire, there is no way to visualize exactly what will happen. For example, two cups with only slightly different bodies, made at the same time, glazed with the same glaze, fired at the same temperature in the same part of the kiln can still be startling in their difference when lifted out (Color Plate 15, p. 210D).

Tests can be done on small tiles to try out a variety of bodies. Before mixing a large amount of clay either by hand, foot, mule, or electric power (Figure 7-6), you should mix a small amount of clay, changing the ingredients slightly for each test, noting carefully what materials each test contains and in what proportions so that you can compare them after firing. You may need to continue testing for a year or more to get exactly the clay body that suits your particular need.

Mixing Clay

Once the desired clay body is decided on, it must be mixed in larger quantities. Today you might mix your clay from bags of dry ingredients, or you might, like Dutch sculptor Helly Oestreicher (Figure 8-31), have a friend bring you the raw clay from a distant clay bed—in this case, from France, which has excellent stoneware clay. Often, local clay can be used just as it comes from the earth, with some temper added. But if there are too many large impurities in it, then a method has to be devised to screen them out. In a village in Greece, the clay is dried into lumps (Figure 1-22),

Figure 7-6 Early potters harnessed water power to ease the work of mixing clay and grinding glaze materials. Some potters, like Paul Philp, of Wales (Figure 10-3), are turning to water mills again for power. Cipriano Piccolpasso, *The Three Books of the Potter's Art,* 1556. *Courtesy, Victoria and Albert Museum, Crown Copyright.*

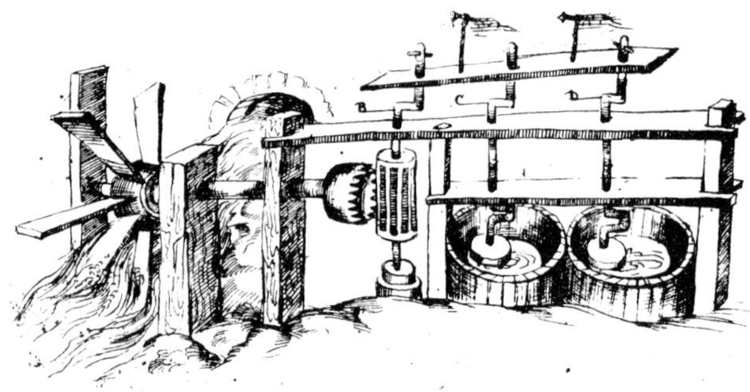

Figure 7-7 Potters in Thrapsanon, Greece, spread clay in the sun to dry to working consistency after digging, drying, pulverizing, and soaking it.

Figure 7-8 (*Left*) Maria Martinez, of San Ildefonso, New Mexico, in a photo taken around 1940, mixes the dry, pulverized clay with temper. **Figure 7-9** (*Right*) She moistens the clay and temper with enough water to make it workable, then kneads it to remove lumps and drive out the air. *Photos courtesy Collections in the Museum of New Mexico.*

pulverized, then soaked until it can be poured through a screen, after which it is spread out in the sun to dry to working consistency (Figure 7-7).

Maria Martinez, of San Ildefonso, New Mexico, mixed her pulverized dry clay and temper together, then added water to soften it and continued kneading by hand (Figures 7-8 and 7-9). Other traditional potters often knead the clay with their feet.

However, it is more likely that you will be using dry clay that comes in bags from a distributor, as does Stephen De Staebler, who uses large quantities of clay, mixing the dry fire clay, ball clay, and sand with water in a power mixer at his studio. If you use clay in large enough quantities or are in a school or cooperative workshop, the cost of such a machine might be economically justifiable. On the other hand, U.S. sculptor Louise McGinley (Figure 8-5) buys a ton of wet commercial sculpture mix in plastic bags jointly with a friend, getting it directly from the distributor, while Jill Crowley, of England, prepares her own clay, mixing crushed bricks in it to add texture (Figure 8-7).

The dry clay is best added to the water, just as kitchen flour is added to milk; otherwise it makes lumps that are hard to remove. Once the clay is mixed with enough water, it becomes a creamy slip that you can pour through meshes of varying sizes, depending on the particles you want to screen out.

After the slip is screened, it can be left to settle so that the clay falls to the bottom, leaving the water on top. Once the water is poured off, the sticky mass of clay can be spread out on flat plaster of paris areas, or **bats,** which soak up the water quickly.

But if you are mixing from dry ingredients that are already pulverized and you have no need to change the particle size, you can skip this part of the process and mix the dry ingredients together directly. Finely ground dry clays can be mixed together by hand or in a large container with paddles until the dry ingredients are blended. Then the clay can be added slowly to the water, much as one adds flour to milk when making bread. The clay can then be set aside, like bread, not to rise, but to age.

The clay can later be wedged to the right consistency (Figures 7-9 to 7-12). In a studio using large quantities of clay, a **pug mill** may be used to recycle scraps of clay, mixing them with water, blending them, and extruding the mixed clay ready for **wedging.**

Wedging

Wedging, to carry the kitchen parallel further, is like kneading bread. It gets rid of lumps and drives out any air that may be trapped in pockets or bubbles in the clay, but most important, it homogenizes the clay. Although the deairing process is important, air bubbles can be dealt with on the wheel or slab by puncturing them with a pin. But if you are throwing a pot and find a moist area on one side of the wall and a dried, hard lump on the other, there is no way you can throw it. Even if the clay body has been well mixed, it may not be homogeneous. Perhaps the bag it came in had been sitting on the manufacturer's shelf for a long time, or perhaps there is a small puncture in the plastic bag. Or the clay may have been left exposed to the air for a while, and although the interior is moist enough, the exterior may have dried out a little. So you have to wedge—and wedge a lot.

You can find out if there are air bubbles by cutting through the clay, but that does not tell you about the consistency. An easy way for a beginner to see how wedging blends the clay and to find out how long to wedge is to take two colors of clay and wedge them until they are completely blended. Like most of the pro-

Figure 7-10 (*Left*) Pushing and lifting the clay on a wedging table using the "ram's head" method. (*Right*) Pushing the clay against a canvas wedging surface gets rid of lumps, forces out trapped air, and makes the clay uniform in consistency.

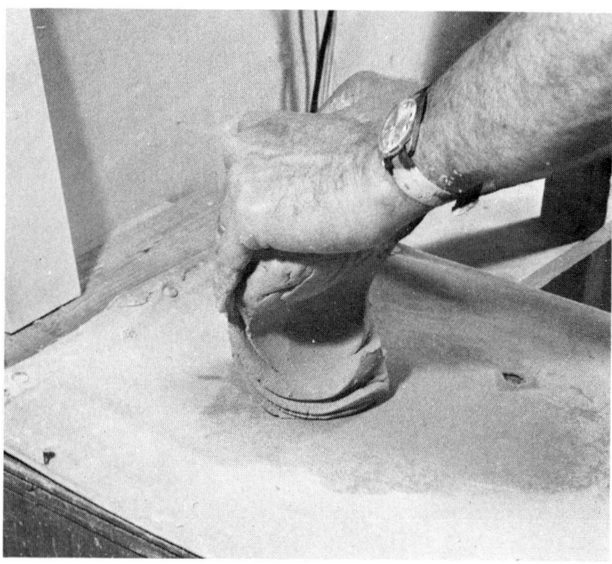

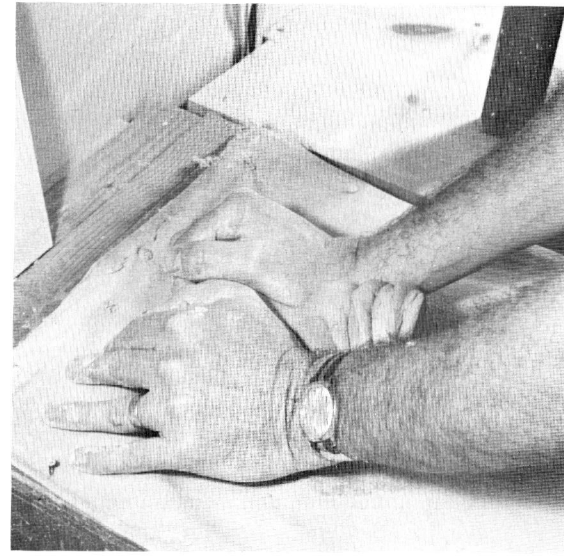

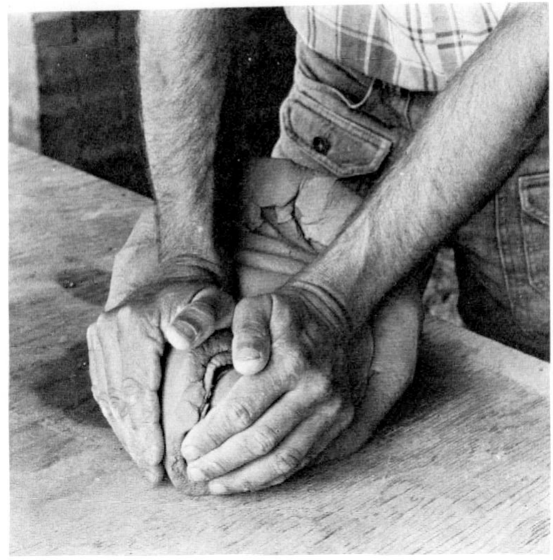

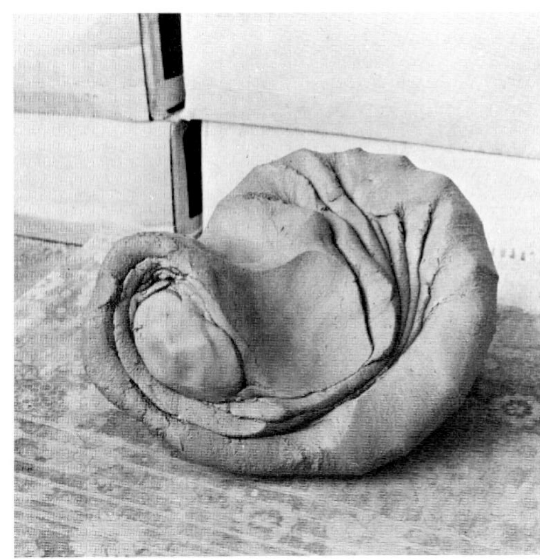

Figure 7-11 (*Left*) Wedging clay into a spiral with a slight twist of the hands opens up all parts of the clay ball, allowing any air bubbles to escape. Ron Judd, U.S.A. **Figure 7-12** (*Right*) Some potters feel that spiral wedging makes the clay easier to throw on the wheel because it lines up the clay particles in the direction the piece will be thrown.

cesses involved in working with clay, wedging does not have to be complex or mysterious. Any method is satisfactory as long as it accomplishes the purpose. Cutting the clay on a wire and slamming it down on a solid surface or wedging table to push it together is adequate for some hand-building methods, but since it separates rather than tightens the clay particles, it does not make the clay cohesive enough for wheel throwing.

Spiral and Ram's Head Wedging

You can use any method of wedging that works (Figure 7-9), but two frequently taught methods of wedging, the "ram's head" and spiral methods, are illustrated in Figures 7-10 to 7-12. Either method will prepare clay for throwing, although some potters say the spiral method does a better job because it lines up the particles of clay in one direction. Pushing methods like these not only de-air the clay and take out lumps, but they also tighten the clay up into a firm, compact ball ready for throwing.

Wedging should be done on as low a surface as is comfortable, so that you can use the weight of your body as well as your wrists and arms. Your back must be involved in the rolling action; otherwise you will tire yourself at the wedging board before you even sit down to throw.

The wedging board should be firm and well anchored, or else it will move too much. The surface can be plaster, which will soak up a lot of moisture from the clay, but some potters prefer canvas as a surface, as they feel there is a danger of picking up bits of plaster from the table and mixing them in the clay.

Whatever method you use, wedging serves another purpose. It brings you into contact with the clay you are going to use, and to some potters and sculptors, this is a very important part of the process. They feel that the

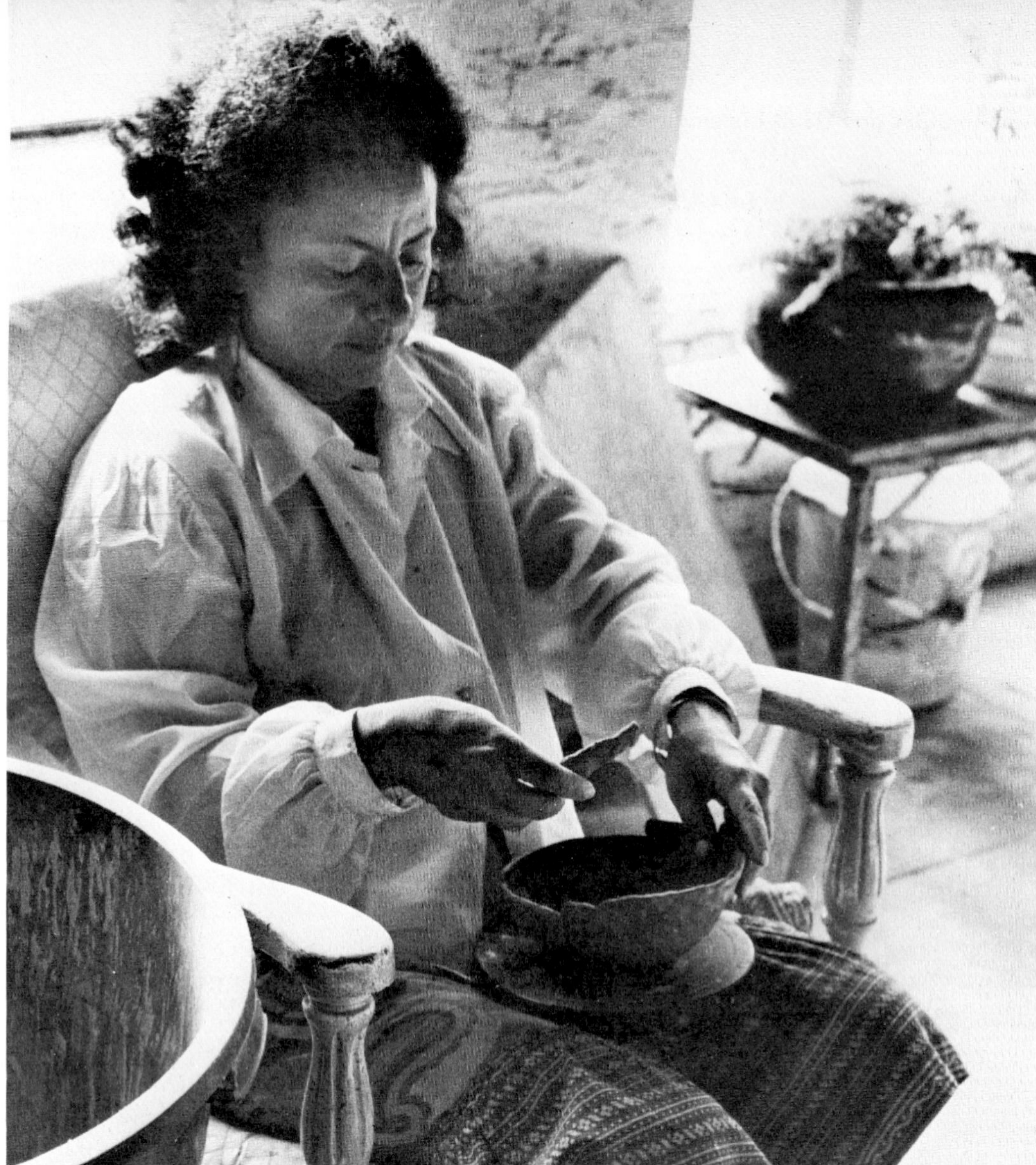

Figure 7-13 Magdalena Suarez, of the United States, sits in her studio, making a pot by pinching and adding pieces of clay. This method lets one make pots almost anywhere with little equipment. *Courtesy of the artist.*

time spent wedging the clay and the rhythmic action of the body give them a chance to think about how they are going to work the clay. They find that if they turn the wedging over to someone else, they miss it and cannot approach their creative work with as positive an attitude. Stephen De Staebler tried having help with wedging and laying out his slabs, but, he says, "I discovered that it was helping me in terms of time, but hindering me in terms of thinking."

Your Body and Clay

Before you start to pinch and shape a lump of clay, think about your hands. Look at the way these remarkable tools can do the simplest as well as the most delicate and complex tasks. Touch your thumb to your fingertips and think of the smallest thing you might be able to pick up with them. Press them together and see how much pressure you can exert between thumb and finger.

Since the change from hand-powered tools to tools driven by some impersonal form of harnessed energy, we humans have lost an awareness of our sense of touch. Machines have become an extension of our hands for even the simplest action. But the sensitivity is still there, the power is still there. They only need to be developed to make our clay experience become "claying, an on-going dialogue between man and earth."*

Open your fingers and look at your palm. What can you do with an open or cupped hand? With your hands flat, push down on a table with your upper body and feel the strength coming from your arms, your shoulders, your whole body. Hands are not only an extension of your arms, but of your entire being. Marvelous tools by themselves, they also need the physical and psychic direction that comes from you.

Sculptor Stephen De Staebler sees his whole body as a tool. Using it to press the clay into the forms he desires, he says,

> I have a feeling that what makes clay an especially satisfying material to work with is that it is so responsive to force. I can't think of any other sculptural medium that has such a vulnerability to force.

So now you will use some of that pressure and force to shape the clay.

* U.S. potter Lawrence Jordan (Figures 7-23 and 7-24).

Figure 7-14 "Salt Rose" was formed while Mary Caroline Richards was sitting on a beach. Pinched out of a 16-inch ball, it allows the finger strokes to show as part of its dynamic form. Salt glazed. *Courtesy of the artist.*

Hand-Building Methods

Hand-building methods include pinching, coiling, and slab building. Each method can be used alone on individual pots, or all three methods can be combined in making one pot.

Pinching

Pinching is a simple method of working with clay, but with it you can learn to make beautiful pots (Figure 7-14) or to build up large pieces of sculpture (Figure 8-14). It is a good way to begin to work because it is direct, allowing you to feel the way the clay responds. A pinched pot or a life-sized sculpture grows out of the concentration of your own being in that piece of clay. Pinching helps you feel the clay walls build up between your thumb and fingers. While pinching, you will discover a great deal about the clay: just how stiff it needs to be to hold its shape as you pinch it, how moist the edge needs to be to keep from cracking. But you may also find that you want to let the clay collapse, may want to let the edge crumble and crack, if that says something important about how you feel. Clay holds not only the imprint of your fingers and your hands, but also the imprint of your personality. Joy, anxiety, confidence, uncertainty, despair, love, conflict, or integration—whatever you are, whatever you feel, it is captured in the clay. (See Figures 7-13 to 7-22.)

Figure 7-15 Louise McGinley, of the United States, pats a ball into shape for pinching. Too-moist clay will collapse and too-dry clay will crack, so if you want to make a symmetrical, smooth pot, the consistency must be just right.

Figure 7-16 In opening the ball, your thumb should be held as straight as possible and the ball rotated. Leave enough clay at the base so that you can later shape it into the form you desire.

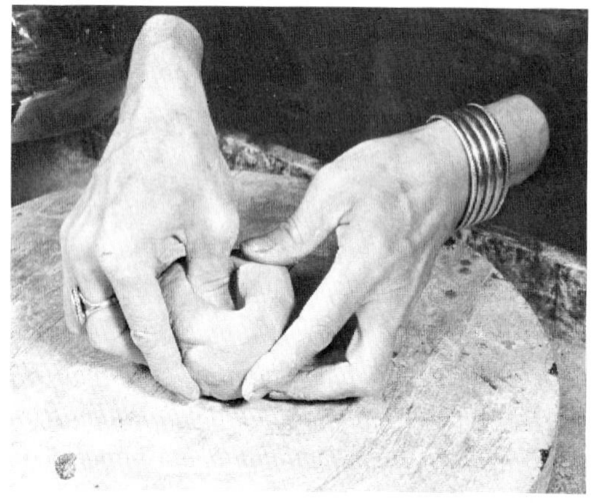

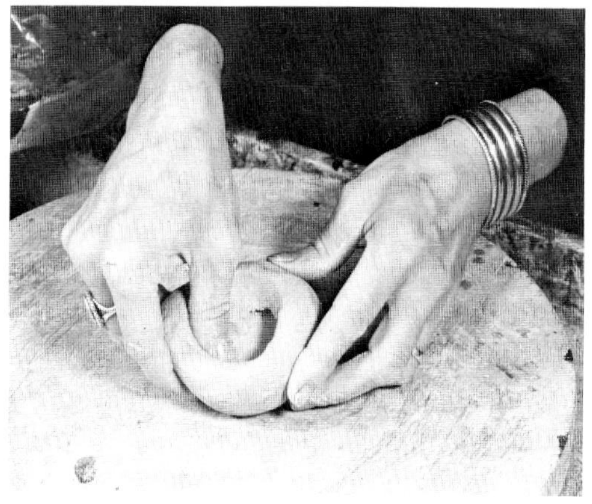

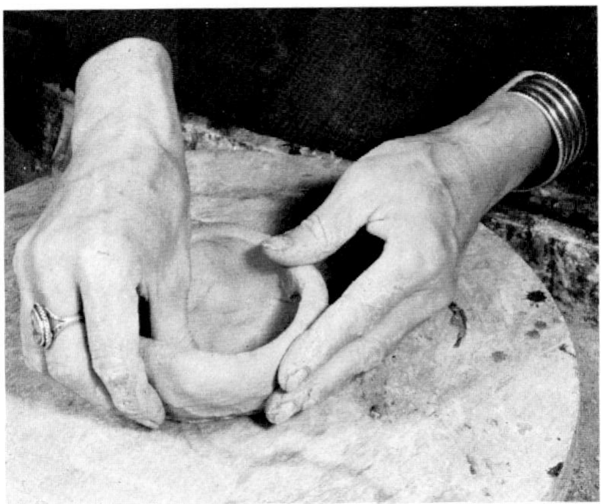

Figure 7-17 McGinley rests the clay on a flat surface as she rotates and pinches the pot.

Figure 7-18 You can feel the thickness of the walls between your thumb and fingers.

Figure 7-19 McGinley adds pieces of clay to a pinched base, then smooths and shapes the sides with a metal rib.

Figure 7-20 As she builds, she begins to form the shoulders and neck of the pot.

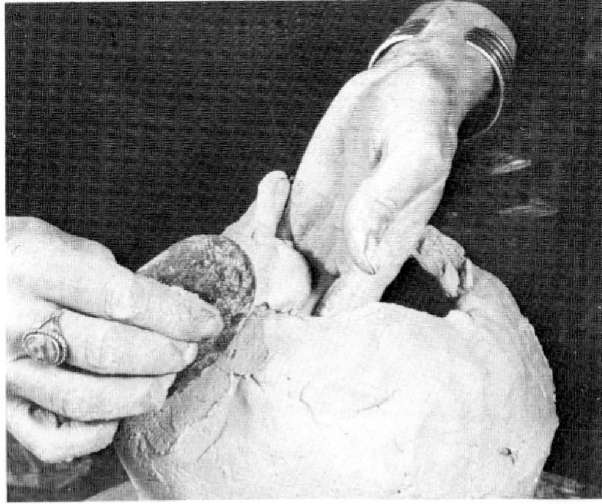

Figure 7-21 She starts to narrow in the neck of the pot, supporting the clay from the inside as she smooths it.

Figure 7-22 A finished hand-built pot becomes part of her sculptural group "Summit Conference" (Figure 8-14).

Figure 7-23 Lawrence Jordan begins his pots with a solid clay cylinder weighing about 50 pounds. The clay body is roughly one third fire clay, one third ball clay, and one third fine sand. He adds a band of porcelain, melding it to the stoneware. Moving around the pot, he pulls up the clay from inside, adding the gouged-out clay to the rim. As he pushes out from the inside, surface cracks appear on the exterior. *Photo by Louie La Fonde, 1978. Courtesy of the artist.*

Coiling

As we saw in Part One, coiling has been used to shape clay into useful and beautiful vessels for thousands of years. Combined with pinching, scraping, and paddling, it gives you a chance to develop a whole range of shapes, from huge, functional storage jars (Figure 2-3 and 2-4) to delicate, nonfunctional bowls enjoyed for their beauty alone (Color Plate 9, p. 146D). From Africa to China, to Scotland, to New Mexico, potters have used this method in a variety of ways (Figures 4-4, 3-2, 1-23, and 5-16).

Today, many potters still find it satisfying and pleasurable to coil-build pots. Before you start to build with coils, study the photographs of coiled pottery of the past presented in the first three chapters as well as in this section. Think about how you can use coiling methods, perhaps in combination with thrown forms and slabs, to shape clay into satisfying pots that reflect both the way they were built and your personal response to the material. Perhaps you see pots as columns (Figure 7-24) or as curving, full forms like those of Kenneth Beittel (Figures 7-28 and 7-31), who says of the potter:

> His forms innovate through subtle
> differences of individuality within
> the world's infinite and pervasive
> Roundness. . . . The movement of eye
> and finger, hand and arm, foot and leg,
> head and trunk, body and mind, love
> and dialogue, is curved.

Figure 7-24 (*Left*) Hand-built pots by Lawrence Jordan show the variety and subtlety of form possible with hand-building methods. Jordan wipes iron oxide on the bisqued form, sometimes adding splashes of cobalt or umber. He then wipes off most of the oxide, leaving it concentrated in the cracks. *Photo by Louie La Fonde. Courtesy of the artist.*

Preparing to Coil

Although wedging is not as important for coiling as it is for wheel throwing if your clay is well mixed, it is still a good idea to use well-wedged clay, making sure it has no lumps or air bubbles. You can use clay that comes mixed with a good deal of **grog**, or you can wedge some into the clay yourself (Figures 7-8 to 7-12).

You may choose to form the base by pressing lumps of clay into the bottom of an old broken pot (Figure 7-26) or plastic bowl or by making a special plaster base mold to your own desired shape. You can also make a flat base by pounding the clay into a slab on a board or table covered with cloth or plastic and cutting it to shape.

Whether you want to work in your lap (Figure 7-13), on a box as you kneel before your work (Figure 7-26), or using a more modern turntable to make coiling simpler (Figure 7-30), the process is basically the same. First, you will want to decide on the general shape before you begin building. Although some potters shape their coiled pots as they go along, others, like Maria Martinez, build a basic cylinder and later gently push out the walls to the desired curve (Figure 7-25).

Figure 7-25 Cross section shows coiling method used in pueblos of the Southwest. (1) Clay is pressed into a base mold. (2) Coils are added to inside of the walls. (3) Walls are built up into cylinder. The bottom can be smoothed easily while cylinder is open. (4) Pot is then shaped and smoothed and the walls thinned. The hand smoothing the outside exerts pressure while the inside hand presses outward.

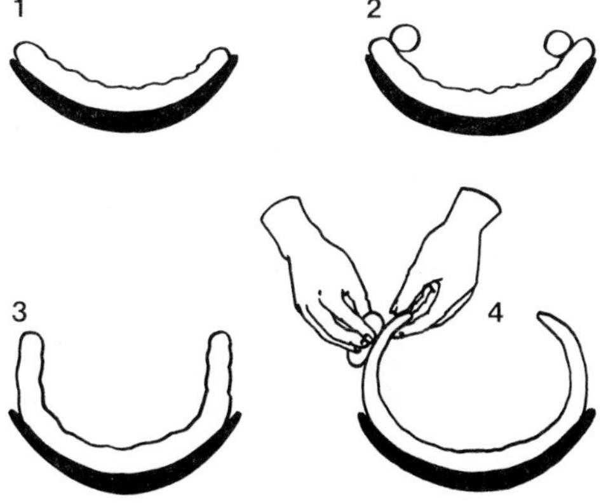

Instead of being formed from one cohesive lump of clay like a pot pinched from a ball, a coiled pot is made up of a lot of separate pieces joined together with seams. This means that when the pot dries, unless the seams are properly joined, cracks can appear as the coils shrink and pull away from each other. In addition to joining the seams carefully and melding the clay together as much as possible, you must be careful to dry the piece very slowly, keeping it wrapped in plastic or letting it sit in a damp closet for a few days.

Making the Coils

Once the base is formed, you will have to decide what thickness of coils you should make, depending upon how thick you want the walls to be. Making the coils requires no equipment but your hands and a flat surface. Squeeze a piece of clay into a "snake," supporting it so that it does not break, turning it as you go along. Some potters make their coils only by squeezing, while others prefer to roll them out on a damp surface with their hands. You will develop the method that works best for you. At first, you will probably make the coils as you go along, but as you become more adept and know how long and how thick you need them to be for a particular piece, you may want to make a batch ahead of time, keeping them under a damp paper or cloth while you build. How long the coils should be also depends on what you find most comfortable. Some people make them long enough for only one ring at a time, while others build a long coil up in a spiral.

As you add the coils to the base and build them up on each other, it is wise, at least until you become experienced, to place each coil

slightly inside the coil below (Figures 7-26 and 7-27). Otherwise, you may find that the pot tends to build outward too quickly, becoming floppy and eventually collapsing. You need patience to build a large pot, because you cannot build on the lower coils without first letting them stiffen enough to support the added clay. But the slow, easy pace of coiling is one of its joys; if you are impatient and want to see your pot take shape quickly, coiling is probably the wrong method for you.

Shaping a Coiled Pot

When your basic cylinder is made, you can begin to shape it, scraping the outside,

Figure 7-26 Working on a low surface, Maria Martinez presses clay into a base mold before starting to coil a pot, turning the base as she works. *Photo by Wyatt Davis. Courtesy, Collections in the Museum of New Mexico.*

Figure 7-27 She adds coils to build up the walls, attaching the first roll on the inside of the walls. Her curved scraping and thinning tools wait in extra base molds of various sizes. *Courtesy, Collections in the Museum of New Mexico.*

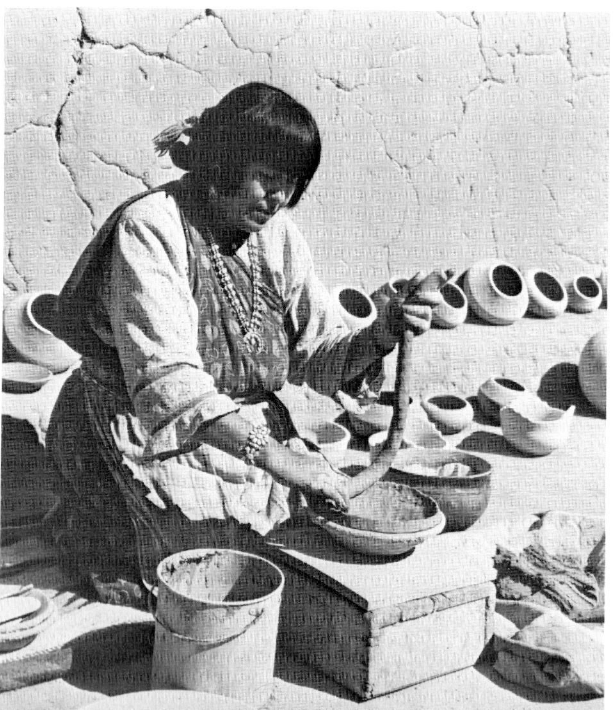

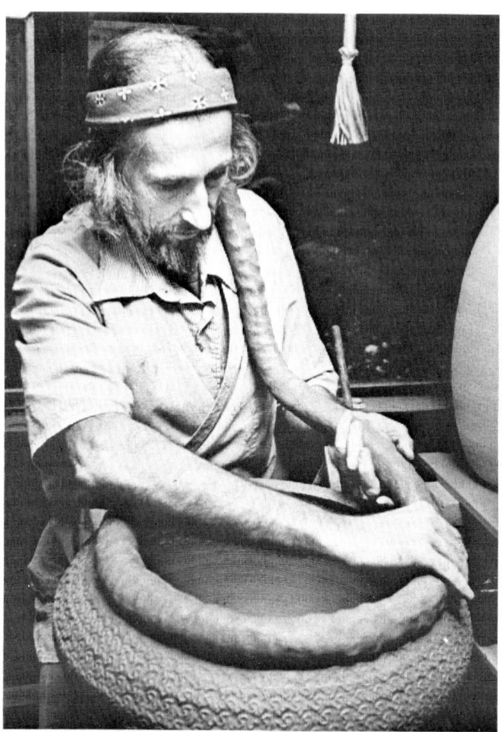

Figure 7-28 Kenneth B. Beittel, of the United States, adds a coil to a large pot made with a combination of techniques—throwing, coiling, and pinching. Supporting the coils on his shoulder, he starts to curve in the upper part of the pot. *Courtesy of the artist.*

Figure 7-29 (*Left*) Alev Siesbye, of Denmark, uses flattened coils, placing each new coil inside the already-formed walls. She carefully joins them, pressing the clay together to be sure that no cracks develop at the seams. **Figure 7-30** (*Right*) Siesbye carefully smooths the outside of the walls with a saw blade, turning the cylinder on a revolving turntable. *Photos by Mogens S. Koch, Copenhagen.*

Figure 7-31 (*Left*) "Gathering of the Ancients," thrown, coiled, pinched, and stamped pot by Kenneth Beittel. Base and neck are thrown, the rest of the piece is hand built. Stoneware with black stain, ash glaze, blue overspray. 19½ X 16½ in. (49.5 X 41.9 cm). *Photo by Joan Novosel-Beittel. Courtesy of the artist.*
Figure 7-32 (*Above*) Finished hand-built bowl has thinned and smoothed walls, glazed interior, and areas of glaze on the outside. Alev Siesbye, Denmark. *Photo by Mogens S. Koch.*

smoothing it as you press out gently from the inside, developing the curve of the walls. This also firms up the walls, tightening the clay particles that may have separated as you worked. Paddling the outside while you hold your hand or a smooth rock inside against the walls will also tighten the clay and alter the curve. Some people use paddles wrapped in fabric, or carved paddles, giving texture to the walls.

Decorating Your Coiled Pot

Once the pot is formed, while it is still damp but stiff enough to hold its shape, you can add texture and decoration to the surface. Potters throughout history have pressed their fingernails into the clay, drawn shells across the surface, marked it with sticks, pressed cords into it, or rolled corn cobs on it to make impressed designs. You can do any of these. Or you can stamp the surface with clay stamps that you have formed and fired or with objects you find around your house—bolts, screws, bottle caps, forks. What you do with the surface after the pot is formed depends on your creativity and on a careful consideration of the appropriateness of the texture or design to the final shape of the pot. (See Figures 7-24, 7-31, 7-32, 7-33, and 7-34.)

Figure 7-33 Coiled pot with thrown base and neck. Once-fired stoneware with iron, cobalt, and chrome oxides wedged into the clay. Red iron oxide is wiped into impressed areas on the outside. Sandra Blain, U.S.A. Height 22 in. (55.9 cm), diameter 20 in. (50.8 cm). *Photo by Roger Smith.*

Figure 7-34 Glazed jug decorated with lines that echo the coiling method used to form it. Raku, alkaline-tin glaze, cobalt inlay. Dan Arbied, England. *Courtesy, Alphabet and Image. Photo by C. Borlase.*

Making Slab Pots

Whether pressed or rolled, joined when leather hard or draped while damp over a hump mold, slabs of clay can be very responsive and enjoyable to work with if you know how to handle them. Slabs are not only useful for making sharp-edged, straight-sided pieces, but they can also be used to form rounded or flaring bowls, plates, or pots, and can be combined with pinched or thrown shapes. (See also the discussion on slabs in Chapter 8.)

You can make slabs in a variety of ways. Some people roll their slabs, others press them with their hands. Some flip and throw the clay on a table to flatten it, others cut slabs off blocks of wedged clay with wire. There are those who find a mechanical slab roller is the answer to their needs, while others say they would never use one.

The clay you use to make slabs should have some grog in it, for that opens the pores of the clay, reducing shrinkage and making it less likely to warp as it dries. Whatever method you use to form the slabs, wedge the clay first. Slabs that are to be formed in or over molds need to be worked while they are still quite damp, or else they will crack as you form them into a curve. But slabs that are built up need to be firm enough to stand upright, and rolling or pressing them on an absorbent surface like plaster or canvas will remove some of the moisture from the clay, making it possible to work with them sooner.

Rolling not only shapes a slab, it also tightens up the clay. If, instead of just rolling it to shape, you continue rolling and periodically tighten up the sides with pressure from a piece of wood, you will firm up the clay so that the slab will stand up even before it becomes leather hard. Rolling also brings trapped air to the surface so that you can puncture the bubbles. And rolling the slabs on a textured material—wrinkled plastic, rough weaves of cloth, crinkled damp newspaper—will transfer the texture to the slab. (See Figures 7-35 to 7-60.)

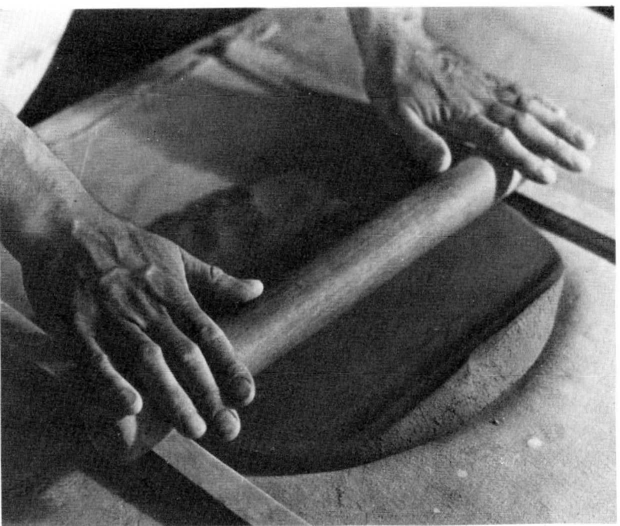

Figure 7-35 A kitchen rolling pin or a large dowel rolled along strips of wood will help you maintain an even thickness of slabs. Michael Woods, England. *Courtesy, Alphabet and Image.*

Figure 7-36 Pricking out air bubbles, compressing the edges with a board, then rolling for a long time, Ruenell Foy Temps, of the United States, prepares a slab for building.

Using Molds With Slabs

Slabs can be formed into round shapes by either draping them over hump molds or pressing them into convex molds. The mold must be made of a porous material so that the clay will not stick to it, or there must be plastic, damp cloth, or newspaper between the clay and the mold. When a convex mold is used, the clay, as it dries, shrinks away from the walls of the mold, making it easy to lift out. But if the clay is formed over a hump mold, you must watch as it stiffens, for if it is allowed to stay too long on the mold, it will crack as it shrinks.

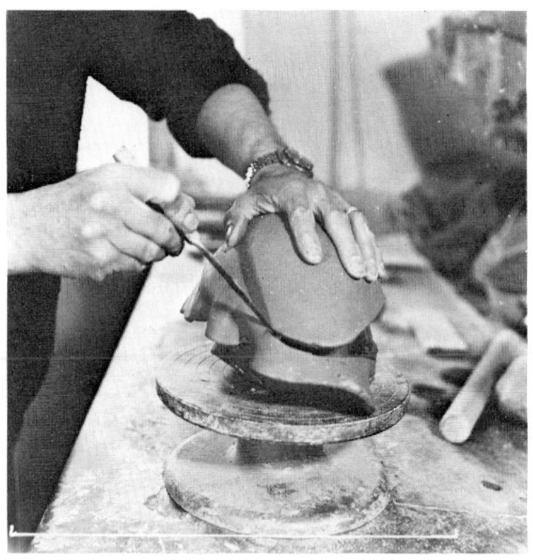

Figure 7-37 Slabs can be draped over hump molds to shape them. Use a rounded stone or the bottom of a bowl—whatever gives the shape you need. Michael Woods, England. *Courtesy, Alphabet and Image.*

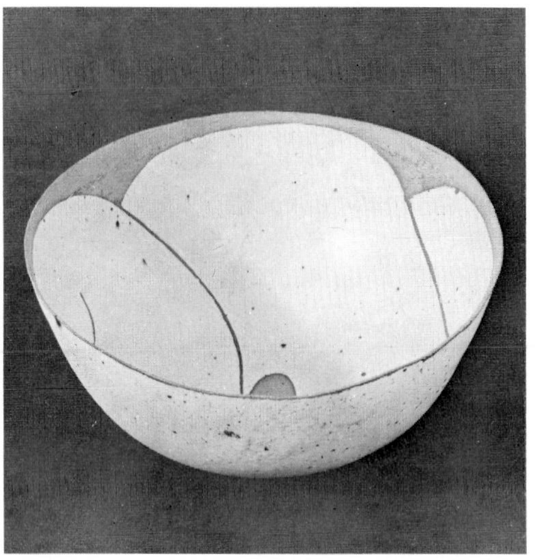

Figure 7-38 Thin-walled bowl formed by pressing a slab over a hump mold. Jane Reumert. *Photo by Mogens S. Koch.*

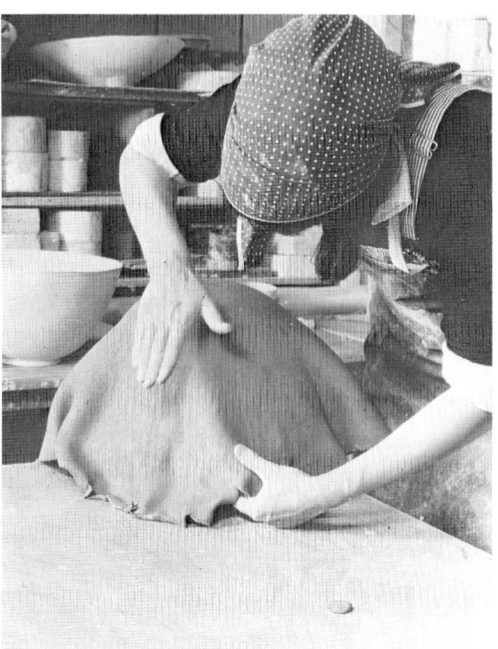

Figure 7-39 (*Left*) Jane Reumert, of Denmark, uses hump and press molds to make her pots. She lifts a thinly rolled slab on plastic to place it over the mold. **Figure 7-40** (*Right*) Patting and pressing, she forms the bowl. *Photos by Mogens S. Koch.*

Figure 7-41 (*Left*) A plastic bag full of vermiculite or styrofoam beads propped on a solid base makes an excellent hump mold for pots or sculpture. When the clay stiffens, the bag can be opened, the vermiculite or Styrofoam beads poured out, and the plastic pulled away from the clay. Sandra Blain, U.S.A. *Photo by Margaret Fernea.* **Figure 7-42** (*Right*) Stoneware pot formed over vermiculite bag mold, wheel-thrown spouts and base, fabric imprint. Sandra Blain. Height 12 in. (30.5 cm). *Courtesy of the artist.*

Figure 7-43 Slabs can also be shaped in any convex form. (*Left*) Sandra Blain using kitchen colander. *Photo by Madge Guffey.* (*Right*) Michael Woods using plaster mold. *Courtesy, Alphabet and Image.*

Figure 7-44 (*Left*) Gunhild Aberg, of Denmark, pounds slab into plaster mold with a smooth stone to form a multisided pot. *Photo by Mogens S. Koch, Copenhagen.* **Figure 7-45** (*Right*) Texturing the clay in a press mold with a notched wooden tool. Michael Woods, England. *Courtesy, Alphabet and Image.*

Figure 7-46 (*Left*) Saw blade pulled across the slab produces rough texture. Gerd Hjorth Petersen, Denmark. **Figure 7-47** (*Right*) Saw-textured slab is pounded into shape. Petersen sometimes uses inner tubes as press molds. *Photos by Mogens S. Koch.*

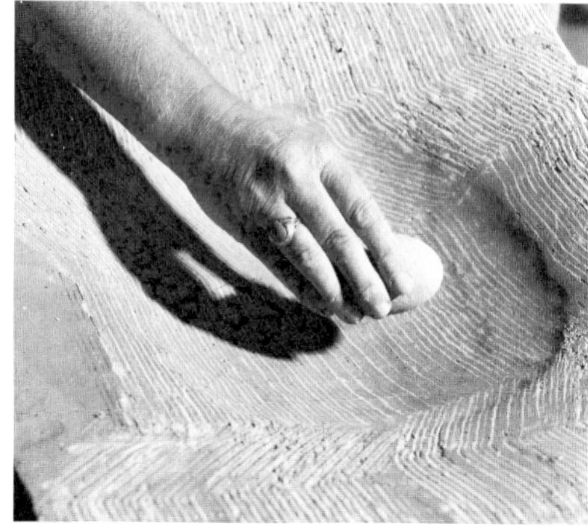

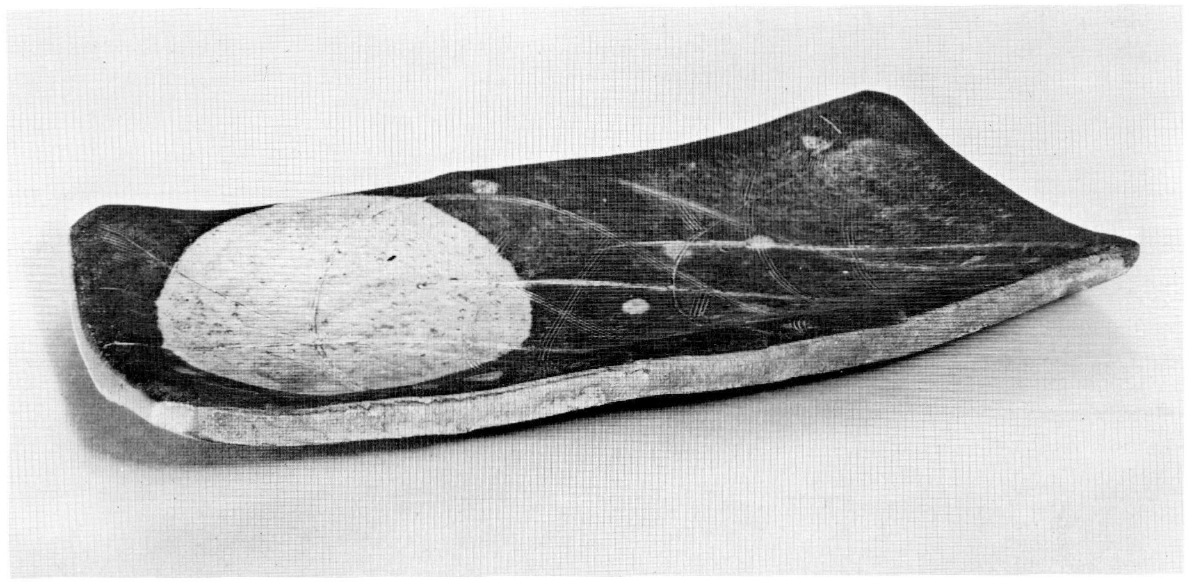

Figure 7-48 "Chop dish with moon and grasses" made from a slab. Bizen firing. Kitaoji Rosanjin, Japan (1883-1959). *Courtesy, Art Institute of Chicago.*

Figure 7-49 Decoration on slab plate emphasizes the linear pattern of its texture. Gerd Hjorth Petersen. *Photo by Mogens S. Koch.*

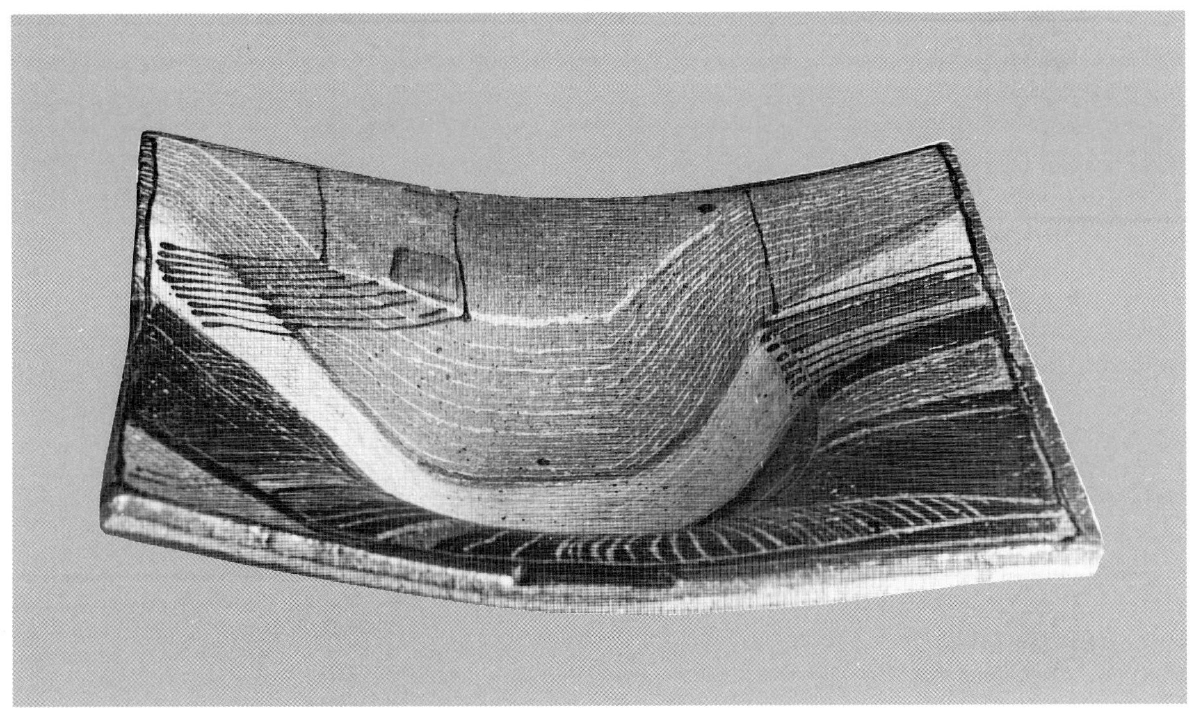

Building With Slabs

The sharp, precise edges made possible with slab building make it a useful method for creating forms that are hard to make in any other way with clay (Figure 8-27). You can also make use of the characteristic straight, sharp edges while contrasting them with rounded, draped forms. More slab constructions are illustrated in Chapter 8.

If you plan to build a form in which it is important to keep the edges sharp, it helps if you cut them precisely, using a ruler, paper pattern, or an inverted bowl for round shapes. Since the edges will probably lose some of their definition as you build, starting out with crisp edges makes it easier to keep them that way, scraping or paddling them as you go along.

Joining Slabs

Joints and seams can cause a lot of trouble during drying, so you must give them special attention. Unless the sections have been securely attached to each other, as the clay shrinks the seam will open. Slab builders have different ideas about the best way to join slabs. Some of them score both sides deeply, others

Figure 7-50 (*Left*) After impressing decorative grooves with edge of a board, Ruenell Foy Temps, of the United States, lifts a slab and begins to ease it carefully into a curve. **Figure 7-51** (*Right*) Carefully easing the slab into shape, she brings the edges together before scoring them. Temps uses a vinegar and water solution often, spraying it on the slab and on the seam edges before scoring them.

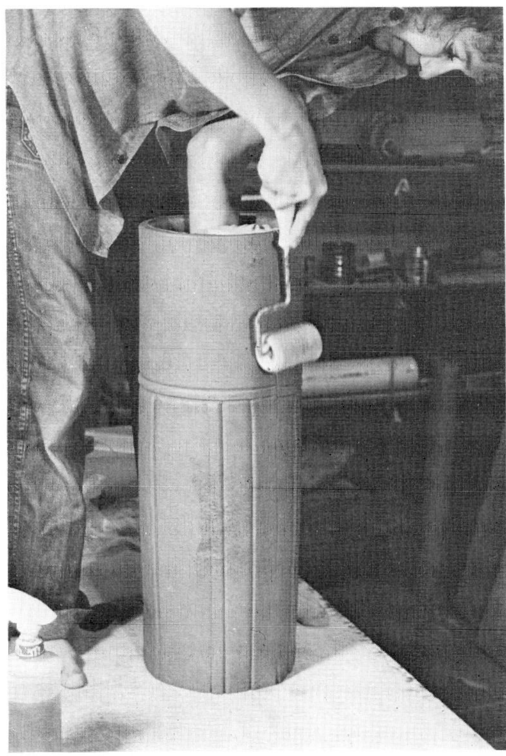

Figure 7-52 (*Left*) After pressing the seam together, she uses a paint roller to tighten it, pressing against a cardboard tube held inside. **Figure 7-53** (*Right*) Scraping the inside of the seam with a rib while supporting the clay with a cardboard tube covered with the sleeve of a sweatshirt, Temps works on the seam to make a tight join.

more lightly. Some paint a lot of slip on the edges of the slabs before pressing them together, others use only water to moisten the scored edges. Ruenell Foy Temps (Figures 7-50 to 7-55) finds that a mixture of vinegar and water sprayed on the scored edges of a well-aged and rolled slab makes slip unnecessary.

Sometimes a joint needs extra strength, in which case you can put a thin roll of clay along the seam and work it in as an added reinforcement. If you want to keep the seam very fresh, work from the inside to meld the clay edges, or accept the characteristics of your material and make the seams express it on both sides (Figure 7-60).

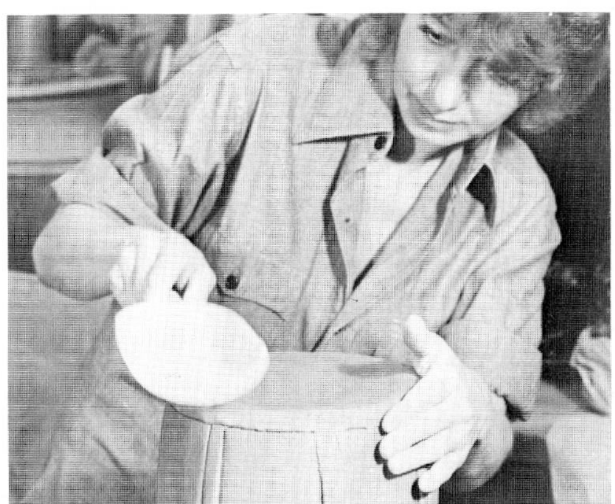

Figure 7-54 After attaching a strip of clay inside the base to strengthen it, she joins the base, paddling it well. Temps uses no slip, only vinegar and water.

Figure 7-55 Vase transferred to wheel for final shaping. The base is refined, lines are sharpened, and the neck is curved on the wheel. Temps says she works with slabs in order to make large pieces she could not throw.

Figure 7-56 Erik Gronborg, of the United States, builds pots from slabs, adding sculptural forms and figures. He says: "To me there is an important distinction between 'ceramics' and sculpture made of clay. Ceramics means that the work is part of the particular thousand-year-old tradition of making utilitarian objects. . . . It also means that the formal involvement is with decoration and pattern, and the relationship between the decoration and the form, and some involvement with the nature of utility." *Courtesy of the artist.*

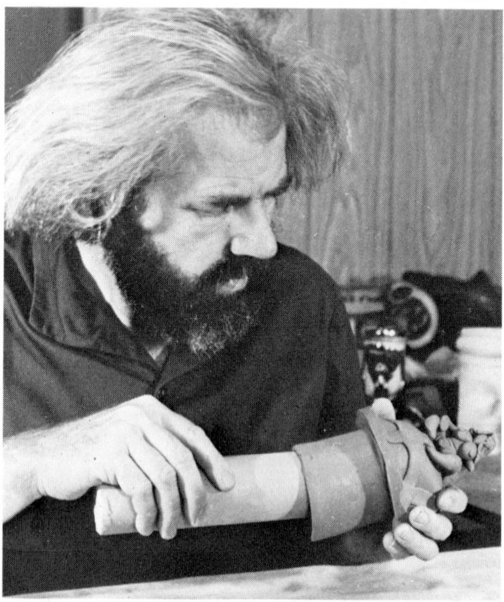

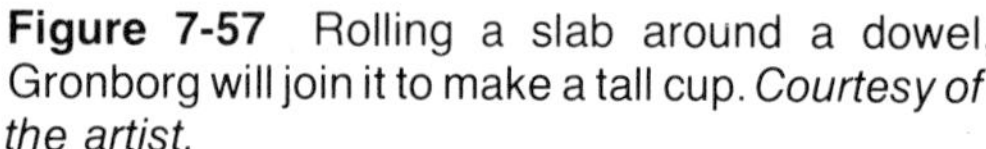

Figure 7-57 Rolling a slab around a dowel, Gronborg will join it to make a tall cup. *Courtesy of the artist.*

Figure 7-58 Erik Gronborg adds a foot to a slab bowl. *Courtesy of the artist.*

Figure 7-59 Greek sculptor-potter Maria Voyatzoglou's slab-formed *stelae* were inspired by ancient Greek grave monuments. She mixed sawdust, coal dust, or ash into the clay to produce localized reduction in her electric kiln. The glaze is either painted on the surface or sometimes even mixed into the clay. Once-fired stoneware. Tallest height 23½ in. (60 cm). *Courtesy of the artist.*

Figure 7-60 Large slab-built vessel by Stephen De Staebler, of the United States, made in four sections, joined at the legs. De Staebler keeps the seams as fresh as possible, leaving finger marks. He was delighted to find, on peeking into an ancient Etruscan sarcophagus, that the seams were joined in the same way and still show hand prints.

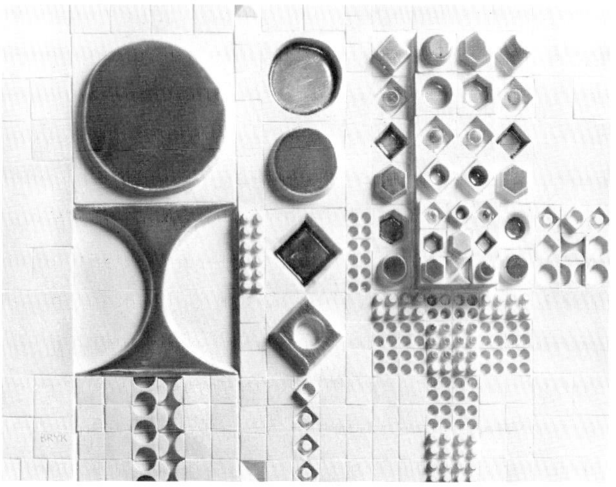

Figure 7-61 "Valpuri," porcelain wall plaque by Rut Bryk, of Finland. White, green, red, turquoise, and yellow glaze. 17 x 13 in. (43.3 x 33 cm). *Courtesy, Arabia, Finland, City of Helsinki Collection.*

As you can see, delicate slab pieces can be made in molds, and rounded forms can be shaped over hump molds (Figures 7-37 to 7-42). Slab forms can be thin and light or thick and heavy (Figures 7-41 and 7-60), and slabs are especially well suited to building up in modules to achieve large-scale installations (Figure 8-31).

Tiles

Tiles are a form of slab module and have been used on walls, on stoves, and in other applications throughout history (Figures 3-27, 6-14, 7-61, and 7-62). If you are making tiles, be careful how you dry them, for they are apt to warp. Unless you want to take advantage of warped edges in your composition, you should dry tiles very slowly in plastic or between pieces of gypsum sheet rock until they are leather hard, then dry them on a rack.

Figure 7-62 Theo Dobbleman, of the Netherlands, designs outdoor environments for schools. Tiles and bricks are coated with bright-colored, heavy-duty glazes developed at De Porceleyne Fles factory, in Delft, where Dobbleman is Director of the Experimental Studio. *Courtesy of the artist.*

Grooves cut on the back of the tiles will help keep them from warping and will provide a good bonding surface when they are cemented to the wall. Although we usually think of tiles as squares or rectangles or other regular shapes fitted together, they can also be cut along curved lines to emphasize a composition.

The Extruder

The extruder is a machine that forces the clay through a nozzle, shaping it into a hollow tube. Different types of nozzles will make the tubes angular or rounded, large or small. Smaller extruders produce solid ribbons, which can be applied as decoration. How extruded tubes are used can make all the difference—from using the machine merely as an aid in forming multiples to using it as a creative tool (Figures 7-63 and 8-46).

As you can see, there are certain things a slab can and cannot do; but if you respect these limitations and use slabs at the right consistency for the particular piece you want to make, you will find that they will respond to your creative needs. (See Figures 7-35 to 7-62.)

Figure 7-63 Porcelain box made from extruded tube. Sliced lengthwise, sprigged decorative features added, it is a humorous adaptation of classic Chinese materials—white porcelain body and celadon glaze. Larry Murphy, U.S.A. Height 4 in. (10.2 cm), length 7 in. (17.8 cm).

Chapter Eight

Creating Sculpture

Clay seems to have an almost magical effect on human imagination, releasing it, allowing our innate creativity to flow through our bodies into our hands. Children are closer to this source of creativity in us all, so that their response to clay is direct and uninhibited. Watch a child pick up a lump of clay. Immediately, an image begins to take shape in his hands—animal or human, tree or pot, house or car. And more often than not, the child will make up a story about the image, telling us what it is, what it is doing, how it feels. So, too, humans in many places and many periods have responded to this urge to make expressive or decorative sculpture in clay. Fragments of unfired clay sculpture dating from about 8000 to 7000 B.C. tell us that the desire to create clay images goes back thousands of years. In some ways the easiest of all sculptural materials to work, in other ways extremely difficult, clay has always intrigued and challenged sculptors everywhere.

Shaping Clay Expressively

The urgent human emotion caught in African clay, the grace of a Tang dancer, the play of light and shade on nonobjective forms—all these reflect the varied ways that sculptors have responded to the material (Figures 4-1, 3-13, and 8-26).

Perhaps much of the appeal of clay is the intimate and direct relationship the potter or sculptor develops with this malleable material. Unlike stone or metal, you can model clay with few tools or intermediate processes to separate you from your work—you can use just your hands to pinch, to coil or to make slabs into any size of sculpture. And many other clay-shaping methods require only a few simple aids. Clay is a material that responds willingly to your touch.

In your daily life you touch things constantly, but how often do you actually *feel*

Figure 8-1 (*Right*) "Standing Man with Brown Knee." Sculptor Stephen De Staebler, of the United States, uses the force and pressure of his whole body as a tool when forming his slab sculpture. "I am tempted to work even bigger than my body can relate to, but if I insisted on going much past the optimum scale that permits my body to be involved, I'd have to change my idea of form—that form that can be arrived at through forces imposed on the clay—or I'd have to develop mechanical means to get the forces. But the price is too great. It is the difference between being out on the field and being on the bench as a coach, and I'd rather be in the field." High-fire clay, 1977. Height 96 in. (2.44 m). *Photo by Susan Felter.*

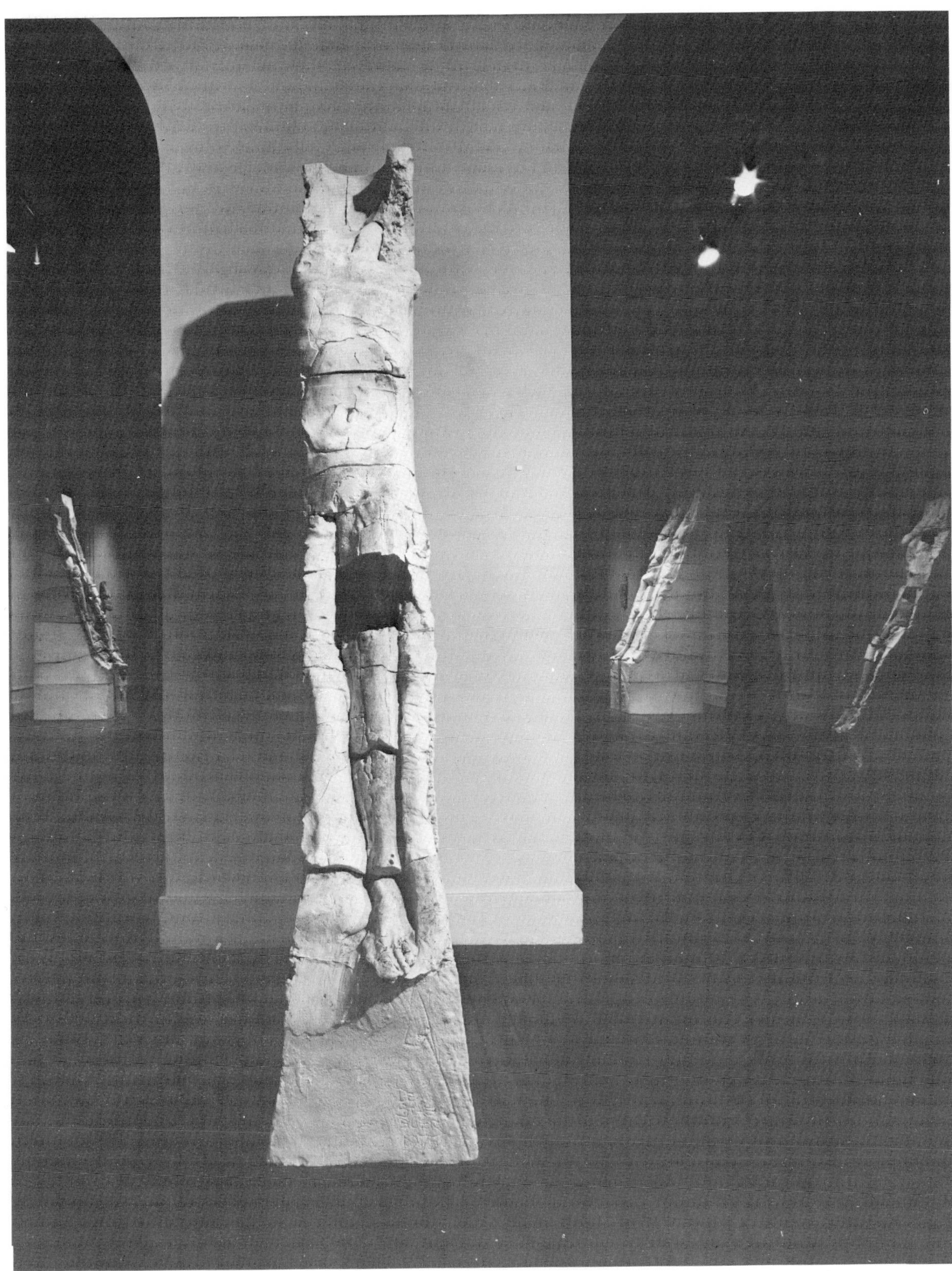

them? You were probably cautioned in childhood to keep "hands off." Now change that to "hands on," and at the same time develop a new awareness of your tactile sense. Your hands—holding the smooth, mechanical surface of a steering wheel, feeling the pitted texture of an orange skin, lifting a mass of wet laundry, holding a baby—touch and experience so many surfaces, masses, and forms in a day, yet how often do you remember what your fingertips feel? To bring vitality to your sculptured clay forms, enrich your tactile imagination and tactile memory by becoming newly aware of these sensations.

New Attitude Toward Clay

The attitude toward clay as a sculptural medium has undergone quite a change since the nineteenth century, when a serious sculptor used clay only to build models for metal sculpture or to make quick life sketches (Figure 8-29).

In the late 1950s and 1960s, the work of sculptors like Peter Voulkos, of the United States (Figure 8-16), brought a new energy, a new importance to clay, influencing many other potters and sculptors to question and experiment. Others explored low-fire clays and glazes, as well as china paints and lusters, using these time-tested techniques and materials in contemporary expressions. This new freedom produced an explosion of ceramic sculpture created with methods ranging from cast china and porcelain to extruded rods (Figures 8-36, 8-37, and 8-46). New attitudes and styles current in the art world— mixed media, pop, minimal, and conceptual—all have influenced contemporary ceramic sculpture. Clay is no longer associated only with pottery or preliminary clay models for metal sculpture. This interest in new methods and new surface techniques has, in the eyes of some people, obscured clay as a sculptural material in its own right, but others feel that the new attitudes have already given back to clay an importance it has lacked for centuries.

Working in Three Dimensions

Whatever method you use, whether you form expressive sculpture or useful pots, you will have to train yourself to think in three dimensions. Many of us tend to think of space as framed in two dimensions, perhaps because we are so used to looking at paintings, photos, or television screens. But when you make even the simplest piece of sculpture, you have to deal with forms in actual space, and therefore you must learn to expand your visual and tactile imagination. You may have the exasperating but challenging experience of working happily on one part of a sculpture, feeling quite pleased that you are expressing your idea so clearly, only to discover when you turn the sculpture or walk around it that from a new angle the forms and their relationships are confused and unresolved. Most people have to make a conscious effort at first to move continually and consider their work from all angles.

How you work out the forms within the sculpture and in relation to the space around it and how you relate them to the surface of the clay are considerations you must deal with in your own way. Working through a few exercises with very simple geometric forms will help you learn to compose masses in space. In addition to observing how tensions develop between flat and curved areas, notice what the *negative* space between the forms contributes to the expression of your idea or emotion. Whether you later work with realistic figures or abstract forms, an understanding of these relationships is essential. Study sculpture of the past and present and develop a critical eye. Ask yourself as you work whether a particular formal relationship "works" or not, and if not, how you could change it.

Sculptural Techniques

To begin with, you will have to learn to overcome some of the structural problems posed by the clay itself. Just getting it to stand up takes practice! Probably the easiest way to start making sculpture is to turn back to the methods used by early sculptors and children—the pinch, pull, push technique.

Pinching and Coiling

You can pinch very small sculptures solid. However, if you want to build anything larger than hand-sized, it is wise to build it hollow, making the walls all the same thickness. A thick section, of course, will not dry at the same rate as a thin one, so if walls are uneven, tensions are set up that can cause warping. The thicker the form, the more slowly it must be dried.

The way you dry a piece of sculpture is as important to the total process as forming it, for hours of work can be destroyed by careless drying. There is one trick you can use to get around this need to build clay hollow. You can slice a leather-hard, not-too-large piece down

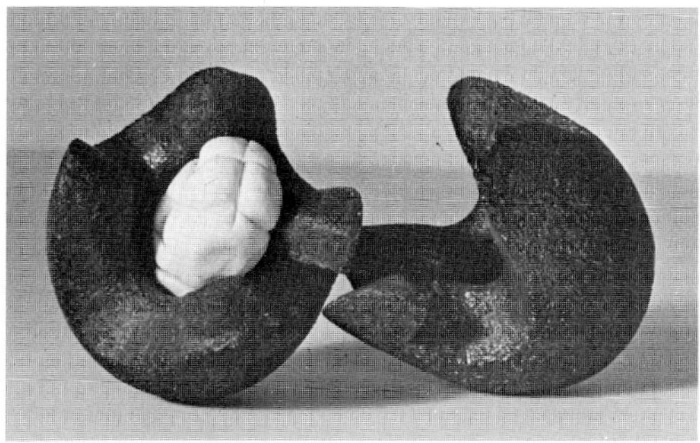

Figure 8-2 Tiny fertility figures, formed of solid porcelain by Eileen Lewenstein of England, rest in an interlocking egg-shaped container. Egg: stoneware, brushed with manganese oxide. Figures: unglazed porcelain. 1977. Length closed 3½ in. (8.9 cm).

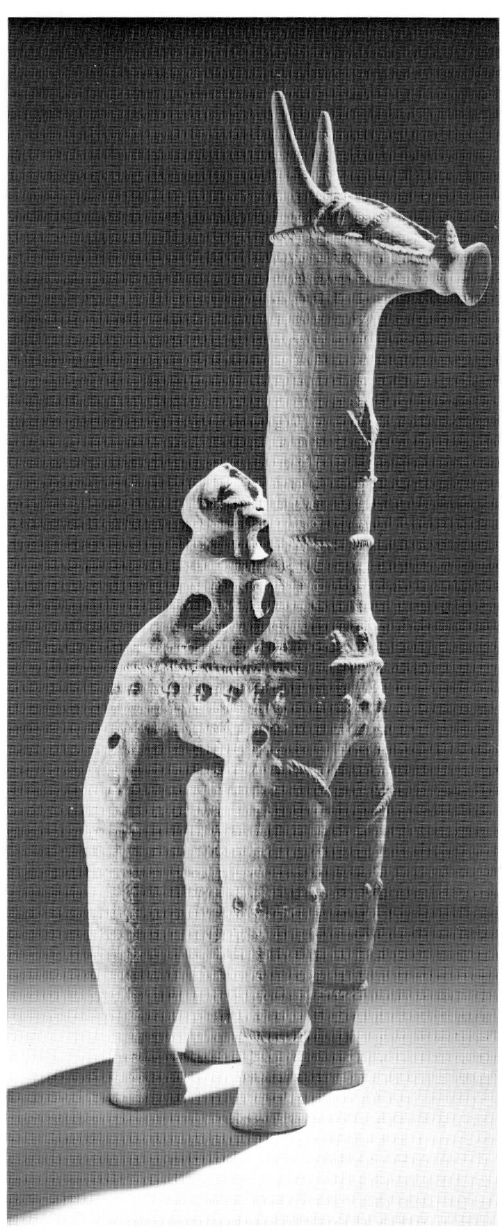

Figure 8-3 Large votive horses are formed by village potters in twentieth-century India as offerings made to gods or heroes to obtain health, children, or protection for their fields. Such horses, possibly echoing the fears of ancient invasions from the horse-riding tribes of inner Asia, continue an ancient tradition. Votive horse and rider, terra cotta, Bhil tribe, India, 20th century. Height about 3 ft (91.4 cm). *Courtesy, Philadelphia Museum of Art.*

Figure 8-4 Pinching the clay, building it into hollow forms, joining them as she builds, Louise McGinley, of the United States, forms a sculptural group. (*Left*) Bodies are built of pinched sections. (*Right*) Sections are joined while still soft, avoiding need for scoring or slip.

the middle, hollow it out, then rejoin the two halves with slip. This is really a make-do solution, however, and is most useful if you have made quick sketches in solid clay and later decide you want to preserve them by firing.

When using pinching, coiling, or slab methods to build up your sculpture hollow, you will have to deal with the plastic quality of clay and will learn to respect the material. The plasticity of clay can bring you joy, can challenge you, and can also drive you nearly wild with frustration. You will have to develop patience, waiting until the clay is ready to let you continue, letting the earlier parts dry out a little so that they stiffen enough to support additional clay.

By working with clay so directly, you will learn what kinds of forms you can or cannot build. You may find that you have to alter your original concept, or even abandon it. Sometimes, also, you can build the form you want, but will find it will not fire. Clay that lets you build strong, rugged slab constructions does not take easily to thin, extended forms. It is a material of the earth, seemingly reluctant to leave the ground and soar into flying shapes.

Figure 8-5 Roughly shaped with fingers, bodies begin to take shape. Using sculpture tool, McGinley adds detail to figures.

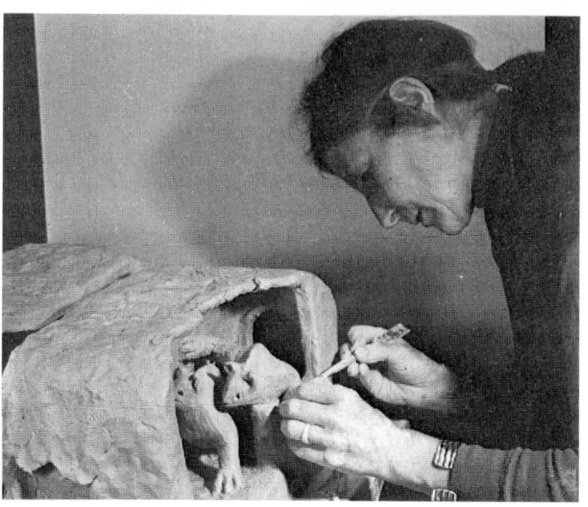

Figure 8-6 Group of small, pinched figures. Louise McGinley, low-fired figures. Heights 6 in. (15.2 cm).

Figure 8-7 "Tom," by Jill Crowley, of England, was coiled, pinched, and hand built of clay mixed with crushed red brick. Bisque-fired, painted with colored slips and underglazes before second firing. Oxidized stoneware, 1976. *Courtesy of the artist.*

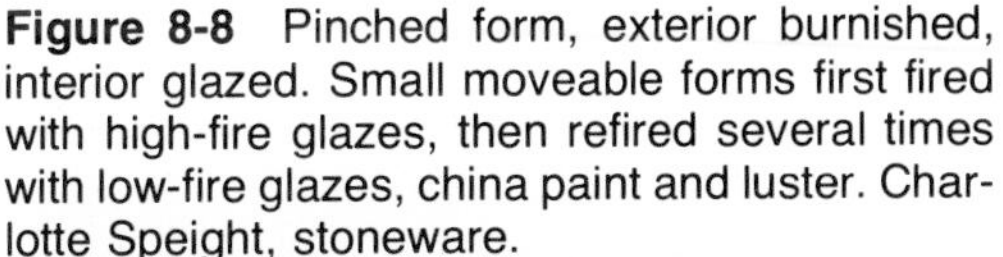

Figure 8-8 Pinched form, exterior burnished, interior glazed. Small moveable forms first fired with high-fire glazes, then refired several times with low-fire glazes, china paint and luster. Charlotte Speight, stoneware.

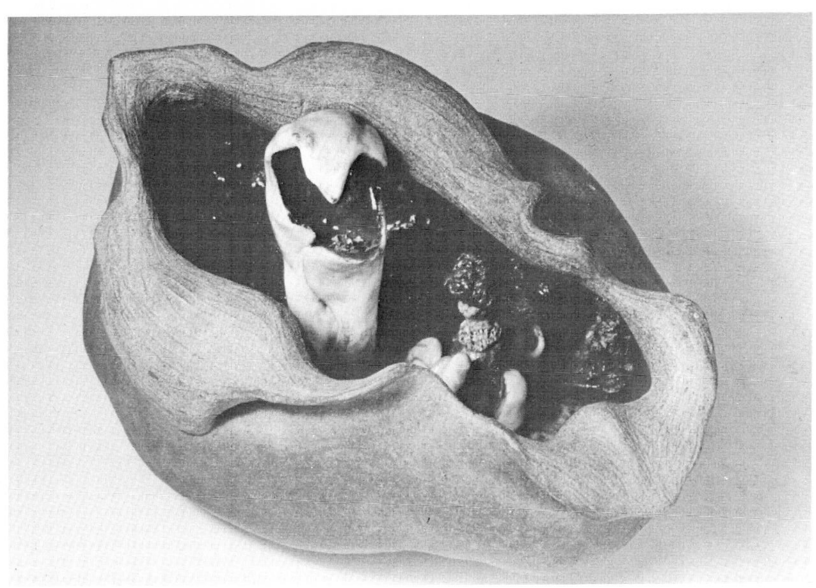

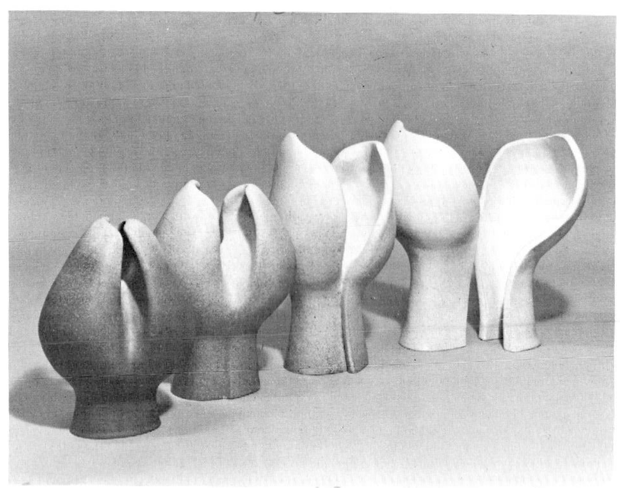

You may be discouraged at first, because clay has a will of its own that may at times fight with yours; but eventually you will come to terms with it, find out what it can do, what you can do, and what you can best express with it. Working simply, pinching the clay, adding more clay and melding it to the earlier sections, possibly paddling the walls to shape them, you will learn the limitations of the material. Then, if you want to try to go beyond those apparent limitations, you will know just what you are challenging. (See Figures 8-2 to 8-14.)

Figure 8-9 (*Above*) A group of glazed sculptures carry a simple organic form through a series of rhythmic variations. Magdalena Winiarska-Gotowska, Poland. 13 X 16⅞ in. (33 X 43 cm). *Courtesy, Concorso Internazionale della Ceramica d'Arte, Faenza, Italy. Photo by Borchi.*

Figure 8-10 Stoneware garden sculpture was fired in sections in a small electric kiln (23¼ X 23¼ X 29½ in., 60 X 60 X 75 cm), then moved to the grounds of the Provincial Government building in Utrecht, the Netherlands. The lines of the joints become part of the composition. Nicholas van Os, 1978. *Courtesy of the artist.*

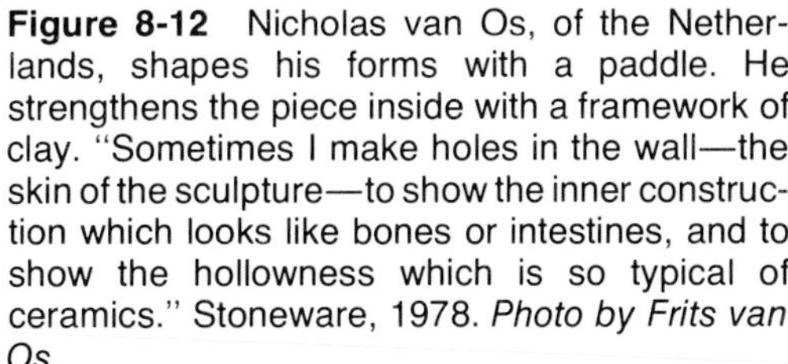

Figure 8-11 Detail from "Estadio Chile," a group of three hundred Chilean faces, expressing the sculptor's outrage and sympathy with the people of Chile after the military coup. Jeff Schlanger, U.S.A. 1975 to 1977. Clay fired in New York, 1977. *Photo by Jeffoto.*

Figure 8-12 Nicholas van Os, of the Netherlands, shapes his forms with a paddle. He strengthens the piece inside with a framework of clay. "Sometimes I make holes in the wall—the skin of the sculpture—to show the inner construction which looks like bones or intestines, and to show the hollowness which is so typical of ceramics." Stoneware, 1978. *Photo by Frits van Os.*

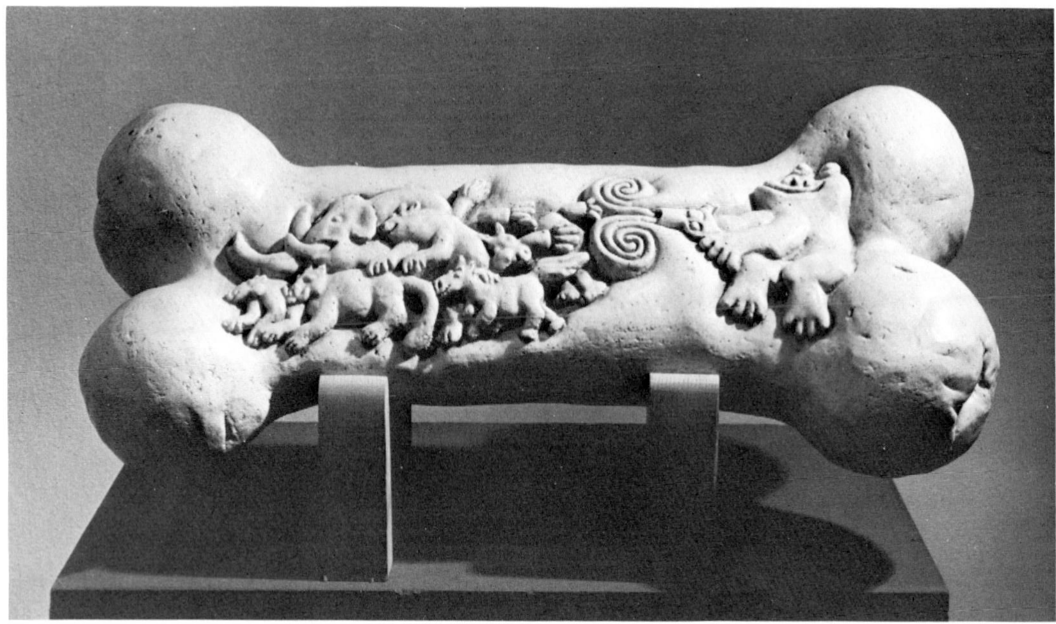

Figure 8-13 "The Early American Hunter." David Gilhooly's sculptures take us into a mythological and satirical "Frog World," entirely populated by frogs and their pet pigeons and toads. Low-fired, glazed. Length 24 in. (61 cm). *Courtesy, Hansen Fuller Gallery.*

Figure 8-14 (*Left*) "Summit Conference" by Louise McGinley was low-fired and painted with acrylic paint after firing. (*Right*) Small figures are study models for the final group. 1978.

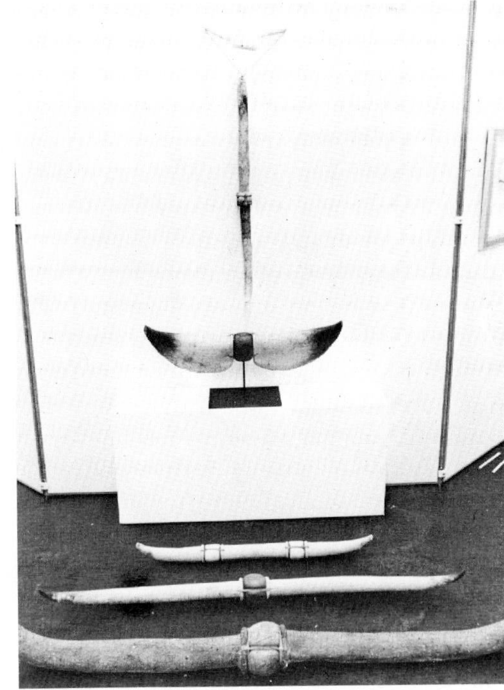

Figure 8-15 (*Left*) Paddling and scraping, Ernst Häusermann, of Switzerland, refines his stoneware forms, assembling them later into mixed-media constructions. (*Right*) Hardwood is carved to look soft, as if squeezed by the clay forms. Häusermann says, "I like to change materials, giving them another quality, not their natural quality." Local clays and minerals are paddled into surface. Stoneware, wood, and string. *Courtesy of the artist.*

Building Slabs

Slabs, made by hand or rolled out with a pin or a mechanical roller, are by their very nature strong and dense. They are also already pressed to a suitable thickness for walls of sculpture. The ways you can use them are limited only by your creativity and patience. For instance, you can drape them over any convex form if you put plastic, fabric, or paper between the clay and the form to keep them from sticking together. In this way you can shape slabs over rocks, over crumpled paper, or in fabric slung like a hammock. You can even drape them over parts of your body and lie in the sun until the clay stiffens. If it helps you develop your forms, use the energy of all your muscles to develop pressure to form the clay, even turning your whole body into a tool.

You can also press slabs into concave plaster molds, into plastic-lined pits dug in earth or sand, or into any concave form you can find; you can roll clay out into slabs, cut it into carefully engineered shapes using paper or cardboard patterns, and join the slabs; you can make slabs into meticulously finished hard-edged forms or into rough-textured, freely shaped constructions. The possibilities are almost endless.

Explore the qualities of clay slabs, observing how far they can be extended without collapsing, how complex compositions can be built up from several slabs, or how you can change a slab with pressure and force. (See Figures 8-15 to 8-28. Additional information about forming and joining slabs can be found in Chapter 7.)

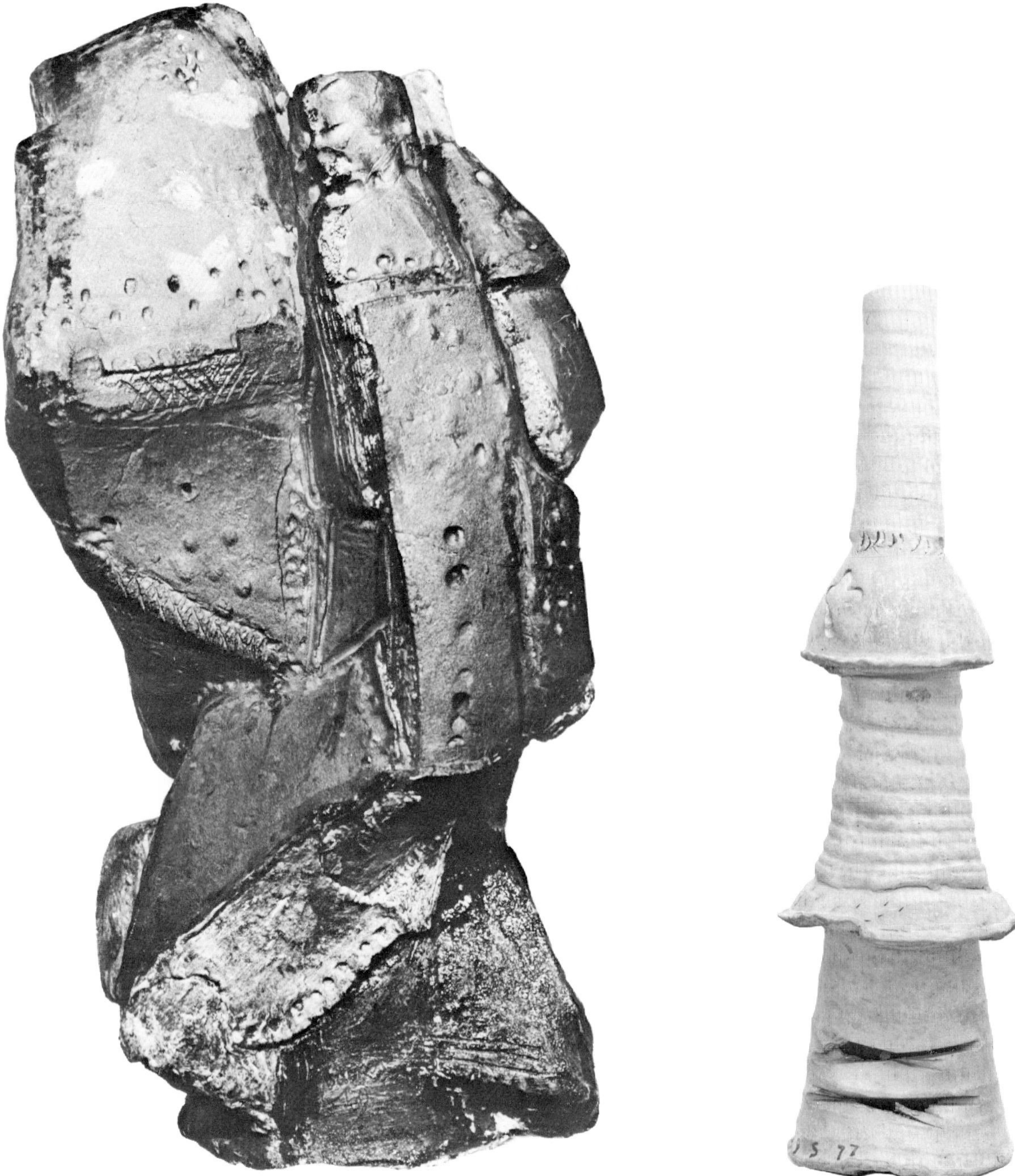

Figure 8-16 (*Left*) "Little Big Horn," by Peter Voulkos, of the United States, 1959. Stoneware. Iron, white, and cobalt slip, clear glaze. 60 X 40 X 40 in. (152.4 X 101.6 X 101.6 cm). *Courtesy, Collection of the Oakland Museum. Gift of the Art Guild of the Oakland Museum Association.* (*Right*) "CALV," by Peter Voulkos, 1977. Height 42 in. (106.7 cm). *Courtesy, Braunstein/Quay Gallery.* In the late 1940s and 1950s, Voulkos used clay as a serious sculptural material, moving back and forth between pottery and sculpture. His work revolutionized American attitudes toward clay, opening up new ways of working for both sculptors and potters.

Figure 8-17 Thrones are made from slabs draped over slab-built pedestals and formed by body pressure—by sitting in them. For these, De Staebler usually mixes two parts of fire clay to one part of ball clay and one-half part sand, a mixture that gives him a wide firing latitude.

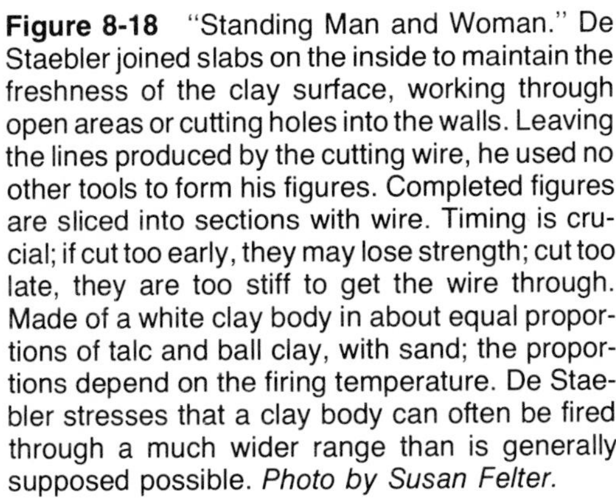

Figure 8-18 "Standing Man and Woman." De Staebler joined slabs on the inside to maintain the freshness of the clay surface, working through open areas or cutting holes into the walls. Leaving the lines produced by the cutting wire, he used no other tools to form his figures. Completed figures are sliced into sections with wire. Timing is crucial; if cut too early, they may lose strength; cut too late, they are too stiff to get the wire through. Made of a white clay body in about equal proportions of talc and ball clay, with sand; the proportions depend on the firing temperature. De Staebler stresses that a clay body can often be fired through a much wider range than is generally supposed possible. *Photo by Susan Felter.*

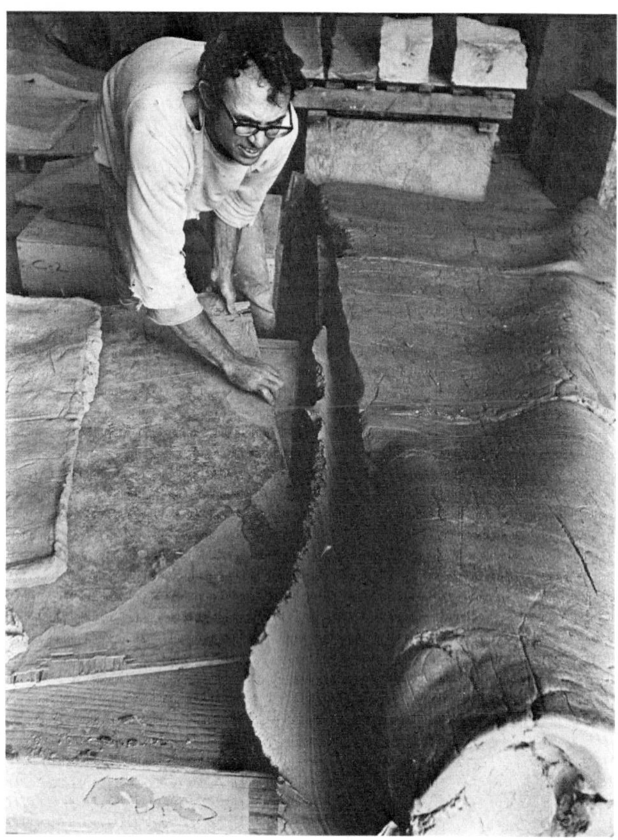

Figure 8-19 (*Left*) Stephen De Staebler presses and joins smaller slabs to form large, thick sheets from which he forms his figures, pots, or thrones. (*Right*) He uses whatever part of his body will best serve as a tool to achieve desired forms. *Photos by Susan Felter.*

Figure 8-20 "Repose of a Vase." Exploiting the plastic quality of the material, Carlo Zauli, of Italy, drapes and ruptures damp clay. Undulating contours suggest living organisms stirring beneath it. White-glazed stoneware. Length 17¾ in. (45 cm), width 12¼ in. (32 cm). *Photo by Antonio Masotti. Courtesy of the artist.*

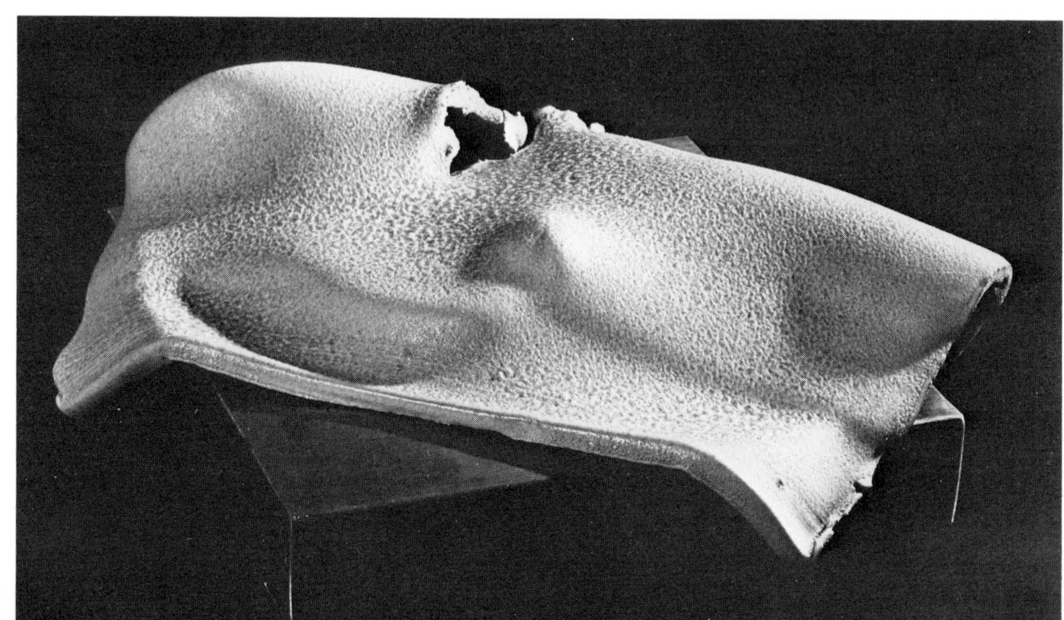

Figure 8-21 (*Above*) Contrasting sharp-edged slab forms with the rough texture of clay and pitted glaze, Carlo Zauli developed a series of visual and tactile relationships, carrying the viewer's eyes along a wall in a hotel in Bologna, Italy. Stoneware, "Zauli white" glaze. Height 59 in. (1.5 m), length 29½ ft (9 m). 1974. *Courtesy of the artist.* (*Below Left*) Zauli works on part of a large relief that will be fired in sections. Faenza, Italy, 1978.

Figure 8-22 Clay pressed into a mold to form a sculptural relief. The cross pieces strengthen it without adding unnecessary weight. Carlo Zauli, Italy.

Figure 8-23 Commenting on the urban environment where he used to deliver newspapers, Bryan Newman, of England, formed "Tenement Block" of pierced slabs. The empty windows are cut into a thick block of clay, which is then sliced, producing slabs with similar window spacing. Stoneware. Height 19 in. (48.3 cm). Ash glaze containing a good deal of china clay. 1280°C, reduction firing. *Courtesy, Alphabet and Image.*

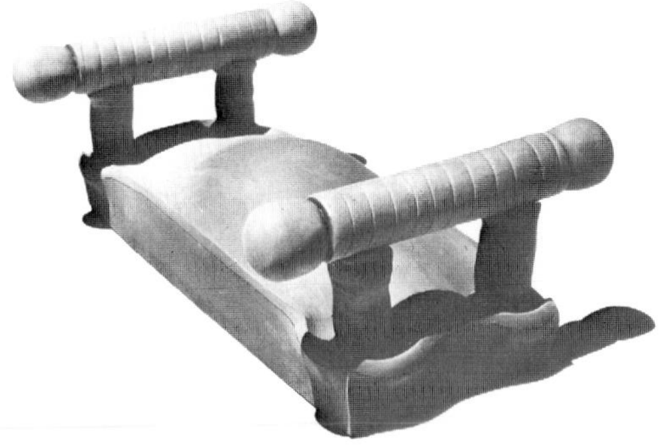

Figure 8-24 Slab form, of unglazed stoneware with iron stain. Hollow handles. Ruenell Foy Temps, U.S.A. Length 2½ ft (76.2 cm). *Courtesy of the artist.*

Figure 8-25 Slab sculpture of grogged stoneware is mounted on iron rod welded to base. Folded and textured slab, red-brown and white. Height 31½ in. (80 cm); width 15¾ in. (40 cm). Francesca Lindh. *Courtesy, Arabia Factory Experimental Studio, Finland.*

Figure 8-26 "Con-Can Tablet #12." For English sculptor Anthony Caro, accustomed to using clay as a basis for bronze sculptures, working in a ceramic studio turned out to be a new experience. Exploiting the qualities of the material, he lifted sheets of clay on canvas, folded them, or allowed them to fall as they would, developing a stock of elements from which he assembled his sculptures. The clay was a heavily grogged stoneware with a small percentage of chopped fiberglas, fired in both reduction and oxidation atmospheres. Gray, cream and tan. *Photos courtesy of Everson Museum of Art, Syracuse, N.Y. Photo by Robert Lorenz.*

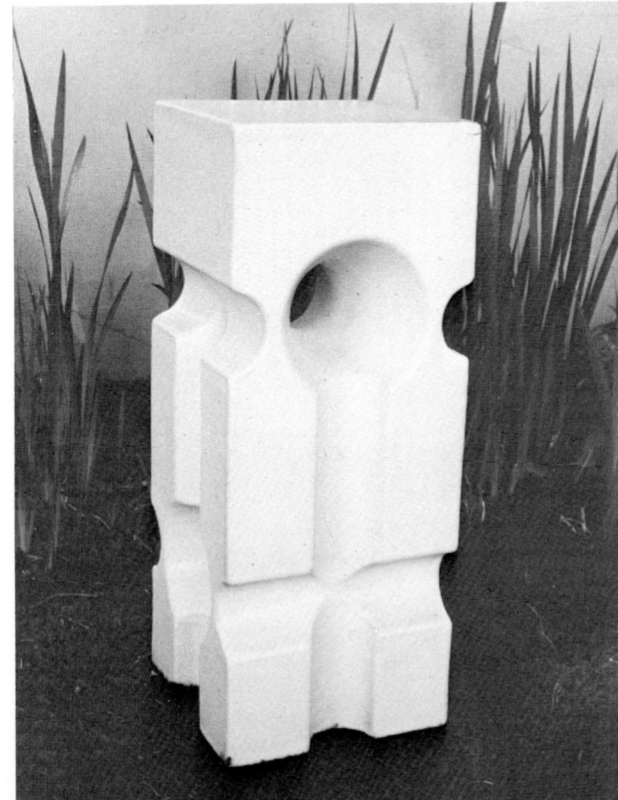

Figure 8-27 Ron Judd, of the United States, built his hard-edged forms in sections in a wooden cradle. This supported the slabs as the seams dried, simplifying the joining process and making it easier to achieve clean, sharp edges. White-glazed stoneware, 1978.

Figure 8-28 Stoneware chair formed of slabs, then glazed. Barbara Grygutis, U.S.A. Height 4 ft (121.9 cm), wing span 3 ft (91.4 cm). *Photo by Glenn Short.*

Figure 8-29 Clay has traditionally been used by sculptors to form the models for cast bronze sculpture. This relief was later cast in bronze, and attached to a concrete slab as a communal memorial. Huguette Etienne-Heldenstein, Luxembourg. Height 5 ft (1.5 m). *Courtesy of the artist.*

Armatures

It is difficult to build large, free-standing figures with clay because their thin legs do not provide enough support for the weight of the body. Although the early Greeks and the Etruscans used clay for large figures on their temples and graves, they usually attached the figures to a wall or tomb. Or if they made them free standing, they had to support and strengthen the legs in some way.

In the West since the Renaissance, however, until artists like Pablo Picasso, Georges Braque, or Piet Mondrian and later nonobjective painters released art from its preoccupation with realistic figures, clay was generally used by sculptors to build a model on an armature as a basis for cast-metal sculpture. The exceptions were usually portrait busts or wall reliefs like those of della Robbia (Figures 6-10 and 6-11).

An armature is a framework of wood, metal, or other stiff substance on which a sculptor builds up clay. With a well-planned armature, a sculptor can use clay in a way that defeats its tendency to collapse—creating shapes that seem liberated from the earth, such as a dancer in movement or a rearing horse. When the clay model is finished, a multisectioned mold is made from it and the final casting of bronze proceeds. The clay on an armature must always be kept damp, for it will shrink as it dries, and since the armature itself does not shrink, the dry, shrunken clay will crack and fall off the wood or metal framework. This type of armature cannot be used for clay sculpture that will be fired. It is possible, however, to support clay as you build with removable or burnable armatures.

Removable Supports

Even if you do not want to make free-standing figures, you may want to build clay into forms that are difficult to maintain upright until they stiffen without some sort of support. Probably the simplest removable support is rolled or crumpled newspaper, which can be tied with string to hold its shape. This will support your clay until it stiffens enough to hold itself, and if the clay shrinks a little while drying, the paper will compress enough to keep the clay from cracking. Then you can either pull the newspaper out or leave it in to burn out in the kiln.

You can make another type of removable armature with a plastic bag filled with Styrofoam beads, vermiculite, or even sand (Figure 7-41). It will give you a domed support, useful if you want to shape a head or other rounded form. But do not pack the bag too tightly—it should be able to give a little as the clay shrinks. Place the bag on a cardboard carton or a fired clay base, making sure that you can get at the opening of the bag easily, because as the clay stiffens, you will want to pour out the sand or vermiculite, leaving the clay to support itself.

Burnable Armatures

Cardboard boxes, tubes, or other containers can provide you with a variety of shapes and sizes from which to build up an armature that can burn out in the kiln. Since the clay must dry completely before it is fired, you will have to provide some sort of compressible material between the clay and the solid framework that allows the clay to shrink without cracking. Layers of newspaper, cellulose sponges, upholsterer's cotton batting, or polyester sleeping bag filler are some materials that provide such a buffer zone. They will burn out along with the cardboard in the kiln.

Some sculptors build up the clay on a Styrofoam armature, either liquifying the foam before firing by pouring solvent through a hole in the clay and letting it drain out, or burning it out in the firing. If you use this method, be very careful with the volatile, fume-producing solvent. And be sure to find out about toxic fumes that may be released during firing before you burn out any synthetic materials.

You can also shape armatures from fiberglas screening, but since the screening is not stiff enough to stand up by itself, you will have to devise a rather elaborate system of suspending the armature in some way as you build up the clay. If it is fired to at least 1222°F (661°C) the fiberglas armature will melt into the surrounding clay rather than burn out, becoming part of the sculpture.

Reinforcing Clay

The idea of reinforcing soft clay by building it on a framework or by adding fibers to the clay to strengthen it has been used in building for thousands of years. Many cultures have made huts out of mud smeared onto a framework of reeds or twigs, and builders in ancient Mesopotamia mixed clay with straw to strengthen sun-dried bricks. Straw, or any other organic fiber mixed into the clay body, will strengthen the clay as you build and as it dries, but will burn out in the kiln. You can also use loosely woven cotton or linen rags to reinforce walls or joints, making sure the fibers are well melded into the clay. Or you can build up a wall to the thickness you want by dipping and redipping cloth or other fiber sheets in clay slip.

Since these fibrous materials burn out during the firing, leaving small spaces, the walls are somewhat weakened. One way to avoid this weakness is to reinforce the clay with fiberglas in a method devised by Daniel Rhodes.* If the clay body is fired at 1222°F (661°C) or more, the fiberglas will actually melt into the clay instead of leaving open pores. You can add the fiberglas in the form of chopped fibers (Figure 8-26) or as fiberglas woven into cloth in an open weave. Adding fiberglas in a percentage of about one-half to

* Daniel Rhodes, *Clay and Glazes for the Potter* (Radnor, Pa.: Chilton Book Company, 1973).

one percent makes the drying process much less tricky, and warping and cracking can be avoided. Take care when working with fiberglas materials, since they can cause skin irritation, and floating fibers may damage your eyes unless you wear protective goggles.

Modules

Although you may not want to work at a life-sized scale, you may nevertheless want to make sculpture that will not fit in your kiln. But even with a small kiln you are not limited to

Figure 8-30 To divide the public entrance to a convent library from the door to the adjoining convent, Eileen Lewenstein, of England, used module units to build a large openwork screen, which could be easily fired in her kiln. Stoneware. Height 20 ft (6.1 m). *Courtesy of the artist.*

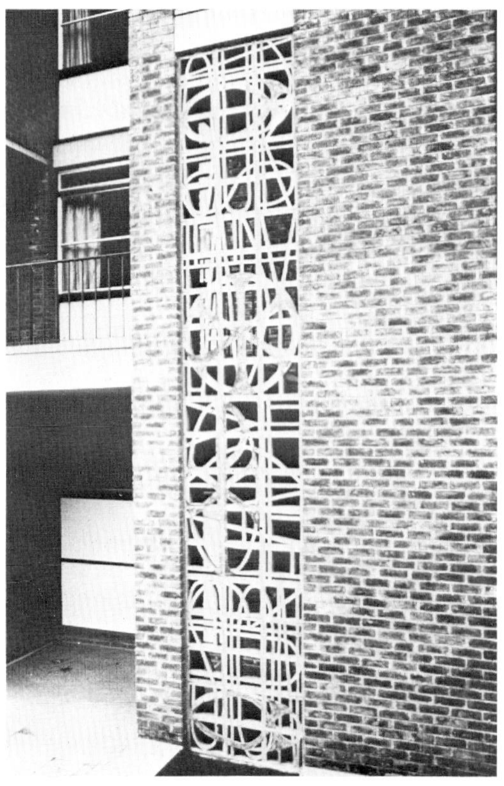

Figure 8-31 Stairwell sculpture by Helly Oestreicher, of the Netherlands. Commissioned for a government building, it was built from small slabs in modular sections. After pressing chunks of clay onto a plaster surface, she sliced the grogged clay with a wire, producing a rough-textured module. These eighteen-inch sections were fired in a small electric kiln, then later assembled on a structure of metal rods. Stoneware, 20 percent grog. Brown glaze with transparent green copper glaze. Installed in the Provinciehuis, Utrecht. Height 118 in. (3 m). *Courtesy of the artist.*

making only small sculpture: you need only figure out how to break a large piece down into modules.

Tiles, of course, are a classic type of ceramic module (Figure 3-27); and with careful planning, you can also engineer quite large three-dimensional sculptures in such a way that they can be made in smaller sections (Figure 8-12). This is not only an advantage in firing, but it also allows you to transport your sculpture more easily. With some ingenuity you can work out a variety of methods to hold the sections together and to allow them to be disassembled. In this way, both Helly Oestreicher and Eileen Lewenstein developed modular sculpture techniques to carry out large architectural commissions, firing the parts in quite small kilns (Figures 8-30 and 8-31). Depending on the installation, a modular piece can be left demountable or cemented together (Figure 8-12).

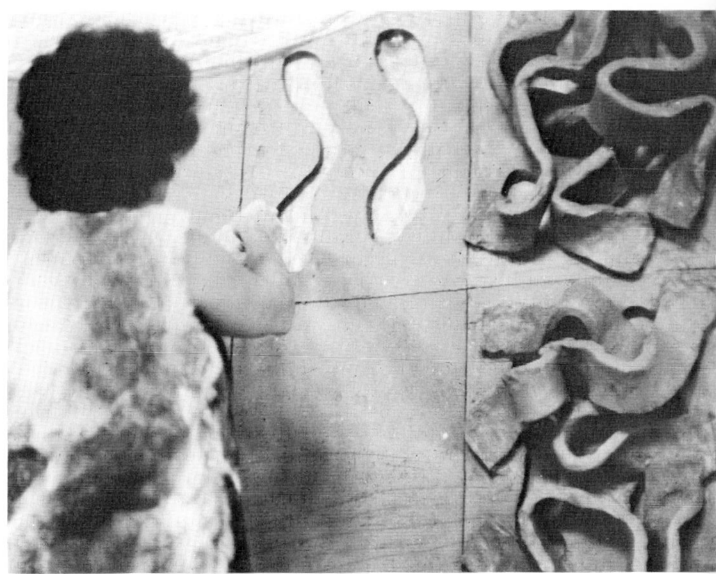

Figure 8-32 Magdalena Suarez, of the United States, works on a composition of modules for a stoneware wall relief. Height 8 ft (2.4 m), length 9 ft (2.7 m). *Courtesy of the artist.*

Figure 8-33 Brightly glazed wall relief adds excitement and color to a dull school wall and door. Maggi Giles, Netherlands, formed sections from industrial clay, fired at 1868°F (1020°C). She mixes industrial glazes to get her own range of yellows, reds, and oranges. Andreas School, Amsterdam, 1976. Length 197 in. (5 m). *Photo by Mieke H. Hille.*

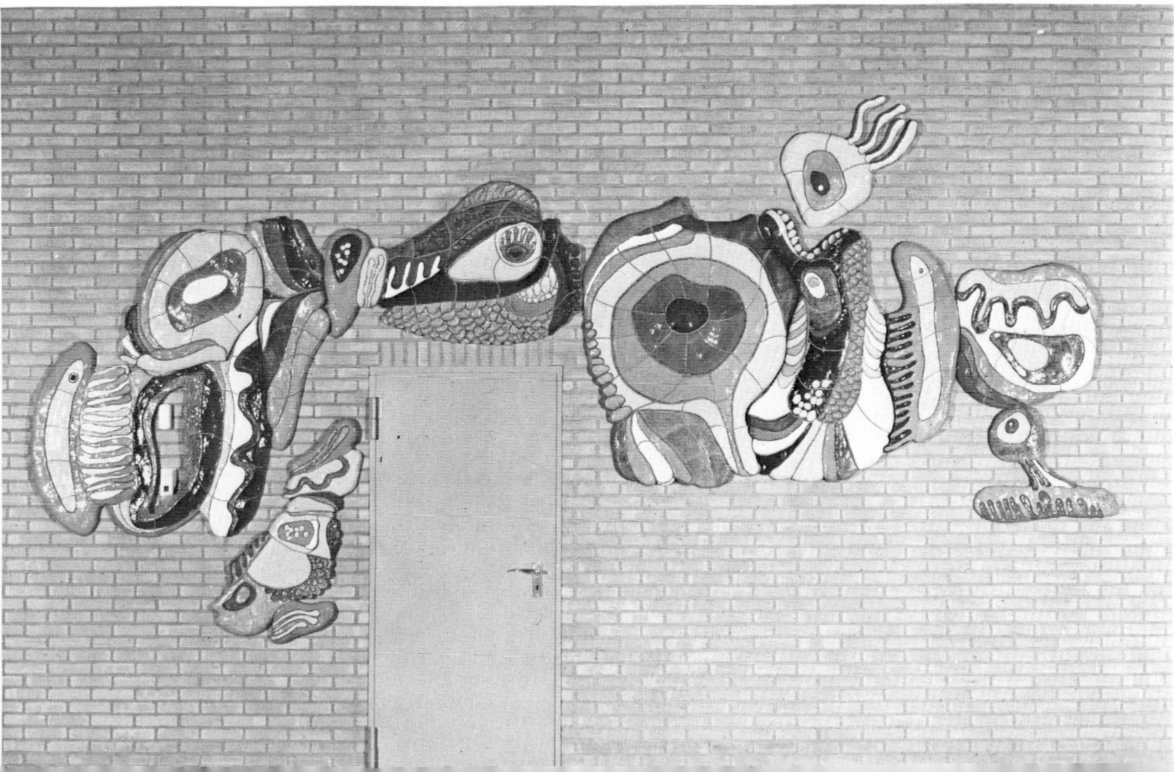

Figure 8-34 (*Left*) Sculptor-potter Ken Williams, of the United States, carved 900 bricks, numbering them for placement on the building. (*Right*) Williams working on one of six sculptured panels for a school administration building. Unfired bricks and clay are from a local brickyard, which also fires his work. *Courtesy, Summit Pressed Brick and Tile Co., Pueblo, Colorado. Photos by John Suhay.*

Figure 8-35 "Springwater Fountain," in hotel lounge in Copenhagen, made up of brightly glazed, thrown forms from which water drips in glistening sheets onto the tiled floor. Fin Lynggaard, Denmark. *Photo by Mogens S. Koch.*

Figure 8-36 (*Above*) Working for a year at the Wedgwood Factory, Glenys Barton, of England, made use of its technical facilities and personnel to produce a series of precise, polished sculptures in cast bone china. (*Below Right*) White and translucent, the polished clay body (a mixture of kaolin, china stone, and bone ash) seems particularly well adapted to Barton's isolated figures. Unglazed, polished bone china, made at Wedgwood, limited edition of four, 1977. Height 14⅛ in. (35.7 cm). *Courtesy, Crafts Advisory Committee, London.*

Slip Casting

Just as you can make multiple pots by pouring slip into molds (Figures 9-70 to 9-74), you can also cast sculpture with slip. Plaster is the traditional material for molds because it is porous, quickly absorbing the water from the liquified clay. Plaster also has the remarkable quality of being liquid one minute and solid the next, so *never* pour plaster down a sink drain and don't pour water into the plaster bin!

If you are going to make your first mold, sculpt your clay into a very simple form with no undercutting and keep this model damp. Prepare plaster by adding the dry powder to water

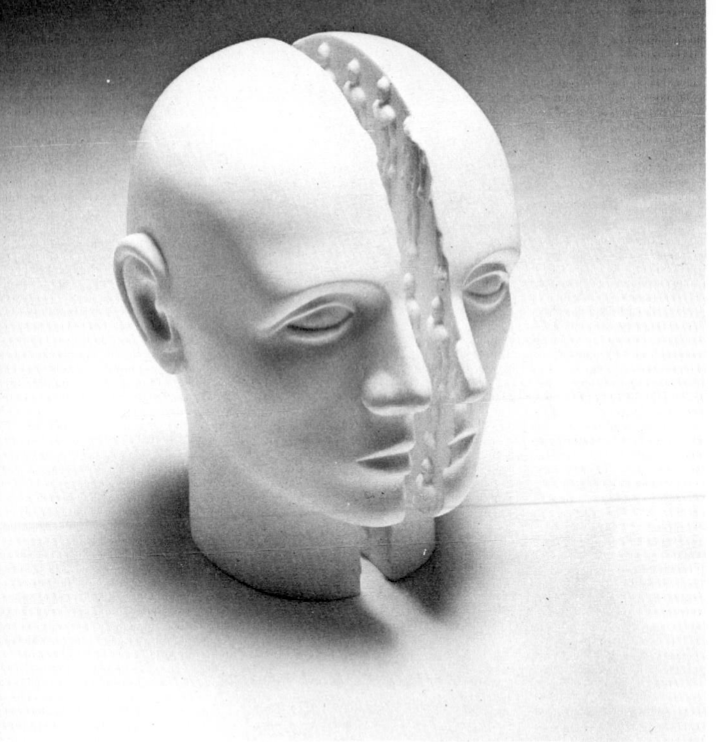

Figure 8-37 Barton sees her work as an optimistic expression of faith in human reason and intelligence. Cast, unglazed, polished bone china head with relief figures. Glenys Barton, at Wedgwood. *Photos courtesy of Crafts Advisory Committee, London.*

in a flexible plastic bowl. Keep adding the dry powder until islands of plaster show above the water. Let it stand a minute or two, then mix it slowly, stirring out lumps, until it begins to thicken. Pour immediately.

To make a very simple two-part mold, pour about one and a half inches of wet plaster into a cardboard box. When it stiffens slightly, but before it hardens, press your damp clay model about one-half inch into the hardening plaster. Then pour more liquid plaster around the clay model until it comes about halfway up the model. When this plaster hardens, carve out several depressions in the plaster surface (Figure 9-77). Smear the top surface of plaster with mold separater (petroleum jelly will work), being sure to coat the depressions as well. Pour on more plaster until it is at least one inch thick above the clay model. When the plaster is hard, separate the mold, dig and wash out the clay, and after a few days when the plaster is dry, you are ready for slip casting. As you become more experienced, you can learn to make intricate multisectioned molds that will reproduce almost any form you wish (Figures 8-36 to 8-40). Refer to a book on sculpture techniques for more detailed instructions on mold making.

Commercially prepared casting slip is the easiest for the beginner to use because it is carefully formulated for the purpose, containing **deflocculants** to keep the clay particles in suspension. Casting slips are difficult to make because it is not easy to get a workable suspension of the clay. Most plastic clays will not work, and even the water used can make a difference.

Figure 8-38 "Stack of Cards on Brown Book." Richard Shaw, a master at casting from the United States, casts porcelain forms, assembling them into magical compositions. Cast porcelain. Height 14 in. (35.6 cm). *Courtesy, Braunstein/Quay Gallery.*

Figure 8-39 "Wednesday—I think your friend that was here last night is a troublemaker." From the "Soap Opera" series of altered industrial forms created by Joe DiStefano while in residence at Kohler Company. Vitreous china, slip cast, soaked, smashed, incised, and glazed with chrome-plated cast brass. 20⅝ X 25¼ X 13⅝ in. (52.4 X 64.1 X 38.4 cm). *Courtesy, John Michael Kohler Arts Center. Photo by Bayens Photo Company.*

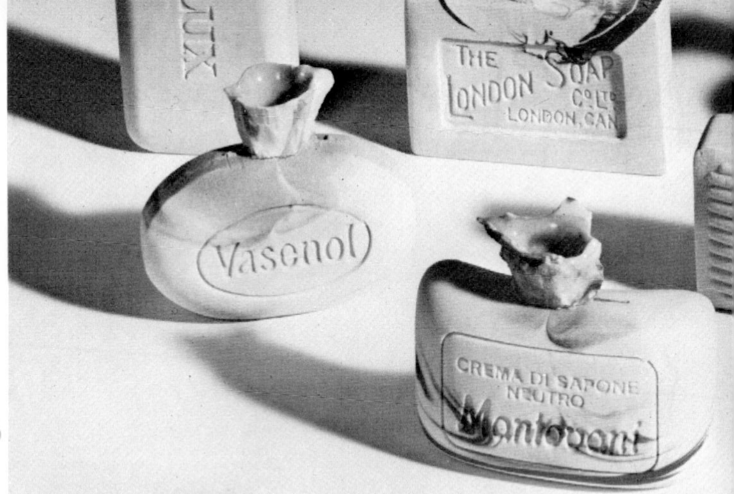

Figure 8-40 "Soap Bottles." Slip-cast, colored, vitreous china, normally used for industrial products, was combined with pinched forms by Karen Massaro while artist-in-residence at the Kohler Company, Wisconsin. Massaro also experimented with the company's glazes and various colored slips. In her journal of the experience, she comments, "There are techniques to be learned, new places where clay cracks or does not crack. New people who also know clay. . . ." Heights from 2½ in. to 4½ in. (6.4 cm to 11.4 cm). *Courtesy, Collection of John Michael Kohler Arts Center. Photo by Bayens Photo Company.*

Your Place in Clay

So you see, you will have to choose from a bewildering variety of techniques and attitudes while you search for your place in clay (Figures 8-29 to 8-52). Use the methods of making sculpture discussed and illustrated in this chapter merely as jumping off points for your own experiments or as inspiration to help you explore your relationship to clay in a totally different manner. Choose the approach that seems most comfortable to you—the one that lets the clay help rather than hinder you in making the strongest personal statement you can.

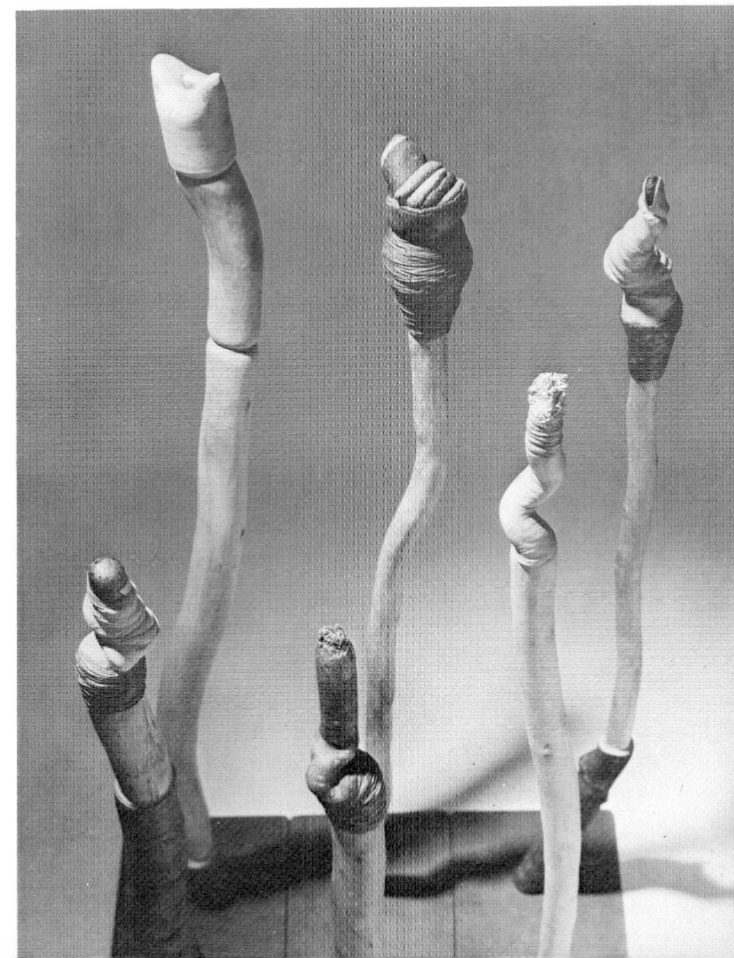

Figure 8-41 Mixed media composition combines carved wood, string, and iron with stoneware. The clay was colored with oxides in the body and on the surface, then glazed with a transparent ash glaze. Ernst Häusermann. *Photo by Werner Erne.*

Figure 8-42 Nineteenth-century roof ornament from the Sepik River Valley in New Guinea combines fired clay, straw, and hair in a fertility figure with mythological bird. Height 19¼ in. (49 cm). *Courtesy, Staatliche Museum für Völkerkunde, Munich.*

Figure 8-43 "Mach II," by Marion Peters Angelica, of the United States, contrasts the movement of feathers and leather strips with solid clay, producing a sculpture that has the appearance of a ritual object. Porcelain, feathers and leather. Length 34 in. (86.4 cm), height 20 in. (50.8 cm). *Courtesy of the artist.*

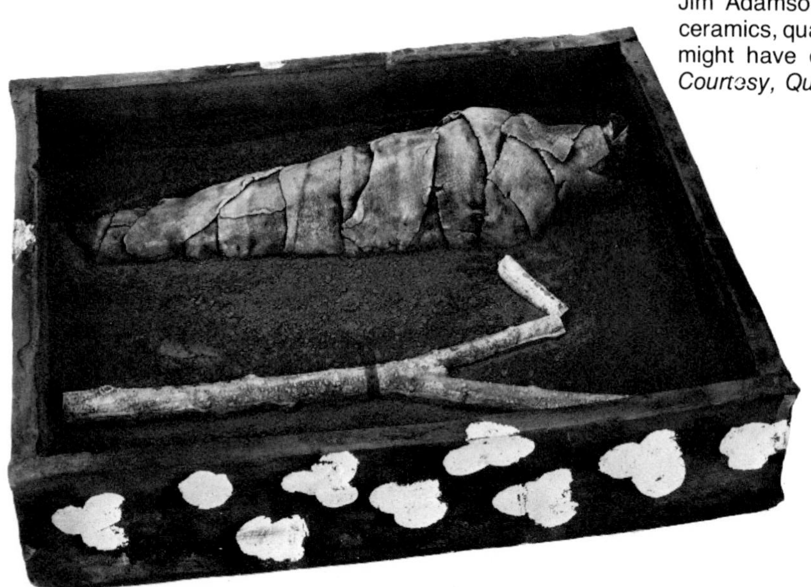

Figure 8-44 In "Cooper's Hawk and Scepter," Jim Adamson, of the United States, combines ceramics, quarry tile, and paint into an artifact that might have come from an ancient civilization. *Courtesy, Quay Ceramics Gallery.*

Color Plate 11 **Maija Grotell,** U.S.A. Copper-blue glazed bowl. 1955. Height 5½ in. (12.7 cm), diameter 9½ in. (24 cm). *Courtesy, Cranbrook Academy of Art/Museum, and Maija Grotell Research Fund.*

Color Plate 12 **Bernard Leach,** England. Stoneware with tenmoku glaze, 1959. Height 14½ in. (36.8 cm). *Courtesy, Victoria and Albert Museum, Crown Copyright.*

Color Plate 13 **Arnold Zahner,** Switzerland.
Crystalline glaze with rutile. *Courtesy of the artist. Photo by Peter Grell.*

Color Plate 14 **Görge Hohlt,** Germany. Blue-glazed plate, 1974, reduction. *Photo by Jochen Schade.*

Color Plate 15 **Larry Murphy,** U.S.A. Glaze tests and cups. The same glaze on two cups made from different stoneware bodies shows color changes due to variation in iron content.

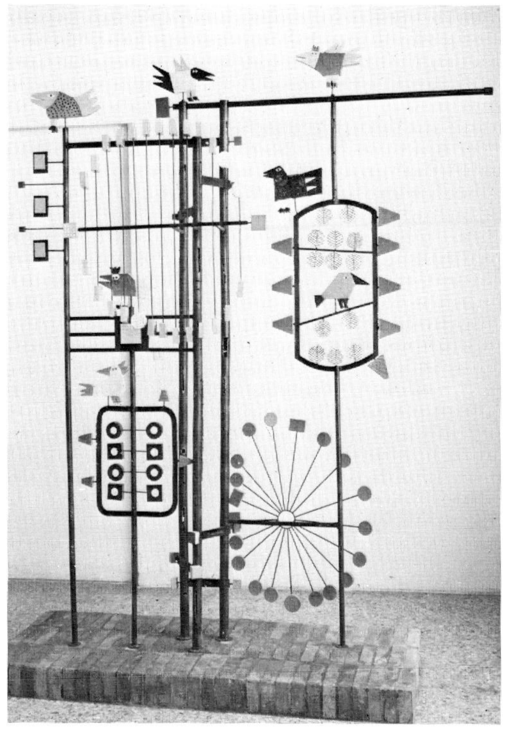

Figure 8-45 Garden decoration. Maiolica on a composition of iron rods. Pravoslav Rada, Czechoslovakia. *Courtesy, Museo Internazionale delle Ceramiche, Faenza, Italy.*

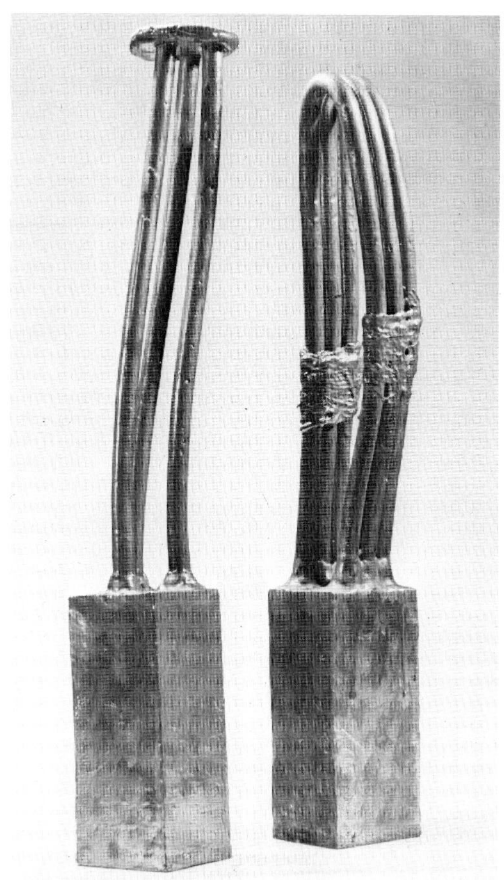

Figure 8-46 Anthony Hepburn's extruded solid-rod sculpture is coated with gold and silver luster. The rods bent and warped in a controlled firing. Stoneware. Height 26 in. (66 cm). *Courtesy, Alphabet and Image. Photo by Eric Webster.*

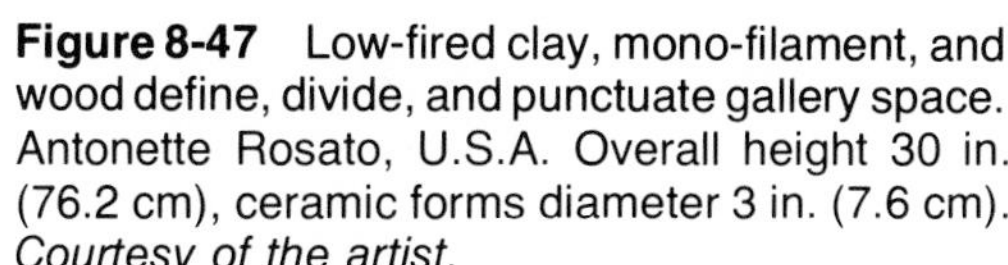

Figure 8-47 Low-fired clay, mono-filament, and wood define, divide, and punctuate gallery space. Antonette Rosato, U.S.A. Overall height 30 in. (76.2 cm), ceramic forms diameter 3 in. (7.6 cm). *Courtesy of the artist.*

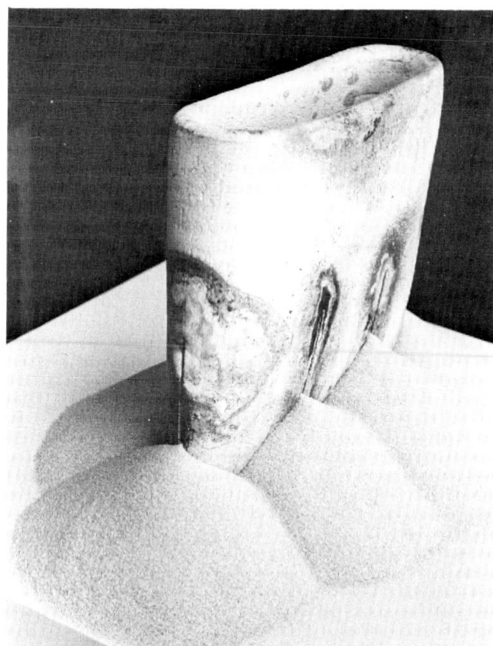

Figure 8-48 (*Left*) Sand pours out of slits, building its own sculptural forms in an appropriate combination of materials that extends our concept of ceramics. Height 18 in. (45.7 cm). (*Right*) Hollow ceramic cylinders become the tool rather than the sculpture. As they roll, they form sand patterns on the floor. William G. Maxwell, U.S.A. Length 15 ft (4.6 m), width 2 ft (61 cm). *Photos courtesy of the artist.*

Figure 8-49 Clay and water piece by George Geyer, of the United States. The water gradually breaks the ropes of clay into separate chunks and crumbling pieces. Geyer, concerned with communicating information about ceramic materials, says, "The ceramic process is in itself the art." Clay, glass, sand, and water. 52 X 82 X 53 in. (132.1 X 208.3 X 134.6 cm). *Courtesy, Santa Ana College Gallery.*

Figure 8-50 "Arch #1," by John Goodhart, of the United States. Rethinking his relationship with clay, he used products derived from clay rather than the raw material of clay. Other pieces "incorporate accidents observed while transporting clay or building kilns." Firebrick and steel, 1976. 20 X 50 X 36 in. (50.8 X 127 X 91.4 cm). *Courtesy, Grinstead Gallery, Central Missouri State University.*

Figure 8-51 "Time Stop Splash," by Michael Arntz, of the United States, translates high-speed photography into solid clay. 1978. *Courtesy, Quay Ceramics Gallery.*

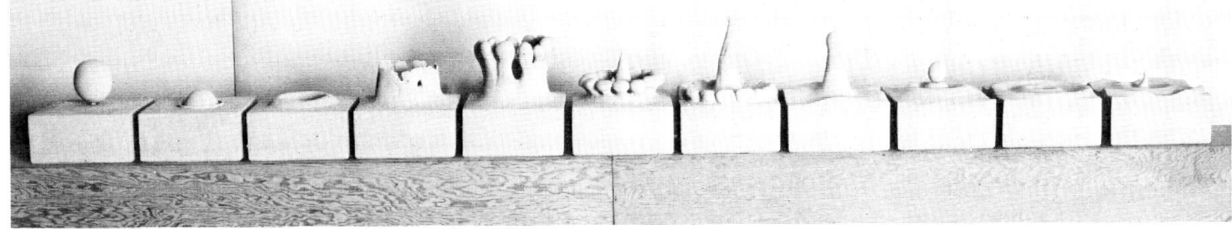

Figure 8-52 In "Fragment of Western Civilization," U.S. sculptor Robert Arneson combines brick and a crumbling self-portrait into a dialogue with himself. "I try not to take myself too seriously, and when I think I might be, it is time to knock over a big piece." This is a continuing piece which changes according to time and place. Terra cotta, 60 X 260 in. (152.4 X 660.4 cm). *Quotation courtesy of John Michael Kohler Arts Center. Courtesy, Hansen-Fuller Gallery, San Francisco.*

Chapter Nine

Working on the Wheel and Casting

Wheels, whether driving a warrior's chariot or a potter's turntable, were a late development in most agricultural communities. Some cultures, otherwise complex, never did harness the power of the wheel. We have seen in Part One how thousands of years of trial and error were needed to develop a fast-moving wheel that would enable the potter to make thin-walled pots more rapidly and easily. (See Color Plates 5, 10, 13, 14, and 17, pp. 146C, 146D, 210B, and 210D).

The image of a potter sitting at a whirling wheel, bringing to life a beautifully shaped vessel from a lump of inert clay, has always appeared quite magical (Figure 9-1). It is an image that both intrigues and awes students, leading them to approach the wheel with fantasies of the marvelous pots they will make. Like any skill, it appears so easy when the experts do it—but when you try it yourself, fantasy, as well as the pot, often collapses in the face of reality!

No one can really teach a physical skill like throwing on the wheel. Only after years of practice will your body become so trained in the movement of throwing, that you can give all your attention to the form of the piece you are making. However, a book such as this can give you basic information about the process to study along with the instruction and guidance of an experienced potter.

Working on the Wheel

Your first question will probably be, What type of wheel should I use? The school or studio where you learn may have both electric and kick wheels. The electric wheel looks so easy, and the kick wheel seems so difficult to manage—like patting your head and rubbing your stomach at the same time. Which type you use is really a matter of personal preference. Some beginners learn more quickly on a kick wheel and feel more in control of its speed. Others are more comfortable on an electric wheel. Find out for yourself which type works best for you. A power wheel can be a boon to one production potter, while another may prefer the kick wheel.

Before you can even begin to think in terms of making a pot, you have to learn to control the wheel, center the clay, and throw a basic cylinder. Resist the impulse to make an object you can point to and say, "That's my pot." Curb your fantasies, and work at the cylinder. It will pay off in the end.

Using a Kick Wheel

Where do you start? Well, first put on rubber-soled shoes before you try to use the kick wheel, then practice getting the wheel in motion. Kick from the inside near the shaft, thrusting out with a rolling motion. In this way, instead of trying to keep up with the outside rim of the kick wheel, which is moving faster, you will make use of the favorable gear ratio close to the shaft (Figure 9-2). Doing this, you will find you can get the wheel moving and keep it going with less effort. Notice how your hair falls in your eyes and your sleeves roll down as you kick. These body movements explain why you should never kick while your hands are on the clay, for that action transferred through your arms to the clay would cause the clay to move off center on the wheel.

A beginner tends to get the wheel up to working speed, then let it slow down almost to a stop, kick it back to speed, then let it slow down again, over and over. It is better to get a rhythm going so that every couple of seconds you take a breath, take your hands off the wheel, and give the wheel a couple of kicks to keep the wheel head moving.

During the first step on the wheel—centering—the wheel should be turning rapidly. The centrifugal force created by the speed will help you **center** the uneven lump of clay. Then with each succeeding step, you will slow down a little bit, until, at the end of the process while you finish the lip, the wheel will be barely moving. When you start out working on the wheel, you may think that if you are having difficulty forming a cylinder, you should kick the wheel faster. But that will just make things worse, for if you speed up the wheel in later stages, then at a time when you are trying to get the walls to rise, the centrifugal force will be trying to flatten them out. So begin fast, then gradually slow down.

Figure 9-1 The strong, sensitive hands of Maija Grotell (1899-1973) giving life to the turning clay. *Courtesy, Maija Grotell Research Fund and Jeff Schlanger.*

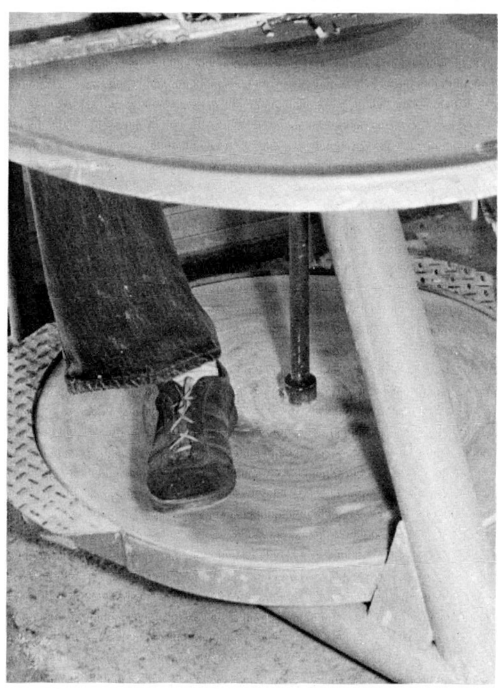

Figure 9-2 To kick a wheel with the least effort, kick from near the shaft, pushing outward.

Centering

When you feel you can control the wheel reasonably well, you are ready to learn to center the ball of clay that you have wedged.

The dictionary defines *center* as "the point around which a body revolves or rotates" or "the point toward which any force, feeling, or action tends, or from which any force or influence takes its origin." Both definitions have meaning in relation to centering clay, and although centering is a physical process involving what you do with your hands, where you press the clay, how fast you kick the wheel, it also has other dimensions. We think of a "centered" person as being steady, comfortable with the inner self, in balance. In the words of poet-potter Mary Caroline Richards,

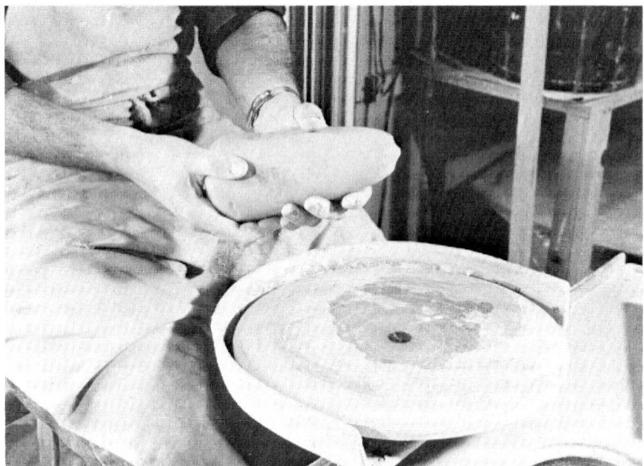

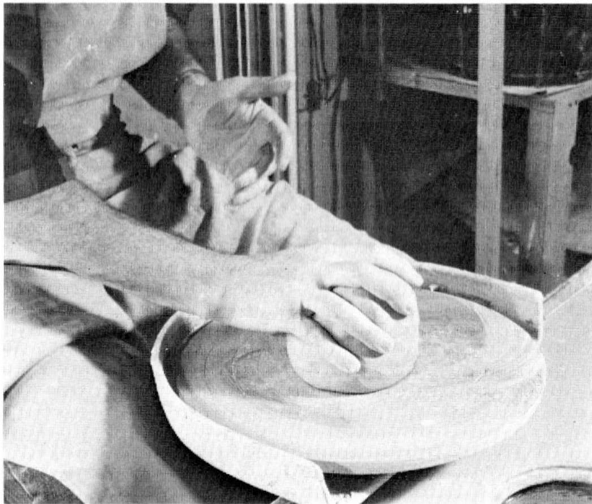

Figure 9-3 (*Left*) Roll the wedged ball of clay back and forth on the wedging table or wheel head to form a cone at one end. **Figure 9-4** (*Right*) Slam the coned end on the wheel, driving the cone up into the lump. This compresses the clay and gives the base added strength to help it resist cracking. Larry Murphy, U.S.A.

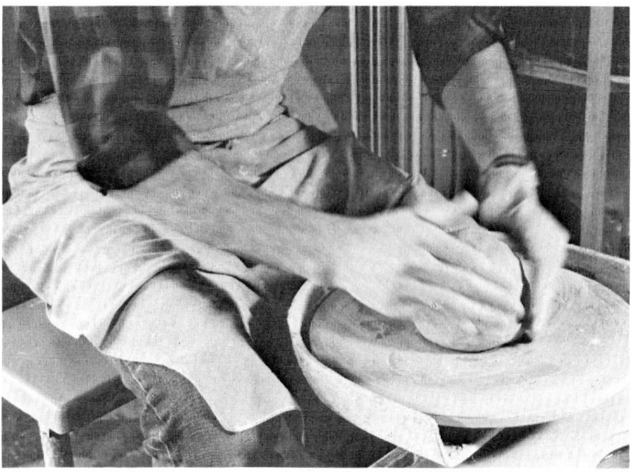

Figure 9-5 (*Left*) Push and pat the clay on the wheel into a beehive shape before starting to center it. **Figure 9-6** (*Right*) Drip some water onto the lump for lubrication, taking care not to get it too wet, for that weakens the clay.

As human beings functioning as potters, we center ourselves and our clay. And we all know how necessary it is to be "on center" ourselves if we wish to bring our clay "into center" and not merely to agitate it or bully it.*

* Mary Caroline Richards, *Centering in Pottery, Poetry, and the Person* (Middletown, Conn.: Wesleyan University Press, 1964).

The principle behind centering is that if an uneven lump of soft clay, turning around the fixed point in the middle of the wheel, comes in contact with a steady force pressing against it—your hands—it will become evenly centered and perfectly round. The importance of centering cannot be overemphasized, for if the clay is not perfectly centered, there is no way you can throw an even pot.

Figure 9-7 (*Left*) To center, the hands should be linked to operate together. One way is to hold the thumb of one hand with the other, pressing down with the heel of your hand on top of the clay and pressing in with the other hand. **Figure 9-8** (*Right*) Centering with the thumbs linked. Eileen Lewenstein, England.

Figure 9-9 (*Left*) Coning up aids centering. Squeeze the clay to make it rise in a cone, but do not repeat too often, as it brings water into the clay and weakens it. **Figure 9-10** (*Right*) When the cone has reached full height, press it back down with one hand on the side, bending it off center a little as you press.

In order to center, you will have to keep your hands perfectly still, so your arms should be anchored in some way. You can anchor them against your upper legs, your sides, or even the wheel frame, whatever is most comfortable. Then your hands should be joined to keep them steady. Whatever method of joining them you use, be sure that they are not working independently, but rather that they work together as one tool. Now you are ready to learn to center a not-too-large ball of clay. (See Figures 9-3 to 9-12.)

Opening

The second step, opening, is not difficult, but it takes concentration. Brace your arms and keep your hands working together. As you press your finger down into the clay, you will form a centered lump of clay with a hole in it—a doughnut. Beginners often make the mistake of trying to throw from this doughnut rather than from a fully opened shape. The clay is not fully opened until you form the bottom of the cylinder and straighten the

Figure 9-11 (*Left*) Press the cone back into the center. Beginners usually cone up regularly, while experienced potters may only cone when centering large amounts. **Figure 9-12** (*Right*) Centered clay. To see if the whole mass is centered, place your hand against the revolving clay and feel whether it is uneven.

Figure 9-13 (*Left*) Opening with the index finger. Press straight in and do not let the hinging motion of your finger pull the clay off center. **Figure 9-14** (*Right*) Cross section showing the action of the index finger as you press down into the clay.

walls. Do this by moving your finger across the bottom parallel to the wheel head. Only now are you ready to pull up the walls. (See Figures 9-13 to 9-21.)

Pulling Up the Walls

This last step is not as difficult as one might think if the earlier steps have been done properly. But if they have not been done with care, then this last step is almost impossible.

To pull up the walls, place your fingers opposite each other on the inside and outside walls of the cylinder. If your fingers are placed so that they force a smaller amount of clay to pass through them than the thickness of the walls, the soft clay will respond by moving, and it has nowhere to go but up. This is what makes the walls rise. Remember that the clay is on a revolving wheel and is being subjected to a centrifugal force that tends to make the walls flare out. In throwing a cylinder, you have to move your hands slightly inward to coun-

Figure 9-15 (*Left*) Opening with the middle finger gives you a little extra depth, useful if you are throwing a large pot. **Figure 9-16** (*Right*) Use either finger, two fingers, or your thumb. Make sure that the tip of your finger presses straight down as if to continue through the clay down the shaft of the wheel.

Figure 9-17 (*Left*) Carefully move your index finger across the bottom of the opened clay about ½ inch above the wheel head to form the base of the cylinder. **Figure 9-18** (*Right*) Cross section showing the position of the index finger inside the pot as the bottom is completed.

teract that force. Imagine a line which goes up the shaft of the wheel, straight up through your clay, and lightly move the clay in toward it.

At the same time that you counteract the centrifugal force, counteract the desire you will feel to start making pots, staying with the cylinder longer than you think is necessary. If you can throw three basic types of cylinders there is no shape you cannot throw. As you become more proficient and begin to think about design, you can start with a cylinder form and go on from there. In this way, your pots will be basically engineered before you start to throw. (See Figures 9-22 to 9-30.)

Figure 9-19 (*Left*) Straightening the wall to a 90-degree angle in preparation for pulling it up to the basic cylinder shape. **Figure 9-20** (*Right*) Cross section showing the position of fingers while straightening the walls before pulling up the cylinder.

Figure 9-21 (*Left*) Cross section of the opened clay showing how to smooth the bottom with a rib. **Figure 9-22** (*Right*) Picking up a bead of clay with your fingers is an easy way to learn the finger position for throwing as well as how much space to leave between them.

Figure 9-23 Starting to pull the walls with your knuckle on the outside and your other hand inside.

Figure 9-24 (*Left*) Pulling up the walls with the fingers holding a sponge. Clay is forced upward through the space between the fingers, causing the walls to rise. **Figure 9-25** (*Right*) Cross section shows finger position as walls are thinned. You may use knuckle on the outside, but fingertips are more sensitive.

Figure 9-26 (*Left*) Always leave a little extra clay at the top. Its weight helps to keep the cylinder centered and the extra clay provides you with material for a lip. **Figure 9-27** (*Right*) Cross section of complete cylinder. Technical skill takes you this far, now the artist in you must take over to shape the cylinder.

Figure 9-28 The three basic cylinder shapes are outlined with heavy lines. You can transform them into any shape.

Figure 9-29 (*Left*) Smooth the walls with a rib. Clay particles become separated as you throw, and pressure from fingers or rib will tighten them. **Figure 9-30** (*Right*) Clean out excess water as you throw with a sponge attached to a long stick. This keeps the water from penetrating and weakening the clay.

Shaping

After you have mastered the basic cylinder shape, you can begin to think about shaping. An experienced potter who knows what is coming, what technical problems must be contended with, can combine the two processes. But a beginner will have to separate the throwing of the cylinder and the shaping.

A basic cylinder is like a stretched, clean white canvas waiting for a painter's first brush stroke. Now your creativity comes into play. And as a painter uses a sketch book as a source of ideas, you, too, will find a sketch book is a good place to work out images before you touch the clay. With it beside you, you can jot down observed forms as you see them. A rock, a tree trunk, a human figure, machinery, or smoke stacks—almost any form in nature or the mechanical world may give you the germ of a pot form.

Once you have shaped the basic cylinder, you can concentrate on the form and design of the pot. Move back from it occasionally to see how it is progressing. Remember, too, that clay loses its plasticity if it is overworked, and if

Figure 9-31 (*Right*) In a motion expressing the intimate relationship between his body and the clay, Michael Cardew, of England, removes a just-thrown bowl from his wheel. For centuries, potters have lifted their finished ware with just such a joyous gesture. *Courtesy, Crafts Advisory Committee, London.*

your desired shape does not grow after a reasonable amount of time, start over with a new ball of clay. Keep it alive and not weakened by too much water or stretching. At the same time, do not think that you can correct a badly designed pot by trimming it later. The shape must grow organically from the action of your hands on the clay as it spins on the wheel (Figure 9-33). If it doesn't, throw it away and start over again. To take a piece off the wheel, pull a wire under it and lift it off.

Figure 9-32 (*Left*) "Writing Stones" bowls by United States potter Mary Caroline Richards were inspired by the name of a park in Canada containing petroglyphs. "I made some pots, stoneware, and wrote on them. Then I put the ladders in them. Why? Later they seemed to me to resemble kivas, the round underground ceremonial chambers where Indian men go to perform their rituals."

Figure 9-33 (*Below Left and Right*) An expert like Ron Judd, of the United States, can throw a complex shape, repeating the size and form exactly to form a matching set.

Making Domestic Ware

When you have learned to make a basic cylinder, you can begin to think about designing pottery to use in your home: cups, teapots, casseroles, or any of the many useful objects one can make out of clay (Figures 9-33 and 9-34). Or you may want to consider becoming a full-time production potter. To make domestic ware, there are certain skills you must learn, aesthetic questions to solve, and practical aspects you must consider.

The Production Potter

Production potters have many problems to deal with beyond those posed by the clay, glaze, and fire. They must be capable of making domestic ware of a high standard, but they must also face the considerations of marketing, building up a clientele, producing items to order, formulating glazes, procuring materials, uncertain income, overhead, kiln construction, studio maintenance, business management, and taxes. At the same time they must continue to grow as artists, improving their forms and exploring new glazes. Many also teach part-time. It is a life with compensations, but the potter who is considering it must be aware of all its aspects.

Figure 9-34 Coffee pot made from a basic cylinder. Stoneware, matt ash glaze. Tony Gant, England. *Courtesy, Crafts Advisory Committee.*

Making a Teapot

Although making a teapot is not a project for beginners, it is shown here because it illustrates most of the skills a production potter needs (Figures 9-35 to 9-51). Just what are these skills?

First, you must be able to form the basic cylinder into a shape that will be pleasing as well as functional. You must learn to balance the handle and the spout; the handle should be large enough to fit the hand, but not so large as to be out of scale visually with the spout. You will have to form a spout that pours well, attaching it so that it stays attached (Figures 9-44 to 9-47). You must also learn to make a lid that fits and doesn't fall off when you pour. Learning to control the thickness of the walls is also important, for walls that are too thin will not have the insulating qualities so characteristic of a ceramic teapot, and walls that are too thick will make it too heavy to lift comfortably. Finally, you must learn to trim the finished piece. When you are able to deal with these considerations satisfactorily, you are ready to make just about anything.

Throwing Off the Hump

Throwing "off the hump," although not essential, is a good technique to learn, especially if you want to throw a series of pieces quickly. It also saves time in wedging and centering. Instead of wedging and centering new lumps of clay for each piece, you merely center the top section of the hump, throw the piece, cut it off, and continue throwing (Figures 9-35 to 9-39).

Figure 9-35 (*Right*) Throwing off the hump saves time, as you only need to center the top of the clay.

Figure 9-36 (*Left*) To form the lid of the teapot off the hump, you can use either finger on the outside.
Figure 9-37 (*Right*) Measuring the lid of the teapot with calipers helps to assure a good fit.

Figure 9-38 (*Left*) When the lid is finished, cut it off the hump with a wire held taut.
Figure 9-39 (*Right*) Collar in the spout like the neck of a bottle, then shape it with a metal rib.

There are some potters who feel that it is best to throw a teapot, spout, and lid from the same piece of wedged clay. Whether or not there is an actual physical advantage, it is a satisfying idea to some potters to make all the parts from the same cohesive lump of clay.

Trimming

Trimming is an important aspect of all pottery making, but it is a skill that must not be relied on too heavily to correct clumsy throwing. Although good trimming may give the last crisp definition to a piece, the form will be much fresher and more alive if it is shaped on the wheel rather than trimmed to shape (Figures 9-40 to 9-43).

As you progress with learning to throw the basic cylinder, you can begin studying the techniques shown here and be thinking ahead to the pots you may want to make; thinking about how you will design them and about the skills you must learn in order to create them.

Figure 9-40 (*Left*) Measure the teapot rim to fit the lid, then dry the lid, spout, and pot until leather hard.
Figure 9-41 (*Right*) Place hardened lid in the opening of the teapot to keep it in place while trimming.

Figure 9-42 (*Left*) A chuck holds the teapot steady on the wheel. A jar lid held on the base distributes finger pressure. **Figure 9-43** (*Right*) Be careful not to trim the bottom too thin. Thickness can be judged by sound when the bottom is tapped.

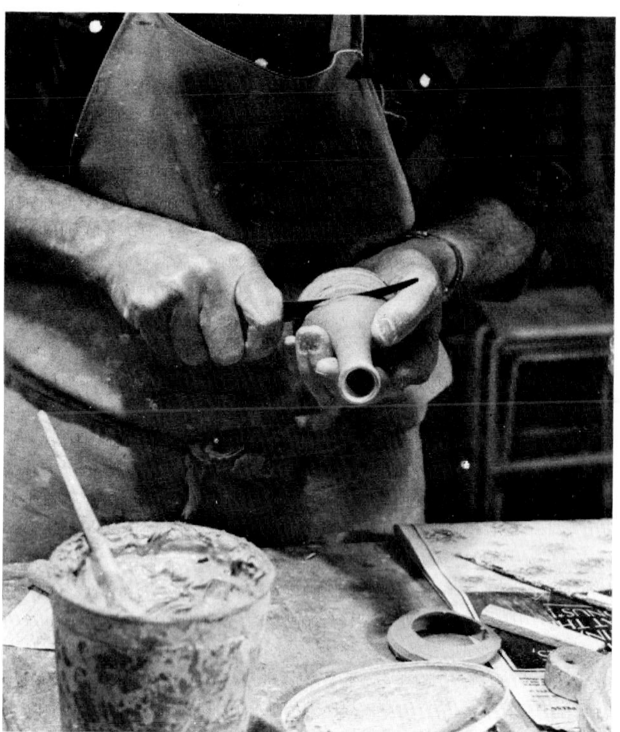

Figure 9-44 Slice the spout to fit the shape of the teapot with a curved fettling knife.

Figure 9-45 Score the teapot and the end of the spout before painting with slip and joining.

Figure 9-46 An old pen nib makes an excellent tool for cutting strainer holes.

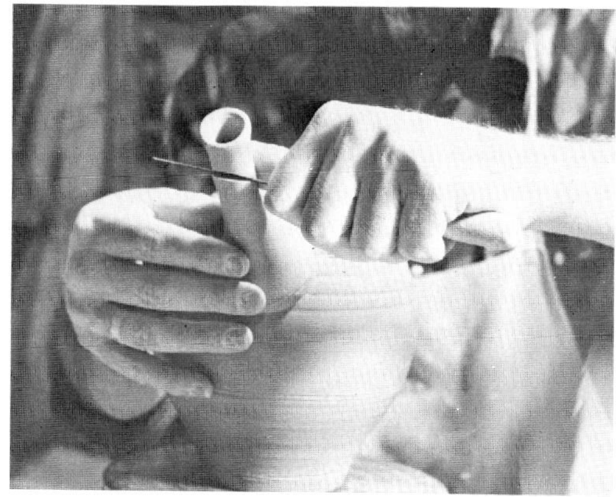

Figure 9-47 To compensate for the slight unwinding that occurs on firing, cut the spout at an angle.

Spouts

The form of a spout can change the whole appearance of a coffeepot or teapot. A spout can be elegant and formal, simple and functional, or perky and cheerful. At the same time, the skill with which it is shaped can make pouring a satisfying or frustrating experience (Figures 9-44 to 9-47).

A spout, or any part that is thrown separately and attached to another shape, will unwind slightly as it is fired. Since the spout is attached firmly at one end, the free, or pouring, end will make about a 10- or 15-degree turn as it fires. If you plan to make a spout that is shaped at the lip rather than left round, and want it to pour tea into the cup instead of on the tablecloth, you must take this into consideration. Slicing off the end at an angle will solve the problem, but you will have to learn, by trial and error, the proper angle at which to cut (Figure 9-47).

Handles

Graceful, pleasing handles that complement the shape of a cup or a pot are important accents, and making sure that they are securely attached is a vital skill to learn (Figures 9-48 to 9-56). Nothing could be more embarrassing to a potter than having a handle fall off a pot as the tea is poured! When you attach a handle with slip, you must be sure that both parts of the clay are ready to absorb the moisture of the slip, so that the scratched and scored clay on both parts will blend together into a complete bond.

Figure 9-48 Attach the moist handle to the scored teapot with a small amount of water.

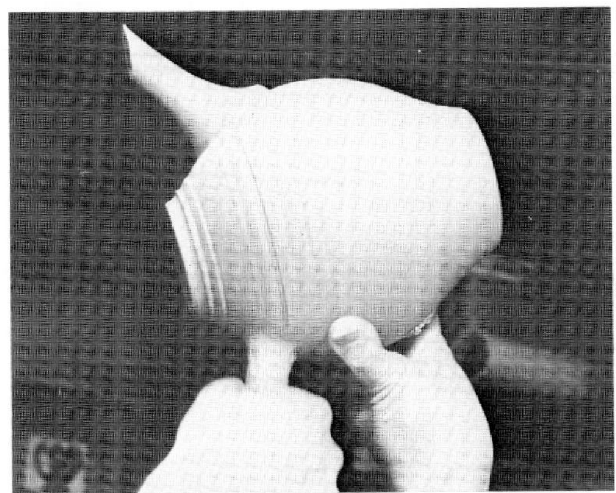

Figure 9-49 After attaching the handle pull out the clay, using a wiping motion.

Figure 9-50 Larry Murphy gently strokes the handle to the desired length and thickness.

Figure 9-51 The teapot is almost complete as Larry Murphy attaches the handle at the bottom with pressure, leaving his fingerprint in the clay.

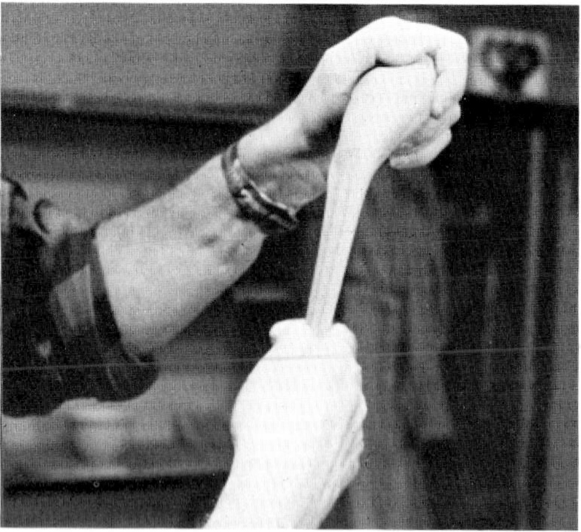

Figure 9-52 (*Left*) Center leather-hard cup on wheel before trimming bottom. Lumps of clay hold it firmly.
Figure 9-53 (*Right*) Pull the cup handle from well-wedged clay, then gently stroke it to shape.

Figure 9-54 (*Left*) Attach cup handle with slip and thumb pressure after both are scored.
Figure 9-55 (*Right*) With handle attached, smooth the clay at the join. Potter's stamp adds final touch.

Figure 9-56 Handles can be both decorative and functional. On this soup tureen and candle warmer the ribbon-like loops provide a light touch that contrasts with its simple shape. Larry Murphy, U.S.A.

Pitcher Lips

Making an attractive and functional pouring lip on a pitcher is another skill you must learn if you are to make a wide range of domestic ware. Once you have shaped the body of the pitcher—whether it is a small, delicate porcelain creamer or a robust stoneware pitcher that evokes images of warm milk right from the cow—you will want to make a lip that says "Pour Me" (Figure 9-57). Most beginners are so delighted when they produce a nice round rim that they cannot bear to change its line with a lip. As a result, they make timid little indentations that would hardly pour the satisfying streams of water, wine, or milk you want to see.

You must learn to be bold about lips, and to expect to spoil a good many before you develop your own strong shape.

Figure 9-57 Wipe with a bold motion to form pitcher spout as your finger and thumb press the lip.

Altered and Composite Forms

Although we are inclined to think of wheel-thrown ceramics only in relation to domestic ware or the classic shapes of the past, wheel shapes can become the basis for a great variety of other forms. A wheel-thrown shape can be altered slightly, giving it new and unexpected relationships of space and outline while still remaining functional. German-born British potter Hans Coper, for example, confines himself to basic wheel-thrown forms, which he alters and combines into new compositions, repeating similar shapes in a variety of subtle combinations (Figure 9-66). Peter Voulkos, of the United States (Figure 9-59), slashes and punctures his pots, while Carlo Zauli, of Italy, frequently alters his pots totally —smashes them, in fact. (See Figures 9-58 to 9-65).

Basic wheel-thrown shapes can be combined with other wheel-thrown shapes or they can be combined with hand-built sections, allowing a freedom not possible with wheel shapes alone. For example, slabs, molded sections, extruded pieces, and sculptural areas can be joined to wheel-thrown sections to create works ranging from the fantasy worlds of an Ian Godfrey to the formal columns assembled by Ruenell Foy Temps. (See Figures 9-66 to 9-69).

Figure 9-58 A wheel-thrown pot may be wrapped with string to alter it as it dries. Bryan Newman, England. *Courtesy, Alphabet and Image.*

Figure 9-59 Stoneware plate by Peter Voulkos, of the United States. Wheel-thrown, altered, colored with cobalt and chrome, then covered with clear glaze. 1962. *Courtesy, Collection of The Oakland Museum. Gift of the Art Guild of the Oakland Museum Association.*

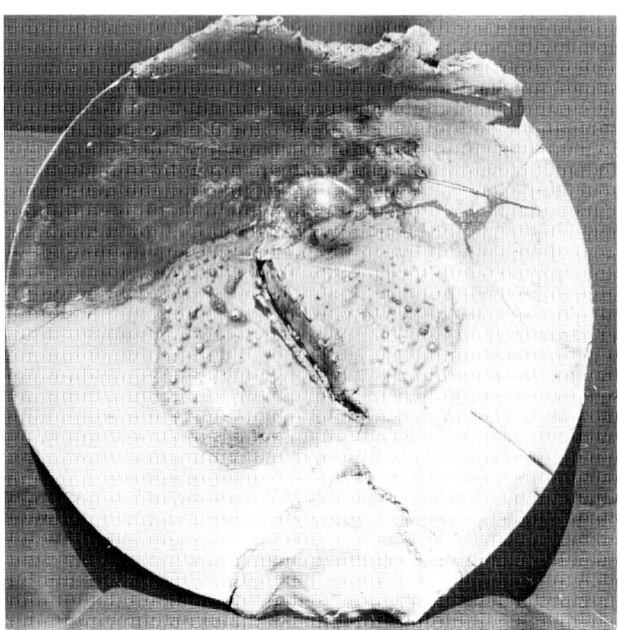

Figure 9-60 A classic bottle has been altered slightly from a round, swelling shape to one with flattened sides. Tatsuzo Shimaoka, Mashiko, Japan. *Photo by James Aliferis.*

Figure 9-61 "Aquacise" plate is altered with sculptural additions. Robert Arneson, U.S.A. Diameter 18 in. (45.7 cm). *Courtesy, Hansen Fuller Gallery.*

Figure 9-62 Thrown stoneware forms are bases for houses, landscapes, and animals. Stoneware with dolomite glaze. Oxidation firing, electric kiln, at 2336°F (1280°C). Ian Godfrey, England. *Courtesy, Alphabet and Image.*

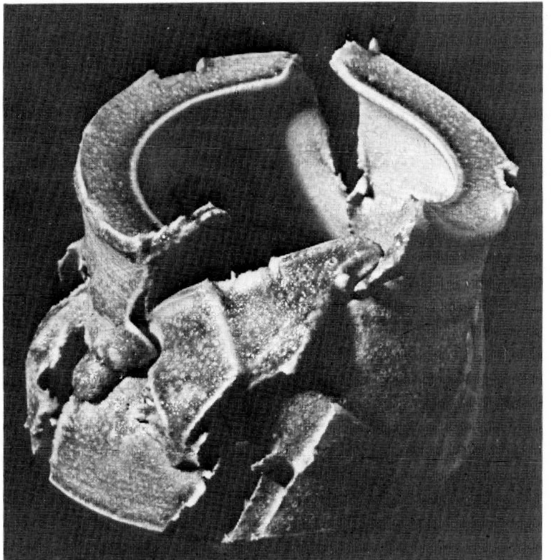

Figure 9-63 White-glazed stoneware pot is totally transformed in the hands of Carlo Zauli, of Italy. Stoneware, 10¼ X 8¾ in. (26 X 22 cm).

Figure 9-64 (*Left*) Her thrown and altered sculptural pots surround Petra Weiss as she works in her studio. **Figure 9-65** (*Right*) Altering may also take the form of additions to the basic shape. Petra Weiss, Switzerland, stoneware bowl. Circumference 11¾ in. (30 cm). *Courtesy of the artist.*

Figure 9-66 Composite stoneware pots made from altered wheel shapes. Subtly varied, flattened pots are attached to cylindrical bases, colored with manganese and white slip. Hans Coper, England. *Courtesy, Alphabet and Image.*

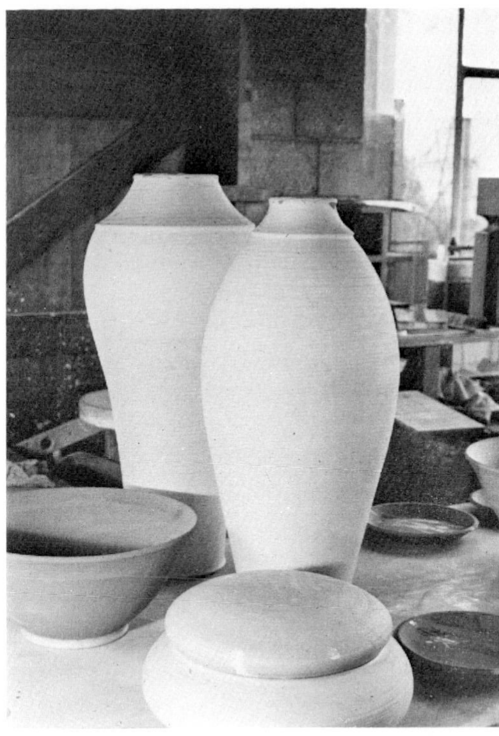

Figure 9-67 Large pots, as yet unglazed, were thrown in sections. Joined rim to rim, the necks were formed from extra clay at the bottom of the inverted pots. Ron Judd, U.S.A., stoneware.

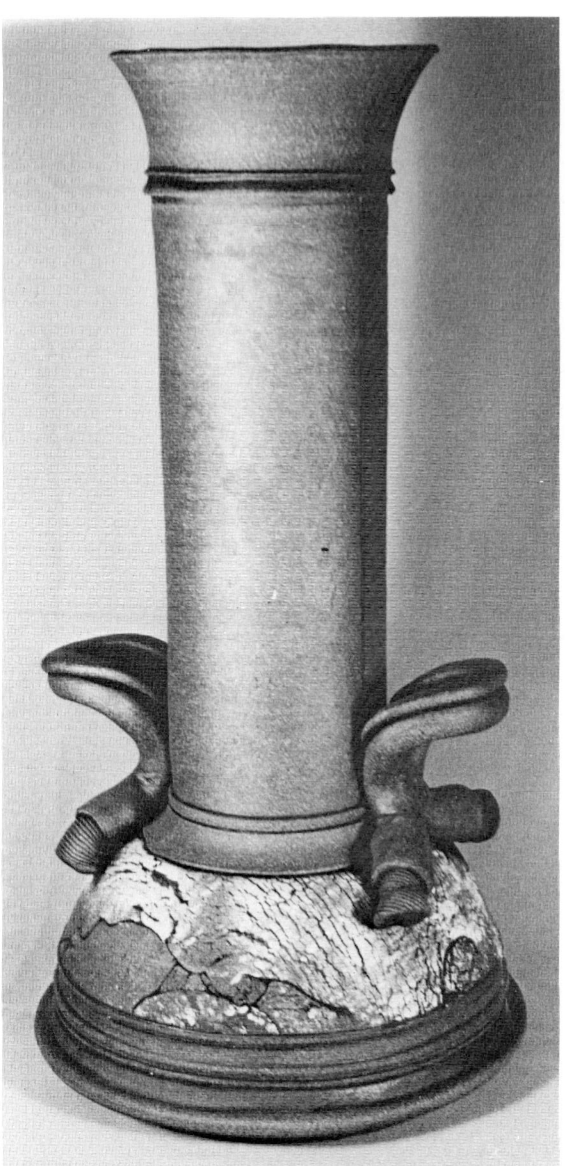

Figure 9-69 Composite stoneware vase combines slab cylinder, press molded top and base, and thrown foot into a classic column. Handles are extruded tubes. Ruenell Foy Temps, U.S.A. *Courtesy of the artist.*

Figure 9-68 (*Left*) Composite wheel-thrown pots achieve a freedom of form not possible with those thrown in one piece. Wood ash and china clay glaze. Tony Birks-Hays, England. *Courtesy, Alphabet and Image.*

Making Multiples

Press molds and mold making are explained briefly in Chapter 7, and a specialized book on casting methods in sculpture will give you more complete instructions for making plaster molds. Here we will explain the basics of slip casting.

At some point you may want to try casting a piece of pottery or a small piece of sculpture in a mold with liquid clay, or slip. It is best to start out with a one- or two-piece mold and learn to use that first. Then you can progress to making **piece molds** and casting more complex shapes. Piece molds are made in sections so that they can be lifted off without damaging the cast piece or the mold. A mold is keyed with small knobs on one side of the mold and matching sockets on the other, so that when it is assembled, the fit will be exact. (See Figures 9-70 to 9-74).

When you first start casting, you will probably use a commercially prepared casting slip, although you can make your own from dry ingredients. Clay slip for casting is made with the addition of a deflocculant material such as sodium silicate, which keeps the clay particles in suspension and reduces the amount of water needed to form the slip. This slip is creamy in consistency and is made out of a less-plastic clay than that used for throwing on the wheel. Pick the slip best suited to your needs and firing range: low-fire, middle range, or porcelain; but remember that the lower ranges are best to start with, as warping problems are not as great.

Slip Casting

First, dust the inside of the mold with talc* to make it easier to remove the cast piece, brush or blow out any residue of talc, then assemble the mold. A two-part mold should be held together with string, wire, or large rubber bands, and the cracks should be sealed with clay. Then pour the slip in and wait while the plaster absorbs the water from the clay. As this happens, you will see the clay becoming firm around the edges. As soon as the walls are thick enough, pour out the excess slip. For a thin piece you will probably need just one pouring, while for a thicker piece you may want to pour in more layers while the inside clay is moist. Wait until the piece is stiff enough to hold its shape, then remove the mold and let the piece dry. Remember that you will have considerable shrinkage as the water evaporates, so make your mold larger than the final size you want to cast. If you don't remember to do this, you may end up with a wine goblet that can only hold a mouthful of wine.

Although it appears basically simple, slip casting is a process that requires the experience of trial and error. In the hands of an experienced caster, complex and extremely fine pieces can be cast (Figures 9-73 and 9-74). Both sculptors and potters use this basic method to form multiples, either creating their own models from which to make the molds, or making molds from found objects and combining the cast shapes into new compositions (Figures 8-36 and 8-37).

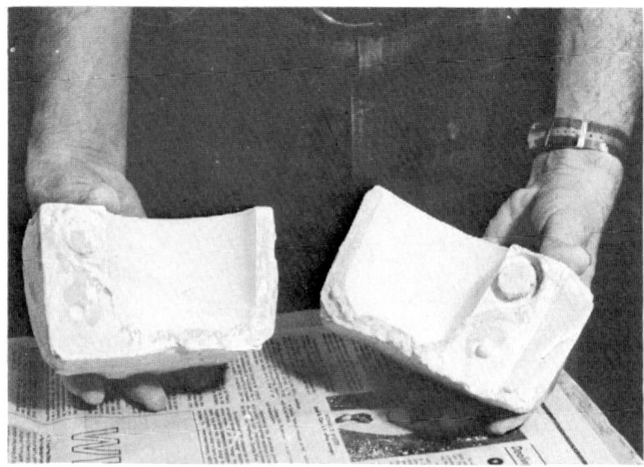

Figure 9-70 Two-piece mold is fitted together, knobs fitting into sockets, then filled with slip.

* Wear a mask, or be careful not to breathe the talc.

Figure 9-71 As the walls build to the desired thickness, the slip is poured off. After clay hardens, mold is removed and cast piece is dried slowly.

Figure 9-72 Jacqui Poncelet, of England, assembles a five-piece mold for one of her thin, bone china cast pieces. Partly assembled mold shows registration keys and carved stripes, which will appear on the final piece as raised stripes.

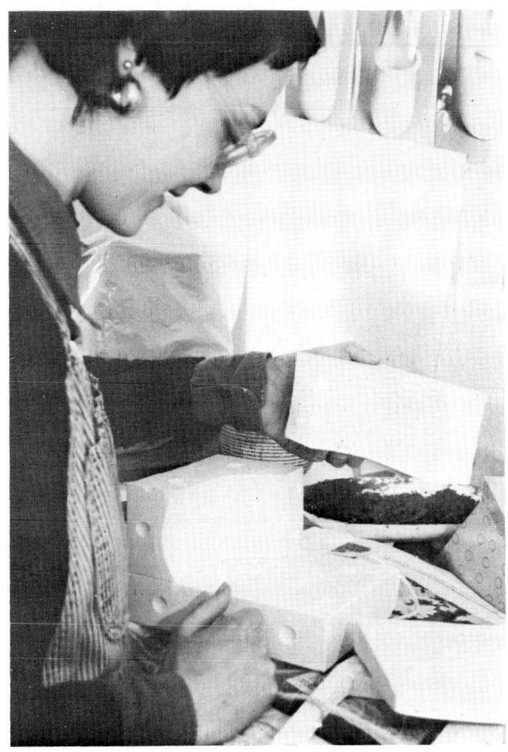

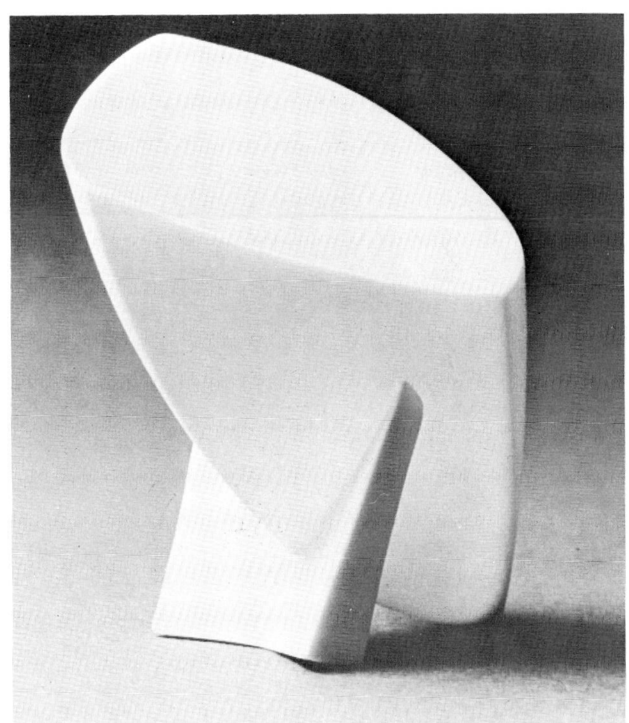

Figure 9-73 Poncelet often pours first one layer of white bone china slip into the mold, then a layer of pale, stained slip over that, sometimes carving through the white. The final pieces have a translucent, subtle color. Jacqui Poncelet, cast bone china. *Courtesy of the artist.*

Figure 9-74 To get this effect, Poncelet poured the stripes of stained slip first, then a layer of white slip. Such thin walls are susceptible to warping, and the different tensions between the stained and unstained slips can cause separation during drying.

Factory Methods

Factory methods for making multiples include casting, hydraulic-press forming methods, and **jiggering.** In jiggering, a plaster mold is placed on a wheel, and a machine presses a slab of clay onto it. As the wheel turns, a shaped pattern called a template then trims the piece to the desired shape.

Hand potters do not generally use the power-driven machines, but some production workshops do adapt factory methods to speed up their work, combining them with hand methods. This has been done throughout history. For example, in Rome, and later elsewhere in Europe, potters formed pieces in revolving molds, pressing in the clay and smoothing it by hand. Factory-made ceramics is beyond the scope of this book, but it should be pointed out that factory methods can produce well-designed and functional shapes. Although factory ware can never have the direct quality of hand-made pottery, some individuality may be obtained in the glazing and decoration (Figure 9-73).

The Potter in the Factory

Good design and an interchange between factory personnel and individual artists have for some time been characteristic of several European ceramics factories. Companies like Bing and Grøndhal in Denmark, De Porcelyne Fles in Holland, and Arabia in Finland have maintained experimental studios where sculptors and potters work on their own individual pieces and may or may not design for the company. This exchange between artist and industry is now being tried in various American companies like the Kohler Company and Syracuse China Corporation, among others, which have given artists opportunities to work with their facilities (Figures 8-26 and 8-40).

Figure 9-75 Factory-produced Ruska ware by Arabia, Finland, designed by Ulla Procopé. The glaze on this stoneware is blown on individually so that there are no two pieces alike in the series. *Courtesy, Arabia, Finland.*

Chapter Ten

Texturing and Coloring Clay

From the very beginning of ceramics, potters and sculptors have not only shaped clay creatively, but they have also combined clay forms, clay textures, and the colors of clay or glazes into satisfying compositions.

Form and Expression

Although the potter is usually more concerned with function and the sculptor more interested in the expression of an idea or emotion, both have to make decisions about the visual aspect of their work. Of course, the clay crafter may be both potter and sculptor, and the object may be either functional or nonfunctional or a combination of both, but the problems of design are basically the same.

The motivation that impels people to work in clay may change from place to place, from time to time. Religious needs, functional needs, or emotional needs may vary tremendously, but the aesthetic considerations remain very much the same whether the clay-crafter is making a ritual figure, a water jug, a teapot, or a large sculpture. Looking at the clay objects of the past and at contemporary ceramics, we can see how the human hand and mind have been challenged in a difficult but satisfying relationship with clay. In this relationship, the task is to create an object—whether coffee cup or temple sculpture—so that each part, the relationship between them, and all the parts together effectively express the crafter's original idea or need.

Changing Motivations

Throughout history, one of the strongest motivations for building with clay has been to supply what the local culture needed, whether it was a figure of a rain god or a cooking vessel. Today, however, when machines produce the bulk of our functional containers and self-expression for itself is considered valid, we have the freedom to explore unlimited relationships between form and material, between idea and form.

Perhaps it was easier to judge success in terms of rigid cultural needs or the traditional dictates of "beauty," "harmony," or "function," but we no longer live in an age of absolutes. Now we are forced to evaluate our work in relation to our *own* motivations and in relation to the clay itself. However, exploring new ideas and new techniques has long been valid in the crafts. For example, the Chinese would never have developed porcelain without centuries of exploration and innovation, nor would the Rhenish potters have discovered stoneware or salt glazing without an experimental attitude. This sense of discovery, the impulse to push the craft further and further, is nothing new.

Choosing Your Own Approach

If you decide to tear apart traditional relationships, to break down historical continuity, perhaps to deal only with the *idea* of clay, then choose carefully whatever means you use to implement your ideas, and use them with integrity.

Everyone is born with sensitivity to form, color, and texture and their relationship to each other. Although you may have lost some of that sensitivity, you can redevelop it and listen to it. Get to know yourself, and create whatever will best express your idea, regardless of the rules. To do this you may have to face your own evasions and question your own motivations. Clay is such a direct material, you cannot hide behind it.

If, on the other hand, it is traditional satisfaction of eye and hand that motivates you, to continue rather than break tradition, then you will need to consider all the parts of your piece in relation to each other. How does the spout of a teapot echo the curves of the body and handle? Do the rhythms throughout a piece of sculpture offer us the enjoyment of repetition punctuated by enough surprise to keep an exploring eye or hand interested? Does the decoration add vitality to the surface without detracting from the shape? Does the color of a glaze relate to the shape so intimately that you can imagine no other possible color or texture on that one piece of fired clay?

Whichever approach you choose, learn to edit your own work, to throw away a cherished idea, a delightful bit of decoration, or a luscious color if it does not contribute to the whole. Ask yourself if it really adds anything to the expression of your idea. If not, THROW IT OUT.

Surface Treatments of the Clay Body

Before you consider the many ways you can treat the surface of your already formed clay object, you might want to think about the changes you can make in the clay body itself before you shape it. First, your choice of clay depends not only on technical considerations of forming and firing but also on what you want to say. Obviously, if yours is to be a rough, strong statement, coarse earthenware or heavily grogged stoneware would be your choice; but if delicacy is important, a fine clay like porcelain would be more appropriate. You can usually buy ready-mixed clay in the color you want, but if you prefer to mix your own, you can change the color by adding oxides. To change the texture you can mix in grog or other substances. Jill Crowley, for example, mixes her own clay, adding crushed brick so that the surface of her sculpture becomes rough, with various-sized extrusions (Figure 10-1). Ernst Häusermann adds a variety of natural materials, which he gathers from the woods and fields of the Swiss valley where he lives, experimenting and making tests to see what new and interesting textures and colors he can develop in his stoneware clay body (Figure 8-15).

Color in the Clay

In addition to using oxides for color, you can change the color of your clay body with commercial body stains, which come in a wide range of colors. By using these stains with a white clay, you can achieve considerable brilliance of color in the clay body itself. You could, for example, form a whole piece out of blue-stained clay, or you could, like Paul Philp or Hans Munck Anderson, combine colored clays in a variety of patterns. (See Figures 10-2 to 10-4.) If you use this technique, you will have to experiment and learn how to keep the various clay bodies separate yet at the same time melded together enough to keep cracks from developing at the point where the two colors meet. Too much stain can change the clay body so much that one color may shrink at a different rate from the others, causing warping and cracking along the joints.

Figure 10-1 To create "Cabbage Cup With Soil Saucer," Jill Crowley, of England, hand shaped clay that had been textured by adding crushed brick. Raku fired. *Courtesy, Crafts Advisory Committee, London.*

Figure 10-2 Agate-ware stemmed dish by Paul Philp, of Wales. Colored clay with a variety of commercial stains. Philp uses a complex layering process to achieve his marbled colors. *Courtesy, Crafts Advisory Committee, London.*

Figure 10-3 Paul Philp presses agate slabs into molds to form these tiny boxes, which open to show interiors with different clay patterns. Philp, who has always been interested in the colors and textures of minerals as well as the patterns visible through a microscope, gave up working in stoneware in order to use stains in white earthenware. *Courtesy of the artist.*

Figure 10-4 (*Above Left*) Hans Munk Anderson, of Denmark, twines stained clay coils into a rope, preparing to form an agate-ware bowl. (*Above Right*) He coils colored clay ropes to make a base, carefully melding them together to preserve the pattern of the clay. (*Right*) Anderson presses coils into a plaster mold, building up the bowl. *Photos by Mogens S. Koch, Copenhagen.*

Textures on Damp Clay

The earliest potters usually decorated pots by pressing a fingernail, a stick, or a cord into the damp clay. Impressing, incising, carving, or stamping are still used to change the surface of the clay, to add decoration or texture to the piece while the clay is still soft. You can use the simplest tools to scratch lines into a still-damp pot, or you can make the most elaborate clay or wood stamps to impress texture or designs. You can also look around, in your home, or outdoors and find a great variety of everyday objects to leave interesting impressions in the clay (Figures 10-5 to 10-9). Like any decorative effect, if used with restraint, stamping can give your piece greater surface interest; overdone, or poorly composed, it becomes distracting.

When you have completed your piece, you can also let it dry longer—until it is still damp but hard enough to handle easily—**leather hard.** It is at this point that you can carve into it easily. Also, at this point, you can score the damp surface, moisten it with water, slip, or a mixture of water and vinegar, and add raised decoration, a process called **sprigging** (Figure 7-63). (See Figures 10-10 to 10-13).

Figure 10-5 Ladi Kwali, of Nigeria, demonstrating how she combines incised lines and textured areas to decorate a water jar. With an unerring sense of design, she breaks the swelling form of the pot at just the right points to emphasize its form. The roughened areas also make it easier to lift if the jar is wet and slippery. *Courtesy, Field Museum of Natural History, Chicago.*

Figure 10-6 A small, basket-shaped jar from prehistoric Thailand, decorated with cord impressions and a coiling snake, reminds us that the urge to add decorative or symbolic touches is an ancient response to clay. Northeast Thailand, 2nd century B.C. to 2nd century A.D. Height 3¾ in. (9.5 cm), diameter 3¾ in. (9.5 cm). *Courtesy, Asian Art Museum of San Francisco, The Avery Brundage Collection. Gift of Dr. and Mrs. James Alexander Hamilton.*

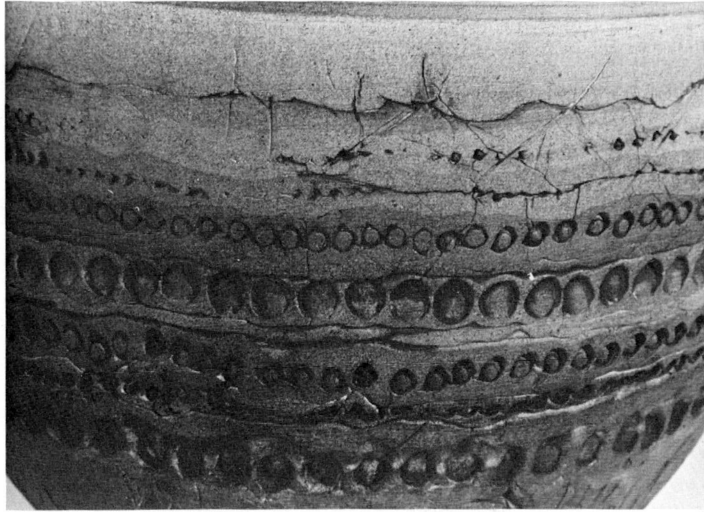

Figure 10-7 Detail of a coiled pot with wheel-thrown base and rim by Sandra Blain, of the United States. The joining lines of the coils form a decorative pattern along with the rows of stamped marks. Natural or household objects, such as seed pods, bottle tops, or hardware items, can be pressed into damp clay to form decorative textures. Stoneware, 1977. *Photo by Roger Smith.*

Figure 10-8 Erik Gronborg, of the United States, rolls his slabs out with a rolling pin, then impresses them with patterns and images from many sources—newspaper zinc plates, wooden printing blocks, or textured fabrics. *Courtesy of the artist.*

Figure 10-9 Rolf Overberg, of Germany, stamped a dark manganese-colored clay body with metal printing plates to form the middle area of "Book." Stamped area is unglazed, while the surrounding area is covered with wood ash glaze with copper oxide. Height 33½ in. (85 cm), width 25½ in. (65 cm). *Courtesy of the artist.*

Figure 10-11 Vase by the late Italian potter Anselmo Bucci (1887–1959), decorated with undulating bands carved in relief. Brown, with silver luster. *Courtesy, Museo Internazionale delle Ceramiche, Faenza.*

Figure 10-10 Italian sculptor-potter Carlo Zauli carves flowing, linear decoration to enhance a textured band on a simple cylinder. *Courtesy of the artist.*

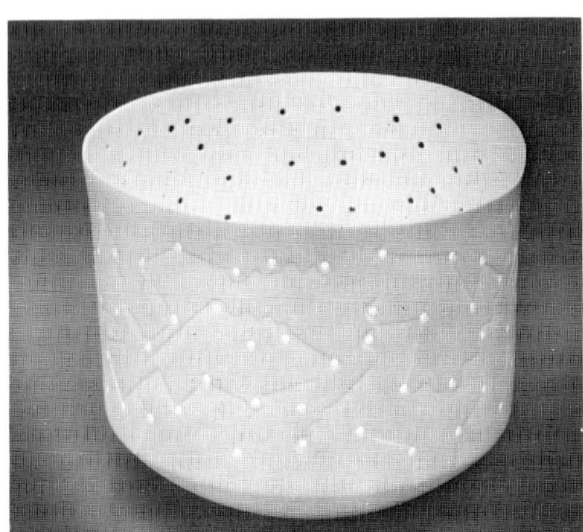

Figure 10-12 Jacqui Poncelet, of England, carved and pierced this translucent bone china bowl, adding to its delicacy. However, since they are high-fired, her pieces are strong, and she safely ships or carries them in tins. Cast bone china, hand polished, unglazed. Height 3¼ in. (8.32 cm), diameter 4 in. (10.24 cm). *Courtesy, Crafts Advisory Committee, London.*

Figure 10-13 Relief decoration, carved and glazed, decorates bowl by Ray Wakeland, of the United States. Stoneware. Height 6½ in. (16.5 cm), diameter 15 in. (38.1 cm). *Courtesy, Southern Highland Handicraft Guild, Tennessee.*

Slips and Engobes

Slip is basically a mixture of clay and water. It was used by early potters to cover the reddish color of earthenware clay, so that many of the early slips were apt to be white or cream. But slip can also be dark and can be used to produce a variety of decorative effects. Correctly, the term **engobe** is applied to any slip that covers the whole of a pot or sculpture, while the term *slip* refers to a clay and water mixture used only for decoration. However, the term *slip* is frequently used for both.

Fitting the Engobe or Slip

When using slip or engobe, it is usually a good idea to use the same clay body as was used for the pot. Since clays vary in their shrinkage rates, an engobe or slip made of a different clay may not have the same rate of shrinkage, so may peel off after firing. This is the problem faced by early potters when they tried to make white or cream engobes to cover the red earthenware body. To mix lighter engobes and slips, you can add light-colored clays like kaolin, bentonite, and ball clays in varying proportions (see Making Multiples, Chapter 9). But each of these has a different rate of shrinkage, so you might have to add flint to counteract shrinkage or borax to help the engobe adhere to the pot before and during firing.

If you use a cream or buff clay body and a darker slip, then you have still more options. For example, you could use a light-colored body and color the contrasting slip with oxides or stains, or you could reverse it, coloring the body and using a light slip for decoration. If you want to make an opaque white slip, you will have to experiment to find the right amount of opacifier to use. Obviously, then, working out the best slip or engobe to use with a particular clay body involves making a series of tests.

Decorating With Slip

It is usually easier to create appropriate decoration with slip rather than with glaze because the clay slip is so similar in quality to the clay body of the pot. Slip decoration has a visual relationship to clay, and with a simple transparent glaze over it, the material is left to make its own statement. Some ways of using slip decoratively are illustrated in this chapter, but look also at other photographs in Part One, and at pieces in museums.

Slip can be trailed on, rather like writing "Happy Birthday" on a cake, or it can be brushed on or painted over **wax resist.** To use this last method, paint with wax whatever area of the dried pot you want to remain the color of the clay body. Then when you brush the slip over the waxed pot, the color will only adhere to the areas of the dried pot that were not waxed. The wax burns out in the fire, leaving the contrasting body color. (See Figure 11-42 for the same wax resist method used with glaze.)

Figure 10-14 Harvest jug, probably made by John Bird of Bideford, England, in 1775. The design and inscription are scratched through a white slip coating to the brown earthenware body using sgraffito technique. The inscription reads:

Harvis is com all bissey
Now Mackin your
Barley mow when men do
Laber hard and swet good
Ale is better far than meet
Bideford April 28, 1775 M–W

Lead glaze over slip. Height 13½ in. (34.3 cm). *Courtesy, Royal Albert Memorial Museum, Exeter, England.*

Figure 10-15 Early American slip cup used for trailing slip designs onto earthenware and stoneware. Filled with clay mixed with water to the consistency of cream, the cup allowed the slip to run out through a quill set in the neck of the cup or in a cork.

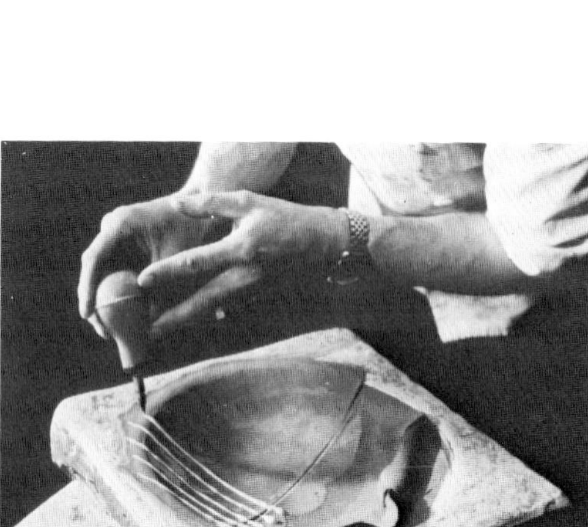

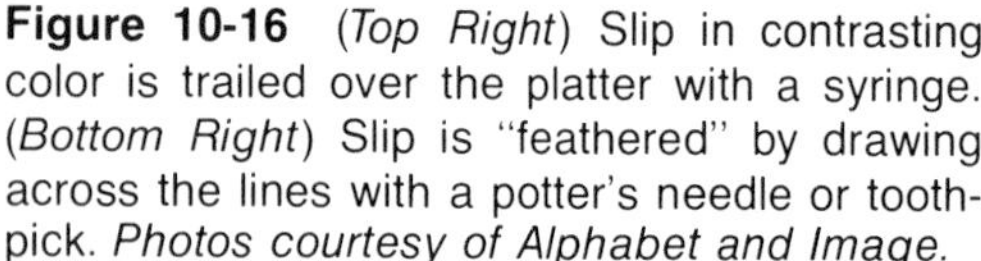

Figure 10-16 (*Top Right*) Slip in contrasting color is trailed over the platter with a syringe. (*Bottom Right*) Slip is "feathered" by drawing across the lines with a potter's needle or toothpick. *Photos courtesy of Alphabet and Image.*

Figure 10-17 Sandra Blain used newspaper to mask off some areas on this pot, then sprayed it with Albany slip. After the pot was bisque fired she applied blue-green matt slip, then rubbed it off the top surfaces. After reduction firing, the pot has a surface that combines matt and gloss textures. Slab formed, thrown base; Albany slip, matt slip. Height 16 in. (40.6 cm), diameter 18 in. (45.7 cm). *Courtesy of the artist.*

Another method is to coat the whole pot with a contrasting engobe and scratch designs into it with a sharp instrument. This sgraffito technique allows the darker or lighter clay body to show through wherever you scratch (Figure 10-14).

You can also paint slip around areas, leaving the body its natural color to produce the design. Or you can paint matt slip on a burnished body, producing a contrast in surface rather than color. This is a method used with skill by Southwest Native American potters like Maria Martinez (Color Plate 9, p. 146D). And look as well at the way in which early Nasca and Moche potters used slip to decorate their pots, then work out your own methods, testing and experimenting, for that is the only way to learn what clay materials can do. (See Figures 10-14 to 10-20 and Color Plate 8, p. 146C.)

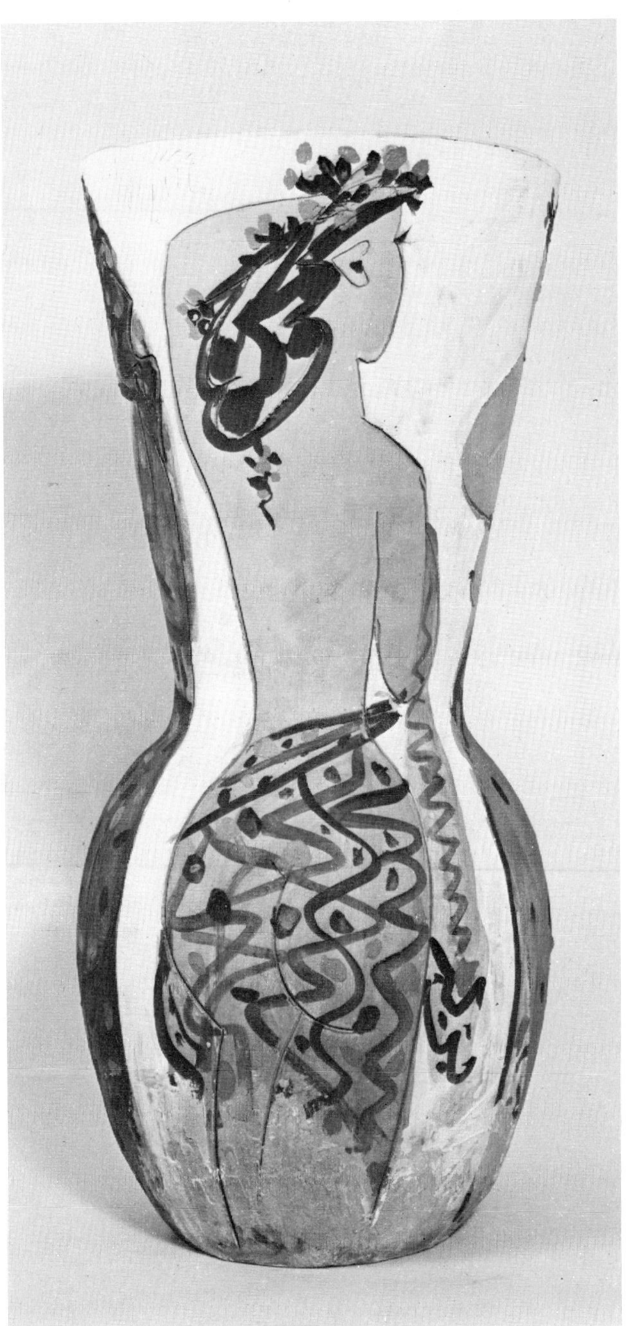

Figure 10-18 "Vase with Four Seasons," painted by Pablo Picasso with white, red, brown, and black slip with sgraffito lines. Once-fired earthenware, France, 1954. *Courtesy, Museo Internazionale delle Ceramiche, Faenza. Photo by Minarini.*

Figure 10-19 (*Left*) Jules Olitski, "Brown Slab Two." Working mainly in gray, black, white, and brown slips, United States painter Jules Olitski creates a painterly surface on stoneware slabs. "I myself find no romance or virtue or mystery in any particular material. All I want from any material is that it give the work the look I want it to have." Height 30 in. (76.2 cm), width 13½ in. (34.3 cm). *Photo and quote courtesy of Everson Museum of Art. Photo by Stuart Lisson.*

Figure 10-20 (*Below*) Jules Olitski, working at a joint Syracuse University–Everson Museum project, which brought painters into a new relationship with clay, said of the experience ". . . clay and paint draw my hands in, as though by necessity. In the work I did at Syracuse I think I had this experience more than ever before, especially with the spreading of colored slips on the surfaces of the slab pieces." *Photo and quote courtesy of Everson Museum of Art. Photo by Stuart Lisson.*

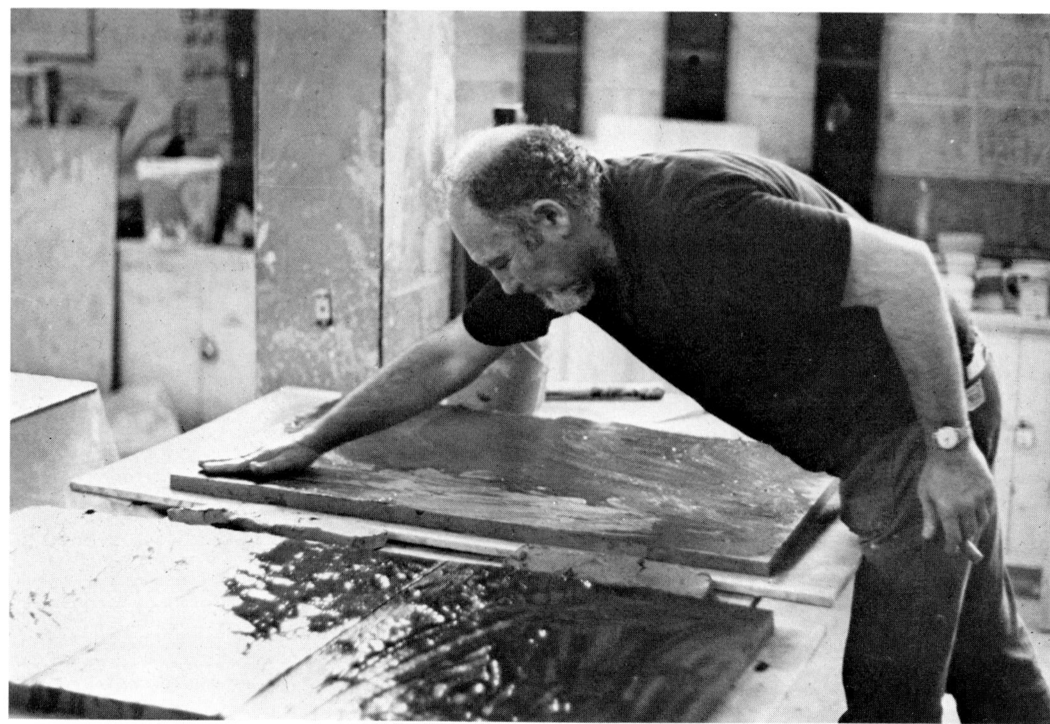

Decorating With Oxides

An **oxide** is, as its name suggests, a combination of any basic element and oxygen. Over a period of time, almost all the basic elements on earth have formed a chemical combination with oxygen. We have already seen that some oxides, such as iron, act as fluxes, lowering the fusion point of clay bodies as well as coloring them, and we will see in the next chapter how oxides are used in glazes.

These chemical compounds—the oxides—are also useful for decorating. Even if you were limited to iron oxide alone, you would find you could create a remarkably wide range of effects. But there are also cobalt, copper, and manganese oxides, among others, which alone or in combination allow you to develop a considerable range of colors.

Oxides have been used throughout history, either alone or in combination with glazes, to bring surface interest to ceramics. Depending on the opacity or transparency of the glaze used, the oxide decoration may show up best if you paint it over, rather than under, the glaze. Another reason for doing this is that if the glaze is applied over the oxide, it may not adhere properly.

To use oxides for decoration, you can choose from a variety of techniques. You would usually paint oxide decoration on a pot after the clay has been through a bisque firing, although you can also paint it on the dried, unfired clay. You can brush, sponge, or spray oxides onto a piece, or you can carefully paint into scratched lines. You can also effectively add depth and definition to textures or carved areas. For instance, you can sponge on an oxide so that it fills the grooves of a textured area, then wash it off the top of the clay, leaving oxide in the grooves. Or you can cover up parts of the pot with masking tape, wax, or liquid latex compound, paint over it with oxide, and on removing the masking you will have a design that contrasts the color of the clay body and the oxide.

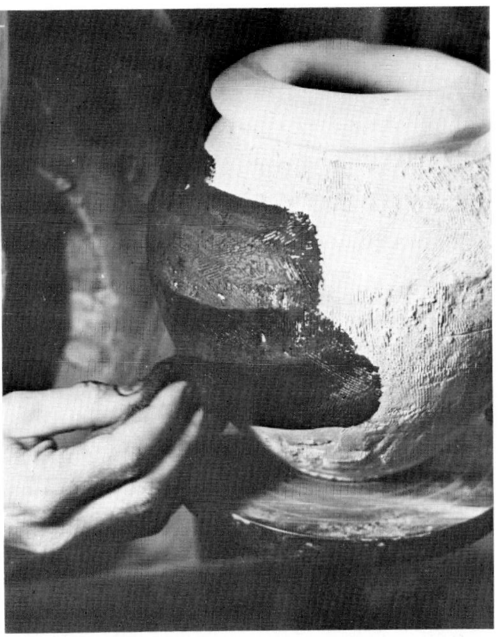

Figure 10-21 Oxides can be wiped onto the pot with a sponge. Textured areas allow some of the clay body color to show through, adding surface interest. *Courtesy, Alphabet and Image.*

Figure 10-22 Metal oxides are used to color glazes, but they can also be used alone under or over glazes. This plate shows the effects produced with a variety of brushes or cords dipped in oxide. *Courtesy, Alphabet and Image.*

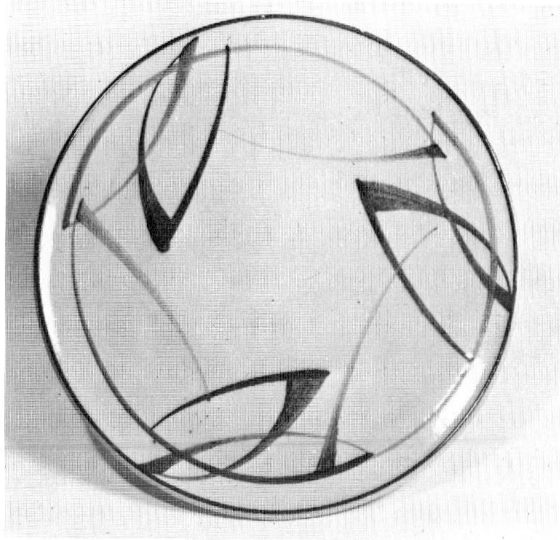

Figure 10-23 Plate by A. Craiger-Smith, of England, decorated with iron and copper oxides. Tin glazed. *Courtesy, Alphabet and Image.*

Figure 10-24 Pam Wright, of England, fashioned a miniature sewing kit of semiporcelain, engraving it with intricate patterns. Leaving the exterior unglazed, she emphasized the engraved designs with manganese oxide and iron oxide. The interior of the boxes, which hold thread reel, four buttons, and a thimble, are glazed white. Height 2¼ in. (5.7 cm), length 4½ in. (11.4 cm). *Courtesy of the artist.*

Freely applied brush decoration with oxides is a traditional method of decorating ceramics. Look at ceramics from the past—especially from the Orient—to see what a variety of effects can be achieved with oxides. Throughout history, brushes, feathers, chewed cactus leaves, and a variety of other methods have been used to apply oxides. For example, the early American potters who made stoneware crocks decorated them with cobalt, sometimes by brushing, but often by trailing the oxide on with a slip cup (Figure 10-15). You can also enrich the color of a piece of sculpture by brushing on an oxide or a combination of them. As in other areas of ceramics, tests are really the only way you will discover exactly how to produce the effects you want with oxides. (See Figures 10-21 to 10-24.)

Underglaze Colors

In addition to the oxides, a wide range of commercial underglaze colors is available. Generally these underglaze colors are formulated for low-fire clays, because at higher temperatures some of the warmer colors will burn out. These commercial colors are mixed with flux and a **refractory,** to help them adhere to the body, and also with gum or some other binder. Painted on either greenware or bisque, these underglaze colors produce rather pastel "ice cream" colors. Underglaze pencils and crayons can also be obtained, so that you can draw in detail or add shading (Figures 10-25 to 10-29 and Color Plates 16 and 20, pp. 274A and 274C).

Decals printed on transfer paper with underglaze colors are available commercially in a wide variety of designs. You can also print underglaze colors on the bisque with rubber stamps or with a silk screen. Photographs can also be transferred to the clay through a silk screen process that uses either underglaze or overglaze colors.

Using one or more of these decorative methods, you can add interest and vitality to your formed clay. At first the temptation may be to overdo the decoration, but soon you will find your own style, your own way to texture the damp clay, to trail on slip, or to brush on an oxide, using the simplest, most direct expression possible.

In Chapter 11 you will learn about the visual aspects of glazes, as well as their functional uses. Glazes give you another whole range of decorating possibilities to explore.

Figure 10-25 (*Left*) "Mars Plate," by Janet Lowe, of the United States. White, low-fire clay, decorated with poured pastel slips. After it was bisque fired, Lowe drew on it with underglaze pencils, then gave it a transparent Wollastonite glaze. Next, she overglazed it with orange and mother-of-pearl luster, adding details with black china paint. Diameter 10 in. (25.4 cm). *Collection of Anona Carey. Courtesy of the artist.*

Figure 10-26 (*Right*) On "Ohio Boy," sculptor Jack Earl used underglaze pencil to create an illusion of texture on smooth, cast vitreous china. Created at Kohler Company, 1976. 15⅞ X 17¾ X 11⅞ in. (40.3 X 45.1 X 30.2 cm). *In collection of John Michael Kohler Arts Center. Photo by Bayens Photo Co.*

Figure 10-27 "You Captured My Heart," by Patti Warashina, of the United States, is a combination of two-dimensional painting and sculptured forms painted with underglaze colors. The figure is painted on a flat background, with nose, arms, and hands in relief, while mouth is recessed. Low-fire clay, wooden arrows, oxidation firing. Height 30 in. (76.2 cm), width 18 in. (45.7 cm), depth 15 in. (38.1 cm). *Courtesy of the artist.*

Figure 10-28 "Billy Bowman," porcelain painted with underglaze. Chris Unterseher, U.S.A. Height 15 in. (38.1 cm), length 7 in. (17.8 cm), 2 in. (5.1 cm) thick. *Courtesy, Quay Ceramics Gallery.*

Figure 10-29 Detail of "Baroque Oak" was drawn with underglaze pencil by Allan Widenhofer, of the United States. He then carefully airbrushed layers of transparent glaze over the drawing and fired it in raku firing. *Courtesy of the artist.*

Chapter Eleven
Glazing

You may be surprised the first time you see a glazed pot ready for the fire. Most people think that the potter has a palette of colors like a painter and need only pick out a color, paint it on, and the pot will come out of the fire the same color. Instead, there sits a chalky, grayish-white pot waiting to be fired. The transformation from this powdery, unfired glaze coating on the bisque ware to a richly colored, perfect surface accounts for much of the satisfaction in a potter's work and a good deal of the frustration. You will soon experience the combined excitement and anxiety of waiting for a kiln to open, of waiting to see how a glaze has responded to the fire (Color Plate 15, p. 210D).

Glaze Function and Composition

How and why glazes act as they do may seem totally mysterious at first, and, confronted with chemical formulas and tables of molecular weights, you may decide to leave the subject to the experts. But if you want to work creatively with glazes, you will probably want to learn how to formulate your own, or at least how to make changes in the glaze formulas you get from books, magazines, or other potters. Since it is unlikely that you will plunge immediately into glaze formulation, detailed information about the methods of glaze calculation and the steps a potter goes through when calculating a glaze formula has been placed in the Appendix. (Also in the Appendix is a list of the most common chemicals and materials used in ceramics, along with charts of molecular weights, firing ranges, and other necessary information.)

Modern chemistry helps us analyze the composition of a glaze and learn exactly what materials are needed to change its composition to achieve certain effects. So, glaze testing is simpler and faster now because we can start out with this basic chemical knowledge. It is still necessary to test, however, and you may find that your best glaze is the result of experimentation. Indeed, there is no reason why you cannot make excellent glazes by measuring out the basic ingredients within the generally known proportions, adding or subtracting materials, and then testing the glaze. Measuring cups and spoons and a creative approach can be successful for those who wish to avoid chemistry, and there is no need to be put off by the "mystery" of glazes. Glaze making is not some form of alchemy performed by wizards in peaked hats.

In this chapter we will give you some basic information to help you understand what happens when you coat your bisque-fired pot or sculpture with that apparently mysterious mixture and trustingly place it in the kiln. In the meantime, you can also learn the process of mixing glaze ingredients by using school formulas that have been translated into **batch** recipes. Or you may decide to avoid mixing altogether and choose from the many commercially prepared glazes: low-fire, leadless glazes, which are a safe way to make earthenware watertight and usable; or high-fire glazes, which presumably will fire to the same color as the sample tile in the store. However, you will find that choosing a glaze is not like choosing paint from a color chart, for the action of the fire or the clay body under the glaze can change its color.

Figure 11-1 Three pots by Janet Leach, of England, show a variety of surface treatment. (*Left*) Scratched decoration, poured glaze. (*Center*) White porcelaneous body, heavy crackle glaze with brown iron splash. (*Right*) Unglazed brush decoration, early 1970s. *Courtesy, Crafts Advisory Committee, London.*

Why Glazes Are Used

Glazes are not only functional, making the fired piece impervious to liquids and giving it a durable surface, but they add color and visual interest to pottery or sculpture. No glaze, however, can make an unsuccessfully formed pot into a thing of beauty.

Glazes can be glossy or matt, transparent or opaque, while the color range possible extends from subdued earth tones to brilliant reds and blues (Color Plate 2, p. 50B).

A glaze can be applied very thinly, allowing the texture of the clay to show through, or so thickly that it develops its own texture quite apart from the clay (Figure 11-9). The decorative effects that are possible with glazes vary from accidental drips running down the sides, often really controlled by the potter (Figure 11-17), to carefully painted designs (Figure 11-40). As you study the glaze examples in this book, consider how you could use each type most effectively in your own work (Figures 11-16 to 11-34). For example, the brilliant glossy red of a Chinese glaze might be very beautiful on a small, simple form, but it would hardly suit a large, heavily grogged slab piece. Or if the pot or sculpture has heavy carving or modeling, a glossy glaze will destroy the impact of the forms through confusing reflections and highlights; on such a piece, a matt surface would be the best solution. (See Figures 11-1 to 11-12).

Safety

Function and safety must also be considered when choosing a glaze. For instance, food collecting in pits or cracks of a casserole or bowl can be a health hazard, so glazes chosen for the interiors of such pieces should be smooth and carefully applied. Also, if the interior glaze on a bowl or cooking vessel is light colored, food particles are easier to see and wash off. Lead, which contributes many desirable qualities to a glaze, is poisonous if leached from the glaze by the acids in fruit juices or other foods, so it should not be used for food containers. What's more, raw lead is dangerous to work with in the studio. So it should not be used by an inexperienced potter. There *are* ways to work safely with lead and to make safe lead glazes, but great care must be taken in the glaze formulation and firing to produce a safe, nonsoluble surface that cannot release lead into foods. For these reasons, it is wise for a beginner to stay away from lead.

Composition of Glazes

A glaze is basically a glassy, impervious coating that is fused to the surface of the clay by heat. The separate materials that you have mixed together gradually melt and fuse as the kiln temperature is raised and eventually combine into a completely new material—the glaze. The oxides of silica, alumina, and others such as calcium, sodium, or zinc play important roles in the formation of glazes. The main glass-forming ingredient in glazes is silica, which is highly resistant to heat (Figure 11-2). A glaze could be made of silica alone, but since its melting point is so high, that is impractical; few clay bodies could withstand the heat, and few kilns could fire that high.

Figure 11-2 Silica, the main ingredient of glazes, is extremely resistant to heat. These cubes of special silica insulation will protect NASA's space shuttle from intense heat when it returns to the earth's atmosphere. They cast off heat so quickly that a technician can hold a cube seconds after it leaves a 2300°F (1260°C) oven. (*Left*) 10 seconds after removal from oven. (*Center*) A few seconds later. (*Right*) Less than 30 seconds out of the oven the cube is turning gray at the edges although still red-hot inside. *Courtesy, NASA.*

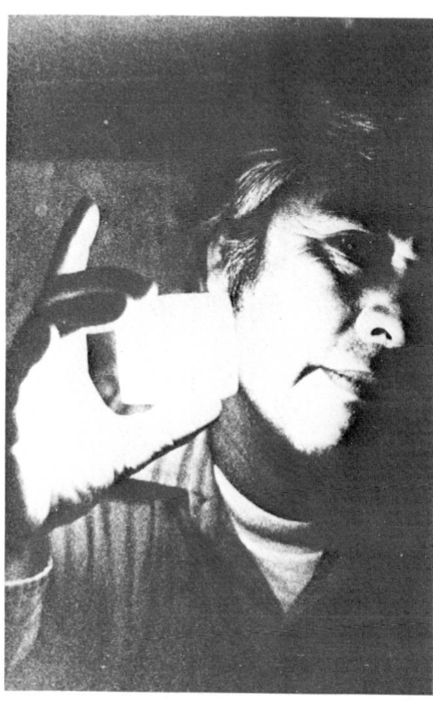
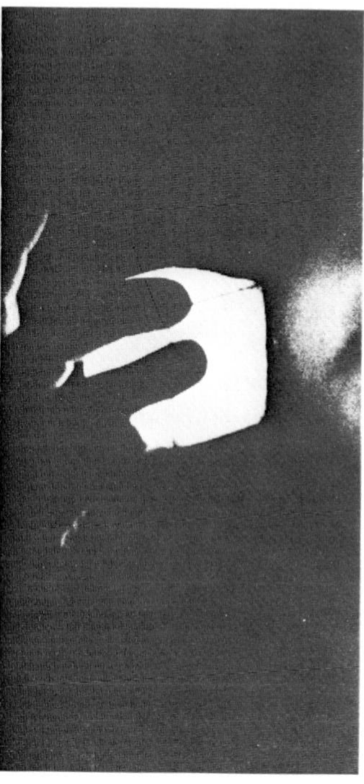
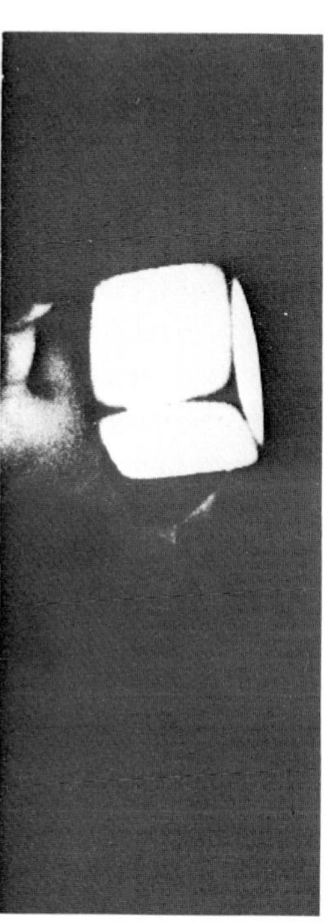

The proportion of silica in a high-fire glaze can be greater than in a low-fire glaze, because at low temperatures too much silica would keep the glaze from melting. Generally, as much silica as possible is used, because silica adds to the durability of a glaze and helps it resist the attack of chemicals. Therefore, in order to lower the melting point of the silica, another ingredient must be added—flux. It is a fact that many combinations of materials have lower melting points than the same materials used alone, and this is a basic factor in glaze making. The melting of a glaze is a result of the interaction of the oxides in the glaze when they are exposed to heat. Thus the fusion temperature of a glaze may be lowered considerably depending upon what fluxing oxides are used in combination and upon their proportions in relation to the silica. At this point, we are talking about oxides as glaze components, not as coloring agents. However, the oxides used to color a glaze can also bring extra fluxing action to the glaze, lowering its melting point even further. There are just over a dozen oxides used in making basic glazes (not for coloring them), but the possible combinations of these are almost endless.

The third ingredient necessary to most glazes is a refractory (high-melting) material, alumina. This oxide, even used in very small amounts, adds strength and durability to the glaze and keeps it from being too runny. Without it, the glaze may run down the sides of the pot during firing. Also, without alumina, glazes crystallize during the cooling process and are apt to become opaqued or mottled. However, sometimes the potter wants crystals to develop for decorative reasons; in that case the alumina content is reduced (Color Plate 13, p. 210C).

Each of these three basic glaze ingredients may be introduced to the glaze by adding any of a variety of ceramic materials. Each of these materials has individual properties and reacts in its own way with other materials (see Chemicals and Materials list in the Appendix). For example, zinc oxide (ZnO) is an active flux at temperatures above 2109°F (1154°C). It can also make a glaze matt and opaque if you add it in larger amounts. If used in small amounts, it can add smoothness to a glaze, but if too much is used alone as a flux, it can make the glaze **crawl** on the pot or cause pinholes to develop. Zinc interacts well with copper to help produce bright turquoises; but if it is used with chrome, it sometimes produces brown rather than chrome green. It is clear from this example that the properties

Figure 11-3 Pale greenish bands are produced by copper carbonate in the clay body of these agate porcelain vases by Lucie Rie, of England. Spiraling bands are created in the throwing and show through the semimatt white glaze, emphasizing the multiple curves of the vases. Once-fired porcelain 2282°F (1250°C). Heights 6 in. (15.2 cm) and 11 in. (27.9 cm). *Courtesy, Alphabet and Image.*

and behavior of each material must be understood fully, and the effect it will have on the other glaze ingredients must be considered. Such understanding comes only through experience and testing; and although potters today rely on chemistry more than their predecessors, they must still test glazes to see how they act on a particular clay or in a certain firing situation.

Glaze Tests

Until comparatively recently, all glaze formulation was based on trial and error. With this laborious method the Chinese potters developed their subtle celadon (Color Plate 1, p. 50A) and brilliant **flambé glazes,** the Near Eastern potters developed bright blue glazes (Color Plate 4, p. 50D), and the Europeans perfected colored decoration on tin-glazed earthenware (Color Plate 5, p. 146A). Although modern chemistry has given the potter much useful information about the behavior of glaze materials, the potter still depends on trial and error and testing. Slight changes in the amounts of certain ingredients can change a glaze radically, and there is no way to be sure what a particular glaze will look like without making a test or series of tests. Tests allow you to change the proportion of one material slightly and see what happens to the glaze. All potters, no matter how experienced, test constantly, always looking for new and better glaze formulas.

Figure 11-4 Tenmoku glaze on a slab bottle by England's Bernard Leach. Leach's years in Japan brought him mastery over such oriental glazes, and his influence has made them popular in the West. Stoneware, 1970. *Courtesy, Crafts Advisory Committee, London.*

To make a series of tests, you will need bisqued tiles. Make the tiles out of the same clay body on which the glaze will be used. Shape them so that they will stand up and allow you to see how the glaze acts on a vertical surface, for you want to see how much it runs, as well as to test it for color and surface. You can make tiles by cutting up a slab and bending it into an L shape, or you can throw a low basic cylinder and slice it into sections (Color Plate 15, p. 210D). Male a hole in the tile so it can be hung up for easy reference, and record the proportions in a notebook or write them on the tile with an underglaze pencil or iron or cobalt oxide.

To see what happens to a glaze when you change the proportions of its ingredients, run a series of tests. Get a basic glaze recipe from your instructor, another potter, or from any glaze book, or use the example given on page 263 (Example of Changing the Flux). It is important, however, to choose a glaze with known results. You will be testing it by changing only one ingredient a small amount at a time and recording the results. This is how a potter experiments with a glaze, adapting it to individual needs or trying to find new effects. Keep track of the materials and the amounts you change, recording how these changes affect the glaze.

Figure 11-5 White, matt wood ash glaze enhances the shape of a thrown bowl by Doucet-Saito, of Canada. Stoneware. Height 4 in. (10 cm), diameter 8⅝ in. (22 cm). *Collection of Tatsuzo Shimaoka, Japan. Copyright Doucet-Saito. Photo by Jean Pierre Boudin.*

Figure 11-6 The glaze treatment on each piece in this group is so well fitted to its size and shape that it is hard to visualize any other. Stoneware vases by Katherine Pleydell-Bouverie, bowl by Nora Braden, both of England. 1935. *Courtesy, Victoria and Albert Museum, Crown Copyright.*

Figure 11-7 (*Left*) Brilliantly colored, shiny glaze emphasizes the simple forms of a stoneware jar by Lynn Gault, of the United States. Red oxide glaze. Height 21 in. (53.3 cm). *Courtesy, Southern Highland Handicraft Guild.*

Figure 11-8 Deep blue and rich brown glazes fit the form of a vase by Nils Thorsson, of Denmark. Stoneware, c. 1952. Royal Copenhagen Porcelain Factory. *Courtesy, Museum of Decorative Art, Copenhagen.*

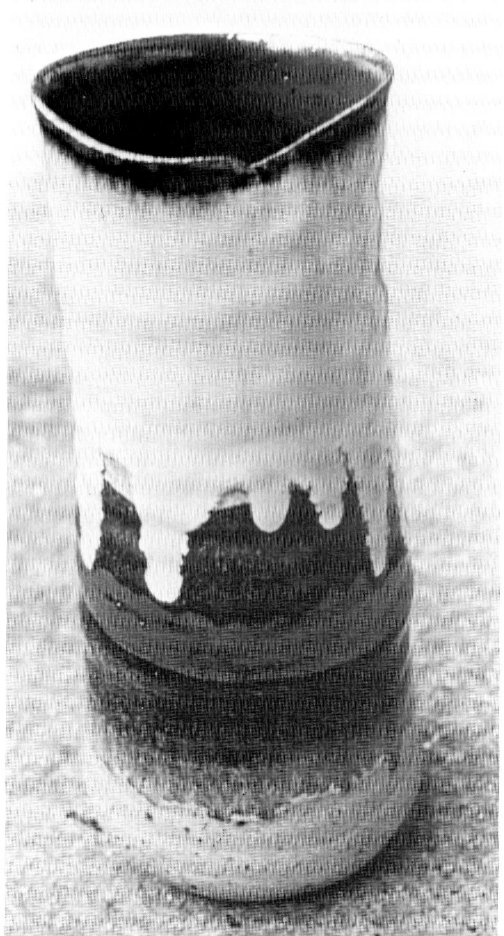

Figure 11-9 Iron slip under an ash glaze applied in varying thicknesses on a basic cylinder form. Glaze shades from thick buttery white through black to browns, with the clay body left unglazed at the bottom for contrast. Local materials and wood-stove ash, tested and retested, provide Ernst Häusermann, of Switzerland, with many of his glaze effects. Stoneware, 1977.

Figure 11-10 "Cat," by U.S. potter Mary Caroline Richards, captures feline grace and pride with a few strokes of a brush. The glaze application allows the throwing ridges to show through, repeating the rhythm of the drawing. Stoneware, brush decorated. *Courtesy of the artist.*

Figure 11-11 Ron Judd, of the United States, first poured Albany slip glaze over the whole surface of this large vase, giving a reddish brown background. Next, he poured Albany slip with rutile, producing yellowish brown areas. These show through the final light-tan matt glaze.

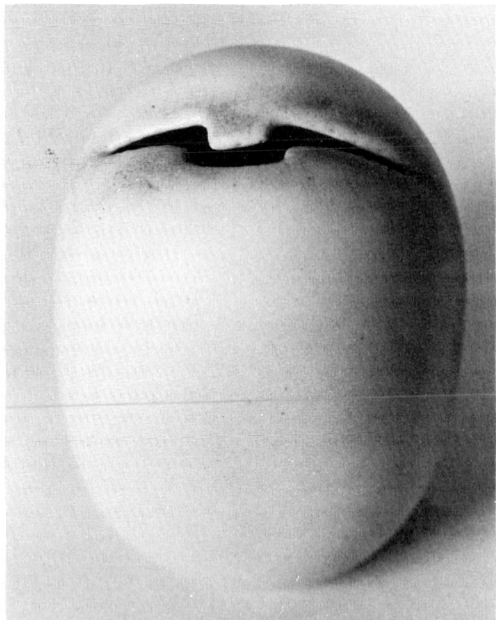

Figure 11-12 Simple form and glaze treatment of miniature egg serve to focus attention on the crack—suggesting further opening. Val Barry, England, white porcelain, raw pink glaze. Height 5 in. (12.7 cm). *Photo by Ian Yoemans. Courtesy of the artist.*

Mixing a Glaze for Tests

Mix a large enough batch of your selected glaze so that small variations caused by mixing or spilling will not change it too much; you will probably want a minimum of 500 grams. To mix the ingredients, use a balance scale (Figure 11-13). Weigh out the dry ingredients, then add them to a small quantity of water to form a thick, soupy mixture. Next, put this mixture through a sieve with a number 60 or 80 mesh, refining the materials and mixing them thoroughly. Add more water to bring the mixture to a good consistency for dipping or brushing the glaze onto the tiles—a mixture rather like thick cream is generally satisfactory. Many potters use a hydrometer to measure the water content (Figure 11-14). By doing this, they can keep the water content constant and the glaze at the same consistency at all times, adding more water as it

Figure 11-13 Balance scale is essential for proper measuring of glaze ingredients.

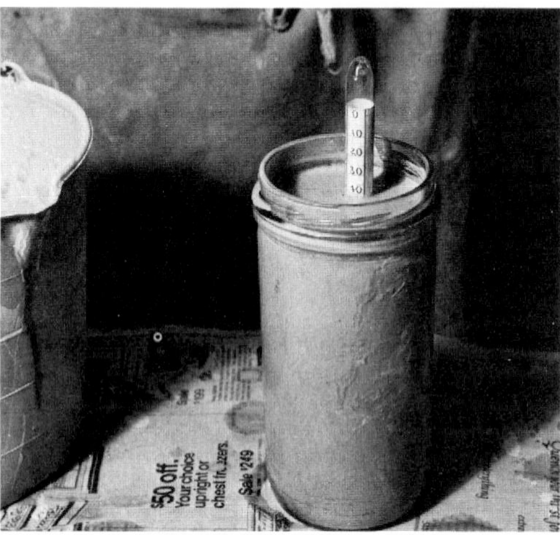

Figure 11-14 Water content of glazes should remain constant to keep consistency of color and surface in repeat glazing. A hydrometer from a wine shop measures the amount of water, allowing the potter to replace the correct amount of water as it evaporates.

Figure 11-15 Paint mixer attachment on an electric drill works well to keep glazes stirred and mixed. Be sure drill is grounded.

evaporates. Mix the ingredients thoroughly and keep them mixed, or else the solid ingredients will settle on the bottom. Brush some of this mixture on a tile, or better yet, dip the tile (Color Plate 15, p. 210D). Tiles made in an L shape will catch any glaze that may melt in the fire and run down the vertical wall. As you change the ingredients in the glaze, number each tile with an underglaze pencil or with cobalt or iron oxide, and keep a record of the changes.

Changing the Ingredients

Now you are ready to vary the proportions of the glaze ingredients. You can either increase one of the ingredients already in the glaze, or you can add a new ingredient in increments equal to 5 percent of the dry weight of the glaze. Remember that it must be effective in your firing range. Record what and how much you have added, then glaze and test fire the tile. When these tiles are fired at the temperature range normally used for that glaze, you will see changes in the glaze, depending on what materials you used. By referring back to your records, you can easily see what effect a change in one of the ingredients can make.

Example of Changing the Flux

Here is an example that you can follow, which alters the type and amount of flux in the glaze. Notice that the formula is given as the number of parts of each ingredient in relation to a total of 100 parts—that is, a percentage of the total. This method of listing ingredients by percentage gives the potter the option of mixing a batch in any amount. Thus the 35 parts of feldspar could be 35 grams, pounds, or tons, while the relationship remains the same. For your purpose, to yield 500 grams, you would multiply each number by 5, although actually you are multiplying each percentage by 500. Here is a basic cone 10 reduction glaze:

Potash feldspar:	35% (.35)	× 500	175
Whiting:	24% (.24)		120
China clay:	28% (.28)		140
Flint:	13% (.13)		65
Total	100%		500 grams

After mixing this batch, add coloring materials in the following proportions:

Rutile:	8% (.08)	× 500	40 grams
Tin:	1% (.01)		5 grams

Dip a tile and mark it. Then add 25 grams of talc, which is a high-fire flux as well as an opacifier. Dip a tile in this mixture and mark it. Add 25 more grams of talc, dip and mark, and repeat for two or three more tests. Fire the test tiles at cone 10 in a reduction firing and compare the results.

Color in Glazes

When it comes to color, there are really no firm rules. The coloring materials used in glazes are undependable because of the many factors influencing them. Glaze color is produced by the interaction of certain oxides and by the effect of the kiln atmosphere on them, with each oxide reacting differently. For example, one oxide may burn out in the kiln, while another may hold its color intensity. It is not enough to consider what color each oxide will produce by itself, but what it will do in combination with other glaze materials or in particular firing conditions. And because coloring oxides exist in clay bodies as well as in glazes and can affect the color of any glaze applied over them, that is one more factor to consider in glaze formulation.

As an example of the various colors an oxide can produce, consider the range of iron. It can yield creams, yellows, red-browns, and also the gray-greens so popular in ancient China (Color Plate 1, p. 50A). It can also produce the black and brown tenmoku (Color Plate 12, p. 210B). Copper oxide, on the other hand, can add turquoise tones in alkaline glazes, but in lead glazes it may produce greens. However, in reduction firing it can give the copper-red glazes of China (Color Plate 3, p. 50C).

Color Tests

To find out exactly what effect a certain oxide has on the color of a glaze, you can test it by making changes in its proportions in the glaze. Remember, however, that an oxide that produces a certain color alone may in combination with another oxide give a totally different color. For example, cobalt alone in certain glazes will yield a brilliant blue, but in combination with vanadium it can give a mustardy yellow.

The glaze color that an oxide will produce will also vary depending on the color of the clay body under it, on how finely the oxide is ground, on how the glaze is applied, and on how it is fired. So it is obvious that testing of glaze colors is a long process. There are so many factors involved in color formation that the only way you can be sure of an oxide is to test it in *your* glaze, on *your* clay, in *your* kiln, or even in one section of your kiln.

Working with one oxide at a time and changing its proportions will give you an idea of how certain colors develop in glazes. However, many effective glazes depend on several oxides in combination for their color. When several oxides are used, however, the amounts usually have to be decreased, for oxides in combination may produce dark or dingy colors.

Because even a small change in the proportion of a colorant can change a glaze color quite radically, it is best to add only a small amount of the new material at a time. If you follow through the cone 10 reduction glaze below, you will see what happens when a potter tests to vary the color of a glaze.

Feldspar:	49% (.49)	× 500	245
Kaolin:	19% (.19)		95
Flint:	11% (.11)		55
Whiting:	21% (.21)		105
Total	100%		500 grams

Mix 500 grams of this glaze, dip one tile, and mark it. Then, on a series of tiles, make the following changes:

Add 5 grams red iron oxide, dip, and mark it "1% red iron"

Add 5 grams more red iron oxide, dip, and mark it "2% red iron"

Add 5 grams more red iron oxide, dip, and mark it "3% red iron"

Fire these tiles at cone 10 (2381°F, 1305°C) and see what effects the changes in the iron content produce. Now to this 3 percent iron mixture add:

5 grams rutile, dip, and mark it "3% red iron 1% rutile"

5 grams more rutile, dip, and mark it "3% red iron 2% rutile"

5 grams more rutile, dip, and mark it "3% red iron 3% rutile"

Now fire these tiles to see what color changes appear.

Tests like these will give you some idea of what the potter can expect when modifying and changing glaze ingredients. Remember, however, that there are many variables, and results can vary tremendously. Out of many tests, you may get only one glaze that you like, but in the process you will learn a great deal about glaze colorants. Don't be surprised, though, if the glazes do not always give the colors listed in Chart 1 in the Appendix. For example, copper produces red in reduction, but you may have to fire it a good many times before you find the right kiln conditions to produce copper red.

Frits

A **frit** is a combination of glass-forming materials that is fired, fractured by immersing it in water while still hot, then ground up. The reason for doing this is that some **raw glaze** materials, like lead, are poisonous, and some, like borax, potash, and soda ash, are alkalies which are soluble in water. Lead in its raw state is dangerous for the potter to use, and if it is not fritted, it can also be dissolved from the glazed ware by acid foods and if ingested can cause illness or death. Other soluble materials can also cause various problems if used in the raw state. For example, soda ash is caustic and can injure the potter working with it. Or a soluble material can sink into the absorbent bisque, thereby changing the chemical combination of the glaze. In addition, soluble materials are hard to store, since they absorb water and form lumps. However, if these glaze ingredients are fritted, then these problems and hazards are avoided. So it is wise to use them as frits rather than as raw materials.

Frits also lower the temperature at which soluble materials can be used, and since the materials in a frit have already been melted once, there are no volatiles left to cause pinholes or pits as they burn out. Frits can be bought in ceramics supply stores, and in many cases the supplier publishes the formulas of the frits. This means that the potter can use them easily in combination with other materials to formulate a glaze. If the formula of a frit is not known, it is necessary to work out its effects on a glaze through trial and error or tests.

Types of Glazes

There are two basic types of glazes, low fire and high fire. The potter also can choose from a variety of specific glaze types such as ash glazes, **slip glazes, matt glazes, crystalline glazes,** and salt glaze.

Low-Fire Glazes

Ever since the early potters in Egypt and the Near East developed first alkaline, then lead and tin glazes, potters have used low-fire glazes to make earthenware watertight or to add color to household vessels (Figures 3-28 and 6-3). Many of today's sculptors, as well, turn to the low-fire glazes to provide bright, smooth colors with which to enliven their work. These glazes flow well, covering the clay and obscuring any imperfections. They have a much wider range of colors than high-fire glazes, and they generally have a glossy surface. These characteristics make them ideal for certain types of pottery and sculpture (Figures 11-28 and 11-30 and Color Plates 19, 21, and 22, pp. 274B and 274C).

As the name implies, low-fire glazes melt at low temperatures (1391°F to 2048°F, or 755°C to 1120°C; cone 016 to 02), and two types of fluxes are used to give them their low-melting characteristic. **Alkaline glazes** depend on an alkali such as sodium or potassium to melt them. These alkaline glazes, although they produce brilliant colors when coloring oxides are added to them, are rather soft and easily scratched. They are, in addition, hard to fit to the clay body because they expand and contract with the temperature changes in the kiln. This means they are apt to craze, or develop small cracks over their whole surface. This may be decorative, but it weakens the glaze, which, with use, may wear or weather off. Therefore, alkaline glazes are generally used on nonfunctional, decorative pieces, where their brilliant colors will not be subject to wear.

Lead is an extremely useful flux, for glazes made with it melt at a low temperature, fit the clay well, and take color well. Combined with tin, lead made possible the cream-colored and white glazes that early Italian potters used so successfully on their maiolica ware as the background for bright-colored glazed decoration (Figure 6-3 and Color Plate 5, p. 146A).

Unfortunately, the poisonous nature of lead makes it very hazardous to work with. A great many people, including young children, died of lead poisoning as a result of working in European pottery factories. How many more throughout history were made ill by eating off improperly fired lead glazes used on food containers we will never know. Using lead in fritted form is safer for the potter, but this does not mean that lead cannot later be released from the glaze. Merely melting the glaze components to form a frit does not necessarily ensure that it has been made insoluble in acids. Improper firing (in this case, not high enough or long enough), improper application (too thick), or the addition of copper to a lead glaze can all increase the dangers of lead release.

Some suggested rules are: *never use lead in its raw form; check any glaze you purchase for its lead content; and never add copper to a lead glaze.* In addition, it is wise never to use lead on anything that could possibly be used as a food container, even though you did not design it as such. Some people even recommend that potters put a hole in any lead-glazed convex form that might hold liquid, so that a child cannot possibly use it for drinking. Some of the glazes used in raku firings contain lead, and even if they are made with frits, they are fired at such low temperatures for such a short time that they are not safe as food containers.

High-Fire Glazes

These glazes are made to be fired between cone 6 and cone 14 (2232°F to 2491°F, or 1222°C to 1366°C) and are used on stoneware or porcelain clay bodies. Unlike the low-fire glazes, which always remain as a surface coating, high-fire glazes actually form a union with the clay body, creating an inseparable coating. If you could look at a cross section of your pot's surface under a microscope, you would see that there is an area between the glaze and the clay body where the materials in both have interacted. This is desirable because it helps the glaze adhere to the body. It can, however, cause problems. Certain ingredients in the glaze can dissolve materials in the clay, and as they move up into the glaze, they may change the glaze considerably. For example, a glaze color may be muddied as a result of "impurities" in the clay. Or glaze ingredients acting on the clay may cause alumina from the body to enter the glaze, making an opaque glaze transparent.

As the kiln cools, the glaze materials form the glassy surface we see on glazed stoneware and porcelain (Color Plates 11 and 14, pp. 210A and 210D). Because they are so strong and impervious to liquids and acids, the high-fire glazes make very durable coatings for tableware. For these reasons, they are especially popular with potters who specialize in domestic ware.

Ash Glazes

Ashes that were blown onto the shoulders of pots from the wood fires in early Chinese and Japanese stoneware kilns often formed accidental glazes. Observing this, potters started to experiment, gradually developing glazes using ashes deliberately (Figure 3-9).

Nowadays, potters continue to use ashes to make attractive and interesting glazes. Ashes are rich in glaze-forming ingredients such as potash, lime, alumina, and silica, as well as various oxides that provide color. You can obtain the ashes for glazes by burning wood, berry canes, grasses, sawdust, corncobs, or even fruit pits. Because each type of ash has a different chemical composition, they should be kept separate and tested separately. Even the locality where the tree is cut may make a difference, as the soil composition affects the chemicals in the tree.

You can experiment with ashes alone, perhaps from grass cuttings; and if you use the glaze on a clay that has a lot of silica, you may find that it makes an adequate and beautiful glaze without any additions. Or you may want to add feldspar, clay, and perhaps whiting as additional flux. Generally, the proportions suggested are 40 percent ash, 40 percent feldspar, and 20 percent clay. To prepare ashes for glazes, you should first soak them in water to leach out the soluble materials. This resulting lye water can burn your skin, so be careful pouring it off. Even if you use dry ashes without soaking, it is wise to wear rubber gloves. After the ashes are soaked, put them through a sieve and mix with the other ingredients. Although you can add small percentages of ash to low-fire glazes, the best effects with ashes come with high-firing temperatures, where large amounts can be used (Figures 11-9, 11-16, and 11-22).

Natural Glazes

Some clays or powdered rocks make a glaze when used alone. For example, feldspars are natural frits that can form a glaze if fired at high enough temperatures; but feldspar's melting point is so high, it may require additional flux. The clays that form slip glazes usually fire in the brown range because they contain iron and manganese. In these slip glazes, the iron works as both a flux and a colorant. **Albany slip,** a natural clay glaze that comes from near Albany, New York, was used widely in the early stoneware potteries in New York state, where salt-glazed ware was often coated with Albany slip glaze on the interior surface. Today it provides an earth-toned glaze that can be used decoratively (Figure 11-11).

The decorations painted on ancient Greek vases that were fired to a rich, glossy black, first in a reducing atmosphere and then an oxidizing atmosphere, were produced by painting the earthenware with a slip glaze. In addition, Japan's famous tenmoku glaze, still widely used today, is a slip glaze whose spotted effects are produced from **blisters** that break and then heal in the firing (Figure 3-23 and Color Plate 12, p. 210B).

Matt Glazes

Some nonshiny, or matt, glazes give the fired ware an attractive satin surface that is hard and durable without having a strong gloss. These, along with "buttery" or "fat" matt glazes, are often sought after for certain types of pottery. The matt effect is produced by large numbers of tiny crystals in the glaze, too small to be seen by the naked eye, which break up the light. Matt glazes may be created by increasing the alumina, silica, calcium oxide, or magnesium or by adding barium. (Barium is poisonous and must be handled with care.) A long, slow cooling also helps in the formation of matt glazes (Figures 11-3 and 11-5).

Crystalline Glazes

Although crystalline glazes can be highly decorative, they are best used on strong, simple pottery forms (Color Plate 13, p.210C), since the crystals in the glaze catch the light and reflect it, visually breaking up the glaze surface. To create these glazes, the alumina content is reduced, and borax, soda, zinc, rutile, or iron can be added. For example, Arnold Zahner of Switzerland used a zinc and titanium glaze on his simple spherical vase, firing it to 2372°F (1300°C) and reducing it with Propan in his electric kiln. The crystals were created by rutile in the glaze (Color Plate 13, p. 210C). Because they contain little alumina, these glazes are very runny and require special precautions in firing to keep them from sticking to the shelves. In order to achieve the snowflake effects, the kiln temperature must be lowered very slowly.

Salt Glaze

Salt glaze, developed in Germany in the Middle Ages, was for a long time used on utilitarian ware in Europe and early America (see Chapter 6). Produced by throwing salt into the heated kiln, it is formed of sodium that is released when the salt vaporizes (Figure 12-18). The sodium fills the entire kiln, and as the heat sends it swirling around like snowflakes in a high wind, it settles on the pots, the shelves, and the kiln walls (Figure 12-17). The sodium combines with the silica and alumina in the clay, forming a thin glaze on everything in the kiln. Salt-glazed pottery often has a mottled and pitted orange-peel surface texture. Or it may be thin and smooth instead, a surface that is especially effective on pieces that have carving or incised decoration, as it does not obscure the design.

Because salt releases chlorine when it vaporizes, the large nineteenth-century pottery factories, where many kilns were fired at the same time, polluted the air. Since the kiln itself becomes coated on the inside, special kilns must be used, and salt should never be used in electric kilns. Also, the studio should be well ventilated. Today, salt glazing is popular with some potters who like the effects it produces (Figures 11-22, 12-14 to 12-17).

Overglazes

After you fire your pot or sculpture with either high-fire or low-fire glazes, there are ways you can change the surface color further by using enamels, china paints, and lusters on top of glazed ware (Color Plates 17, 19, and 20, pp. 274B and 274C).

Enamels and China Paints

Enamels and china paints are basically very-low-fire glazes that are painted on top of an already-fired glaze. They were used in the past to add decoration on household china, which is why they are often grouped together and called **china paints.** However, the word **enamels** correctly refers to overglaze colors that are opaque, while china paint is the correct name for transparent overglaze. Opaque overglazes may be applied so thickly that they actually produce raised areas, while the transparent overglazes can be used like watercolor paints to brush on thin washes of color. These overglazes melt in a short, low firing, so it is easy to add another coat and refire several times (Color Plate 19, p. 274C). With the contemporary interest in colored surfaces on ceramic sculpture, overglazes have become popular, and china painting, which used to be associated with Victorian ladies painting flowers on teacups, has become a quite different process in the hands of contemporary sculptors.

Lusters

Lusters are made from metallic salts, which require some form of reduction to develop their characteristic opalescent surface. Lusters fired in a reduction atmosphere were developed by Persian potters and eventually spread to Spain and on to Italy and the rest of Europe (Figure 3-30). Although various firing methods can be used to develop lusters, today the easiest and most commonly used method is to apply a ready-mixed commercial luster, made with a reducing agent mixed in the glaze. With the use of these local reducing agents, luster effects can be produced at low heat in an electric kiln instead of depending on reduction firing. Like so many traditional techniques, lusters have now been given totally new applications and are used in a free and imaginative way by contemporary potters and sculptors (Figures 11-27 and 11-32 and Color Plate 17, p. 274B).

Other Overglaze Effects

In addition to enamels, china paints, and lusters, contemporary potters and sculptors often use commercial processes, such as photolithography, decals, and silkscreen, to add more surface interest to their pieces (Figures 11-27 and 11-32). One potter has even experimented with electroplating his ware with copper (Figure 11-31).

Figures 11-16 to 11-32 There are so many types of underglazes, glazes, and overglazes available to the potter that the decorative possibilities are endless. Throughout the book there are many illustrations of glazes and the manner in which potters have used them throughout history. The following examples show some of the many possible effects.

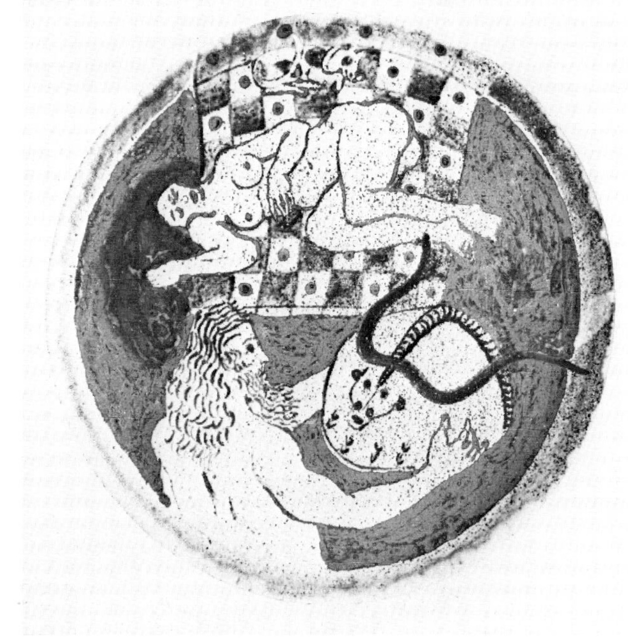

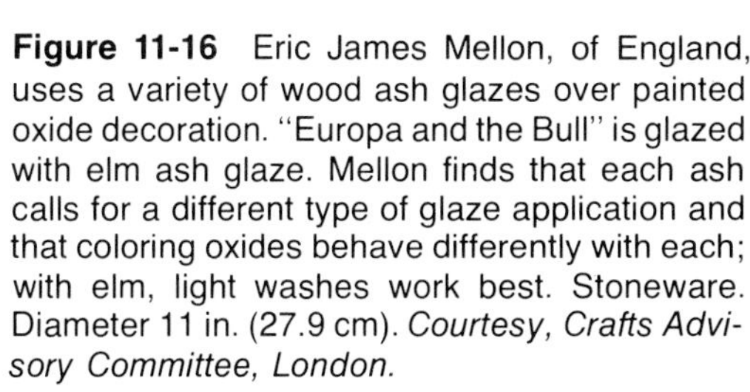

Figure 11-16 Eric James Mellon, of England, uses a variety of wood ash glazes over painted oxide decoration. "Europa and the Bull" is glazed with elm ash glaze. Mellon finds that each ash calls for a different type of glaze application and that coloring oxides behave differently with each; with elm, light washes work best. Stoneware. Diameter 11 in. (27.9 cm). *Courtesy, Crafts Advisory Committee, London.*

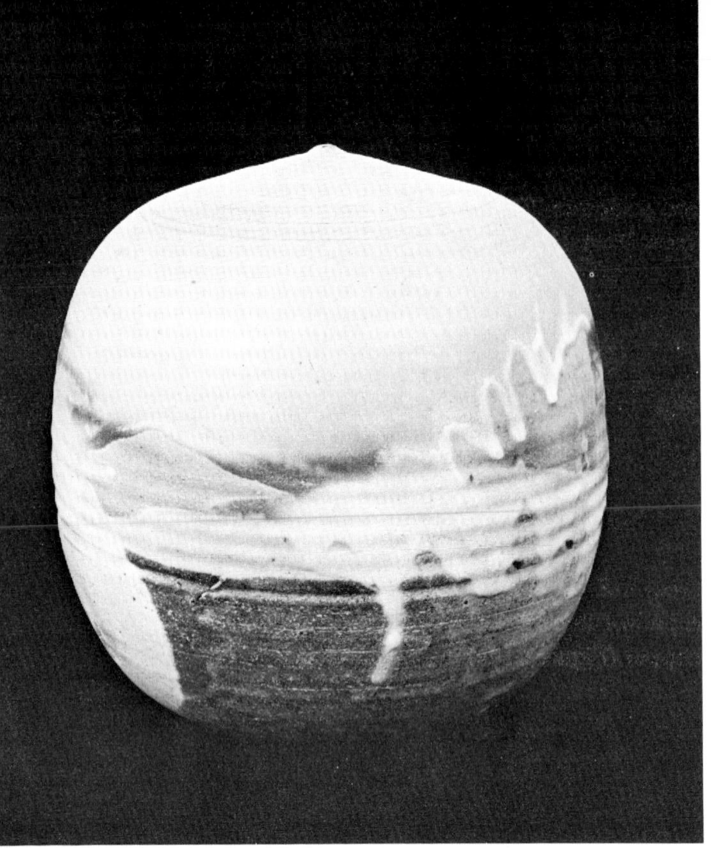

Figure 11-17 Toshiko Takaezu, of the United States, allows glazes to run and mix in an apparently casual manner. Her years of experience with glazes make possible such subtle effects. Stoneware. 12 X 12 in. (30.5 X 30.5 cm). *Photo by Thomas Haar. Courtesy of the artist.*

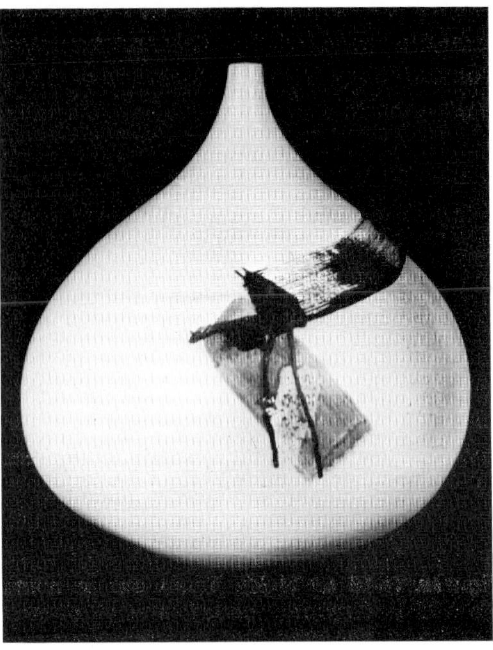

Figure 11-18 Charles McKee, U.S. potter, decorates a white stoneware vase with a few free brush strokes. *Courtesy, M. H. DeYoung Museum Art School. Photo by Jim Stevenson.*

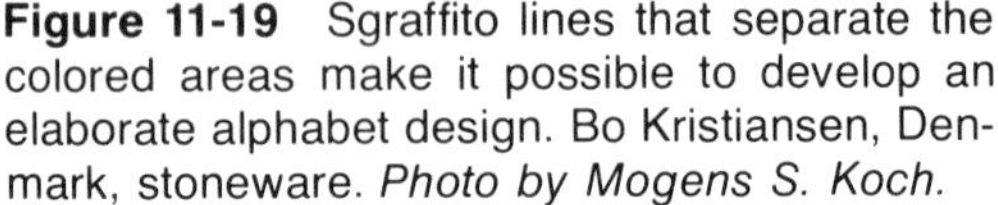

Figure 11-19 Sgraffito lines that separate the colored areas make it possible to develop an elaborate alphabet design. Bo Kristiansen, Denmark, stoneware. *Photo by Mogens S. Koch.*

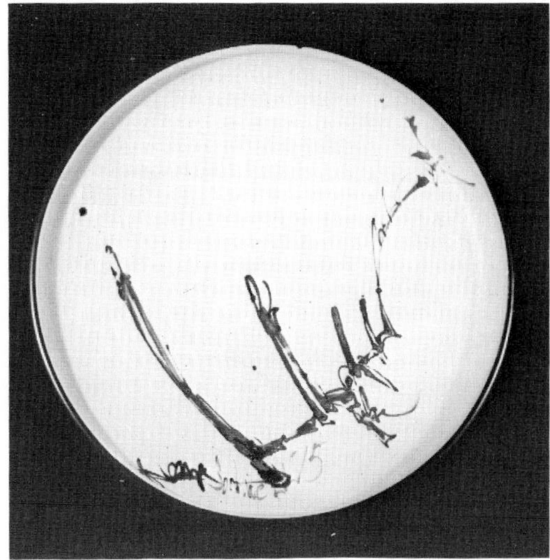

Figure 11-20 Porcelain plate decorated with calligraphic design. James Sockwell, U.S.A. Diameter 16½ in. (41.9 cm). *Courtesy, Southern Highland Handicraft Guild.*

Figure 11-21 Karen Karnes, of the United States, used salt glaze to add visual interest to this simple stoneware vase. Strong forms can handle the pitted, mottled surface of glaze. Stoneware. Height 16 in. (40.6 cm). *Courtesy of the artist.*

Figure 11-22 Salt and ash glazes on a vase by Joe Hoffman, of the United States. Smooth, greenish ash glaze from the bay tree behind it contrasts with rough, brown lower surface. Stoneware, 1978.

Figure 11-23 Slabs present contrasting textures and glaze surfaces in a wall relief by Maria Voyatzoglou, Greece. In order to fire with a slight reduction in her electric kiln, she mixes up to 10 percent of sawdust, coal dust, or ash either in the clay body or in the glazes. Stoneware. Height 23⅝ in. (60 cm), length 68⅞ in. (1.75 m).

Figure 11-24 (*Right*) "American Vase: The Winning of The West," by U.S. potter-sculptor Erik Gronborg. Gronborg says, "I do not strive for novelty of technique, but for a personal, well crafted use of conventional processes, including some modern industrial techniques, such as making my own photo decals." Porcelain, with photo decals and luster. *Courtesy of the artist.*

Figure 11-25 "Mao Tse Toad." Line drawings of frogs on base contrast with highly glazed bust. David Gilhooly, Canada, 1976. 31 X 19 in. (78.7 X 48.3 cm). *Courtesy, Hansen-Fuller Gallery.*

Figure 11-26 Glenys Barton's "Time at Yagul" contrasts an unglazed, polished figure with the glazed photo lithographic transfers of clouds. Cast bone china on press molded base, made in limited edition of four at Wedgwood Factory, England. Height 6⅞ in. (17.4 cm). *Courtesy, Crafts Advisory Committee, London.*

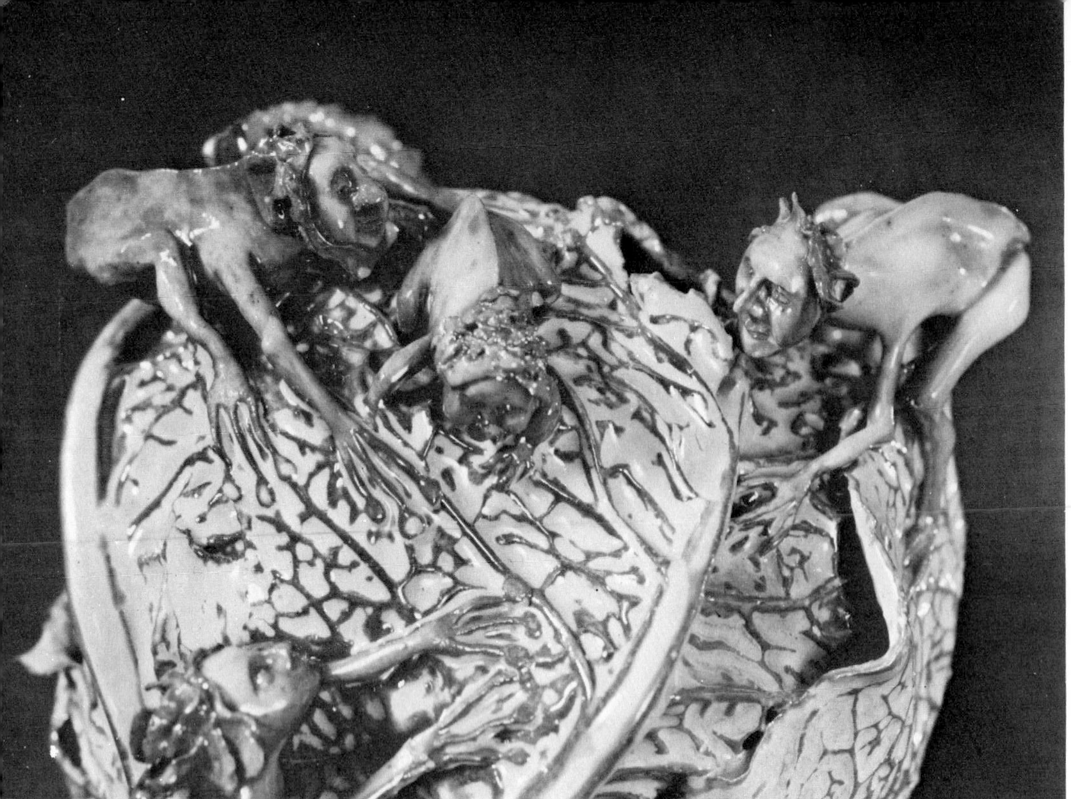

Figure 11-27 Alan and Ruth Barret-Danes, of Wales, collaborate on small narrative sculptures. Her sculptured figures are combined with press or slip-molded cabbage leaves. The alkaline-base glazes are colored with metallic salts that produce lusters when fired in reduction. Chemical luster, blue with cobalt sulfate reduced at 1760°F (960°C). *Courtesy, Alphabet and Image.*

Figure 11-28 Richard Moquin, of the United States, covered earthenware body with thick white glaze. "Sun Glasses for a Super Star." Earthenware, 1975. 4½ X 10 X 7½ in. (11.4 X 25.4 X 19.1 cm). *Courtesy, M. H. DeYoung Museum Art School. Photo by Robert Hsiang.*

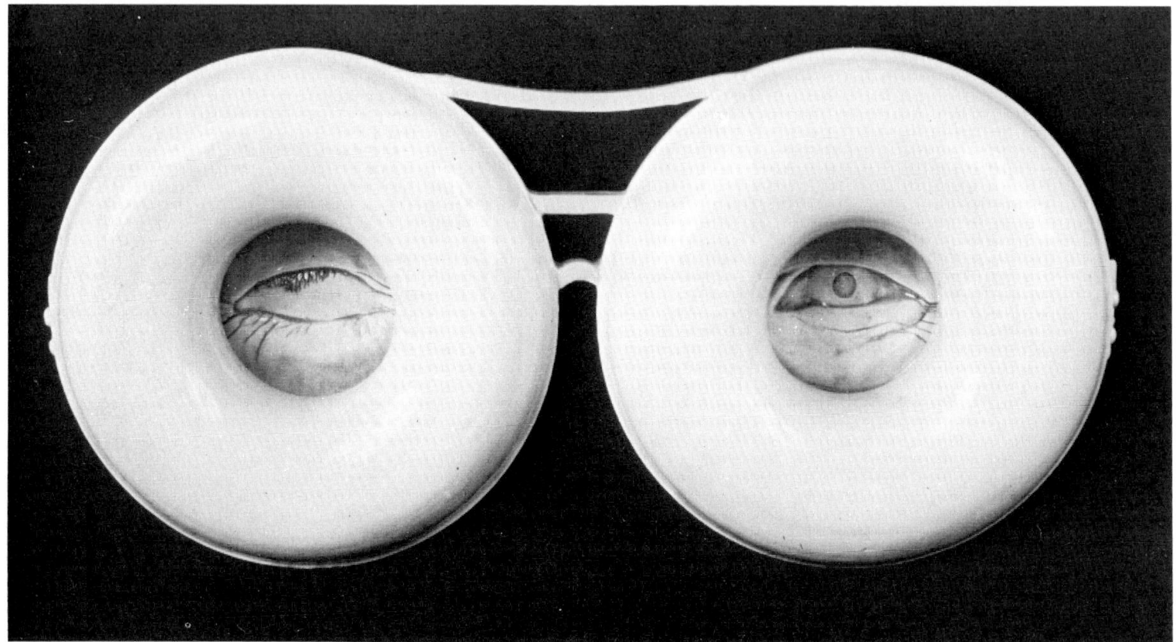

Color Plate 16 **Patti Warishina,** U.S.A. Low-fire clay with underglaze painting on back panel and on sculptured forms. *Courtesy of the artist.*

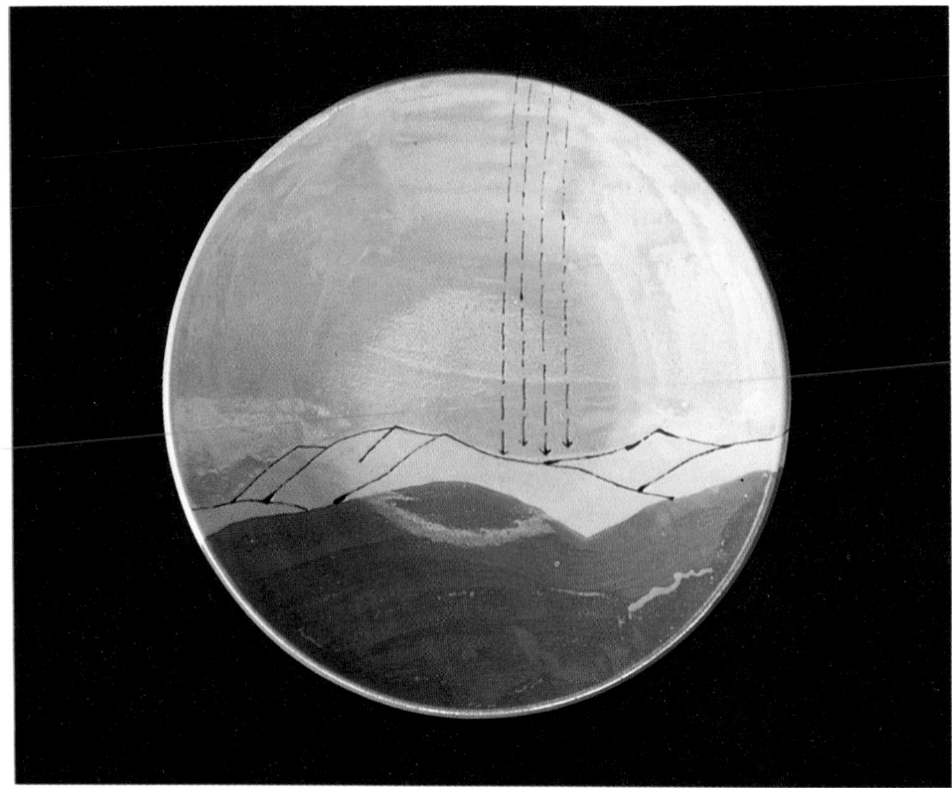

Color Plate 17 **Janet Lowe,** U.S.A. Plate with underglaze, china paint and luster decoration. *Courtesy of the artist.*

Color Plate 18 **Miriam Licht,** U.S.A. Burnished, low-fire teapots. Uneven firing in sawdust caused decorative fire marks. Amethyst set in lid. *Courtesy of the artist.*

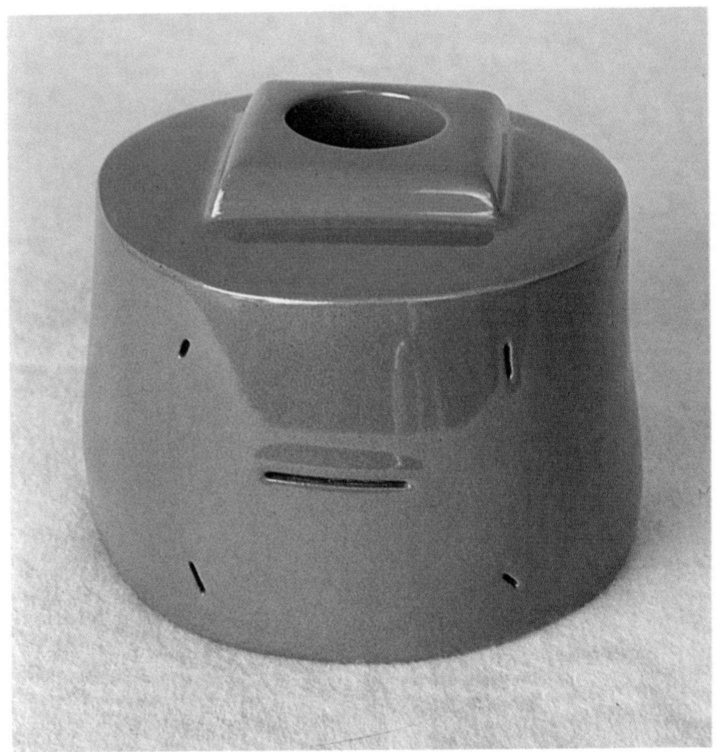

Color Plate 19 **Ron Nagle,** U.S.A. Low-fire clay with sprayed china paint. Height 3 in. (7.6 cm). *Courtesy, Quay Ceramics Gallery. Photo, De Young Museum Art School.*

Color Plate 20 **Allan Widenhofer,** U.S.A. "Bicentennial Plate," stoneware with underglaze pencil drawing and sprayed china paint. *Courtesy of the artist.*

Color Plate 21 **Erik Gronborg,** U.S.A. "American Plate," stoneware with low-fire glazes. Height and width 13 in. (33 cm). *Courtesy of the artist.*

Color Plate 22 **Ron Cooper,** U.S.A. "Four Skydivers," Earthenware. Diameter 24 in. (60.9 cm). *Courtesy of the artist. Photo, De Young Museum Art School.*

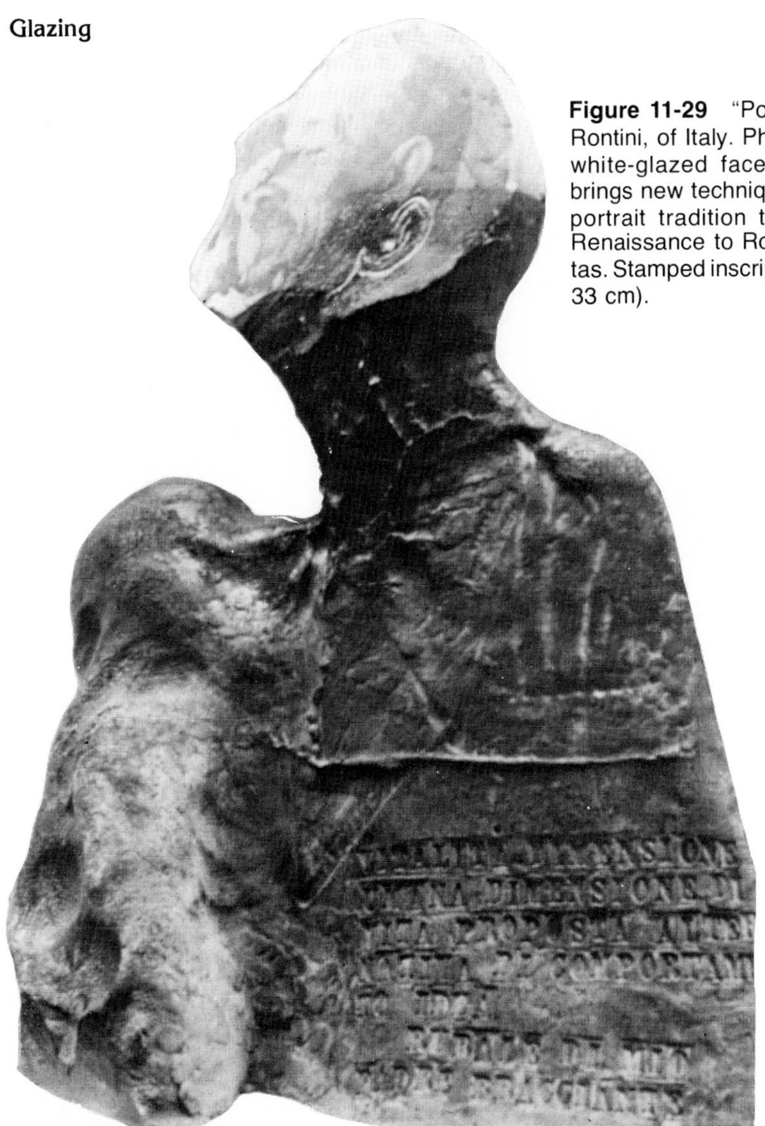

Figure 11-29 "Portrait of My Father," by Aldo Rontini, of Italy. Photograph is printed in red on white-glazed face using silk screen. Rontini brings new techniques and images to the Italian portrait tradition that goes back through the Renaissance to Roman and Etruscan terra cottas. Stamped inscription, 1977. 17⅜ X 13 in. (44 X 33 cm).

Figure 11-30 "Nose Lamp" is an electric lamp surrounded by highly glazed ceramic noses. Clayton Bailey, U.S.A., earthenware, low-fire glazes, 1968. Height 11½ in. (29.2 cm), diameter 13½ in. (34.3 cm). *Courtesy, M. H. DeYoung Museum Art School. Photo by Robert Hsiang.*

Figure 11-31 "Motorcycle Platter." Allan Widenhofer adapted electroplating methods to coat sculptured areas of his platters with copper. Process requires careful masking of unplated areas to avoid damage to clay from plating chemicals. Stoneware. Diameter 22 in. (55.9 cm). *Courtesy of the artist.*

Figure 11-32 "Snail Shell Goblets" of porcelain with luster interiors, by Susan Wolf, of the United States. Height 13 in. (33 cm). *Collection: The Lannon Foundation. Courtesy, Quay Ceramics Gallery.*

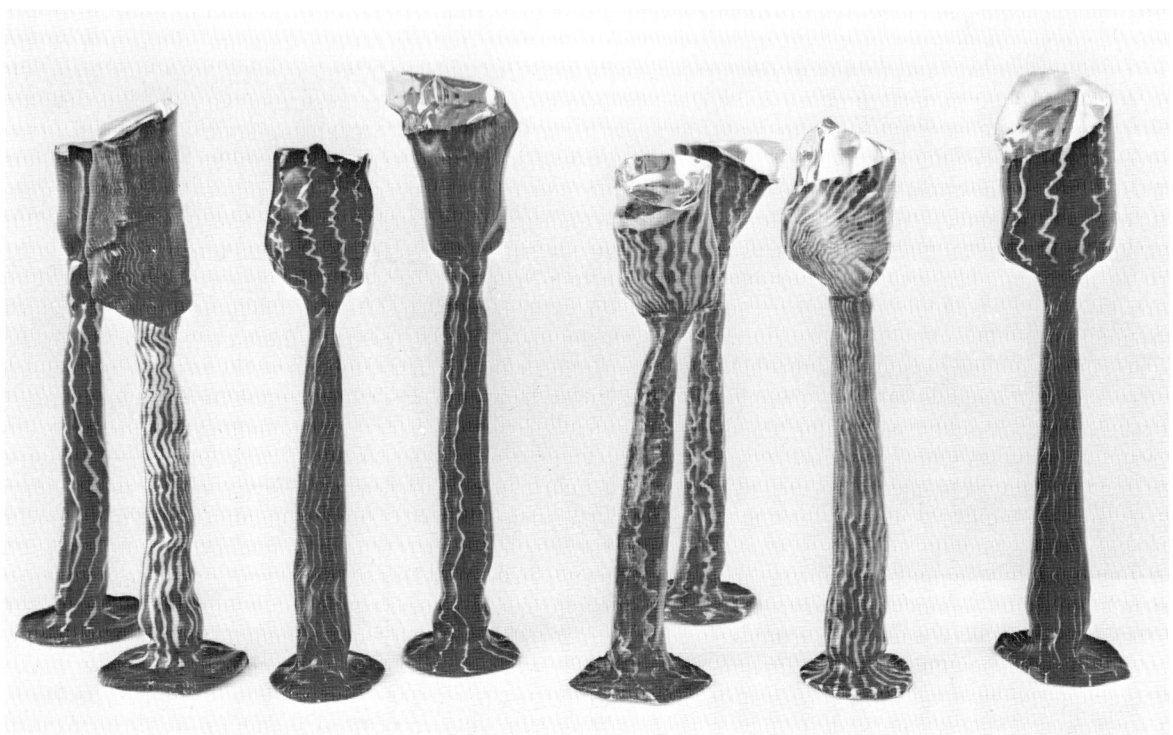

Mixing Glazes

Assuming that you are using a glaze recipe from a book, from another potter, or have even calculated your own, it is relatively simple to measure and mix the dry ingredients once the recipe is arrived at. To mix a glaze, you need a good balance scale (Figure 11-13) and some method of measuring the water content of the glaze in order to keep the glaze at the same consistency at all times (Figure 11-14). Add the dry ingredients to the water in a large enough container, so that you can mix comfortably. Whether you stir it with a paddle or mix it with a wire kitchen whip or electric mixing device, be sure it is stirred thoroughly, because the heavier glaze ingredients fall to the bottom (Figure 11-15).

Applying Glazes

It is possible to glaze a piece before it is bisque fired, as **greenware** or unfired clay, and there are some advantages to this single-firing method; but there are also enough problems involved with it, such as the brittle condition of the greenware, that it is best to bisque fire your ware first. Once the glaze is mixed, there are several ways it can be applied to the bisqued piece.

Your bisque piece should be free of dust and handled as little as possible to avoid oily fingerprints. Wipe it off with a damp sponge or rinse it quickly under a tap. You want to dampen it slightly, as well as clean off dust, because it should not absorb too much glaze. Experienced potters can mix glazes to a consistency that does not require the pot to be damp and can often dip or pour expertly enough to dispense with damping, but the less experienced usually dampen first.

Because glaze becomes runny in the kiln, it can run off the bottom of a pot, actually fusing it to the kiln shelf. To avoid this, either dip the bottom of the pot in melted wax before glazing or clean the glaze off the bottom with a sponge, also removing about one-quarter inch of glaze up the side of the pot. Commercially prepared wax-resist products, which can be brushed on, are available in ceramics supply stores.

Dipping

Dipping the piece in a bucket of glaze is one way to apply the glaze (Figure 11-33). Each person works out a glaze consistency and method of dipping that is most comfortable. Some dip once, others mix the glaze thinner and double dip, a process that will cover any pinholes that may appear in the first coat. How

Figure 11-33 Dipping a stoneware teapot in a large bucket of glaze. The length of time it is held in the glaze and the amount of time between dips are determined by trial and error and experience. Larry Murphy, U.S.A.

long you hold the piece in the glaze—usually only a few seconds—and how long you let it dry between dips if you double dip will affect the way the glaze will turn out. Any finger marks left on the piece can be covered by touching up with a brush, but if you hold the piece carefully at the bottom while dipping, there should be no problem. For certain pieces that are hard to hold, you can use metal tongs (Figure 11-43). After dipping, shake the piece to get rid of the extra glaze.

Pouring

Pouring is the only way you can get the glaze into tall, narrow vases, and it is a good way to glaze the inside of a bowl with one glaze and the outside with another. You can also get interesting effects by pouring more than one glaze on the exterior of a piece or by pouring glaze on only part of a piece, allowing some of the clay body to show through (Figures 11-11 and 11-35).

Figure 11-34 Ron Judd pouring a second Albany slip glaze on a large stoneware bowl. Judd frequently uses two Albany slip glazes and a light matt glaze in combination.

Figure 11-35 (*Left*) Judd pours light matt glaze over one coat of Albany slip to lighten interior of large stoneware jar. (*Right*) Even a large jar must be turned constantly in order to ensure even glaze application.

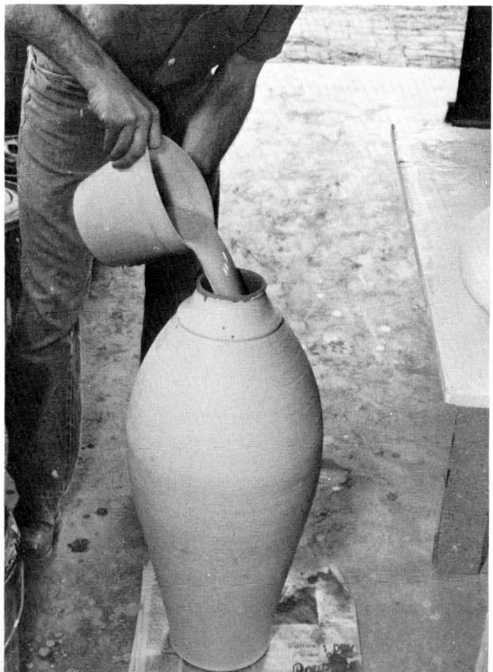

Figure 11-36 (*Left*) Spraying glaze outdoors to avoid breathing glaze materials. (*Right*) Air brushing a thin coat of glaze over underglaze drawing in a spray booth. Exhaust fan removes sprayed chemicals. Allan Widenhofer. *Courtesy of the artist.*

Spraying

Before air compressors and spray guns were developed, potters sprayed over-all glazes or areas of glaze onto their pottery by blowing it through a wooden or metal tube. All spraying should be done outside or in a well-ventilated **spray booth** to avoid inhaling the glaze materials. Spraying allows you to develop gradations in color, just as the airbrush does with paint. However, it does take considerable practice to learn to spray the glaze on evenly, for the glaze has to be built up gradually (Figure 11-36). Very subtle effects can be achieved by spraying china paint on top of fired glazes and refiring (Color Plate 19, p. 274C).

Figure 11-37 Larry Murphy paints cobalt oxide on white glaze. After test firing, Murphy discarded the glaze as too bland. Even experienced potters constantly test new glazes or variations of old formulas, searching for better glaze characteristics or more attractive decorative effects.

Brushing

By brushing on a glaze with a wide brush, you can control the thickness of the coat you apply, but it is difficult to get the coats even. Usually, brushing a glaze evenly requires two

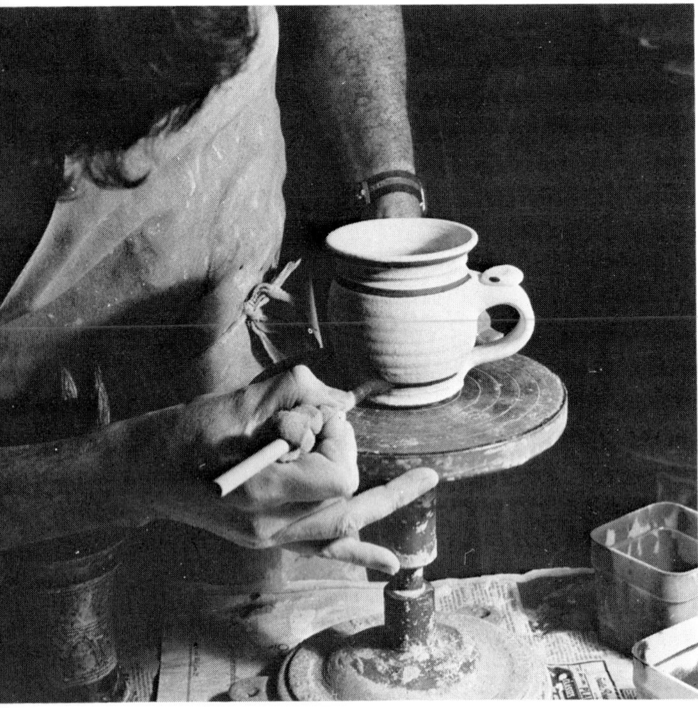

Figure 11-38 Banding wheel makes it easier to apply stripes evenly. The same decorated cup can be seen fired in Figure 12-10.

or three coats, applied before the lower coat is dry. Brushing can also be used to add a second or third glaze, as well as to apply decorations to a glazed pot (Figures 11-39 and 11-40). Trailing is a method that works equally well for applying slip or glaze (Figure 11-41).

Resist Methods

Many decorative effects can be achieved by using resist methods to cover parts of the piece so that they cannot become coated with glaze during brushing, dipping, pouring, or spraying. Areas of a piece can be masked off with paper or tape, so that either parts of the clay body will remain unglazed or an already-glazed area will not receive an additional coating.

Another method makes use of melted wax or wax-resist compounds, which can be bought at a ceramics supply store. In this method, the potter paints certain areas with the wax. When the piece is dipped or poured, the areas painted with wax will repel the glaze (Figures 11-42 to 11-45).

Figure 11-39 (*Left*) Julie Høm, of Denmark, paints glazes onto stoneware birds. In order to keep the glazes from running together, she has outlined the decorated areas with incised lines. **Figure 11-40** (*Right*) The color and texture contrasts between the glazes and the stoneware body bring vitality to these bird forms. Julie Høm, Denmark. *Photo by Mogens S. Koch.*

Figure 11-41 (*Left*) Using a syringe, Ron Judd trails a contrasting Albany slip glaze on the interior of a bowl (*Right*) Syringe next to glaze in cup.

Figure 11-42 (*Left*) Using the wax-resist method, Judd paints wax on a plate that has already been dipped and trailed with two Albany slip glazes. Waxed areas will resist third, bluish glaze and will show the red-brown and yellow-brown of the Albany slip glazes. **Figure 11-43** (*Right*) Dipping the wax-painted plate in the same glaze colored with a different oxide—cobalt. The iron in the slip mutes the strong cobalt, causing it to fire a softer blue or greenish blue.

Figure 11-44 (*Left*) Areas that were coated with wax repel the glaze; small bubbles of glaze form on the wax. Judd cleans these off before firing, finding that instead of adding interest, droplets just look messy when fired. **Figure 11-45** (*Right*) Fired plates now show the trailed glaze pattern along with wax-resist areas. Judd's sensitive use of color keeps the relationships between the glazes subtle so that the design never becomes busy.

Glaze Defects

The way a glaze is formulated, how it is applied, and how it is fired may all cause problems when it is fired, so it is often difficult to know just what went wrong. Like everything else in ceramics, experience is the best teacher. A few precautions, however, may help you anticipate some of the more common problems.

Crazing, which causes fine cracks in the fired glaze, may be the result of several factors. For example, certain oxides have a higher rate of expansion and contraction than the clay body, so a glaze containing these oxides may not fit the clay. This is often true of the low-fire alkaline glazes. In high-fire glazes, lowering the feldspar content may help. On the other hand, a defect may be turned into a decorative effect, and crazing is then called crackle (Figure 11-1). The Chinese appreciated the surface cracks and deliberately increased certain ingredients in order to produce them, learning to control the spacing of the cracks and even rubbing color into them for emphasis.

Crawling can occur when the raw glaze shrinks more than the body. The glaze actually crawls off parts of the pot, leaving unglazed areas. This defect can also be caused by dust, dirt, or oily fingerprints on the bisqued body, by placing still-moist glazed ware in the kiln, or by adding too much of some materials with high shrinkage rates to the glaze, such as clay, zinc oxide or colemanite. Crawling can also occur over areas painted with underglaze, especially if it has been applied thickly.

Pinholes and pits in a fired glaze are sometimes caused by applying glaze to a bisque that is too porous; during firing, air or moisture escaping from the pores causes holes to develop as it bursts through the glaze, rather like the bubbles that erupt and burst when you boil a thick sauce. Volatile materials escaping through the glaze as gases can also cause pinholes and pits; this is another reason for using frits rather than certain soluble materials in a glaze. These tiny holes sometimes also appear in a glaze that has been intentionally underfired to achieve a matt effect. Too much zinc oxide or rutile can also cause a glaze to pit. Adding more flux, applying the glaze less thickly, increasing the heat, or lengthening the firing may all help to avoid pinholes.

Precautions

Many of the oxides used in glazing are either poisonous or dangerous if absorbed into the body. They may be hazardous to breathe or to get in your eyes or mouth. This does not mean that you should not use them—just take a few commonsense precautions.

While working with glaze ingredients, keep your hands away from your face, and especially your eyes, and avoid inhaling any dust in the studio, for even nontoxic dusts can damage the lungs. Wearing a mask or a respirator while mixing dry ingredients is a wise precaution. Keep the workshop clean, keep your hands clean, and if you have any cuts on your hands, keep the chemicals out of them. It is also wise to vacuum workshop floors rather than to sweep them, and to use a damp rag or sponge instead of a brush to clean the work surfaces. Keep the glaze area ventilated, and do not spray glazes, except in a booth or outdoors. Don't smoke or eat near glaze chemicals, and wash your hands after using them. It is also a good idea to wear a smock or old shirt over your clothes while you are working and remove it when leaving the glaze area.

Although the chemicals and materials list in the Appendix identifies certain materials as particularly dangerous, *all* materials in a ceramics studio should be treated with respect. By taking these precautions, however, you can avoid dangerous exposure and can use glaze materials with safety.

You will probably find glazing rewarding and exciting, and gradually, with experience, it will seem less complex. After all, the master potters of the past were not magicians, but ordinary human beings. Although they usually spent their childhoods in their parents' workshops, absorbing centuries of passed-on knowledge as they helped around the shop, now we can use modern chemistry to help us instead.

Chapter Twelve
Firing

So far, your relationship has only been with the clay and glaze—learning to understand them, to work with them, and to control them to a certain extent. Now another participant enters the process—fire. It makes its own demands, and imposes its own limits on your work. Excitement, delight, frustration, and awe—you will probably feel all of these as you see what has happened to your pots in the fire. Early humans believed fire to be a gift from the gods, and from the ancient Greeks to contemporary Native Americans, each people has had its myths and beliefs surrounding fire. Many of these cultures considered metalworkers and potters who worked with fire to be magical or supernatural beings. As you experience the excitement of your first kiln watch and kiln opening, you will probably agree, for fire indeed has a life of its own that will totally transform—or destroy—your carefully shaped clay (Color Plate 18, p. 274B).

It is unlikely that you will be firing alone at first, so the information in this chapter is designed only to give you a basic understanding of how kilns are used. For more detailed information about kilns and kiln construction, consult some of the books listed in Suggestions for Further Reading.

Single Firing

As we saw in Part One, pottery often was, and still is, fired only once to a relatively low temperature. This produces a porous earthenware that is not watertight. Depending on the heat and duration of the fire, the pottery may be fired barely beyond a sun-dried state or it may be brought to maturity. If you live in an area that permits open fires, you may want to try the traditional **open-fire** method used in Fiji or Africa (Figures 1-43 and 1-44). Or you can build a simple kiln of bricks and then fire with sawdust (Figures 12-1 and 12-2). It is even possible to fire earthenware in the grate in your home fireplace or wood stove, using charcoal briquettes or synthetic logs.

If you experiment with some of these methods, you will learn first-hand some of the effects of fire on clay: how the pot is transformed from dried, brittle soluble clay into a hard, dense insoluble material; how the pot may blow up if it is heated too fast or is not dry enough; how the wind may cause uneven firing, causing oxidation in places so that some parts of a pot are reddish while other parts are black from reduction. The density of the fired pottery depends upon the type of clay used as

Figure 12-1 (*Left*) Miriam Licht, of the United States, fills a burnished pot with fuel before firing it in one-half sawdust and one-half peat moss. Fire is ignited with twigs or strips of newspapers, then allowed to burn and cool over a fifteen-hour period. **Figure 12-2** (*Right*) Firing complete, she lifts pot from the kiln. Sawdust has burned down, leaving the pots in a few inches of ashes. Some of them fire black in a local reduction, while others have warm reddish areas. As wind blows through cracks between the bricks of the kiln, the fire blazes up and consumes the oxygen, leaving these fire marks (see Color Plate 18, p. 274B). *Photos by Tom Bong. Courtesy of the artist.*

well as on the fuel used in the fire and how high a temperature can be produced by the burning straw, wood, peat, sawdust, or manure.

There is no rule that says that any clay or glaze cannot be fired in a single firing. Certainly fuel, time, and labor are saved if the **bisque firing** is skipped. But because there are problems in glazing greenware caused by absorption of water into the dry clay and risk of breaking the fragile greenware, single firing is best confined to sculpture or other unglazed pieces.

Thorough drying of the greenware is crucial, and when a thick-walled piece is to be fired, the drying process cannot be hurried. The piece can be given extra drying with auxiliary heat, or the kiln can be brought up to full heat very slowly, with the door of the kiln left partly open to allow any moisture to escape.

Firing Ranges

The type of clay you use will dictate to some extent how high the temperature of a single firing can go. But the range possible with most clays is considerably wider than labels or recipes suggest. Remember that there is no one way to proceed in this as in so many areas of ceramics. For example, the proportions in a body composed of fire clay, ball clay, and sand can be varied to fire it through a wide range of temperatures; it has strength at bisque, but Stephen De Staebler has taken it to cone 13.

Figure 12-3 (*Above*) Stephen De Staebler, of the United States, loads "Lavender Throne" into his large gas kiln. Loading a kiln when the piece weighs several hundred pounds involves applying principles of physics—or access to a hydraulic lift. **Figure 12-4** (*Below*) Final push gets the throne over the kiln threshold. Fire bricks at left will be used to close the kiln opening.

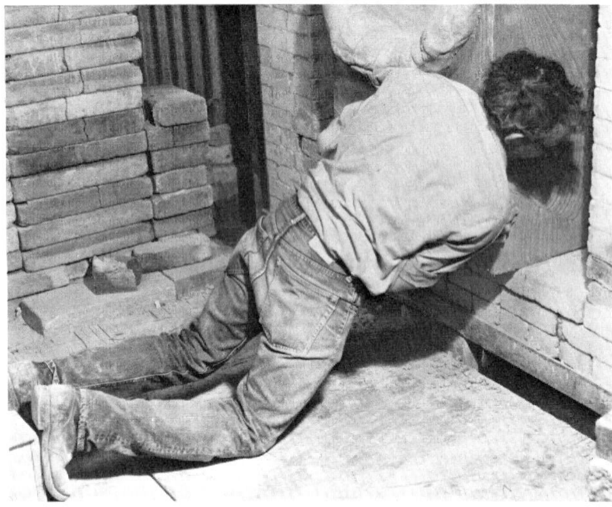

Also, the white body that he uses for his figures—a mixture of ball clay, talc, and sand—can be fired at varying temperatures. "It is a good body because it has some of the same characteristics as a high-fire body, it has good plasticity and is pretty tough. . . . Proportions can be about equal, but if you want to take it higher, you add more ball clay. I have fired it up to cone 10. . . ." Just as there are many ways to work in clay, so firing ranges should not be taken as absolutes. You may lose more pieces if you have an experimental attitude, but your knowledge of what can be done in collaboration with fire will be extended.

Loading Sculpture

Loading a large piece of sculpture into a kiln can be a complicated process, and for this reason many sculptors build their pieces in

Figure 12-5 (*Right*) Throne is loaded, and a structure of bricks and shelves holds the slab pot. The heater at right will be lowered to the front of the kiln and left running for two or three days to dry out the throne completely, although it has dried for several months in the studio. De Staebler checks the draft.

sections (Figures 8-10, 8-11, and 8-18). If this is not practical, then various devices can be used. Louise McGinley, whose outdoor kiln is down one story from her studio, has built a trolley that is raised and lowered on a sloping track by pulleys (Figure 8-14). Steven De Staebler sometimes borrows a hydraulic lift from the factory next door to his studio, but he prefers to load his chairs himself, using wooden platforms and levers, since loading without mechanical means puts less strain on the sculpture (Figures 12-3 to 12-5). If the piece cannot be moved for some reason, it is possible to build a temporary kiln around it, fire the piece, then take down the kiln brick by brick to reveal the finished work.

Another consideration in firing any sculpture is the possibility of extended forms slumping during firing. If a piece has such problem areas, supports made of the same clay body should be propped under them in the kiln.

Bisque Firing

Whether you single fire your work or bisque fire and then glaze it depends, of course, on how you intend to use the finished piece and on what visual effects you want to achieve. Assuming you have made a piece that you want to preserve and glaze, your first experience with bisque firing will probably be in a school or workshop situation.

Pinched, coiled, slab-built, or thrown, the piece should have dried slowly until it is completely dry to the touch. At this point it is called greenware and is ready for the bisque firing. Although a bisque firing is not as dramatic as a **glaze firing,** it is still exciting to see your work change from a crumbly bit of clay to a solid pot ready for you to decorate. Although some potters do glaze pots when they are green, only firing them once, greenware is usually given a first firing to somewhere between 950°F and 1300°F (510°C to 705°C). In a school, where

Figure 12-6 (*Above*) Preliminary bisque firing to between 950°F (510°C) and 1300°F (704°C) drives out moisture as well as the water that is chemically combined with the molecules of clay. The bisque kiln can be loaded tightly with pieces touching each other or nested. (*Below*) Drawing shows how heat is radiated through the ware from the electric elements.

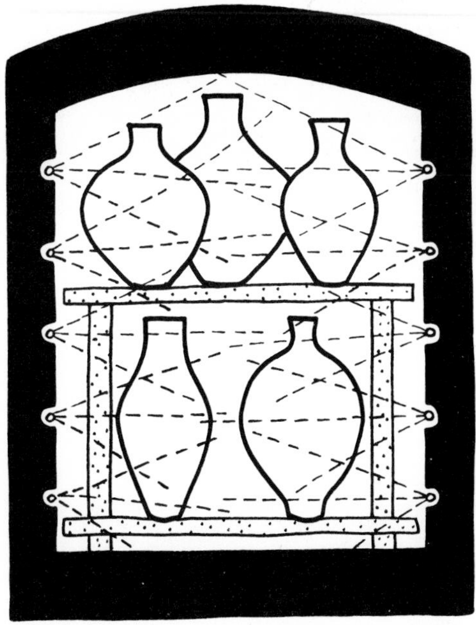

large numbers of pots need firing, or in a pottery workshop that must turn out a large amount of ware, two kilns are almost a necessity: one for bisque firings and one for glaze firings. Bisque firing can be done in any type of kiln, but many potters find it convenient to use an electric kiln for bisque firing even if they use gas for glaze firings (Figure 12-6).

Loading a bisque kiln is not as difficult as loading a glaze kiln, because without any melting glaze to make the ware stick together, the pots can be stacked tightly and inside each other.

As the heat slowly increases to about 400°F (200°C), all the physical water that is still left in the clay is driven out. If the heat is raised too rapidly during this period, the pot can explode as the steam escapes. The more temper there is in the clay, the more porous it is, and the easier it is for the steam to escape. For this reason, thick-walled pots or sculpture should be made with a good deal of grog or sand in the clay. As the temperature continues to rise slowly, the chemical water that has combined with the clay ingredients in their molecular structure leaves the clay along with gases from any organic materials.

Mullite Crystals

As the kiln gets hotter and reaches bisque temperature, crystals of alumina and silica start to form in the clay. Called **mullite crystals**, they are one reason the clay becomes hard in the fire. They are, however, only partially formed during a bisque firing, and you would have to continue to heat the clay to a much higher temperature—depending on the clay—for them to form completely. Stoneware, for example, matures at around 2350°F (1290°C). However, a bisque firing does not reach such a high temperature because you want the ware to be left absorbent enough for the glaze to adhere to it.

Cones and Pyrometers

How do you know when the kiln has reached the necessary temperature for either bisque or glaze firings? If you were experienced, you could tell by looking at the pots through a peephole, but it is best to use **cones** or a **pyrometer** or both.

A pyrometer is a device for measuring the temperature of the kiln, and with it a potter can control both the heating and the important cooling process. But a pyrometer can only measure temperature, and to get a good glaze, it is not enough just to heat the kiln quickly to a certain temperature and let it cool. Glazes need time to go through a process of starting to melt, bubbling, then smoothing out as they melt. A **pyrometric cone** will tell the potter that the time and temperature have both reached the correct point for glaze maturity (Figure 12-8).

Cones are made of ceramic materials that are calculated to fuse and bend over at a certain degree of heat saturation. They really measure the total effect of the heat on the clay or glaze materials, rather than measuring the temperature. America's Orton cones and Europe's Seger cones are calculated to bend according to the work done by the heat during a certain temperature rise per hour—the numbers given to the cones represent the point at which they bend over. Orton cones cover temperatures from about 1085°F to 2383°F (585°C to 1306°C). (See Appendix for Seger and Orton cone table. Numbers used in the text are for Orton cones.)

For a bisque firing, you would usually fire to between cone 010 and cone 06, depending on the clay body. Three consecutively numbered cones, placed in a series in a wad of clay, will warn you as you get near the point at which you must stop the heat. As the first cone collapses, you know you should watch the middle one carefully, because you are approaching the desired temperature. If the third cone

Figure 12-7 (*Left*) Glazed ware loaded on shelves at back of down-draft gas kiln. Fire-resistant shelves rest on three posts; shelves and posts make it possible to accommodate any size pot. Notice the test tiles on the second shelf. **Figure 12-8** (*Right*) Kiln loaded, Larry murphy places cones on shelves, positioning them opposite peepholes in the front of the kiln. As firing progresses, he can watch them and control the heat. His kiln is warmest at the middle, where the flames shoot over the top of the bag wall, so he places ware that is coated with glazes that can stand slightly higher temperatures here.

bends, you know you have overfired. When the kiln reaches the correct temperature, if it is electric you must shut it off unless you have an automatic shut-off system. If it is gas you close the damper, then turn it off.

Once the bisque firing is done, the kiln must be cooled very slowly, probably overnight, and you must resist the temptation to open the door too soon, or the ware will crack. But when you do open the door or lid, there is your pot, hardened and ready for decoration. Store it where it will collect a minimum of dust until you glaze it, handling it as little as possible, because oil from your fingers may keep the glaze from adhering properly.

Glaze Firing

After you have applied glaze to your pots and they have dried (Chapter 11), they are ready for the glaze firing. Before loading the kiln, be sure it is clean and that the brick kiln lining has no loose fragments that can fall on the ware.

Loading the Glaze Kiln

Before you start to load a kiln, you will have to learn to build up the kiln shelves on posts to fit around your pieces (Figures 12-7 and 12-8).

Three points of balance make for a less wobbly support, so use three, rather than four, posts for each shelf. Kiln shelves, which can be bought at a supply store, may also rest on a structure of fire bricks (Figure 12-5). New kiln shelves must be coated with a **kiln wash,** a mixture of one-half china clay (kaolin) and one-half flint. Later, when the shelves have collected drops of glaze from several firings, they will probably need a new coating of wash.

The bottom of a piece must be kept free of glaze—either by dipping it in wax before glazing or by wiping it after glazing. If, for some reason, the bottom is to be glazed, then **stilts** are used. These are sharp, triangular supports on which the piece is balanced on the kiln shelf and which leave only pin-sized marks in the glaze. Porcelain, or some high-fire stonewares, must be supported on a flat surface, as they soften in high temperatures and would warp if placed on stilts. Glazed pieces must not touch each other, or they will stick together.

Where you place the ware in the kiln can make a difference in the glazing. Each kiln, electric, gas, or other fuel, has its individual peculiarities, and you will have to get to know the kiln you use in order to get the best results. Many kilns have hot spots where certain glazes would be overfired. Since most glazes have a firing range that can extend over as much as two or three cones, this allows for some variation in the heat, and a potter learns from experience which glazes fire best in certain parts of the kiln (Figures 12-10 to 12-12).

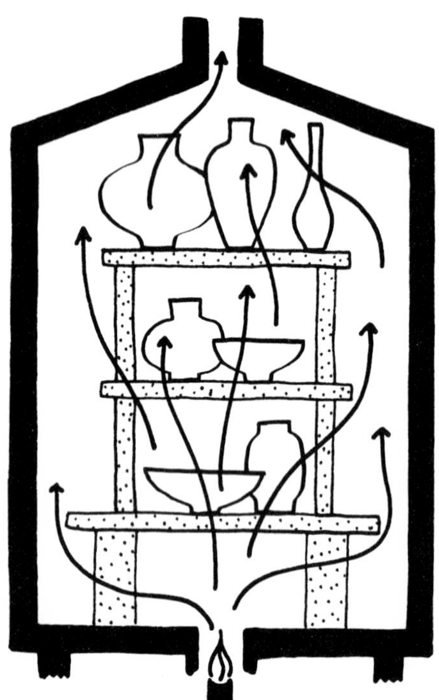

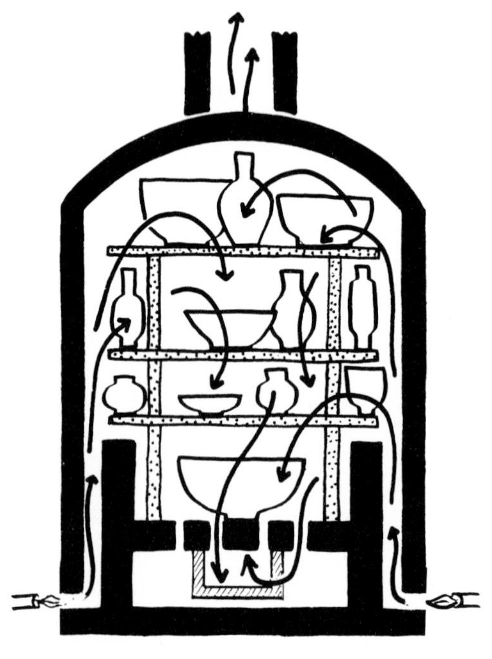

Figure 12-9 (*Left*) Cross section of up-draft gas kiln shows how the heat goes up through the ware and out the stack on top. **Figure 12-10** (*Right*) Down-draft gas kiln sends the heat up; then the heat is drawn down through the ware to the flue at the bottom and finally out the stack behind the kiln. The bag wall inside the outer wall directs flames upward to provide even circulation.

Glaze in the Fire

When you place your glazed pots in the kiln, you give up what control you have had over your work. Now you must trust the fire. Although experience and knowledge of glaze materials make it possible for potters to control the effects of the firing up to a point, any firing brings surprises. This part of the ceramics process involves letting go, and it is a humbling experience. As the time for opening the kiln approaches, the tension mounts in the workshop, and friends and colleagues gather around for the moment when the door is opened and the glazed ware appears (Figures 12-15 and 12-17).

But before the kiln is opened, you can look through a **peephole** and watch the glaze melting. In this active stage, it bubbles and boils, and you wonder if it will ever settle down into the smooth, glossy surface you want (Figure 12-11). It usually does, and the bubbles generally smooth out as the melting process continues, assuming, that is, there are no problems with formulation, fit, or application.

How long it takes to bring the heat of a kiln

Figure 12-11 Down-draft gas kiln during firing. Peepholes are left in the bricked-in front for observing the cones. To starve kiln of oxygen and produce reducing atmosphere, Murphy closes the damper. Air is trapped, backs up, and allows no new oxygen to enter. Kiln could also be reduced by closing burner ports so no new air could enter.

Figure 12-12 Kiln opening reveals shelves of glazed ware. Cones are bent, showing that the kiln fired to a little less than cone 10; at cone 10 the third cone would have bent over. Murphy reduces his kiln for about one-half hour at 1400°F (760°C), then fires it at slight reduction for about 3½ hours while the kiln gets to cone 7 or 8. He then opens damper and lets kiln go up to final temperature in oxidation.

Figure 12-13 When covers are fired in place, even if a piece warps, the covers will fit. Glaze must be cleaned off any touching surfaces, or no mallet will separate them. Tapping lightly with wooden (or hard leather) mallet will loosen cover.

to the necessary cone to mature a glaze varies from kiln to kiln and glaze to glaze, but as it begins to get near the correct cone, you must watch carefully. The cones should be placed where they can be seen easily and also out of the direct flame or drafts to make sure they give correct readings. As the cones start to bend, the kiln must be carefully controlled so that enough time is allowed between cones. After the correct cone is bent, some potters keep the kiln at that heat for a **soaking** of about one-half hour, while others never soak.

Firing Atmospheres

We have seen in Part One that throughout history, potters and sculptors have fired with either a reducing or an oxidizing atmosphere. Which one they used often depended on what type of kiln was available to them. As firing techniques improved, potters learned to control the firing atmosphere, until today they can usually choose which type of firing they wish to use. Some localities, however, will not allow wood-fired or gas kilns, so potters there are limited to electric kilns and therefore generally to an oxidizing atmosphere.

Oxidizing and Reducing Atmospheres

Any burning is a result of oxidation. As materials such as wood, straw, or grass burn in an open fire, there is usually plenty of air entering the fire. This produces an oxidizing atmosphere, in which the fire burns bright and clear. However, if the same open fire is smothered so that most of the air is shut off, then the incomplete combustion produces a reducing atmosphere. This means that the carbon and carbon monoxide that are formed have to draw oxygen from the materials that form the clay and the glaze. When this happens, some of the oxides that color the clay or glaze change their color radically.

As closed kilns were developed and improved, it became easier to control the atmosphere in the kiln, and the reduction process was perfected to produce a great variety of glaze effects. For a dramatic example of how reduction can change a glaze ingredient, see what happens to copper in a reduction fire. Fired in an oxidizing atmosphere, copper is green, but in proper reduction, it becomes red.

Depending on the kiln, or on the potter's preferred methods, the kiln atmosphere in a gas or wood kiln is changed from oxidizing to reducing either by controlling the air flow into the kiln or by cutting down on the draft. Closing the damper forces the air to back up and prevents new air from entering the kiln. The oxygen in the kiln is consumed, and when it is gone, the fire draws oxygen from the oxides, causing them to "reduce" back to their metallic state.

It is possible to induce reduction in an electric kiln by adding smoke-producing materials. In Europe, where stringent fire regulations prohibit gas kilns in the cities, potters have experimented with different ways of producing reduction in electric kilns. Some have placed the pots in saggars, enclosing various materials in the saggars, from grasses to mothballs* to mustard seeds; others add various reduction materials to the clay or glaze (Figures 7-59 and 11-23). It is also possible to throw reduction materials into the kiln or insert a gas-burning poker. Any of these methods make it possible to reduce pieces in an electric kiln. However, constant reducing can wear out the electric elements; heavy-duty elements last the longest, but even with these the kiln should always be fired several times under oxidizing conditions after each reduction firing. The protective coating that oxidizing builds up on electric elements is eaten away in a reducing firing, and it takes a good many oxidizing firings to build it back up.

Fuels

Potters throughout history have used any fuel available to them. In arid lands this might be sparse vegetation or manure from the herds; in lush tropical areas, it could be palm fronds (Figure 1-44). When European potteries began using coal as kiln fuel, fires could reach higher temperatures. By the early 1900s, some kilns burned oil, and later, gas and electric kilns were developed and perfected. With these developments and improved kiln design, the potter has been able to achieve greater control and has been liberated from the constant stoking that kept Renaissance potters and their assistants so busy (Figure 6-9). However, with increasing costs of fossil fuels and growing awareness of their ultimate scarcity, alternatives are now being explored. Some potters have returned to wood (Figure 3-41), others are experimenting with waste oil and solar heat, and still others with new insulating materials that will enable a kiln to fire with less fuel. Ceramics and craft magazines are a good source of information on these experiments.

* These produce dangerous fumes.

Safety

A gas kiln, or any open-flame kiln, always involves a fire hazard. Obviously, the kiln must be built or placed at a safe distance from combustible materials. The chimney must not send hot air too close to dry foliage and should not exhaust fumes into a room, as carbon monoxide produced in reduction firing can be fatal. In addition, the usual precautions taken while lighting any gas appliance and around open flame should be observed near a gas kiln. This means that long hair and flammable clothing should be kept from the flame, and eyes should be protected from both flame and radiation when peering into peepholes (Figure 12-11).

Although electric kilns are simple to operate and do not use open flames, any high heat can be dangerous, and the chemical changes in the materials being fired will cause gases to escape from any kiln—electric or gas. So, aside from obvious precautions, such as not placing a kiln too near combustible materials, *all* kilns should be operated with adequate ventilation. Also, remember that whether the kiln is electric or gas, the pots inside are *hot*. Even when the kiln appears cool, curb your desire to grab your beautiful pot with bare hands, as it may be hotter than you think.

Salt Glaze Kilns

Salt glazing, developed in Germany, popular in England, and brought to America by immigrant potters (Figure 6-21), has recently been revived by studio potters (Figures 11-22 and

12-14 to 12-17). Since salt fumes are irritating and corrosive, a salt kiln should not be built where the chimney can release the fumes too near people or buildings. Although it is possible to build a kiln using a calcium alumina lining, which can be used for bisque and glaze as well as infrequent salt firings, usually a special kiln is used for salt glazing. This is because the salt is introduced into the kiln, rather than applied to the ware, so the whole interior of the kiln is subjected to glazing. Since the sodium vapors released when the salt is heated combine with the silica and alumina of the clay to form the glaze, they also combine with these materials in the lining bricks (Figure 12-17). If the kiln is used for ordinary glaze firing after a salt glaze firing, the glaze from the fire bricks in the kiln would melt again and cause problems in the new glaze. The shelves and kiln walls can be protected somewhat by a wash of aluminum oxide. Electric kilns cannot be used for salt glazing, as the elements would be damaged.

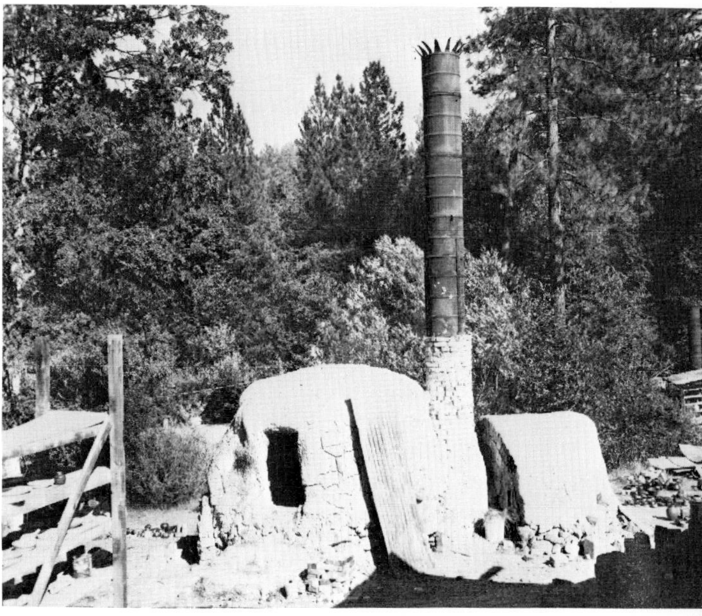

Figure 12-14 Salt glaze kiln at Earth Air Fire Water Workshop in Nevada, with stack extended with metal-drum chimney. *Photo by Anne Henry.*

Figure 12-15 (*Left*) Joe Hoffmann, of the United States, removes cast sections from the door of his cooling salt kiln. Kiln was fired with a combination of propane gas and diesel oil. The oil is turned off after the kiln reaches cone 9 or 10 and the salting is done with only the propane on. This is done to keep a relatively oxidizing atmosphere with the dampers constricted in order to retain the salt vapor in the kiln.
Figure 12-16 (*Right*) Old burner ports at the bottom of the sides of Hoffmann's former stoneware kiln are now used to throw in the salt. The new propane-diesel burners fire from the rear, parallel with the bag wall.

Figure 12-17 Upper shelf of Hoffmann's opened salt kiln shows a porcelain piece by Dean Taylor and a section of a stoneware piece by Ron Judd with characteristic salt-fired surfaces. Also visible is the build-up of salt glaze on the bricks of the kiln after only five firings.

Raku

The term *raku* correctly refers to the ware made by members of a Japanese family. It means "pleasure." In the sixteenth century, that family was given permission to use that stamp to identify their pieces (Figure 3-36). Descendants of the family still make pottery in Japan, carrying on the tradition and using the honored name.

Western potters and sculptors have adapted the raku firing process, using it as a way to get interesting surface effects. As usually practiced now, except by traditional Japanese potters, bisqued and glazed pieces are fired quickly at a low heat in any kiln that will allow easy access to the ware. The glazes used are ones that will mature at a very low temperature. The pot or sculpture is pulled from the kiln when the glaze has melted, then placed in a container of straw, sawdust, or any material that will burn quickly (Figure 12-19).

After the pot is placed in it, the container is covered immediately to smother the fire, thus reducing the glazes as a result of the lack of oxygen. This means that interesting reduction effects can be produced even with an electric kiln, because the pieces are reduced after being removed from the kiln. Iridescent luster areas appear and fire marks often enrich the surface. If the ware is dipped in water to cool it rapidly, crackle patterns can develop. The speed with which pots become glazed, and the fact that it is possible in some kilns to watch the glaze melt in the fire, have made raku firings a popular way to initiate beginners into the firing and glazing process. But experienced potters also use it to create subtle or rich surfaces (Figures 12-20 to 12-27).

Special kilns that can be raised and lowered easily to allow quick access to the ware simplify raku firing. These can be purchased ready-made or built in an outdoor area. Using modern equipment, raku-type firings are today often done under conditions that would have amazed the first Raku, Jokei—conditions that allow much greater control, making it possible to achieve refined and subtle glaze effects (Figures 12-20, 12-23 and 12-24).

Figure 12-18 Light-weight wire and kaowool kiln is lowered onto large glazed bowl made by Allan Widenhofer, of the United States. Kiln is fired with gas, and heat-proof protective clothing makes handling the kiln and ware easy and safe. *Courtesy of the artist.*

Figure 12-19 (*Top Right*) Allan Widenhofer's large bowl is removed from kiln and placed on a bed of newspaper, which ignites from bowl's heat. (*Middle Right*) Wire ring with kaowool insulation is lowered over bowl. Metal drum would do as well, but bowl was so large it needed specially built cover. (*Bottom Right*) Sheet metal is placed over ring to smother fire and cause reduction. *Photos courtesy of the artist.*

Figures 12-20 to 12-25 Raku has traditionally been associated with rough textures and accidental effects like those on Japanese teaware. The following illustrations, however, show that in the hands of contemporary potters and sculptors, the range of raku has been extended.

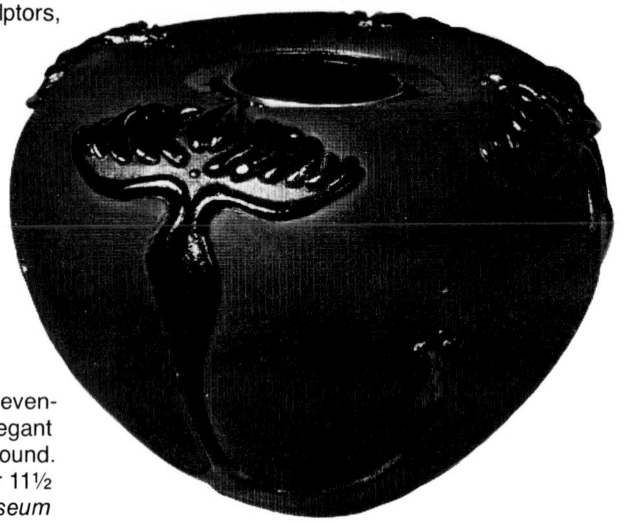

Figure 12-20 (*Right*) Barbara Andino Stevenson, of the United States, contrasts elegant glossy black relief with matt black background. Raku firing. Height 9 in. (22.9 cm), diameter 11½ in. (29.2 cm). *Courtesy, M. H. DeYoung Museum Art School. Photo by Jim Stevenson.*

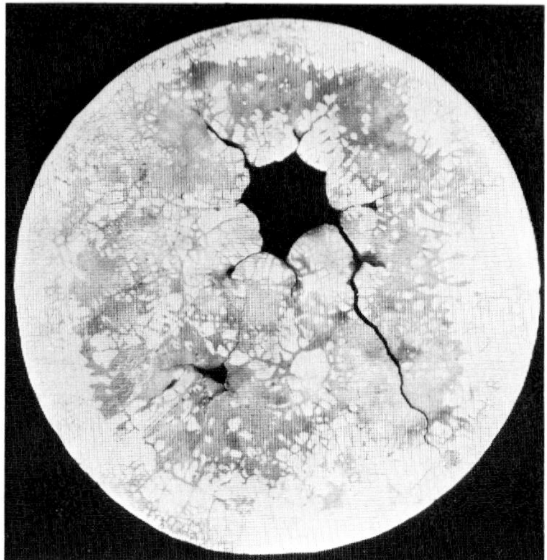

Figure 12-21 Rory Nakata, of the United States, takes advantage of carbon in the crackles to create a moonlike surface on "Raku Disc." Raku firing. *Courtesy, M. H. DeYoung Museum Art School. Photo by Robert Hsiang.*

Figure 12-22 The iron found-object that encircles the cover on this piece combines well with the clay. Because the raku firing is done at such a low temperature, the metal will not melt in the kiln. Ernst Häusermann, Switzerland.

Figure 12-23 "Raku Lady." Woven coils form the frame for an underglaze pencil drawing. Allan Widenhofer, raku firing. Diameter 23 in. (58.4 cm). *Courtesy of the artist.*

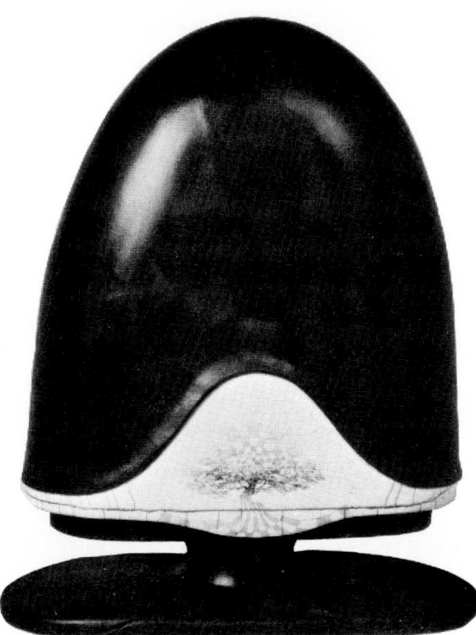

Figure 12-24 "Checkered Arch Tree" with underglaze pencil drawing, by Allan Widenhofer. Raku firing. 16¼ X 14 X 16 in. (41.3 X 35.6 X 40.6 cm). *Courtesy of the artist.*

Figure 12-25 Portable raku kiln can easily be transported to beach from workshop. Already-bisqued ware is glazed on the spot, then dried thoroughly on expanded metal shelf. *Courtesy, M. H. DeYoung Museum Art School. Photo by Tad Sekino.*

There are those, however, who prefer to do their raku firings under somewhat different conditions, preferring the accidental effects that may result. A wood-burning kiln works well for raku , because the low melting point of the glazes means that the fire does not have be very hot or kept at full temperature very long. A beach with plenty of dry driftwood is a good place to fire (Figures 12-25 to 12-27). In these surroundings, with the sound of surf and a crackling wood fire, it is easy to feel a bond with early clay-crafters. Here we become part of a tradition reaching back thousands of years and stretching ahead into the future for as long as there is earth for human hands to shape and fire to transform it.

Figure 12-26 (*Left*) Kiln is building up heat, and glazed ware is ready to place in the kiln for short firing during which students can watch their glazes melt in the fire. **Figure 12-27** (*Right*) After firing, glazed ware is removed from kiln and plunged into sawdust to reduce it. Iridescent areas often develop in reduction. The speed and spontaneity of raku-type firings make them popular. *Courtesy, M. H. DeYoung Museum Art School. Photos by Tad Sekino.*

Appendix One

Calculating Glazes Using Chemical Analysis

You will need to use some chemistry if you want to make your own glazes from scratch or do more than make the simple changes in glaze ingredients discussed in Chapter 11. For generations, potters have made glazes by trying out various combinations of materials and firing them to see what happens. This is a valid, but time consuming, way to work. Now modern chemistry enables us to break down the composition of a glaze into a formula that represents the chemical, rather than physical, proportions of its ingredients. Using such formulas, we can first analyze and compare glazes in a more detailed and logical manner, then test them in the kiln. This method of calculation involves some understanding of chemistry and of the basic atomic and molecular composition of materials. It is also a great help to have a calculator handy.

The following example of glaze calculation shows how a potter who works with high-fire stoneware glazes goes about analyzing, calculating, and testing a glaze. Because the method is the same whether the glaze is high-fire or low-fire, matt or glossy, transparent or opaque, by working through this example, you will learn how to apply the basics of glaze calculation to any glaze.

Before going into the calculations, however, it is necessary to understand something about the chemical composition of the earthy materials used in glaze making. With the development of modern chemistry, these materials have been analyzed and tested, and their chemical structure, as well as their behavior in the kiln, has been observed and recorded. Rules have been established to express their chemical relationships, making it easier for the potter to supply the needed chemical components of a glaze from the available ceramic materials.

Elements and Compounds

The earth's crust, from which these materials come, is made up of elements and compounds. An element is a substance that cannot be separated into substances different from itself by ordinary chemical means, containing only one kind of atom. The atoms of the 106 known elements have been assigned weights in relation to the lightest element—hydrogen—which was given the weight of 1. In order to calculate glazes, you must use the atomic weights of the elements (see Chart 2 in Appendix 3).

The elements, however, rarely exist in pure form, but rather in compounds. Made up of combinations of different elements in a definite proportion, these compounds have been formed by natural forces and may exist as gases, liquids, or solids. The compounds with which the potter is mainly concerned are oxides produced when various elements become chemically combined with the oxygen that is so plentiful in our environment.

Atoms and Molecules

Molecules are the smallest particles of a compound that retain chemical identity with a substance in mass. The weight of a molecule consists of the total combined weights of all the atoms in that molecule. For example, water, which is made up of two atoms of hydrogen to one atom of oxygen, is written as H_2O. Since the atomic weight of one atom of hydrogen is 1, the weight of two atoms is 2. Add that 2 to the atomic weight of one atom of oxygen, which is 16, and you have a total molecular weight of 18. It is this concept of molecular weight that you will be concerned with in glaze calculation.

It helps to remember that the gram weight is the actual physical weight of the materials you will use when mixing a glaze, while the molecular weight is the chemical weight based on the atomic structure of the molecules. When making changes in a glaze, which is made up of different compounds, it is necessary to convert all calculations to molecular weights, since the weight of a compound in molecular terms differs markedly from its physical weight. If you simply mixed by gram weight, you would not achieve the desired result. Here we are concerned with the chemical reactions determined by the *proportion* of molecules of the various substances, rather than with the gross amounts of the substances.

Example of Glaze Calculation

Now let's follow a potter through a calculation:

I need to calculate a cone 10 glaze for the interior of casseroles and cups. I want a glaze that is glossy and either colorless or a very light gray or off-white. Most glazes that don't have glaze-coloring oxides (such as cobalt, iron, or copper oxide) added to them turn out to be clear or light gray. I will test a glaze without coloring oxides, fire it, and see what it looks like. Later I can add a colorant or an opacifier if I wish and test again. Experience has given me some basic knowledge as a starting point. I know, for instance, that most cone 10 glazes have ingredients, by weight, in the following very general proportions:

Feldspar (either soda or potash)	35-50%
Clay (china clay or ball clay)	5-20%
Additional flux for texture (whiting, colemanite, talc, dolomite, etc.)	15-30%
Flint (quartz)	5-25%

Each of these ingredients functions in one or more ways in a glaze:

Feldspar 35-50% This is an extremely useful and important material that is present in most glazes. In high-fire glazes it is usually the main flux because feldspars have a relatively low melting point (around 2264°F, 1240°C). Feldspar lowers the point at which the silica fuses and will also bring some additional silica and alumina to the glaze. Used with another flux, the fusing point can be lowered even more.

Clay (china clay, or ball clay) 5-20% This is the main source of the refractory, alumina, in a glaze. China clay is white, so for my particular glaze, I would use china clay rather than ball clay, which fires to a gray or cream. The clay, along with the feldspar, will generally supply all the alumina needed in a glaze.

Additional flux 15-30% One of several high-fire fluxes can be used, such as talc, whiting, dolomite, or colemanite. The additional flux may lower the melting point of the glaze by a cone or two, or even more if large quantities are added, and will also bring other oxides to the glaze. Talc, for instance, contains magnesia and silica, while colemanite yields calcium and boric oxide. When you use feldspar alone as a flux, the fired glaze surface is usually "glassy." If additional fluxes are used, the surface of the fired glaze changes. Potters use terms like "buttery," "satin," or "soft matt" to describe these glaze surfaces.

Flint 5-25% This is the main source of silica, the glass-forming oxide. It is best to use as much silica as possible in order to give a glaze the desired qualities of durability, hardness, and resistance to acids.

Using these proportions as a rough guide, I'll select the ingredients from those available to me, mix a glaze by gram weight, and test it.

These are the proportions I choose:

Kingman feldspar Because it is the principal and most efficient flux material, used to lower the melting point of silica.	45%	(.45)
China clay Because it is the source of the refractory and it is whiter than ball clay.	15%	(.15)
Talc Because in combination with the feldspar it is a stoneware flux that promotes highly glossy textures at cone 9 or 10, as well as being an opacifier.	15%	(.15)
Flint Because it is the source of silica, the glass former.	25%	(.25)
	100%	

Since I want to have enough glaze to dip the tiles, I'll mix up a batch of 500 grams. To do this, I'll multiply the above proportions by 500, to get the following amounts in grams:

Feldspar	225 grams
China clay	75 grams
Talc	75 grams
Flint	125 grams
	500 grams

Now I measure out these ingredients on my balance scale and add them to enough water to form a soupy mixture (see Chapter 11). This mixture is the basic glaze. After mixing these ingredients, I dip some test tiles in the glaze and put them in the kiln with pottery I am ready to fire to cone 10.

After I have fired the kiln and looked at the test tiles, I can see that the glaze has some characteristics that I want to change. I'm unhappy with its rather bland, glassy, and uninteresting texture. I feel it lacks the smooth, rich quality I like in a stoneware glaze. So I decide to make some alterations in the glaze ingredients.

Since the proportions of feldspar, china clay, and silica are constants in most stoneware glazes, I decide not to change them. This means I'll have to make my alterations in the additional flux, which in this case is talc. But in order to decide how much to change the proportions of the talc, I have to get involved in some chemistry. I'll have to examine the molecular makeup of the glaze, as well as take into consideration certain known limits of amounts of materials, altering the formula of the glaze accordingly. Before I do that, I'll explain some basic procedures that apply to glaze calculation.

Empirical Formula

For the purposes of glaze calculation, the materials used in a glaze are divided into three categories, according to their function in glazes. In Table 1, these categories are arranged in columns. The fluxes (both high- and low-fire) are listed under the heading RO/R_2O (also called bases); the refractory materials are listed under the heading R_2O_3 (also called neutrals); and the main glass former is listed under the heading RO_2 (also called acid). In this method of listing the ingredients, the R symbol represents the element and the O represents oxygen.

Notice that the oxides in the flux column (RO/R_2O) are all made up of one or two atoms of the element for each atom of oxygen (for example, MgO, PbO, Na_2O). Some of these fluxes, like lead, are only effective in low-fire glazes. The second column (R_2O_3) contains the oxides that make up the refractory ingredients in the glaze. Notice that these oxides are all formed with two atoms of the element to three atoms of the oxygen. The third column, which contains the glass-forming agent (silica), is called the RO_2 column because the oxide in it consists of the element combined with two atoms of oxygen.

This grouping of glaze materials into three columns is called the empirical method, and glaze formulas that list ingredients in the same three-column arrangement are called empirical formulas. Later, when we discuss the unity formula and limit formulas, we will see that the three-column (empirical) method of writing formulas provides a convenient format for checking the proper proportions of glaze ingredients.

TABLE 1 Glaze Oxides

Flux	Refractory	Glass Former
RO/R_2O (bases)	*R_2O_3 (neutrals)*	*RO_2 (acid)*
Oxides of:		
Lead, PbO	Alumina, Al_2O_3	Silica, SiO_2
Sodium, Na_2O	Boric oxide, B_2O_3*	
Potassium, K_2O		
Zinc, ZnO		
Calcium, CaO		
Magnesium, MgO		
Barium, BaO		
Lithium, Li_2O		
Strontium, SrO		

*This is a neutral that can function as an acid or a base. It is an effective flux in both low- and high-fire glazes.

Atomic and Molecular Weight

As we have seen, because ceramic materials vary so widely in weight, you cannot merely take so many grams of that material or so many grams of this. If you did, you might get many more molecules of the heavier material than you wanted. Unless you know the weight of the molecules in each of the materials you cannot select 1 or 20 or 500 or 10,000 molecules.

We have seen that each of the 106 known elements has been assigned an atomic weight in relation to hydrogen (examples given in Chart 2, Appendix 3). Since the atomic weight of hydrogen is 1 and oxygen 16, calcium 40, and silica 28, the atomic weight of oxygen is 16 times the weight of hydrogen, while calcium is 40 times the weight of hydrogen, and silica is 28 times the weight of hydrogen. Unfortunately, ceramic materials are not conveniently made up of pure elements, but rather combinations of elements. In order to find the molecular weight of each material, I must first refer to its chemical symbol in Appendix 2, to see the kind and number of atoms that compose the material. For example, the symbol for silica (or flint) is SiO_2, and that, I know, means that there are 1 atom of silicon (Si) and 2 atoms of oxygen (O_2). By looking at Chart 2 in Appendix 3, I can see that the atomic weight of silicon is 28 and the atomic weight of oxygen is 16. Doing some arithmetic, I can figure out the molecular weight of flint. To do this, I first multiply the atomic weight of silicon by 1 atom:

Silicon: 28 X 1 = 28

Then I multiply the atomic weight of oxygen by 2 atoms:

Oxygen: 16 X 2 = 32

Added together these come to 60, which gives me the weight of one molecule of silica (that is, the molecular weight of SiO_2). However, I don't have to go through this arithmetic each time, for the molecular weights are listed in Chart 3 of Appendix 3.

Equivalent Weights

You will notice that there is also a column of equivalent weights in Chart 3, and that for some of the materials, the equivalent weight is not the same as the molecular weight. The reason for this is that some materials are structured in such a way that they would yield more or less than one molecule of the desired oxide. In these cases, an altered, or equivalent, weight has been assigned to the material in order to introduce one molecule of the desired oxide into the glaze formula (and other oxides in proportion). In these cases, the equivalent weight should be used because it will yield precise quantities for the purposes of glaze calculation.

The Unity Formula

Before I do the necessary calculations to change my glaze, there is one more procedure I must explain. You have seen the reason for the empirical formula and the three-column arrangement, and also how to express the materials in molecular weights. However, in a formula based on the relationship between three groups of materials, there must always be one constant for purposes of comparison. Remember, it is the *relative* amount of the materials that is important in formulating a glaze. So, arbitrarily, it has been decided that the RO/R_2O column will always represent 1—or *unity*. By accepting this, and by comparing this column to the other two columns, the relationships of the materials in a glaze will always be clear. Remember my glossy white glaze? Its original recipe was

Kingman feldspar	45%
China clay	15%
Talc	15%
Flint	25%
	100%

In order to be able to work with molecules, I will divide these percentages of the materials by their molecular weights (or their equivalent weights). By consulting charts 3 and 5 (Appendix 3), I see that the molecular weight of Kingman feldspar is 575, that of China clay is 258, that of talc is 379, and that of silica is 60.

Now, taking each material in turn, I do the necessary arithmetic to find out the existing proportional amounts of the glaze ingredients:

	Molecular Proportions		
Kingman feldspar	45 ÷ 575	=	.078
China clay	15 ÷ 258	=	.058
Talc	15 ÷ 379	=	.039
Silica	25 ÷ 60	=	.417

The numbers in the right-hand column express the molecular proportions.

Now I can consult Chart 3 for the formulas of each of my ingredients. I know what materials I am using and the molecular proportion of each one in this particular glaze. The formula for talc, for example, is $3MgO \cdot 4SiO_2 \cdot H_2O$, and I have already worked out that its molecular proportion in this glaze is .039. With this information, I can now construct a chart of my own glaze, which will give me a clear picture of its contents and the relationship of the parts to each other. I can do this by multiplying the molecular proportion of each raw material by the quantity of each oxide in its formula. For example, in the case of talc, which has 3 parts of magnesium, I multiply 3 by .039. This shows me that the talc will contribute .117 parts of magnesium oxide to this glaze (3 X .039 = .117).

There is one complication. Feldspars are composed of many oxides, so I must be sure to have the correct formula for the type of feldspar I use. Ceramic material suppliers usually provide the necessary information about the composition of various feldspars, but these formulas may vary somewhat depending on where the feldspar is mined. Also, they usually have to be brought to unity. I have worked out that the empirical formula for Kingman feldspar is

RO/R_2O	*R_2O_3*	*RO_2*
Na_2O, .260	Al_2O_3, 1.05	SiO_2, 6.35
K_2O, .740		
CaO, trace*		
FeO_2, trace*		

*small amounts can be ignored

This means that there are .260 parts of sodium oxide and .740 parts of potassium oxide in the Kingman feldspar formula, as well as 1.05 parts of alumina and 6.35 parts of silica.

Now I make up a table in which I arrange the ingredients down the left side next to the molecular proportions for my particular glaze (see Table 2). Across the top I list the oxides that my materials will yield. This table makes it possible for me to see very clearly the quantity of each oxide that is present in my white glaze. Since water and gases burn away or change in the firing, they are not included in the calculations, nor are the small amounts of other elements in the feldspar.

TABLE 2

Material	*Molecular Proportion*	*Oxides* K_2O	Na_2O	Al_2O_3	MgO	SiO_2
Kingman feldspar	.078	.057	.020	.082		.50
China clay	.058			.058		.116
Talc	.039				.117	.156
Flint (silica)	.417					.417
Totals		.057	.020	.140	.117	1.189

Now, again using the three columns, I arrange my oxides according to the empirical formula:

	RO/R₂O	*R₂O₃*	*RO₂*
	K_2O, .057	Al_2O_3, .140	SiO_2, 1.189
	Na_2O, .020		
	MgO, .117		
Totals	.194	.140	1.189

As I said before, I want to make a unity formula by expressing the RO/R_2O column as a unit of one. Now it adds up to .194. How do I fix this? By dividing everything in the above formula by .194, I get a true unity formula. Here it is:

	RO/R₂O	*R₂O₃*	*RO₂*
	K_2O, .294	Al_2O_3, .722	SiO_2, 6.129
	Na_2O, .103		
	MgO, .603		
Totals	1.00	.722	6.129

Limit Formulas

Now I can see my glaze expressed in a unity formula that can easily be analyzed and compared to other glazes. The amount of each oxide in the glaze can also be checked easily against the limits suggested in Chart 4, Appendix 3. These limit formulas have been worked out as guides to show the amount of each oxide that occurs in a particular type of glaze maturing at a particular temperature range. Remember, however, that although limit formulas are generally accurate, there are many glazes that exceed either the upper or lower limits but which can still be successful glazes. These limits should be taken only as broad guidelines and should not keep you from experimenting. However, in order to solve my problems with this particular glaze, it will help me to look at the proportions of the materials in the unity formula of my glaze and compare them to the limits suggested in the limit formula for stoneware or porcelain glazes in the cone 8 to 12 range (Chart 4, Appendix 3).

Cone 8 to 12 Stoneware Limit Formula

KNaO	.2-.40	Al_2O_3	.3-.5	SiO_2	3.0-5.0
CaO	.4-.70	B_2O_3	.1-.3		
MgO	0-.35				
ZnO	0-.30				
BaO	0-.30				

Looking at the two sets of numbers and comparing the formula of my glaze with the limit formula, several facts become apparent.

1. My sodium and potassium are within limits. I combine these two ingredients by addition to get the total of the KNaO:

K_2O	.294
Na_2O	.103
	.397 versus a limit to .2-.40

2. My magnesium is very high: .603 versus a limit of .35
3. My alumina is high: .722 versus a limit of .5
4. My silica is high: 6.129 versus a limit of 5.0

So now I can figure out that the combination of high silica and high flux made a very shiny, glassy glaze, but it did not run off the test tile because the alumina was also high.

Analyzing the Glaze

I now examine the glaze ingredients closely in view of their functions. This will give me some information about how to change the glaze so that it may suit my purposes better. After firing, I saw that the glaze was glossy. This means that despite the fact that the silica was high, the actual proportion of glass (silica) to glass melters (feldspar and talc) was all right. If there had been too much silica and not enough flux, the final product would have been underfired, rough, and granular. On the other hand, if there had been too much flux, the glaze would have run down off the wall of the test tile into a pool at the base of the tile. Also, I see that the glaze is not brittle, nor is it crazing, crackling, or shivering off the clay body. This means that the proportion of the refractory (alumina) must be all right. Too little alumina would have caused the glaze to be brittle and probably shiver, while if there had been too much, the glaze surface would be matt and dull.

The only thing I find wrong with this glaze for my purposes is that I don't care for the texture. I know that texture is controlled largely by the oxides in the optional fluxes (such as calcium, magnesium, zinc, or barium). So, considering the high proportion of magnesium (.603 versus a limit of .35), my decision is to reduce the magnesium to bring it within the usual limits. I'll then substitute another flux for the quantity of magnesium I remove. (Remember that I am still testing, and all experimentation at this point can be modified according to the results that show after the tiles have been fired in the kiln.)

I decide to reduce the magnesium by .30 to a total of .303 and to substitute .30 molecules of calcium. I choose calcium for several reasons: it is easily available in whiting, a staple in most pottery studios; it is known to provide a smooth, matt surface in some glazes; and it is a proven trouble-free stoneware flux. Also, when calcium is added in the form of whiting, it will promote a light color in the glaze, suiting my purpose.

After I have made the substitution, my formula looks like this:

K_2O	.294	Al_2O_3	.722	SiO_2	6.129
Na_2O	.103				
MgO	.303				
CaO	.300				

Converting From Empirical Formula to Batch Recipe

Now that I have decided how to alter my empirical formula to achieve the desired results, I must find a way to supply the ingredients from the dry materials. The way I do this is to construct another table with the ceramic materials and their formulas on the left and the oxides of my empirical formula running across the top. Starting with the oxides that come from single-oxide materials, I continue with the materials that have two or more oxides, putting the silica last. Under each oxide I enter the desired proportional amount needed as I determined them for my altered formula. Table 3 includes notes and comments to clarify the process for the reader. Of course, I would not add these notes if I were working alone in my workshop.

To determine the required amounts of each material, I must fill in the table using the amounts I found in my empirical formula and which I have listed across the top of the table. Starting with the oxides that come from the materials that have only one oxide in them, I determine the required amounts by using the following equation:

$$\text{Materials proportional requirement} = \frac{\text{Amount wanted in formula}}{\text{Amount present in material}}$$

For example, I want .3 CaO. Whiting has one part CaO, so I divide .3 by 1, which of course gives me .3. (If there were any other elements in whiting, I would have to multiply them all by .3 since that is how much I will use of the entire material.) As you can see, my needs for CaO are thus satisfied entirely by the whiting. I can now go on to calculate the proportional figures for the remaining materials.

I need .303 MgO and I find that talc has 3 MgO in its formula. Therefore, I divide .303 by 3 to arrive at the proportional figure of .101 for talc. I then multiply each oxide in the talc formula by .101, which gives me .303 of MgO (satisfying my needs) and .404 of SiO_2. I subtract that amount of SiO_2 from my needed amount of 6.129 and put the remaining needed amount (5.725) in parentheses.

The next material listed in my empirical formula at the top of the chart is Na_2O and I need .103 parts of it. In the Kingman feldspar formula I see that there is .26 available. To get my proportional figure, I divide .103 by .26 and get .397. I then multiply each part in the feldspar formula by .397 to get the equivalent amounts of each part contained in my empirical formula. So I get .103 Na_2O (satisfying the amount needed), .294 K_2O (also satisfying that amount needed), .417 Al_2O_3, which I subtract from the needed amount of .722, and I put the remaining amount needed (.305) in parentheses. Finally I get 2.52 SiO_2 and subtract that from the needed amount of 5.725 and put the remainder (3.205) in parentheses.

Now I have satisfied all my needs except for the remaining amounts of Al_2O_3 and SiO_2. I can complete my alumina needs with china clay by using .305 of it, since it contains one part of Al_2O_3. However, there are two parts of SiO_2 in china clay, and when I multiply by .305, I get .610. I subtract this amount from the needed 3.205, leaving me with 2.595 parts of silica still needed. I complete my remaining requirements by adding the needed amount (2.595) with flint, which is a nearly pure form of silica.

TABLE 3 From Empirical Formula to Batch Recipe

Materials	*Proportional Requirement*	*Remarks*	*CaO* *.3*	*MgO* *.303*	*Na_2O* *.103*	*K_2O* *.294*	*Al_2O_3* *.722*	*SiO_2* *6.129*
Whiting, $CaCO_3$	.3	I need .3 parts of CaO. Whiting has one part CaO, so I divide .3 by 1 to get my proportional requirement.	Satisfied by 1×.3= .3					
Talc, 3 MgO • 4 SiO_2	.101	I need .303 MgO. Talc has 3 MgO. The materials proportion is thus .303÷3 = .101. I multiply each part in talc by this figure. Magnesium is satisfied, but we need more silica.		Satisfied by 3×.101= .303				4×.101=.404 (Still need 5.725)
Kingman feldspar, .26 Na_2O • .74 K_2O • 1.05 Al_2O_3 • 6.35 SiO_2	.397	I need .103 Na_2O. There is .26 Na_2O available in the feldspar. I divide .103 by .26 to get .397. Then I multiply each part in the feldspar formula by this figure. I find I still need more Al_2O_3 and SiO_2.			Satisfied by .26×.397= .103	Satisfied by .74×.397=.294	1.05× .397= .417 (Still need .305)	6.35× .397= 2.52 (Still need 3.205)
China clay, Al_2O_3 • 2 SiO_2	.305	.305 Al_2O_3 is needed. There is one part Al_2O_3 available in china clay. .305÷1 = .305, which is the materials proportion still needed of alumina. China clay satisfies .610 silica. I still need 2.595 silica.					Satisfied by 1×.305=.305	2×.305=.610 (Still need 2.595)
Flint, SiO_2	2.595	Remaining silica needed satisfied by 2.595 of flint.						Satisfied by 1×2.595=2.595

Now that I have determined the proportions required of each material, I simply multiply this amount by the molecular (or equivalent) weights for each ingredient. The molecular or equivalent weights of the most common materials are listed in Chart 3, Appendix 3. Thus I have:

Ingredient	*Material (Proportional Amount)*	*X*	*Molecular Weight (or Equiv. Weight)*	=	*Batch Amount (Grams)*
Whiting	0.300	X	100	=	30.0
Talc	0.101	X	378	=	38.2
Feldspar	0.397	X	575	=	228.3
China clay	0.305	X	258	=	78.7
Flint	2.600	X	60	=	156.0
					531.2 (grams)

A batch recipe is what I started with, and now I have another batch recipe of the altered glaze ready to mix, test, and fire.

Once again I will mix a batch of 500 grams of the glaze, dip some test tiles in the batch, and fire them to cone 10. It is a good idea to dip several tiles and place them in different locations in the kiln. In this way you will see if small variations in kiln atmosphere will affect the glaze.

The fired result of the test is a glaze that has changed somewhat. Its glossy finish has a softer texture. It is a glaze that suits my purpose as a liner glaze at the present time. If I decide to alter it later, I will go through the testing process again. I could, for example, add a little Zircopax (2 to 10 percent) in order to try to introduce some opacity and whiteness to the glaze. Or I could add some other colorants.

What I have followed here is the basic method for testing glazes, using most of the procedures required in order to go from batch recipe to molecular formula and back to batch again. If you have followed this example as it was carried through these procedures, you now have seen the basic process of calculating and analyzing glazes.

As you get into more complex materials and more sophisticated and elaborate glazes, the calculations can become more complex. However, no amount of knowledge of chemistry can substitute for patient testing and retesting of trial formulas in your own kiln, with your own clay body, and with the available materials. The use of chemistry answers many technical questions and gives you a method of formulating a glaze, but experience, patience, hard work, and aesthetic sensitivity are what really create beautiful glazes.

Appendix Two

Chemicals and Materials

The main oxides used in glaze forming and coloring, as well as the materials that yield them, are listed below. The main colorants and opacifiers are listed separately in Appendix 3. The precautions that should be taken when using all ceramics materials are discussed in Chapter 11. Use *all* these materials with care and avoid breathing their dusts. Those materials that are actually poisonous are indicated in this list.

Albany slip A natural clay containing silica, alumina, and flux in porportions that form a glaze when fired between cones 8 and 10. Used in slip form. Fires to tan, brown, or black. Mined near Albany, New York, it was used by Early American potters, frequently in the interiors of stoneware salt-glazed crocks.

Alumina (Al_2O_3) A refractory material that increases the viscosity of glazes, making them less runny. Helps control the melting point of a glaze. Has a high melting point, so only a small amount can be added to a glaze—the proportion can be greater in a high-fire glaze. The quantity of alumina is increased for a matt surface and decreased if a crystalline glaze is desired. Alumina also helps to make glazes more durable. Main sources of alumina are china clay and ball clay.

Antimony oxide (Sb_2O_3) Combined with lead and fired below cone 1, it is an opacifier not often used. Also infrequently used to produce light yellow.

Barium carbonate ($BaCO_3$) A source of barium oxide for glazes. Poisonous in the unfired state.

Barium oxide (BaO) A refractory, although in high-fire glazes it acts as a flux. Helps produce a matt surface. Adds brilliance to certain colors. Poisonous in the unfired state.

Bentonite ($Al_2O_3 \cdot 4SiO_2 \cdot 9H_2O$) A clay of volcanic origin that increases plasticity of other clays. Used in glazes as a deflocculant to keep glaze particles from settling too rapidly. Formula varies according to source.

Bone ash Used in clay bodies to lower firing temperatures and give translucency. Occasionally used as a flux in stoneware glazes. See **Bone china** in Glossary.

Borax ($Na_2O \cdot 2B_2O_3 \cdot 10H_2O$) Generally used in fritted form, since it is soluble in water. A low-fire flux, but small amounts in high-fire glazes can help a glaze melt more smoothly. Source of sodium and boric oxides.

Boric Oxide (B_2O_3) A useful flux that operates at both high and low temperatures. Helps produce a smooth glaze and increases brilliance of colors. Although a glass-forming material, it is also a strong flux at high temperatures. With iron, it may produce opalescent blues.

Boron See **Boric oxide.**

Cadmium sulfide (CdS) Used with selenium in stains and in low-fire frits for overglazes to produce red and orange. Toxic. As it can be released into food, do not use in food containers.

Calcium oxide (CaO) A useful glaze ingredient. Glazes with calcium are durable and resistant to acids. Has a high melting point, but is a very active flux at high temperatures. For this reason, it is used especially in porcelain glazes. In low-fire glazes, usually combined with other fluxes. See **Whiting** ($CaCO_3$).

China clay See **Kaolin.**

Chromium oxide (Cr_2O_3) In glazes without zinc, it yields greens. With zinc, browns and tans. With tin, pink, and in some lead glazes, yellow and red. Reduction darkens the color.

Clay (Theoretical formula $A1_2O_3 \cdot 2SiO_2 \cdot 2H_2O$) Generally used in the form of kaolin or ball clay in glazes to provide alumina and silica. Clay in a glaze helps to keep ingredients suspended and gives some toughness to the glaze when it is painted on the bisque. Amounts of silica and alumina will vary according to the particular clay used.

Cobalt oxide (Co_3O_4) and **cobalt carbonate** ($CoCO_3$) Formula varies. Strong blue colorants that do not burn away. Used for centuries for decoration, cobalt can be fired from low to high temperatures. Cobalt alone gives rather violent blues but can be softened by adding manganese, iron, rutile, or nickel. Cobalt carbonate along with iron chromate or manganese will produce black. (Chinese potters who wanted bright blue had to import cobalt, since the local cobalt contained manganese.)

Colemanite ($2CaO \cdot 3B_2O_3 \cdot 5H_20$) A source of boric oxide in insoluble form, and also provides calcium oxide. A flux in both high- and low-fire glazes, it is popular for the effects it produces in glazes. With rutile, it gives a mottled appearance, and may also give a milky blue.

Copper oxide (CuO) and **copper carbonate** ($CuCO_3$) Copper gives greens, blues, or reds, depending upon the other ingredients in the glaze and the atmosphere in the kiln. In lead glazes, the oxide gives greens but should not be used with lead on any food containers, as it decreases the acid resistance of the glaze. Copper was used in China to produce the famous red oxblood and peachbloom glazes.

Cornish stone (Theoretical formula $K_2O \cdot A1_2O_3 \cdot 8SiO_2$) An English feldspathic material that requires high temperatures to fuse it. Shrinks less than kaolin and feldspar, so is less subject to glaze defects. Helps form tough, hard glazes. Used as a source of silica, it contains varying amounts of it, as well as potassium and sodium. In ancient China, a similar rock, petuntze, made possible the development of porcelain.

Cryolite (Na_3AlF_6) A natural source of sodium. Can be used when both sodium and alumina are needed. Gives brilliant colors, but sometimes glazes containing it are subject to pits.

Dolomite ($CaCO_3 \cdot MgCO_3$) A natural source of magnesium and calcium oxides. Used as a flux in stoneware glazes, it helps produce smooth matt surfaces.

Feldspar (also spelled **felspar**) Yields alumina and silica. Feldspars vary in composition, with some containing potash and others soda. Usually, the formula of a commercial feldspar is available from suppliers, so that one can see what oxides are present. At high temperatures, feldspar is a flux, melting without additional flux at 1250°F (677°C). At lower temperatures, talc dolomite or whiting are added to lower its melting point. Used in porcelain clay bodies.

Ferric oxide and **ferrous oxide** See **Iron.**

Flint (SiO_2) Also called quartz. It is the main source of silica in glazes and combines with a variety of fluxes to fuse at lower temperatures.

Fluospar (CaF_2) Used in some glazes as a source of calcium, it fluxes at a lower temperature than most calcium compounds. Helps develop blue-greens of copper in oxidation firing.

Ilmenite ($FeO \cdot TiO_2$) An ore with both iron and titanium. Usually added to glazes to give specks of dark color.

Iron The colorant in reddish earthenware clays, where its fluxing action lowers their firing temperatures. Also used in glazes for color and to modify other coloring oxides. Most commonly used forms are:

Ferric oxide (Fe_2O_3) Red iron oxide or hematite
Ferrous oxide (FeO) Black iron oxide
Ferrous-ferric oxide (Fe_3O_4) Magnetite

All are used to give warm cream or yellowish tones, tans, red-browns, and black. It also gives the Japanese tenmoku glaze and the gray-greens of celadon, depending on the glaze, firing, and amount used.

Iron chromate ($FeCrO_4$) Usually gives grays and browns. With copper, will yield black. With tin, may give pink or red-brown.

Kaolin (Theoretical formula $Al_2O_3 \cdot 2SiO_2 \cdot 2H_2O$) Also called china clay. The main source of alumina and silica in glazes, it is also used in white clay bodies, since it does not contain iron.

Lead oxide (PbO) Lead is a very active flux at low temperatures and was used for this purpose for many centuries in the Near East, Europe, and the United States. Used in frits with silica, the danger of this poisonous material to the potter is lessened, but even fritted lead glazes must be fired properly to avoid releasing lead in foods. Commercial frits should be checked to make sure there is enough silica in proportion to the lead, at least in the proportion of $PbO \cdot 2SiO_2$. Poisonous.

Lead (red) and **lead (white)** Both are poisonous and are not recommended for studio use except under very safe conditions and only by experienced users. *Never* use on a food container or on anything that might be converted into one.

Lepidolite ($LiF \cdot KF \cdot Al_2O_3 \cdot 3SiO_2$) Formula varies. Used in china bodies and as a flux in some high-fire glazes. It contains lithium and helps make most glazes brighter than soda or potash feldspars. However, it can cause pitting.

Lime (CaO) See **Calcium oxide** and **Whiting.**

Lithium carbonate (Li_2CO_3) A source of lithium in glazes. An active flux at high temperatures, it allows the use of more alumina and silica in alkaline glazes, increasing the hardness of the glaze. It also widens the possible firing range and brightens colors. Although expensive, only a small amount is needed. Low expansion and contraction, so glazes fit well.

Magnesium carbonate ($MgCO_3$) Provides magnesium oxide. Acting as a flux at high temperatures, it is a refractory in lower firings. Increases viscosity and improves the adhesion of glazes. Useful in producing matt glazes.

Magnesium oxide (MgO) A refractory material at low temperatures and a flux at high temperatures. In high-fire glazes, it gives a smooth surface, while at lower temperatures, it helps produce matt, opaque surfaces.

Manganese oxide (MnO_2) Gives purple when used with alkaline fluxes (sodium, potassium, and lithium), but usually brown in most glazes. Used with cobalt, purple or black colors will develop, depending on the other ingredients.

Nepheline syenite ($K_2O \cdot 3Na_2O \cdot 4Al_2O_3 \cdot 9SiO_2$) A useful substitute for potash feldspar. Since it has more potassium and sodium, it melts at lower temperatures. The formula varies depending on sources.

Nickel oxide (NiO) Generally used to dull down other colors, as it does not produce clear colors when used alone.

Opax One of several commercial opacifiers. See **Tin oxide.**

Pearl ash See **Potassium carbonate.**

Potassium carbonate (K_2CO_3) Also called pearl ash. Used in frits as a source of potassium.

Potassium dichromate ($K_2Cr_2O_7$) Acts as a green colorant with boric oxide. With tin in lead low-fire glazes, it is used in frit to develop red and orange. A soluble material that is poisonous in the raw state.

Potassium oxide (K_2O) A flux that operates at all temperatures but has a high coefficient of thermal expansion that can cause crazing if used in large amounts. Available in feldspars or commercial frits.

Rutile (TiO_2) An ore that contains titanium and iron. Gives tans and browns, often in streaks. In glazes with copper, cobalt, chrome, or iron it may produce subtle, grayed colors.

Silica (SiO_2) The essential glass-forming oxide in glazes. Since it gives durability and increases resistance to chemicals, a glaze should contain as much silica as possible. The higher the temperature, the more silica can be used in a glaze, causing high-fire glazes to be more durable than low-fire. At lower temperatures, it is necessary to bring down the melting point of silica with a flux.

Silicon carbide (SiC) Used in glazes to produce local reduction with copper oxide, independent of the general kiln atmosphere. Also, the chief ingredient in heat-resistant kiln furniture.

Soda ash See **Sodium carbonate.**

Sodium carbonate (Na_2CO_3) Also called soda ash. An active glaze flux, usually only used in frit form as it is soluble. Also a defloccant. When used in a clay body, it reduces the amount of water needed, thus reducing shrinkage.

Sodium oxide (Na_2O) Used widely in low-fire glazes as a flux, it can also be used in high-fire glazes. Has a high expansion coefficient that can cause crazing. Glazes high in sodium are apt to weather and flake off. Most useful if used with other fluxes.

Sodium silicate ($Na_2 \cdot SiO_2$) Varies in formula. Used as a deflocculant in casting slips, where it reduces the water needed to form the slip, thus reducing shrinkage on drying.

Spodumene ($Li_2 \cdot Al_2O_3 \cdot 4SiO_2$) A source of lithium in glazes. If used instead of feldspar, it lowers the fusing temperature and helps to eliminate crazing.

Talc ($3MgO \cdot 4SiO_2 \cdot H_2O$) Formula varies. Used widely in clay bodies, it can also be used as an opacifier in glazes. It is an effective high-fire glaze flux as well as lowering the melting temperatures of ball clays, feldspars, and kaolin in clay bodies.

Tin oxide (SnO_2) Gives opaque and semi-opaque white. Has been used since very early times to cover the reddish colors of earthenware. Since it is expensive, commercial substitutes have been developed, such as Zircopax, Superpax, and Opax.

Titanium oxide (TiO_2) An opacifier that will also help create a somewhat matt surface. Gives white and cream opaque glazes. Used alone or in frit form. (Rutile is an impure form of titanium.)

Vanadium pentoxide (V_2O_5) Alone, it gives light yellow, with tin, gives a bright yellow. Reduced, it can produce blue-gray.

Whiting ($CaCO_3$) The main source of calcium oxide in glazes and an important high-fire flux. Small amounts can be added to low-fire alkaline glazes to increase durability.

Wollastonite ($CaSiO_3$) Used in glazes as a source of calcium oxide.

Zinc oxide (ZnO) A high-fire flux that is useful in reducing thermal expansion. Increases strength of glazes and helps produce smooth surfaces. Often used as a substitute for lead, in small amounts it is a useful flux and helps create matt glazes. Too much, however, causes glazes to become dry, pit, or crawl.

Zirconium oxide (ZrO_2) An opacifier, usually fritted with other oxides. Not as strong as tin, but cheaper. Available in various commercial products.

Zircopax Commercial opacifier.

Appendix Three

Charts Relating to Ceramics

CHART 1 Colorants and Opacifiers

Colorant	Colors	Usual % Range
Antimony oxide, Sb_2O_3	In glazes below cone 1 or 2, infrequently used for light yellows. Poisonous.	10–20%
Cadmium sulfide, CdS	Used in low-fire overglazes to produce red. Disappears in firings over cone 010. Usually combined with selenium in a stain. Poisonous.	
Chromium oxide, Cr_2O_3	Greens. With tin, pinks. With zinc, browns. In reduction kilns can darken or blacken colors. Can be toxic. Avoid breathing the dust.	1–3%
Cobalt oxide, Co_3O_4 Cobalt carbonate, $CoCO_3$	Blues. With magnesium, purple. Withstands high firing. Powerful colorant. Higher percentage gives blue-black. Frequently used with iron, rutile, manganese, or nickel to soften its harsh color. Carbonate with manganese, iron, or ochre gives black.	.01–2%
Copper oxide, CuO Copper carbonate, $CuCO_3$	In alkaline glazes, gives blue and turquoise. In lead glazes, gives soft greens, but must *not* be used on tableware because it encourages release of lead in contact with acid foods. In some high-fire glazes, can give blues. In others, browns. Under certain firing conditions and glaze composition, produces the famous red oxblood or peachbloom glazes of ancient China.	1–5%

CHART 1 (continued)

Colorant	Colors	Usual % Range
Ilmenite, $FeO \cdot TiO_2$	Gives brown specks and spots.	1–7%
Iron: Ferric oxide, Fe_2O_3 Ferrous oxide, FeO Ferrous-ferric oxide, Fe_3O_4 Iron chromate, $FeCrO_4$	Iron is the material that causes earthenware clays to fire in the buff and red range. In most glazes it produces a wide range of colors, ranging from tans to reddish brown to black. Added to other oxides, it grays or modifies their brilliance. In certain glazes and under certain firing conditions it produces the Japanese tenmoku or the gray-green celadon of China.	1–10%
Manganese oxide, MnO_2 Manganese carbonate, $MnCO_3$	In alkaline glazes, gives purples. In lead glazes, yields browns or brownish purple. In reduction high-fire glazes, brown. With cobalt, produces violets.	2–10%
Nickel oxide, NiO	Browns and grays. Rather dull colors. Used mostly to modify other coloring oxides. In certain reduction firings in a glaze with zinc, it *may* yield yellows or blues, but results are uncertain.	1–3%
Potassium dichromate (bichromate), $K_2Cr_2O_7$	Soluble. Used in frits in low-fire glazes. With boric oxide, gives greens; with tin, gives reds and oranges.	1–10%
Rutile, TiO_2	Gives tans and browns. Used to produce streaks and mottled effects. With cobalt and sometimes with iron, blue.	2–10%
Tin oxide, SnO_2	Gives soft opaque whites. Used as opacifier in Persian, Spanish and Italian glazes.	5% semi-opaque 10% opaque
Titanium oxide, TiO_2	Whites and creams. Opacifier.	5–10%
Vanadium oxide (pentoxide), V_2O_5	Generally used in frit with tin, it gives opaque yellows.	5–10%

Opacifiers

Antimony, Sb_2O_3; Tin oxide, SnO_2; Zirconium, ZrO_2; Zircopax, Opax, Superfax, etc.

CHART 2 *Atomic Weights of Elements Used in Ceramics*

Element	Symbol	Atomic Weight
Aluminum	Al	26.98
Antimony	Sb	121.75
Barium	Ba	137.34
Bismuth	Bi	208.98
Boron	B	10.81
Cadmium	Cd	112.40
Calcium	Ca	40.08
Carbon	C	12.01
Chlorine	Cl	35.45
Chromium	Cr	51.99
Cobalt	Co	58.93
Copper	Cu	63.54
Fluorine	F	18.99
Gold	Au	196.96
Hydrogen	H	1.00
Iridium	Ir	192.22
Iron	Fe	55.84
Lead	Pb	207.20
Lithium	Li	6.94
Magnesium	Mg	24.30
Manganese	Mn	54.93
Nickel	Ni	58.71
Nitrogen	N	14.00
Oxygen	O	15.99
Phosphorus	P	30.97
Platinum	Pt	195.09
Potassium	K	39.10
Selenium	Se	78.96
Silicon	Si	28.08
Silver	Ag	107.86
Sodium	Na	22.98
Strontium	Sr	87.62
Sulphur	S	32.06
Tin	Sn	118.69
Titanium	Ti	47.90
Uranium	U	238.02
Vanadium	V	50.94
Zinc	Zn	65.37
Zirconium	Zr	91.22

CHART 3 Molecular and Equivalent Weights

Material	Formula	Molecular Weight	Equivalent Weight
Alumina	Al_2O_3	102	102
Antimony oxide	Sb_2O_3	291.5	291.5
Barium oxide	BaO	153.4	153.4
Barium carbonate	$BaCO_3$	197.4	197.4
Bone ash	$Ca_3(PO_4)_2$	310.3	103
Borax	$Na_2O \cdot 2B_2O_3 \cdot 10H_2O$	382	382
Boric acid	$B_2O_3 \cdot 3H_2O$	124	124
Boric oxide	B_2O_3	70	70
Calcium borate (Colemanite)	$2CaO \cdot 3B_2O_3 \cdot 5H_2O$	412	206
Calcium carbonate (Whiting)	$CaCO_3$	100	100
China clay (Kaolin)	$Al_2O_3 \cdot 2SiO_2 \cdot 2H_2O$	258	258
Chromium oxide	Cr_2O_3	152	152
Cobalt carbonate	$CoCO_3$	119	119
Cobalt oxide	Co_3O_4	241	241
Copper carbonate	$CuCO_3$	123.6	123.6
Copper oxide (cupric)	CuO	79.57	79.57
Copper oxide (cuprous)	Cu_2O	143	80
Cornish stone	$CaO \cdot 304$ $Na_2O \cdot 340$ $K_2O \cdot 356$ } Al_2O_3 1.075 } SiO_2 8.10	667	667
Cryolite	Na_3A1F_6	210	420
Dolomite	$CaCO_3$ $MgCO_3$	184	184
Feldspar (potash)	$K_2O \cdot Al_2O_3 \cdot 6SiO_2$	556	556
Feldspar (soda) Feldspar (lime)	$Na_2O \cdot Al_2O_3 \cdot 6SiO_2$	524	524
Flint	SiO_2	60	60
Ilmenite	$FeO \cdot TiO_2$	151.74	151.74
Iron chromate (ferrous-ferric)	$FeCrO_4$	231.4	231.4
Iron oxide, red (ferric)	Fe_2O_3	160	160
Iron oxide, black (ferrous)	FeO	72	72
Kaolin	$Al_2O_3 \cdot 2SiO_2$	222	222
Lead carbonate (white lead)	$2PbCO_3 \cdot Pb(OH)_2$	776	258
Lead oxide (red)	Pb_3O_4	685.6	223
Lead oxide	PbO	223	223
Lepidolite	$LiF \cdot KF \cdot Al_2O_3 \cdot 3SiO_2$	356	356
Lithium carbonate	Li_2CO_3	74	74

CHART 3 (continued)

Material	Formula	Molecular Weight	Equivalent Weight
Magnesium carbonate	$MgCO_3$	84.3	84.3
Magnesium oxide	MgO	40.3	40.3
Manganese carbonate	$MnCO_3$	114.93	114.93
Manganese dioxide	MnO_2	87	87
Nepheline syenite	$K_2O \cdot 25$ } Al_2O_3 } SiO_2 $Na_2O \cdot 75$ } $1 \cdot 11$ } $4 \cdot 65$ $0 \cdot 75\ Na_2O\quad 4 \cdot 65\ SiO_2$	462	462
Nickel oxide	NiO	74.7	74.7
Potassium carbonate (pearl ash)	K_2CO_3	138	138
Quartz	SiO_2	60	60
Rutile	TiO_2	80	80
Silica (flint)	SiO_2	60	60
Sodium carbonate (soda ash)	Na_2CO_3	106	106
Sodium silicate	Na_2SiO_3	122.1	122.1
Spodumene	$Li_2O \cdot Al_2O_3 \cdot 4SiO_2$	372	372
Talc (magnesium silicate)	$3MgO \cdot 4SiO_2 \cdot H_2O$	378.96	378.96
Tin oxide	SnO_2	150.7	150.7
Titanium oxide	TiO_2	80	80
Vanadium pentoxide	V_2O_5	181.9	181.9
Whiting	$CaCO_3$	100	100
Zinc oxide	ZnO	81.3	81.3
Zirconium oxide	ZrO_2	123.2	123.2
Zirconium silicate (Zircopax)	$ZrO_2 \cdot SiO_2$	183	183

CHART 4 Limit Formulas for Various Temperatures and Types of Glazes

RO/R_2O (Flux)		R_2O_3 (Refractory)		RO_2 (Glass former)	
Low-fire Glazes					
Cone 012–08 Lead Glazes		Al_2O_3	.05–.2	SiO_2	1. –1.5
PbO	.7–1				
KNaO	0–.3				
ZnO	0–.1				
CaO	0–.2				
Cone 08–01 Lead Glazes		Al_2O_3	.1 –.25	SiO_2	1.5–2.00
PbO	.7–1				
KNaO	0–.3				
ZnO	0–.2				
CaO	0–.3				
Cone 08–04 Alkaline Glazes		Al_2O_3	.05–.25	SiO_2	1.5–2.5
PbO	0–.5				
KNaO	.4–.8				
CaO	0–.3				
ZnO	0–.2				
Cone 08–04 Lead-Colemanite		Al_2O_3	.15–.2	SiO_2	1.5–2.5
PbO	.2–.60	B_2O_3	.15–.6		
KNaO	.1–.25				
CaO	.3–.60				
ZnO	.1–.25				
BaO	0–.15				
Cone 2–5 Lead Glazes		Al_2O_3	.2–.28	SiO_2	2.–3.
PbO	.4–.60				
CaO	.1–.40				
ZnO	0–.25				
KNaO	.1–.25				
Cone 2–5 Colemanite		Al_2O_3	.2–.28	SiO_2	2.–3.
CaO	.2–.50	B_2O_3	.3–.6		
ZnO	.1–.25				
BaO	.1–.25				
KNaO	.1–.25				

CHART 4 (continued)

RO/R_2O (Flux)		R_2O_3 (Refractory)		RO_2 (Glass former)	
Cone 2–5 Lead Boro-Silicate		Al_2O_3	.25–.35	SiO_2	2.5–3.5
PbO	.2–.3	B_2O_3	.2–.6		
KNaO	.2–.3				
CaO	.35–.5				
ZnO	0–.1				
High-fire Glazes					
Cone 8-12 Stoneware or Porcelain		Al_2O_3	.3–.5	SiO_2	3.0–5.0
		B_2O_3	.1–.3		
KNaO	.2–.40				
CaO	.4–.70				
MgO	0–.35				
ZnO	0–.30				
BaO	0–.30				

CHART 5 Formulas of Some Feldspars

Feldspar	Formula*	Molecular Weight
Albite	1.00 Na_2O • 1.00 Al_2O_3 • 6.00 SiO_2	524
Anorthite	1.00 CaO • 1.00 Al_2O_3 • 2.00 SiO_2	278
Buckingham (Kona A-1)	.79 K_2O • 1.05 Al_2O_3 • 6.45 SiO_2 .17 Na_2O .04 CaO	587
Clinchfield #202	.72 K_2O • 1.06 Al_2O_3 • 7.08 SiO_2 .25 Na_2O .03 CaO	618
Cornwall Stone	.356 K_2O_3 • 1.075 Al_2O_3 • 8.10 SiO_2 .340 Na_2O .304 CaO	667
Custer (Keystone)	.67 K_2O • 1.04 Al_2O_3 • 6.94 SiO_2 .30 Na_2O .03 CaO	694
Del Monte	.40 K_2O • 1.03 Al_2O_3 • 6.42 SiO_2 .39 Na_2O .21 CaO	564
Eureka	.52 Na_2O • 1.07 Al_2O_3 • 8.61 SiO_2 .46 K_2O .02 CaO	703
Ferro Spar #10	.716 K_2O • .984 Al_2O_3 • 7.85 SiO_2 .286 NaO	684
Kingman	.74 K_2O • 1.05 Al_2O_3 • 6.35 SiO_2 .26 Na_2O	575
Kona A-3	.52 K_2O • 1.05 Al_2O_3 • 7.91 SiO_2 .42 Na_2O .05 CaO	660

*Formulas and molecular weights may vary.

CHART 5 (continued)

Feldspar	Formula*	Molecular Weight
Kona F-4 (56)	.58 Na_2O • 1.00 Al_2O_3 • 5.79 SiO_2 .26 K_2O .16 CaO	518
Lepidolite	.39 K_2O • 1.00 Al_2O_3 • 3.74 SiO_2 .06 Na_2O .55 Li_2O	383
Nepheline Syenite	.75 Na_2O • 1.11 Al_2O_3 • 4.65 SiO_2 .25 K_2O	462
Orthoclase	1.00 K_2O • 1.00 Al_2O_3 • 6.00 SiO_2	556
Oxford	.58 K_2O • 1.07 Al_2O_3 • 1.07 SiO_2 .42 Na_2O	660
Petalite	1.00 Li_2O • 1.00 Al_2O_3 • 8.00 SiO_2	612
Plastic Vitrox	.61 K_2O • 1.33 Al_2O_3 • 14.00 SiO_2 .34 Na_2O .05 CaO	1051
Spodumene	1.00 Li_2O • 1.00 Al_2O_3 • 4.00 SiO_2	372
Volcanic Ash	.47 KNaO • 1.09 Al_2O_3 • 9.52 SiO_2 .17 CaO .25 MgO .11 FeO	720

*Formulas and molecular weights may vary.

CHART 6 Comparison of Orton Cones (U.S.A.) and Seger Cones (Europe)

Seger Cone	°C	Orton Cone	Seger Cone	°C	Orton Cone	Seger Cone	°C	Orton Cone
	600	022		923	09	2a	1150	
	614	021	09a	935			1154	1
	635	020	08a	955	08		1162	2
	683	019	07a	970			1168	3
019	685			984	07	3a	1170	
018	705		06a	990			1186	4
	717	018		999	06	4a	1195	
017	730		05a	1000			1196	5
	747	017	04a	1025		5a	1215	
016	755			1046	05		1222	6
015a	780		03a	1055		6a	1240	7
	792	016		1060	04	7	1260	
	804	015	02a	1085			1263	8
	838	014		1101	03	8	1280	9
	852	013	01a	1105		9	1300	
	884	012		1120	02		1305	10
	895	011	1a	1125		10	1320	
	905	010		1137	01	11	1340	

Glossary

Acids Glaze chemicals that combine with *bases* and *neutrals* under heat, interacting in the formation of glazes. In glaze calculation, acids are represented by the symbol RO_2. Silica is the most important acid used in glaze formulation.

Albany slip A natural slip glaze that turns brown to black when fired at stoneware temperatures. Mined near Albany, New York, it was used by Early American potters and is still popular today (Figures 11-11 and 11-34).

Alkalies Mainly sodium and potassium, but also lime, lithium, and magnesia. They act as fluxes in certain glazes.

Alkaline glazes Glazes in which alkalies (mainly sodium and potassium) are used as fluxes. The earliest glazes developed in the Near East were alkaline.

Amphora An ancient Greek vase form. Used for transporting liquids, but also used for prize presentations to Olympic games winners (Figure 2-21).

Antefix An ornament placed at regular intervals along the roof of Greek and Etruscan temples to cover the joints of the tiles (Figure 2-30).

Armature A framework of wood, metal, plastic, or other solid material used to support clay while forming sculpture. Some burnable armatures of cardboard or synthetic materials can be fired.

Ashes Ashes from trees or plants provide fluxes for use in glass and glazes. They contain silica, alumina, and varying amounts of potash, iron, magnesia, phosphorus and lime. Used very early in the Orient, they are still popular glaze ingredients (Figures 3-9, 11-9, and 11-22).

Aventurine glaze A glaze which, when cooled slowly, crystallizes and produces small spangles that catch the light. Aventurine glazes are generally high in iron content.

Bag wall A wall inside a down-draft kiln that separates the firing chamber from the fire, directing the flames upward to produce even circulation and protect ware from flame (Figure 12-9).

Ball clay Plastic, fine-grained, secondary clay. Often containing some organic material, it is used in clay bodies to increase plasticity and in glazes to add alumina. Ball clay fires grayish or buff.

Ball mill A machine for grinding glaze ingredients or pigments. A porcelain jar filled with flint pebbles or porcelain balls that revolves and grinds the material to powder form.

Bas relief Low, three-dimensional modeling on a flat surface.

Basalt ware Black, unglazed stoneware first developed by Josiah Wedgwood in eighteenth-century England (Figure 6-17).

Bases Glaze oxides that combine under heat with the acid substances, acting as fluxes. In glaze calculation, they are represented by the symbol RO. Sometimes a neutral (R_2O) will act as a base.

Bat A plaster slab used to absorb water from clay. Drying bats are large plaster slabs used to dry clay to a workable consistency. Throwing bats are plaster, wood, or masonite disks used on top of a wheel head during throwing (Figures 9-2 to 9-29).

Batch A mixture of glaze materials or ingredients that have been weighed in certain proportions in order to attain a particular glaze or clay body (Figure 11-13).

Bisque (bisquit) Unglazed pottery that has been fired at a low temperature to make handling easier in glazing and to remove all water from the clay body.

Bisque firing The process of firing the body at low temperatures, usually from cone 010 to 05, to produce bisque ware (Figure 12-6).

Bizen Ware produced in Japan showing marks from a deliberately uneven firing. Pots are stacked touching each other, sometimes wrapped in straw, or in saggars containing straw with a high silica content in order to cause fire marks. Ash from the wood fire also settles on them unevenly, causing glazed areas. Bizen is much treasured in Japan for the tea ceremony (Figure 3-35). The term is now applied to any Bizen-fired ware.

Black-figure A style of vase painting used in ancient Greece. Figures and decoration were painted with a clay slip that turned black when the piece was subjected first to reducing, then to oxidizing firing. The black decoration contrasts with the red background (Figures 2-20 and 2-22).

Blistering A glaze defect in which bubbles form in a glaze from rapid liberation of gases during the firing.

Blunger A machine with revolving paddles used to mix slip or glazes.

Body Any blend of clays and nonplastic materials that is workable and has certain firing properties. Clay bodies are formulated for particular purposes and firing temperatures.

Bone china China of high translucency made with a considerable amount of bone ash, which lowers its maturing point. Produced mainly in England, it matures at somewhat lower temperatures than porcelain. Today, it is also used by studio potters and sculptors (Figures 8-36 and 9-73).

Burnishing Rubbing leather-hard clay with any smooth tool to polish it and tighten the clay surface (Color Plate 9, p. 146D, and Figure 5-19).

Calcined In ceramics, material that has been calcined has been heated to a moderate degree to drive off its chemical water or carbon dioxide. The term *calcined* also refers to ceramic materials reduced to a powder by the application of heat.

Casting The process of forming pottery or sculpture by pouring clay slip into absorbent plaster molds (Figures 9-70 and 9-74).

Celadon The European name for a type of glaze first used in China (Figure 3-19 and Color Plate 1, p. 50A) on stoneware and porcelain in an attempt to imitate the color and texture of jade. Its colors depend on a small percentage of iron fired in a reducing atmosphere. Colors range from greens to gray-greens.

Centering The act of forcing a lump of clay by hand into the center of a potter's wheel in preparation for throwing pottery (Figures 9-7 to 9-12).

Centrifugal force The force that tends to impel an object or material outward from the center of rotation. It acts on the clay while it rotates on a potter's wheel.

Ceramics Objects made from earthy materials with the aid of heat, or the process of making these objects.

Chambered kiln A type of kiln, developed in the Orient, built on a slope with several separate chambers opening into each other (Figure 3-41). Also called climbing kiln or snake kiln.

China A word usually used for any white ware fired at a low porcelain temperature. It was developed in Europe to compete with the expensive imported Chinese porcelain.

China clay Primary clay, or kaolin, which is white, refractory, and not very plastic.

Chinoiserie Decoration used in eighteenth-century Europe inspired by the newly imported Chinese crafts. Used on everything from furniture to ceramics.

Clay In theory, $Al_2O_3 \cdot 2SiO_2 \cdot 2H_2O$. Actually, earthy materials formed by the decomposition of granite. See also **Secondary clay** and **Primary clay** (Figure 1-12).

Coiling A method of forming pottery or sculpture from rolls of clay welded together to form the walls (Figures 5-1 and 7-25 to 7-29).

Cone See **Pyrometric cone.**

Cornish stone (Cornwall stone) A material found in England, similar to Chinese petunze. Used in porcelains, it contains silica and various fluxes.

Crackle glaze A glaze with deliberately caused cracks that form a decorative surface. Often color is rubbed into the cracks to increase the effect.

Crawling A glaze defect in which the glaze separates from the body during firing and leaves bare spots. Usually caused by dust or grease spots on the surface of the ware before glazing.

Crazing This glaze defect is caused by the improper fit of glaze to clay body. Unintentional cracks develop all over the glaze surface because the glaze expands and contracts more than the body.

Crystalline glazes Glazes in which crystals form, causing the light to reflect. Slow cooling helps to produce crystals in glazes that are low in alumina (Color Plate 13, p. 210C).

Decal A picture or design printed on a special paper so that it can be transferred to bisqued ware and fired to permanency.

Deflocculant Material such as sodium carbonate or sodium silicate, used in casting slip to help maintain the suspension of clay so that less water is needed to form a slip—an advantage, because less shrinkage will occur in drying.

Dipping Applying a glaze or slip to the body by immersing the piece and shaking off excess glaze (Figure 11-33).

Draw To take fired ware from the kiln.

Dunting The cracking of pots during cooling. Caused by cold drafts, rapid cooling, or by removing the piece from the kiln before it is cool enough.

Earthenware Pottery that has been fired at low temperature and is opaque, porous, and relatively soft, usually red or brown in color. Used world-wide for domestic ware, glazed or unglazed (Figures 3-2 and 6-3).

Enamels Low-temperature opaque glazes (usually lead based) painted over higher-fired glazes.

Engobe Colored slip that is applied over the entire surface of a piece of pottery or sculpture to change the color and/or texture of a clay body. The term is now often used for any slip decoration (Figure 6-38).

Eutectic A combination of two or more materials whose melting point is always the lowest melting point possible with those components.

Faience Often used as a general term for any pottery made with a colored, low-fire clay body covered with opaque glaze. Originally the French name for the tin-glazed earthenware made in the town of Faenza, Italy (Figure 6-4).

Feathering A method of decorating ware by trailing lines of slip over it, then altering the lines by drawing through them in the opposite direction (Figure 10-16).

Feldspar Any of a group of common rock-forming minerals containing silicates of aluminum, with potassium, sodium, calcium, and occasionally barium. Feldspar melts at temperatures between 2192°F and 2372°F (1200°C and 1300°C). Feldspar is used extensively in stoneware and porcelain bodies and in glazes as a flux. (See Appendix 2.)

Ferric and **ferrous oxides** Terms used for the red and black iron oxides that produce reddish and brown colors in clay bodies and glazes. They also produce the greens of the celadon glaze, and can act as fluxes. (See **Iron** in Appendix 2.)

Fire clays Clays that withstand high temperatures. They are used in kiln bricks and also as ingredients in stoneware bodies or in clay bodies for hand building or sculpture.

Firebox The part of the kiln into which fuel is introduced and where combustion takes place.

Firing Heating pottery or sculpture in a kiln or open fire to bring the clay to maturity. The temperature needed to mature the clay varies with the type of body used. Also, heating glazed ware to the necessary point to cause the glaze to mature.

Fit The adjustment of a glaze to a body, causing it to adhere to the surface of the ware.

Flambé glaze A high-fire red and purple glaze produced by firing copper in a reducing atmosphere.

Flues The passageways in a kiln, designed to carry the heat from the chamber to the chimney.

Flux A substance that lowers the melting point of another substance. Oxides such as those of lead, sodium, potassium, lime, zinc, barium, and others combine with the silica and other heat-resistant materials, helping them to fuse. (See Appendix 2.)

Foot The base of a piece of pottery.

Frit (Fritt) Various soluble or toxic materials melted together with insoluble materials, then cooled rapidly, splintered in cold water, and powdered. This makes them nonsoluble and nontoxic for use in glazes. Feldspar is a natural frit.

Galena Lead sulfide, formerly used in Europe to glaze earthenware.

Glaze Any vitreous coating that has been melted onto a clay surface in the kiln. Made of fine-ground minerals, when fired to a certain temperature, the ingredients fuse into a glassy coating. Glazes can be matt or glossy. (See Color Plate 3, p. 50C, and Figure 11-5.)

Glaze firing The firing during which glaze materials melt and form a vitreous coating on the pottery (Figures 12-7 to 12-12).

Glost Ware that has been glazed. *Glost firing* is another term for glaze firing.

Greenware Unfired pottery or sculpture.

Grog Crushed or ground particles of fired clay added to the body to help in drying and to add texture and reduce shrinkage. Used especially in sculpture and hand-built pottery to reduce thermal shock in firing.

Hard paste True porcelain made of a clay body containing kaolin. Fired over 2372°F (1300°C), it is white, vitrified and translucent.

Hematite Iron oxide (Fe_2O_3) used as coloring on much early pottery (Figure 3-1).

Hispano-Moresque Term used to describe tin-lead glazed earthenware produced in Spain in the Middle Ages, frequently with luster decoration (Figure 6-1). Sold in Italy, it influenced Italian potters who adapted the method to produce their own glazed pottery called maiolica (or faience in France).

Jiggering A method of forming multiples. A soft clay slab is placed on a mold, then trimmed to size by a mechanical jigger or metal arm with a template.

Kaolin Also called china clay. Pure kaolin is a white-firing natural clay that withstands high temperatures. An essential ingredient in porcelain, its presence in large quantities in China allowed potters there to develop their fine white porcelain (Figure 3-20).

Keramos A Greek word meaning "earthenware" from which our term *ceramics* is derived.

Kiln A furnace or oven built of heat-resistant materials for firing pottery or sculpture (Figures 2-7, 2-8, 2-23, 3-34, 3-41, 12-7, and 12-26).

Kiln furniture Heat-resistant slabs, shelves, and posts for supporting ware in the kiln during firing (Figure 12-7).

Kiln wash A coating of refractory materials (half flint and half kaolin) painted on the kiln shelves and floor to keep the melting glaze from sticking the ware to the shelves.

Lead In a variety of forms, lead has been used extensively as a flux for low- or medium-temperature glazes. Lead is poisonous and should be used in fritted form. Pottery that will contain foodstuffs should not be glazed with lead glazes.

Leather-hard The condition of a clay body when much of the moisture has evaporated and shrinkage has just ended but clay is not totally dry. Joining slabs, carving, or burnishing is done at this stage.

Luster (lustre) A thin coating of metallic salts usually applied to the glazed piece, then refired at a low temperature in a reducing atmosphere. Developed in Persia, it was brought to Europe by the Moors (Figures 3-31 and 6-3). Used today by potters and sculptors to give a metallic surface to their work (Figures 11-27 and 11-32).

Maiolica (Majolica) The Italian name for tin-glazed ware that was sent from Spain via the island of Majorca. Later, local styles of decoration were developed in Italian pottery centers, such as Faenza and Deruta (Color Plate 5, p. 146A). Now a general term for any earthenware covered with a tin-lead glaze.

Matt glaze A glaze that has a dull, nonglossy finish due to its deliberate composition. Barium carbonate or alumina added to the glaze, along with a slow cooling, helps form matt glazes.

Maturing (maturity) Refers to the temperature and time in firing at which a clay or glaze reaches the desired condition of hardness and density.

Model The original form in clay or plaster from which a mold is made.

Mold Any form that contains the negative shape from which multiple copies of the original model can be cast with slip or from slabs pressed into the mold (Figures 9-70 to 9-74). Molds can be made in one piece or in sections. (Also see **Casting** and **Piece mold.**)

Mullite crystals Crystals of aluminum silicate that start to form in clay between 1850°F and 2200°F (1010°C and 1204°C) and which strengthen stoneware and porcelain when fully developed at high temperatures. They also help in the interaction that unites high-fire glazes and high-fire bodies.

Neutrals In glaze calculation, materials that are neutral and can react as either an acid or a base. Also called amphoteric, they are represented by the symbol R_2O_3.

Opacifier A material that causes a glaze to become opaque by producing small crystals. Tin, zirconium, and titanium oxides are used as opacifiers in combination with various oxides.

Open firing Refers to firing that is not done in an enclosed kiln (Figure 1-44).

Overglaze A low-temperature glaze, usually of bright color, painted over glazed ware and fused into the harder glaze in a second, low-temperature firing. Colors that would burn out at higher temperatures can be used in overglazes. Also called china paint (Color Plate 19, p. 274C).

Oxidation (oxidizing firing) The firing of a kiln or open fire so that the combustion is complete and the firing atmosphere contains enough oxygen to allow the metals in clays and glazes to produce their oxide colors. Electric kilns always produce oxidizing firings unless reduction materials are added.

Oxide A combination of an element with oxygen. Oxides are used both in glaze formulation and for coloring and decoration (Figures 10-1 to 10-24).

Paste (See **Hard paste** and **Soft paste.)** Terms used for the clay bodies of European porcelains of varying degrees of hardness.

Peephole A hole in the wall or door of a kiln through which the potter can watch the pyrometric cones and the firing process (Figure 12-11).

Petunze A type of feldspar rock in China from which, with kaolin, the Chinese formed their porcelains. In Europe and the United States, it is called Cornish stone, Cornwall stone, or china stone.

Piece mold A mold for casting that is made in sections so that it can be removed from the cast object easily.

Pinholes Small holes in a glaze caused by the bursting of blisters formed by gases as they escape from the glaze during firing.

Pithos (plural, **Pithoi**) A Greek term for a large storage jar made of earthenware (Figures 2-3 and 2-10).

Plastic clay See **Plasticity.**

Plasticity The ability of a damp clay body to yield under pressure without cracking and to retain the formed shape after the pressure is released.

Porcelain A translucent, nonabsorbent body fired at high temperature. White and hard, it was first developed in China (Figure 3-20).

Pottery Originally a term for earthenware, now it is used loosely to refer to any type of ceramic ware or the workshop where it is made.

Primary clay Clay that was formed in place, rather than being transported by the action of water. Also called residual clay. Kaolin is a primary clay (Figure 1-12).

Proto-porcelain (also **Proto-porcelaneous**) Refers to an early high-fire ware developed in China as kilns became more efficient and capable of reaching higher temperatures. It preceded true porcelain. (See Figure 3-14.)

Pug mill A machine used to mix clay into a moist, workable consistency. Often used to recycle clay scraps.

Pyrometer A device used for measuring the temperature within a kiln during firing.

Pyrometric cones Small pyramids of ceramic materials formulated to bend over and then melt at certain temperatures. They indicate to the potter when a firing is complete (Figures 12-8 and 12-12). Made from the same basic ingredients as glazes, they measure time as well as temperature and thus give a more accurate indication of the glaze melt than a pyrometer. Orton cones in the United States and Seger cones in Europe have different ranges. (See Chart 6, Appendix 3.)

Raku Originally a name used by a Japanese family who have made tea ceremony ware since the seventeenth century, now the term is used for any ware glazed in raku-type firing. Soft and porous, it is frequently lead-glazed. Placed in a red-hot kiln and quickly withdrawn, it is often reduced in straw or sawdust (Figures 12-18 to 12-25).

Raw glaze Glaze that does not contain fritted materials.

Reduction (reducing firing) A firing in which insufficient air is supplied to allow complete combustion. Under these conditions, the carbon monoxide must combine with the oxygen in the oxides in the clay body and glaze, causing the oxides to change color. This results in the characteristic earthy tones of reduction-fired stoneware, as well as the subtle or brilliant colors of some Chinese high-fire glazes.

Refractory Resistance to high heat and melting. Refractory materials are used in porcelain and stoneware and also for building kilns and kiln furniture.

Reserve A method of painting around an area, reserving it so that it remains the color of the clay body or glaze while the painted area fires a different color. Used by early potters, such as the Greek red-figure painters, and still used today (Figures 2-24 and 6-39).

Roulette A carved wheel that imprints repeated decorative motifs when run over the damp clay surface.

Saggar A refractory container in which glazed ware is placed during firing to protect it from the kiln fire (Figure 3-22).

Salt glaze A glaze formed by introducing salt into a hot kiln. The vaporized salt combines with silica in the clay body, forming a sodium silicate glaze on the surface. It also combines with the silica in the kiln bricks, so it must be used in a special kiln (Figures 11-21 and 12-17).

Sang de boeuf The French name for the oxblood red glazes of China (Color Plate 2, p. 50B).

Secondary clay Clay moved by water or wind from its source and settled elsewhere in deposits. Also called sedimentary clay (Figure 1-12).

Setting Placing the ware in the kiln in preparation for firing (Figure 12-7).

Sgraffito Decoration of pottery made by scratching through a layer of colored slip to the differently colored clay body underneath (Figure 10-14).

Shard A broken piece of pottery. From these fragments, archaeologists can learn much about ancient cultures (Figure 1-4).

Shivering The cracking of a glaze due to greater shrinkage of the clay body than the glaze during firing.

Silica Oxide of silicon, SiO_2. Found in nature as quartz or flint sand, it is the most common of all ceramic materials. (See also Appendix 2.)

Silicate of soda A solution of sodium silicate is used as a deflocculant to help in the suspension of materials in slip.

Silicon carbide Used in a glaze to produce local reduction in an electric kiln. Also used in making kiln furniture.

Slip A suspension of clay in water, usually with sodium silicate. The resulting creamy substance is used for joining leather-hard pieces or for casting in molds.

Slip casting Forming objects by pouring slip into a plaster (or bisqued clay) mold. The mold absorbs the water in the slip so that solid clay walls are formed in a positive repeat of the mold (Figures 9-70 to 9-74).

Slip glaze A glaze that contains a large proportion of clay. Generally one, like Albany slip, that contains enough flux to form a glaze with few or no additions (Figures 10-17, 11-11, and 11-42).

Soaking Keeping a kiln at its hottest temperature for a certain length of time to allow the heat to penetrate the ware fully.

Soft paste A term used in Europe for a porcelain body that fires at a lower temperature than true porcelain.

Soluble Capable of being dissolved in a fluid.

Spray booth A ventilated booth that removes chemicals from the air so that the worker does not inhale them while spraying glazes (Figure 11-36).

Sprigging A method used to attach low-relief decorations of damp clay to an already formed piece (Figure 7-63).

Stilts Triangular supports with fire-resistant metal points, which leave only small marks on the glaze. Used to support pieces of glazed pottery during the glaze firing. Stilts hold the piece above the shelves and keep the glaze from sticking the ware to the shelf.

Stoneware A type of clay body fired to a temperature at which the body vitrifies. A dense body with little absorption, but nontranslucent. It is usually colored by the presence of iron and usually matures at temperatures above 2192°F (1200°C).

Temper Any material, such as sand, mica, or crushed fired pottery fragments called grog, that is added to a clay body to make it more porous (Figure 7-8).

Tenmoku (temmoku) High-fire, saturated iron glaze, black, brown, and yellowish. Used by the Chinese and Japanese, especially on tea ware. Still a popular glaze (Figures 3-23, 11-4).

Terra cotta A low-fire, porous, reddish clay body, frequently containing grog or temper. Used throughout history for common domestic ware, it is also used for sculpture.

Terra sigillata A fine slip glaze used by the Greeks, Etruscans, and Romans to coat their pottery. It is fired red or black according to whether the firing was reducing or oxidizing.

Throwing Forming pieces on the potter's wheel from a plastic clay body (Figures 9-1 to 9-27).

Tin enamel A low-fire, opaque overglaze containing tin oxide. Also called tin-lead or lead-tin glaze (Figure 6-4).

Trailing A method of decorating in which a slip or glaze is squeezed out of a syringe or from a tube inserted in a narrow-necked clay cup (Figure 11-41).

Underglaze Colored decoration applied to bisque ware, then usually coated with a transparent or semitransparent glaze.

Viscosity The ability to resist running or flow. A glaze must have enough viscosity to avoid flowing off the ware when it is melted under heat.

Vitreous Glassy. A vitreous glaze or body is one that has been fired to a dense, hard, and nonabsorbent condition. High-fire glazes vitrify and combine with the glassy particles that form in the high-fire clay body as it approaches vitrification. This results in a glaze that is united with the clay body as compared to a low-fire glaze, which merely coats the surface of the clay.

Ware Any pottery—earthenware, stoneware, or porcelain—whether greenware, bisque, or glazed.

Warping Changes in the form of a clay body. Warping can occur in drying or firing if the walls are built unevenly or if drying or firing is uneven.

Wax resist A method of decoration in which melted wax is painted onto the clay body or onto a glazed piece. The waxed areas resist the next coating of glaze, then melt out in firing, so that the color of the clay or underglaze appears (Figures 11-42 to 11-45).

Wedging Any one of various methods of kneading a mass of clay to expel the air and get rid of lumps (Figures 7-8 to 7-12).

Suggestions for Further Reading

The following books and magazines are suggested to the reader who wants to pursue some of the subjects discussed in this book. Most of these sources also contain bibliographies that will be helpful for those who want to study specialized subjects in greater depth.

Periodicals

Ceramics Monthly. 1609 Northwest Blvd., Columbus, Ohio, 43212.
Studio Potter. Box #172, Warner, N.H. 03278.
Craft Horizons. American Crafts Council, 44 W. 53rd St., New York, N.Y. 10019.
Ceramic Review. 17a Newburgh St., London W1, England.
Crafts. Crafts Advisory Committee, 12 Waterloo Place, London SW1Y 4AU, England.
Antiquity: A Quarterly Review of Archaeology. King's Hedges Rd., Cambridge CBA 2PQ, England.
African Arts. University of California Press, Los Angeles, Ca. 90024.

Books

Part One

World Ceramics. Robert J. Charleston. New York: McGraw-Hill, 1968.
A Dictionary of World Pottery and Porcelain. Louise Ade Boger. New York: Scribner, 1970.
Avenues to Antiquity. Readings from *Scientific American.* San Francisco: W. H. Freeman, 1976.
Earliest Civilizations of the Near East. James Mellaart. New York: McGraw-Hill, 1966.
Prehistoric Crete. R. W. Hutchinson. Baltimore, Md., and Harmondsworth, England: Penguin Books, 1962.
The Techniques of Painted Attic Pottery. Joseph Veach Noble. New York: Watson-Guptill, 1965.
Athenian Black-Figure Vases. John Boardman. London, New York, Toronto: Oxford University Press, 1975.

Nishapur, Potter of the Early Islamic Period. Charles Wilkinson, Editor. New York: Metropolitan Museum of Art, 1974.

Iranian Ceramics. Charles K. Wilkinson. New York: Asia House (Harry N. Abrams, distributor), 1963.

Ceramics from the World of Islam. Esin Atil. Washington, D.C.: Freer Gallery of Art, 1973.

In Search of Persian Pottery. Yoshida Mitsukuni. New York: Weatherhill, 1972.

The Arts of China. Michael Sullivan. Berkeley, Ca.: The University of California Press, 1973.

China: A History in Art. Bradley Smith and Wan-go Weng. New York: Harper and Row, 1976.

Two Thousand Years of Oriental Ceramics. Fujio Koyama and John Figges. New York: Harry N. Abrams, 1961.

A Connoisseur's Guide to Chinese Ceramics. Cécile and Michel Beurdeley. New York: Harper and Row, 1974.

The Ceramic Art of China. William B. Honey. London: Faber and Faber, 1954.

Chinese Ceramic Glazes. A. L. Hetherington. London: Cambridge University Press, 1948.

The World of Japanese Ceramics. Herbert H. Sanders. Tokyo: Kodansha International, 1967.

Chinese Ceramics in the Avery Brundage Collection. San Francisco: M. H. DeYoung Memorial Museum, 1967.

A Potter in Japan. Bernard Leach. London: Faber and Faber, 1960

The Ceramic Art of Japan. Hugo Munsterberg. Rutland, Vt.: C. E. Tuttle, 1964.

Japanese Pottery. Soame Jenyns. London: Faber and Faber, 1971.

Shoji Hamada: A Potter's Way and Work. Susan Peterson. Tokyo: Kodansha International, 1974.

Hamada, Potter. Bernard Leach. Tokyo: Kodansha International, 1975.

African Crafts and Craftsmen. Rene Gardi. New York: Van Nostrand Reinhold, 1969.

African Art. Frank Willett. London, New York, Toronto: Oxford University Press, 1971.

Contemporary African Arts. Maude Wahlman. Chicago: Field Museum of Natural History, 1974.

The Traditional Artist in African Societies. Warren L. d'Azevedo, Editor. Bloomington, Ind.: Indiana University Press, 1973.

The Potter's Art in Africa. William Fagg and John Picton. London: The British Museum, 1970.

Potters of Southern Africa. C. Clark and L. Wagner. New York: Hacker, 1974.

Pioneer Pottery. Michael Cardew. New York: St. Martin's Press, 1976.

Unknown India, Ritual Art in Tribe and Village. Philadelphia: Philadelphia Museum of Art, 1968.

The English Country Pottery, Its History and Techniques. Peter C. D. Brears. Rutland, Vt.: C. E. Tuttle.

Porcelain Through the Ages. George Savage. Baltimore, Md., and Harmondsworth, England: Penguin Books, 1954.

Five Centuries of Italian Majolica. Guiseppe Liverani. New York: McGraw-Hill, 1960.

Museo Internazionale delle Ceramiche. Guiseppe Liverani. Faenza, Italy, 1963.

Majolica. Jirina Vydrova. London: Spring House, 1960.

European Ceramic Art. William B. Honey. London: Faber and Faber, 1949.

A Collector's History of English Pottery. Griselda Lewis. New York: Viking, 1970.

Early New England Potters and their Wares. Lura Woodside Watkins. Cambridge, Ma.: Harvard University Press, 1968.

Art Pottery of the United States: An Encyclopedia of Producers and Their Marks. Paul Evans. New York: Scribner, 1974.

Decorated Stoneware Pottery of North America. Donald Blake Webster. Rutland, Vt.: C. E. Tuttle, 1970.
Bennington Pottery and Porcelain. Richard Carter Barret. New York: Crown Publishers, 1958.
Ancient Arts of the Americas. Geoffrey H. Bushnell. New York: Praeger, 1965.
Precolombian Terracottas. London, New York, Sydney, Toronto: Hamlyn, 1969.
The National Museum of Anthropology, Mexico: Art, Architecture, Archaeology, Ethnography. Pedro Ramiriz Vasquez and others. New York: Harry N. Abrams, 1968.
Mexico: A History in Art. Bradley Smith. New York: Doubleday, 1968.
South American Folk Pottery. Gertrude Litto. New York: Watson-Guptill, 1976.
Historic Pueblo Indian Pottery. Grancis H. Harlow and Larry Frank. Sante Fe, N.M.: Museum of New Mexico Press, 1967.
Pueblo Crafts. Ruth M. Underhill. Washington, D.C.: United States Office of Indian Handcrafts, 1977 (reprint of 1944 edition).
Santa Clara Pottery Today. Betty Le Free. Albuquerque, N.M.: University of New Mexico Press, 1975.
Pueblo Potter: A Study of Creative Imagination in Primitive Art. Ruth L. Bunzel. New York: Dover, 1973.
Pottery Treasures: The Splendor of Southwest Indian Art. Spencer Gill and Jerry Jaka. Portland, Or.: Graphic Arts Center, 1976.

Part Two

Finding One's Way with Clay. Paulus Berensohn. New York: Simon and Schuster, 1972.
Centering in Pottery, Poetry and the Person. M. C. Richards. Middletown, Ct.: Weslyan University Press, 1964.
A Potter's Book. Bernard Leach. Hollywood-by-the-Sea, Fl.: Transatlantic Arts; London: Faber and Faber, 1960.
A Potter's Challenge. Bernard Leach. New York: Dutton, 1975.
Art of the Modern Potter. Tony Birks. New York: Van Nostrand Reinhold, 1977; London: Hamlyn, 1976.
The Potter's Companion: The Complete Guide to Pottery Making. Tony Birks. New York: Dutton, 1977.
New Ceramics. Eileen Lewenstein and Emmanuel Cooper. London: Ceramic Review; New York: Van Nostrand Reinhold, 1974.
Penland School of Crafts Book of Pottery. John Coyne, Editor. New York: Bobbs-Merrill, 1975.
The Invisible Core: A Potter's Life and Thoughts. Marguerite Wildenhain. Palo Alto, Ca.: Pacific Books, 1973.
Pottery for Everyone. Dora M. Billington. New York: Watson-Guptill, 1975; London: B. T. Batsford, 1962.
Ceramics for the Artist Potter. Frederick H. Norton. Cambridge, Ma.: Addison-Wesley, 1956.
Pottery: Materials and Techniques. David Green. New York: Praeger, 1967; London: Faber and Faber, 1963.
Ceramic Science for the Potter. W. G. Lawrence. Radnor, Pa.: Chilton, 1972.

Clay and Glazes for the Potter. Daniel Rhodes. Radnor, Pa.: Chilton, 1973.

Ceramics: A Potter's Handbook. Glenn C. Nelson. New York: Holt Rhinehart and Winston, 1978.

Illustrated Dictionary of Practical Pottery. Robert Fournier, Editor. New York: Van Nostrand Reinhold, 1976.

Stoneware and Porcelain. Daniel Rhodes. Radnor, Pa.: Chilton, 1973.

Terracotta: The Techniques of Fired Clay Sculpture. Bruno Lucchesi. London: Pitman; New York: Watson-Guptill, 1977.

Pottery Glazes. David Green. New York: Watson-Guptill, 1973; London: Faber and Faber, 1963.

Understanding Pottery Glazes. David Green. New York: Praeger, 1967; London: Faber and Faber, 1963.

Ceramic Glazes. Cullen W. Parmelee. Chicago: Industrial Publications, 1951.

Ceramic Review Book of Glazes. London: Ceramic Review Books, 1977.

The Potter's Complete Book of Clay and Glazes. James Chappell. New York: Watson-Guptill, 1977; London: Pitman, 1977.

Glazes for the Potter. William Ruscoe. London: Academy, 1974; New York: St. Martin's Press, 1974.

Glazes for Special Effects. Herbert Sanders. New York: Watson-Guptill, 1974.

The Glazer's Book. A. B. Searle. London: Technical Press.

Ceramic Formulas: A Guide to Clay, Glaze, Enamel, Glass and their Colors. John W. Conrad. New York: Macmillan, 1973.

Glaze Projects. Richard Behrens. Ceramics Monthly Handbook. Columbus, Oh.: Professional Publications, 1976.

Ceramic Glaze Making. Richard Behrens. Ceramics Monthly Handbook. Columbus, Oh.: Professional Publications, 1974.

Salt-Glazed Ceramics. Jack Troy. New York: Watson-Guptill, 1977; London: Pitman Publishing Co.

Primitive Pottery. Hall Riegger. New York: Van Nostrand Reinhold, 1972.

Raku Handbook: A Practical Approach to Ceramic Art. John Dickerson. New York: Van Nostrand Reinhold, 1972; London: Studio Vista, 1972.

Raku: Art and Techniques. Hal Riegger. New York: Van Nostrand Reinhold, 1970.

Kilns. Daniel Rhodes. Radnor, Pa.: Chilton, 1974.

Index

Page numbers in boldface indicate illustrations on those pages.